The Nakshatras

The Stars
Beyond the Zodiac

Komilla Sutton

The Wessex Astrologer Ltd

Published in 2014 by
The Wessex Astrologer Ltd
4A Woodside Road
Bournemouth
BH5 2AZ
England

www.wessexastrologer.com

ISBN 9781902405926

A catalogue record of this book is available at The British Library

Cover design by Jonathan Taylor
Cover photo of Soma, the Moon: Author's own

Acknowledgements

I would like to thank the following for their help and support:

My Guru Dr Ajit Sinha for showing me the light of Jyotish. He will forever be in my heart.

Margaret Cahill for being the best publisher ever. I feel so blessed to know her and have her publish all my books. Thanks too for her excellent editing, inspiration and suggestions that make my books shine.

Paul F. Newman for his editing and incredible eye for detail.

Jonathan Taylor for creating such a beautiful cover.

Keiko Ito and Anna Karlsdottir for their help with the book. I value them both so much.

To my family, especially my mom Inderjit Wirk and my brother Kuldip Wirk for their love and for always being there for me.

Komilla Sutton is a very intuitive and wise Jyotishi and teacher, with a deep knowledge of Yoga and the mind. In this year of Jupiter coming to exaltation position, I would like to recommend her new book on nakshatras which represents all the shaktis of the mind. May all readers receive insights from the book to pierce through the divine mysteries of mind and maya and learn the way to liberation, Peace and Happinness.

Swami Sitaramananda
Acharya, International Sivananda Yoga Vedanta Centers

Contents

Glossary

Agni	Fire, one of the five great elements
Aakash	Ether, one of the five great elements
Amavasya	the 30th tithi, the dark night of the Moon
Apas	Water, one of the five great elements
Artha	practical aim of life, one of the four aims
Ashtamamsha	when planets in Rashi chart move into the 8th sign from themselves in the navamsha/pada
Bhakti	devotion or worship
dik bala	directional strength
Gandanta	the spiritual knot. It refers to special areas or degrees at the junction of Pisces/Aries, Cancer/Leo and Scorpio/ Sagittarius
Graha	planet
Hanuman	Vedic god, devotee of Lord Rama, the head of the monkeys. His form is of the monkey. He represents the ideal devotee.
Janma	birth, often refers to the Moon's nakshatra
Jati	caste, social group, could be professional group too
Kama	passion, one of the 4 aims of life.
Karaka	significator
Kshema	prosperity
Mahadasha	major period of time, top level of dasha
Manasa	mind
Mantra Shastra	scripture on Sacred Sounds
Navamsha	ninth divisional chart
Navatara	a group of nine nakshatras
Pada	feet, division or part, divides one nakshatra into four parts
Panchanga	five limbs of the day
Param mitra	eternal friend
Paryay	cycle
Prashna	the Jyotish technique of interpreting the chart from the time a question is asked
Pratayak	obstacle
Prithvi	Earth, one of the five great elements
Pushkara	refers to special navamsha and degrees that are auspicious
Rashi	sign of the zodiac
Rishi	sage
Soma	the Moon
Vargottama	when a planet is in the same sign in both Rashi and navamsha charts
Vayu	Wind, one of the five great elements, also a Vedic God
Vimshottari	is a system of timing which takes 120 years as the optimum age. It shows what a soul experiences during a life time.

1
An Introduction to the Nakshatras

'Nakshatra' is the original language of the stars with which the ancient sages connected to intangible spirit. They tried to decipher the meaning of life from qualities beyond the zodiac, where the gods and goddesses lived in a world that is free from pain and sorrow. The Sages felt that if they could understand the language of the stars and work with their cosmic patterns they could truly learn to override the daily turbulence of the human life and mind. The word 'nakshatra' literally means a star. Each nakshatra is a group of several thousand fixed stars comprising 13° 20' of the ecliptic – the number of degrees travelled by the Moon in a 24-hour day. One rashi or sign has 2¼ nakshatras within it. Breaking it down further, *Naksha* means 'to get closer' and *Tra* means 'to preserve'. 'Nakshatra' also therefore means 'one that never decays'. The nakshatras' cosmic remit is to be the guardians of the soul during its journey through many human lifetimes, and bring divine knowledge to earth.

The nakshatras represent the mind: the higher and lower energies and daily struggles for peace and calmness amid the uncertainties and pressures. They show the mind's ability to be part of the higher self, the evolution of consciousness, and to be at one with the divine. They also indicate the emotional chaos, unhappiness and sorrows which the mind copes with on a daily basis. The nakshatras deal with karma which is stored in the mind, whose daily fluctuations keep us from developing towards self-realization.

The nakshatras relate to two key aspects – the eternal and the ever changing. They represent the fixed stars which are constant, and the Moon/mind which is always changing. This interaction, if truly understood, can bring deeper knowledge of consciousness, karma and the search for happiness.

Although the Moon's position in a nakshatra is of prime importance, the quality of the other planets is also influenced and altered by their nakshatra position. To study the deeper meanings of life, the nakshatra placements of all planets must be analysed and this will give a better understanding of the inner motivations of the planets in your chart.

Gayatri Mantra and the Nakshatra Loka

The Gayatri mantra, which is the greatest chant in the Vedas, connects to the inner meaning of the world (loka) of nakshatras. This chant is about the three worlds and prays to the solar god Savitur to show us the inner light beyond the visible light of the Sun.

The Gayatri Mantra

ओम् भूर्भुव: स्व: तत् सवितुर्वरेण्यम्
भगों देवस्य धीमहि धियो यो न: प्रचोदयात्

Om bhûr bhuvah svah tat savitur varenyam
Bhargo devasya dhîmahi dhiyo yo nah pracodayât

I pray to God Savitur, who appears through the Sun to show the light that has given birth to all the three Worlds. Please illuminate our intellect and show us the inner light.

This chant tells us of the three worlds which are:

Bhur – Earth
Bhuvah – Sky
Svah – Swarga or heaven

This mantra also teaches us about the Earth, Sun and Moon:

Bhur – the Earth is where the humans live, and Mercury or the intellect is its lord.
Bhuvah – the sky is the path of the Sun and the zodiac.
Svah – heaven, where the nakshatras shine their light and the devas (gods and goddesses) live. Heaven is under the jurisdiction of the Moon.

The Gayatri mantra helps us to understand the concept of Atma, Buddhi, Manas – Soul, Intellect and Mind. Atma is the Sun, Buddhi is Mercury and Manas is Moon. Atma lives in the world of the Sun, Intellect in the Earth and the Mind is beyond these two. Of these, the mind is the most difficult to control. It can block us, make us unhappy and bring instability. Hence chanting the Gayatri Mantra helps in calming the mind and developing its higher nature.

The Myth of the Nakshatras: The Wives of Soma

The nakshatras are the twenty-eight daughters[1] of Daksha Prajapati who became the wives of Soma, the Moon god. Daksha Prajapati allowed Soma to marry his daughters on the condition that he, Soma would treat them equally. Soma visited one wife per day. Soon he started showing preference to Rohini and was spending a little extra time with her, which made the other wives jealous. They complained to Daksha Prajapati and he cursed Soma who started dying. The wives realized their mistake and begged their father to remove the curse. Daksha Prajapati explained that a curse once given cannot be taken back but he modified it so that Soma would die and be reborn every month. This became the waxing and waning cycle of the Moon. When the Moon transits the nakshatras, visiting the symbolic wives of *Soma*, it activates the differing aspects of the human mind, their soul desires and their changing moods.

Nakshatras – The Lunar Mandala

In the beginning there were no equal divisions of the sky. The nakshatras were of varying lengths and their guiding stars were given great importance. In *Vedanga Jyotish*[2], Dr Mishra refers to this and further adds that over time the nakshatras were divided into 28 sections. Then the sages modified the nakshatras and made them equal in size. They decided to make one nakshatra equal to the distance the Moon travels in one day which is 13°20'. They were able to divide the sky into 27 sections and the 28th nakshatra is shorter and is intercalary (outside the nakshatra belt). The nakshatras were usually referred to by the names of their deities and not the nakshatra name. This practice is still prevalent especially in Muhurta and Prashna.

---

1.   Nakshatra Devis are given in *Chatuvarga Chintamani* by Hemandra.

2.   *Vedanga Jyotish* - the oldest written book on vedic astrology. The translation by Dr Suresh Chandra Mishra, published by Ranjan Publication in Delhi is a good one.

The nakshatras are divided into three cycles of nine, which are always ruled by the planets in the same order. The nine planets are Ketu, Venus, Sun, Moon, Mars, Rahu, Jupiter, Saturn and Mercury. The division of the sky into 27 sections relates to the Moon as it stays in one nakshatra for a day.

The 28th Nakshatra

There is also a nakshatra called Abhijit that was part of the original nakshatra mandala. Abhijit is 4°13'20" long and is placed between 6°40' and 10°53'20" Capricorn and it was the most auspicious nakshatra during the ancient times. It was such a powerful nakshatra that if an important activity began when the Moon was in Abhijit nakshatra, it guaranteed unparalleled success.

During the Mahabharata[3], Lord Krishna came to know that Duryodhana was planning to start a war with five Pandava brothers at a time when the Moon was in Abhijit. He was aware of the power of the Abhijit. The Kauravas were planning to begin Mahabharata when it was Amavasya tithi (New Moon) and the Moon was in Abhijit nakshatra; this day would be an extremely potent one to bring a successful outcome. This combination can only happen when the Sun is in Capricorn and is an unbeatable combination for victory over an enemy. Lord Krishna knew that if the Kaurava and Duryodhana started Mahabharata on this day, the Pandava would lose, so he removed Abhijit nakshatra from the nakshatra mandala; he wanted to avoid misuse of this auspicious nakshatra.

This nakshatra was placed beyond the nakshatra belt and so became an intercalary nakshatra. It remains 6°40' to 10° along the side of Uttara Ashadha and 10° to 10° 53'20" by Shravana.

27 or 28 Nakshatras

There are different schemes of nakshatras; one that uses Abhijit and others that don't. Abhijit is not used in natal astrology, but it is important for Panchanga and many other aspects and in Kali Yuga we only use

---

3.   Mahabharata is an epic of the *Dwapara Yuga*. It tells of the war between two opposing sections of the same family. Lord Vishnu comes in the form of Sri Krishna to give the message of Dharma to Arjuna and help the Pandava family.

The 28 Nakshatras

	Nakshatra	Ruler	Degrees of Zodiac	Degrees in Sign
1	Ashwini	Ketu	0°00' to 13°20'	0°00' to 13°20' Aries
2	Bharani	Venus	13°20' to 26°40'	13°20' to 26°40' Aries
3	Krittika	Sun	26°40' to 40°00'	26°40' Aries to 10°00' Taurus
4	Rohini	Moon	40°00' to 53°20'	10°00' to 23°20' Taurus
5	Mrigasira	Mars	53°20' to 66°40'	23°20' Taurus to 6°40' Gemini
6	Ardra	Rahu	66°40' to 80°00'	6°40' to 20°00' Gemini
7	Punarvasu	Jupiter	80°00 to 93°20'	20°00' Gemini to 3°20' Cancer
8	Pushya	Saturn	93°20' to 106°40'	3°20' to 16°20' Cancer
9	Ashlesha	Mercury	106°40' to 120°00'	16°40 Cancer to 0°00 Leo
10	Magha	Ketu	120°00' to 133°20'	0°00' to 13°20' Leo
11	P Phalguni	Venus	133°20' to 146°40'	13°20' to 26°40' Leo
12	U Phalguni	Sun	146°40' to 160°00'	26°40' Leo to 10°00' Virgo
13	Hasta	Moon	160°00' to 173°20'	10°00' to 23°20' Virgo
14	Chitra	Mars	173°20' to 186°40'	23°20 Virgo to 6°40' Libra
15	Swati	Rahu	186°40' to 200°00'	6°40' to 20°00 Libra
16	Vishakha	Jupiter	200°00' to 213°20'	20°00'Libra to 3°20' Scorpio
17	Anuradha	Saturn	213°20' to 226°40'	3°20' to 16°40' Scorpio
18	Jyeshta	Mercury	226°40' to 240°00'	16°40' Scorpio to 0°00'Sagittarius
19	Mula	Ketu	240°00' to 253°20'	0°00' to 13°20' Sagittarius
20	P Ashadha	Venus	253°20' to 266°40'	13°20' to 26°40' Sagittarius
21	U Ashadha	Sun	266°40' to 280°00'	26°40' Sag to 10°00' Capricorn
22	Abhijit		276°40' to 280°53'20''	6 °40 to 10 °53'20' Capricorn
23	Shravana	Moon	280°00' to 293°20'	10°00' to 23°20' Capricorn
24	Dhanishta	Mars	293°20' to 306°40'	23°20' Cap to 6°40' Aquarius
25	Shatabhishak	Rahu	306°40' to 320°00'	6°40' to 20°00' Aquarius
26	Purva Bhadra	Jupiter	320°00' to 333°20'	20°00' Aquarius to 3°20' Pisces
27	Uttara Bhadra	Saturn.	333°20' to 346°40'	3°20' to 16°40' Pisces
28	Revati	Mercury	346°40' to 360°00'	16°40' to 30°00' Pisces

twenty seven nakshatras. But old traditions remain and some techniques still use twenty eight nakshatras.

Abhijit should be seen as another secret link to help us understand the true quality of the soul; a bridge that leads us to deeper, more spiritual concepts – and therefore its knowledge is essential for the more serious astrologer. When we are studying Abhijit, we should think of it existing side by side with Uttara Ashadha and Shravana nakshatras, and all analysis should include both.

Nakshatra and Their Padas

Pada means foot or steps. There are four steps in each nakshatra. As the Moon remains in one nakshatra for one day, the padas reflect the natural divisions of the day: sunrise, midday, sunset and midnight.

Only 27 nakshatras are used for the padas. Each pada is the same as the navamsha and equals 3°20' each. The terms pada and navamsha are often interchangeable. In this book I will mostly use pada.

	Nakshatra	Pada 1 Sign	Pada 2 Sign	Pada 3 Sign	Pada 4 Sign
1	Ashwini	Aries	Tau	Gem	Can
2	Bharani	Leo	Virgo	Libra	Scorpio
3	Krittika	Sag	Cap	Aqua	Pisces
4	Rohini	Aries	Tau	Gem	Can
5	Mrigasira	Leo	Virgo	Libra	Scorpio
6	Ardra	Sag	Cap	Aqua	Pisces
7	Punarvasu	Aries	Tau	Gem	Can
8	Pushya	Leo	Virgo	Libra	Scorpio
9	Ashlesha	Sag	Cap	Aqua	Pisces
10	Magha	Aries	Tau	Gem	Can
11	P Phalguni	Leo	Virgo	Libra	Scorpio
12	U Phalguni	Sag	Cap	Aqua	Pisces
13	Hasta	Aries	Tau	Gem	Can
14	Chitra	Leo	Virgo	Libra	Scorpio
15	Swati	Sag	Cap	Aqua	Pisces
16	Vishakha	Aries	Tau	Gem	Can
17	Anuradha	Leo	Virgo	Libra	Scorpio
18	Jyeshta	Sag	Cap	Aqua	Pisces
19	Mula	Aries	Tau	Gem	Can
20	P Ashada	Leo	Virgo	Libra	Scorpio
21	U Ashadha	Sag	Cap	Aqua	Pisces
22	Shravana	Aries	Tau	Gem	Can
23	Dhanishta	Leo	Virgo	Libra	Scorpio
24	Shatabhishak	Sag	Cap	Aqua	Pisces
25	P Bhadra	Aries	Tau	Gem	Can
26	U Bhadra	Leo	Virgo	Libra	Scorpio
27	Revati	Sag	Cap	Aqua	Pisces

Further Padas Classifications

The nakshatras relate to each other through the sequence of rulership of the padas – nine nakshatras will have the same padas. This is an important connection and it is used in techniques for understanding the nakshatras.

Aries to Cancer padas are within Ashwini, Rohini, Punarvasu, Magha, Hasta, Vishakha, Mula, Shravana and Purva Bhadra. They are ruled by Ketu, Moon and Jupiter. These nakshatras show the various beginning cycles of new levels of the soul's development. They are searching for and creating fresh energies depending on the level of their manifestation.

Nakshatras	Ashwini, Rohini, Punarvasu, Magha, Hasta, Vishakha, Mula, Shravana & Purva Bhadra			
Signs →	Aries	Taurus	Gemini	Cancer
Pada →	1	2	3	4
	Ash 1	Ash 2	Ash 3	Ash 4
	Roh 1	Roh 2	Roh 3	Roh 4
	Pun 1	Pun 2	Pun 3	Pun 4
	Mag1	Mag 2	Mag 3	Mag 4
	Has 1	Has 2	Has 3	Has 4
	Vis 1	Vis 2	Vis 3	Vis 4
	Mul 1	Mul 2	Mul 3	Mul 4
	Shr 1	Shr 2	Shr 3	Shr 4

Leo to Scorpio padas are within Bharani, Mrigasira, Pushya, Purva Phalguni, Chitra, Anuradha, Purva Ashadha, Dhanishta and Uttara Bhadra. Venus, Mars and Saturn nakshatras show the soul's involvement in settling down into a certain way of being and then learning it is not good enough; so sparking the need for change.

Nakshatras	Bharani, Mrigasira, Pushya, P Phalguni, Chitra, Anuradha, P Ashadha, Dhanishta, U Bhadra			
Signs →	Leo	Virgo	Libra	Scorpio
Pada →	1	2	3	4
	Bha 1	Bha 2	Bha 3	Bha 4
	Mri 1	Mri 2	Mri 3	Mri 4
	Pus 1	Pus 2	Pus 3	Pus 4
	P.P 1	P.P 1	P.P 3	P.P 4
	Chi 1	Chi 2	Chi 3	Chi 4
	Anu 1	Anu 2	Anu 3	Anu 4
	P.A 1	P.A 2	P.A 3	P.A 4
	Dha 1	Dha 2	Dha 3	Dha 4
	UB 1	UB 2	UB 3	UB 4

Sagittarius to Pisces padas are within Krittika, Ardra, Ashlesha, Uttara Ashadha, Swati, Jyeshta, Uttara Ashadha, Shatabhishak, Revati. Sun, Rahu and Mercury rule them and they are seeking self-realisation. They are the ending cycles of the soul's development. These nakshatras end one way of thinking and aspire to move to the next level.

Nakshatras	Krittika, Ardra, Ashlesha, U Phalguni, Swati, Jyeshta, U Ashadha, Shatabhishak, Revati			
Signs →	Sag	Cap	Aqu	Pisces
Pada →	1	2	3	4
	Kri 1	Kri 2	Kri 3	Kri 4
	Ard 1	Ard 2	Ard 3	Ard 4
	Ashl 1	Ashl 2	Ashl 3	Ashl 4
	U.P 1	U.P 2	U.P 3	U.P 4
	Swa1	Swa 2	Swa 3	Swa 4
	Jye 1	Jye 2	Jye 3	Jye 4
	U.A 1	U.A 2	U.A 3	U.A 4
	Sha 1	Sha 2	Sha 3	Sha 4
	Rev 1	Rev 2	Rev 3	Rev 4

How Rashi and the Nakshatras Connect

The rashi division (twelve signs from Aries to Pisces) is the solar zodiac, and planets in the rashi show how we deal with Atma, the universal soul.

The nakshatras (Ashwini to Revati) form the lunar mandala and reflect the Jiva Atma, the living soul. The mandala shows how the mind works either with the soul or against it. It can indicate both intuition and blocks.

The rashi and nakshatras are connected by the navamsha and pada; the navamsha is the 9th division of the solar zodiac and the padas are the 4th division of the lunar one. *Nava* means nine and *amsha* means division. Navamsha means nine divisions. Each rashi is divided by nine navamsha that equals 3°20'. One nakshatra is 13°20' and if you divide one nakshatra by four there are four 3°20 pada. So the navamsha division and the nakshatra pada are one and the same division. The nakshatra padas and the navamsha both divide the zodiac into 108 parts.

Rashi, Nakshatra, Navamsha Mathematics
Solar Rasi: 9 navamsha in 12 signs = 108 divisions
Lunar nakshatras: 27 nakshatras each have four pada
(divisions) = 108 divisions
One navamsha = 3°20'
One pada = 3°20'

The Uses for Nakshatras

There are so many ways to use the nakshatra that it is impossible to list them all. Here are some of the important areas where the knowledge of nakshatras is essential.

1) Analysing the natal chart

The nakshatras are the key to Jyotish as they combine the solar and the lunar influences. Nakshatras represent the lunar mandala, and rashis, the solar Zodiac. What the combination of these two reveal is the essence of analysis. This book is focusing on chart analysis and the information given will be of immense use in understanding the self and its connection to the divine.

Knowing the nakshatra placements of your Ascendant and grahas is very important in Jyotish. The study of the nakshatra placements are very personal and understanding their points in your natal chart will lead you to a much deeper understanding of your inner motivation and tensions. They are best reached through their symbols: meditate on them and on their meaning. Their study, even in your own chart, is the work of a lifetime; they work on many different levels and their full meaning is only revealed over time. The nakshatras show the complex working of the mind and the underlying emotional energy behind every planet. In natal chart analysis, there is static and dynamic analysis:

In **static** analysis, we study the nakshatra to ascertain the quality of the mind, not just from the position of the Moon but also for all the other planets. We want to know gandanta positions, ashtamamsha, vargottama, pushkara. There are certain nakshatras that are difficult by nature, so we need to know how to deal with them if we have planets in them. The Moon nakshatra gives us the auspicious name consonant or vowel.

The **dynamic** analysis includes the mahadasha pattern and the transits that we will experience. In Jyotish, one human lifetime falls into a series of phases, the dashas, each one ruled by a particular graha. Calculation of which dashas you will experience in your life (you will not live through them all) and the timing of these life phases, is taken from the exact nakshatra position of the Moon at birth.

The position of the Moon at birth will indicate how the dasha pattern will unfold the soul purpose and timing of events.

2) Panchanga and the nakshatras of the day

The nakshatras form one of the five limbs of the panchanga and most of the aspects of birth panchanga nakshatra will be included in the natal analysis. The Moon travels through a different nakshatra daily. Each nakshatra, and therefore each day, has a different energy, which the Moon reflects and everybody feels throughout that day.

The transit position of the Moon in different nakshatras can make a difference to your life on a very personal level as well. Each day the Moon, as it is moving now, will have a slightly different relationship to the birth Moon and sometimes the aspect will be good and easy, sometimes difficult, and the energy you experience will have a different quality. This cycle is known as tara bala. With the tara bala grid you can use this lunar energy for yourself on a daily basis. You can read more about the Panchanga from my book *Personal Panchanga*.

3) Muhurta – Electional Astrology

Mahurta chooses auspicious times for planned events such as a marriage or the foundation of a new business venture, by setting up a 'birth' chart for them in advance which makes the best possible use of the planetary energies. Knowledge of the nakshatras is essential to this process.

4) Prashna

Prashna is a fascinating branch of vedic astrology where you do not need to know the time of birth or the place. The natal birth chart is not required. The time you visit the prashna astrologer or approach them has the answer as it becomes the birth chart of your question.

Prashna means question. The questioner is asking the astrologer a divine question to understand where his soul is at the present moment.

The birth chart is what we are born with. This gives us the perimeters within which our life works. We can use our given tools beautifully or create problems for ourselves. The question to the prashna astrologer is *Have I created positive karma for myself through expressing my free will or not?* What areas are blocking me and how to resolve them? The knowledge of nakshatras is essential for Prashna.

5) Synastry or relationship astrology
Most marriages in India are still arranged by the families, and the comparison of the charts of the likely bride and groom is an important part of the arrangements. The placement of the grahas, especially the Moon, in the nakshatras is considered when deciding whether the couple would be compatible on a sexual, romantic, practical and spiritual basis.

6) Medical astrology
The gunas, dosha and body parts of the nakshatras provide the key to analysing health. The padas of the nakshatras show how disease can travel in our body.

7) Remedial measures for challenging nakshatras
There are remedies given for all nakshatras, including difficult transits or eclipses. There are some nakshatras that bring issues with them: if your nakshatra is the same as your parents' or your siblings' or if your Moon is in gandanta, then certain remedies are prescribed by Parashara for removing the negativity. The most important element is beginning your remedies when the Moon is in the right nakshatra.

8) For use in rituals and prayer ceremonies
The birth nakshatra is used in all prayers. In yagyas, or in temples, the priests ask for the janma nakshatra so that they can propitiate the deities correctly, and with the connection directly to you. Subtly this helps the mind to calm down and remain like a gentle breeze rather than a destructive hurricane. The birth nakshatra connects you to the original great seer who had a say in your incarnation. This is known as *gotra* and is also used in all prayer ceremonies.

9) Rectification

Drawing up a correct natal chart requires an accurate and precise time of birth. Rectification is an astrological technique used to refine uncertain birth-times. Jyotish uses the nakshatras as an aid to rectification.

The Focus of This Book

In this book I am giving insight into the nakshatras which is immense in itself, the focus is on natal chart analysis.

2
Nakshatra Characteristics

Each nakshatra has its own individual characteristics, made up of many strands which include:

- Devata – ruling deities
- Symbols – secret knowledge
- Planetary rulers
- Puranic myth
- Animal connection – sacred animals and yoni – the animal sexuality
- Gunas or psychological qualities
- Nadi – physical weaknesses or doshas
- Purushartha – four aims of life
- Nama nakshatra – the sacred consonant
- Gana – division into Deva, Manushya and Rakshasa
- Varna – caste
- Quality – sharp, fixed, mutable etc.
- Direction
- Body part
- Panchamahabhuta – the five great elements

Devata – Ruling Deities *Devata* means god or divine dignity. Each nakshatra has a special deity that expresses its characteristic and protects the soul. As the nakshatras are said to reside in Swarga or heaven, where the gods and goddesses live, the devata of the nakshatra is of prime importance. The soul born in a specific nakshatra brings the essence of the deity down to earth. Nakshatra Devata is the deity to be propitiated at times of trouble.

During every yagya, prayer ceremony or visit to temple, the individual gives his/her janma (Moon) nakshatra to the priest so that they are at that moment connecting directly to the heavens; they are receiving the blessings of their nakshatra deity. It used to be a tradition

Nakshatra Devata and Symbol

Nakshatra	Devata	Symbol
Ashwini	Ashwini Kumara	Horse's head
Bharani	Yama	Female sexual organ
Krittika	Agni	Razor
Rohini	Brahma	Chariot
Mrigasira	Soma	Deer's head
Ardra	Rudra	Teardrop
Punarvasu	Aditi	Bow
Pushya	Brihaspati	Flower
Ashlesha	Naga	Serpent
Magha	Pitris	Palanquin
P Phalguni	Bhaga	Fireplace
U Phalguni	Aryaman	Four legs of the bed
Hasta	Savitar	Hand
Chitra	Twatshar	Pearl
Swati	Vayu	Coral
Vishakha	Indra, Agni	Archway
Anuradha	Mitra	Lotus
Jyeshta	Indra	Earring
Mula	Nirriti	Elephant's goad
P Ashadha	Apas	Elephant's tusk
U Ashadha	Vishwedeva	Planks of a bed
Shravana	Vishnu	Ear
Dhanishta	Vasus	Drum or flute
Shatabhishak	Varuna	Hundred stars
Purva Bhadra	Aja Ekapada	Sword
Uttara Bhadra	Ahir Budhnyana	Twins
Revati	Pushan	Fish

to be named after your janma deity. For example if you are born in Uttara Phalguni nakshatra, you could be named Aryaman after the deity. Obviously there are some more difficult deities whose names were not given. This is more the fear of the modern psyche, as in ancient India all energies were honoured. The fiercer the deity, the more blessings it can give if we invoke its inner nature. This name is usually kept secret and only revealed to the priest at the time of prayers.

Symbols

Symbols give the hidden meaning of the nakshatras. There can be more than one symbol connected to each nakshatra. Unravelling these symbols helps us to understand the nakshatra and its many meanings and it is one of the pleasures of studying the nakshatras. Ancient sages talked in the language of symbols, not giving the complete information in case it fell into the wrong hands and was misused. Many of the symbols are connected to the devata of the nakshatra and what they carry in their hands. Agni carries a sword of flames in his hand and one of the symbols of Krittika is a small sword.

The Navagraha – the Planetary Rulers of the Nakshatras

The navagraha, the nine planets, rule the nakshatras. *Graha* means 'to grasp' and *Nava* means nine so the nine planets grasp the energies of the celestial powers. The planets influence our lives and relationships through the rulership of the nakshatras. The nine planets are the Sun and Moon, Mars, Mercury, Jupiter, Venus, Saturn, Rahu and Ketu. One planet rules three nakshatras each. One set of nine nakshatras is known as a *paryay*. Abhijit nakshatra does not have a planetary ruler.

Vedic astrology relies on observable astronomy. The Sun and the Moon, Mars, Mercury, Jupiter, Venus, Saturn are observable by the naked eye so were given rulership of the nakshatras. Uranus, Neptune and Pluto are not observable by eye so they do not rule any nakshatras. Rahu and Ketu (the north and south nodes of the Moon) are astronomical points where the eclipses occur. According to the vedic seers Rahu and Ketu were visible during the solar and lunar eclipses so they too rule the nakshatras.

The nine planet rulership is prevalent in the vimshottari dasha system. In other dasha systems you may come across different planetary rulerships to the nakshatras.

Planetary Rulers

Graha	Nakshatras		
Sun	Krittika	U Phalguni	U Ashadha
Moon	Rohini	Hasta	Shravana
Mars	Mrigasira	Chitra	Dhanishta
Rahu	Ardra	Swati	Shatabhishak
Jupiter	P Vasu	Vishakha	P Bhadra
Saturn	Pushya	Anuradha	U Bhadra
Mercury	Ashlesha	Jyeshta	Revati
Ketu	Ashwini	Magha	Mula
Venus	Bharani	P Phalguni	P Ashadha

Puranic Myth

Puranas are ancient lore which eulogise the many vedic gods and goddesses with divine stories. In the puranas there are many myths connected to the same special aspect of the nakshatras. I will explain one myth per nakshatra to give a better understanding of their qualities.

The Animal Connection – Sacred Animal and Yoni

The animal symbols of the nakshatras are full of deep meanings and esoteric significance. In most books, the animal symbols are only given in connection with the sexual compatibility of the nakshatras. The animal connected to the nakshatras will give an indication of the personality, behaviour pattern, and relationship with other nakshatras not just from a sexual point of view, but the more spiritual connection. The animal talks of the primal energy and the starting point of the nakshatra where much of their energy rests.

Animals play an important part in vedic mythology. All deities have special animals which act as their transport. For example, Ganesha rides a rat. The rat is connected to Ganesha, so the two nakshatras with rats as their animal (Purva and Uttara Phalguni) should have some link to Lord Ganesha. These animal rulerships of the nakshatras show a secret connection between the animal and the deity it carries or is associated with. The presiding deity of all animals is Shiva and in this form he is known as Pashupatinath.

Nakshatra Sacred Animal and Devata

Nakshatra	Sacred Animal	Devata who connects with the Sacred Animal
Ashwini	Horse	Surya
Bharani	Elephant	Brihaspati, Indra
Krittika	Goat/Sheep	Agni
Rohini	Snake	Adishesha
Mrigasira	Snake	Adishesha
Ardra	Dog	Bhairava
Punarvasu	Cat	Shashti Devi
Pushya	Goat/Sheep	Agni
Ashlesha	Cat	Shashti Devi
Magha	Rat	Ganesha
P Phalguni	Rat	Ganesha
U Phalguni	Bull	Shiva
Hasta	Buffalo	Yama
Chitra	Tiger	Ayyappa
Swati	Buffalo	Yama
Vishakha	Tiger	Ayyappa
Anuradha	Deer	Soma
Jyeshta	Deer	Soma
Mula	Dog	Bhairava
P Ashadha	Monkey	Hanuman
U Ashadha	Mongoose	Kubera
Shravana	Monkey	Hanuman
Dhanishta	Lion	Durga
Shatabhishak	Horse	Surya
Purva Bhadra	Lion	Durga
Uttara Bhadra	Cow (Kamdhenu)	Shiva, Krishna
Revati	Elephant	Brihaspati, Indra

Sacred Animals

When analyzing the nakshatras, I started finding that understanding the sacred animal and which deity it is connected to had a major impact on how I understood them. I have included the sacred animal in each nakshatra analysis. In the ancient puranic lores, the gods overcame demonic forces and these became their transport; the deities also established a special connection with a particular animal whose more basic nature could be curbed through divine knowledge and blessings. It is better for everyone to be masters of their lower nature and that is the secret message revealed by the nakshatra animals.

Yoni – The Sexuality

Yoni has several meanings: womb, vulva, vagina, place of birth, source, origin, an abode, a receptacle. There are 13 pairs of animals which are either of male or female gender. The fourteenth animal is the mongoose who has no female counterpart. Each nakshatra has a yoni and the animal connected to it. Planets in the nakshatra vitalize this energy and therefore create a connection between Shiva and Shakti.

In relationship compatibility, the yoni of the couples is matched to study the sexual compatibility. The Moon nakshatra at birth decides your primary animal and its counterpart gender will be the best match sexually. Remember that for long term relationships just matching the yonis is not enough. Note that the mongoose has no female.

Nakshatra Yoni

Animal Sign	Male	Female
Horse	Ashwini	Shatabhishak
Elephant	Bharani	Revati
Goat/Sheep	Pushya	Krittika
Serpent	Rohini	Mrigasira
Dog	Mula	Ardra
Cat	Ashlesha	Punarvasu
Rat	Magha	P Phalguni
Cow	U Phalguni	U Bhadra
Buffalo	Swati	Hasta
Tiger	Vishakha	Chitra
Deer	Jyeshta	Anuradha
Monkey	P Ashadha	Shravana
Lion	P Bhadra	Dhanishta
Mongoose	U Ashadha	

The Gunas or Qualities of the Mind

Each nakshatra has its own guna. *Guna* means strand, the strands of twine that make up a rope. The rope is seen here as an allegory to personality; the various strands, or gunas, entwining to create the individuality of a person. The attribute of each guna is usually seen as mental rather than physical, but the mind has a great capacity to affect the physical side of our life.

Guna also means quality and usually refers to the mental quality of an individual. Gunas help the creative process and the operational qualities of prakriti, how nature unfolds within the human mind. As nakshatras represent the mind, it is essential to know their gunas. The three gunas are:

- Sattva – purity
- Rajas – activity
- Tamas – darkness

It is important to understand the impulses (gunas) of the nakshatras that give them their unique behaviour patterns. Sattva and tamas are inactive and they need rajas to activate them. All the gunas exist within each person, but one will be more prominent. See chapter six for more details.

Nadi – The Doshas of the Nakshatras

Each nakshatra has its own nadi or pulse. In this case it is used to define the ayurvedic dosha of the individual. The Sanskrit word *dosha* means fault or weakness and the term is used in ayurveda, the vedic science of well being, to find the weakness in the nature of man which when aggravated causes diseases. The weakness represented here is physical as well as spiritual; how nature organises itself in a physical body. Each person tends to reflect a dosha in dominance.

We can find our weaknesses by studying the doshas of our Moon nakshatras. This is used in relationships analysis; people with a similar dosha should not marry if they want to have children as the child would inherit too much of the same weakness from both parents. The three doshas are vata, pitta and kapha.

Vata – the Air quality The natural qualities of vata are action, sensation, and enthusiasm. Vata means wind. Vata nakshatras tend to be of a nervous disposition.

Pitta – the Fire quality Fire is required to digest and eat. Pitta produces heat and controls the digestive system. Pitta nakshatras are active, motivated and hot-tempered.

Kapha – the Water quality Water governs the suppleness and structure of the body and protects it from disease if in balance. Kapha nakshatras are philosophical, calm and patient in nature. Laziness and weight can be their problem.

Doshas are important to understand the physical weaknesses in a person, while the nakshatras show how these weaknesses affect the mind. Doshas are the nervous energy indicating certain psychological patterns that make up the physical self. They reflect the temperaments and attitudes, as well as the ability to spiritually connect.

The nadi of the nakshatras are used in relationship compatibility and medical astrology.

Nakshatras and their Doshas

Vata	Pitta	Kapha
Ashwini	Bharani	Krittika
Ardra	Mrigasira	Rohini
Punarvasu	Pushya	Ashlesha
U. Phalguni	P. Phalguni	Magha
Hasta	Chitra	Swati
Jyeshta	Anuradha	Vishakha
Mula	P Ashadha	U Ashadha
Shatabhishak	Dhanishta	Shravana
P Bhadra	U Bhadra	Revati

Purushartha – The Four Aims of Life
According to the vedic tradition, humans have four aims to fulfill in life. This gives meaning to their life and sets them on the path of self-realization. The four aims are known as Purushartha. *Purusha* means both the supreme soul and the human being; *Artha* means the aim or purpose. Purushartha is the true purpose of the soul that is born on earth, the foundation of life. The vedic philosophers considered four basic motivations that guide us to lead a happy and fulfilled life, so the purushartha are what each soul has to deal with; understanding them helps us to navigate life without adding unnecessary karma for future lives. The four aims are:

Dharma – its motivation is virtue
Dharma is the correct action, the right purpose. Dharma is the main purpose of our life, the duty towards ourselves and others, the duty to do the right thing. Dharma is religious, moral and social duty, acting according to our own conscience, following the laws of nature, and upholding the principles of society. Dharma can change according to the sex, caste, nationality, status and culture of the individual. Without Dharma, the other aims of life are useless and do not bring fulfillment or realization.

Artha – its motivation is wealth creation
Artha means purposeful action. Artha relates to wealth, financial matters, material success and the practicalities of life. This is action we take to fulfill a particular purpose. This is goal-orientated activity that leads to prosperity and material success. Wealth creation or prosperity achieved at the cost of ethics and virtue is not regarded as a true expression of Artha.

Kama – its motivation is love and passion
Kama deals with the art of living pleasurably. It also represents fragrances, art, drama and other creative pleasures of life. The path of pleasure awakens the five primal elements (Earth, Water, Fire, Air, and Ether) and their physical organs (eyes, nose, tongue, ears and skin). Kama is what delights the mind, body and soul by seeing, hearing, eating, listening and touching. Kama is passion for life, to enjoy it in every colour and

form, and to fulfill the sexual and sensual desires as well. Kama is both a purushartha and a shad ripu or prime weakness in man. The reason: pleasures and desires that kama awakens can soon overtake an awakening conscience and make them indulgent and materialistic.

Moksha – its motivation is liberation
Moksha is spiritual realization. Moksha means self-realization or liberation, the need to find the highest truths and move towards self-realization. When we attain moksha, we break away from the cycles of births and deaths and live a life of eternal happiness. This is the final purpose of every incarnating soul. Moksha can be achieved once we get the first three right. There is no fast track to moksha.

Purushartha – Four Aims of Life

Dharma	Artha	Kama	Moksha
Ashwini	Bharani	Krittika	Rohini
Pushya	Punarvasu	Ardra	Mrigasira
Ashlesha	Magha	P. Phalguni	U. Phalguni
Vishakha	Swati	Chitra	Hasta
Anuradha	Jyeshta	Mula	P Ashadha
Dhanishta	Shravana	Abhijit	U Ashadha
Shatabhishak	P Bhadra	U Bhadra	Revati

All the purushartha are bound together and are interdependent. One leads to another and one cannot be fulfilled while we neglect the other. The first phase of the aims is dharma, artha and kama. They are bound together and need to be pursued in harmony. Dharma is the most important aim and has to be practised while achieving artha and kama. Virtue and ethics cannot be sacrificed in the pursuit of pleasure and success. Trying to take a fast track to moksha can only lead to failure, as the worldly issues haven't been dealt with; the soul is not fully ready to give up all its responsibilities. The sages always say that we should fulfil the first three purushartha first, and only then should we aspire towards moksha.

Unlike the rashi, the nakshatras are complete in themselves. Each nakshatra has its own aim and its pada reflects all the four aims. These can be used to refine the purushartha where we study the dual influences. The main purushartha is the obvious quality and then the sub-purushartha adds to the analysis. The purushartha of each pada is the following:

Nakshatra Purushartha and Pada Purushartha

Nakshatra	Purushartha	Pada1	Pada 2	Pada3	Pada4
Ashwini	Dharma	Dharma	Artha	Kama	Moksha
Bharani	Artha	Moksha	Kama	Artha	Dharma
Krittika	Kama	Dharma	Artha	Kama	Moksha
Rohini	Moksha	Moksha	Kama	Artha	Dharma
Mrigasira	Moksha	Dharma	Artha	Kama	Moksha
Ardra	Kama	Moksha	Kama	Artha	Dharma
Punarvasu	Artha	Dharma	Artha	Kama	Moksha
Pushya	Dharma	Moksha	Kama	Artha	Dharma
Ashlesha	Dharma	Dharma	Artha	Kama	Moksha
Magha	Artha	Moksha	Kama	Artha	Dharma
P Phalguni	Kama	Dharma	Artha	Kama	Moksha
U Phalguni	Moksha	Moksha	Kama	Artha	Dharma
Hasta	Moksha	Dharma	Artha	Kama	Moksha
Chitra	Kama	Moksha	Kama	Artha	Dharma
Swati	Artha	Dharma	Artha	Kama	Moksha
Vishakha	Dharma	Moksha	Kama	Artha	Dharma
Anuradha	Dharma	Dharma	Artha	Kama	Moksha
Jyeshta	Artha	Moksha	Kama	Artha	Dharma
Mula	Kama	Dharma	Artha	Kama	Moksha
P Ashadha	Moksha	Moksha	Kama	Artha	Dharma
U Ashadha	Moksha	Dharma	Artha	Kama	Moksha
Abhijit	Kama				
Shravana	Artha	Dharma	Artha	Kama	Moksha
Dhanishta	Dharma	Moksha	Kama	Artha	Dharma
S'bhishak	Moksha	Dharma	Artha	Kama	Moksha
P Bhadra	Kama	Moksha	Kama	Artha	Dharma
U Bhadra	Artha	Dharma	Artha	Kama	Moksha
Revati	Dharma	Moksha	Kama	Artha	Dharma

Each nakshatra has its own motivation like Hasta is moksha nakshatra and then its four padas begin with dharma and end in moksha. If the Moon is placed in 15° Virgo, it is placed in Hasta pada 2 so the dual influence of purushartha will be moksha and artha, two opposing aspects, and can be a struggle between spiritual and practical expression.

Abhijit is kama nakshatra and it has only one full pada; we can consider it to be expressing the desires and creativity of kama.

Gana – Deva, Nara and Rakshasa (Gods, Humans, and Demons)

Gana means a tribe or multitude, and in this instance it means the tribe of humans. They are classified under three headings: *devas* (gods), *nara* (humans) and *rakshasa* (demons). Gods are kind, humans imperfect and mostly trying to fulfill their ambitions, whereas demons are only concerned with their own needs, never caring for others. Humans tend to move between godliness and demonic behaviour. These sections also reflect the temperament and nature. The gods were soft and sensitive, demons were ambitious, rough and ready. Humans can be both, struggling with their weaknesses and moving between fine and harsh natures. Gana are also followers of Shiva. The lord of the gana is Ganesha. In this case the gana of the nakshatra refers to a group.

Ganas

Gods	Humans	Demons
Ashwini	Bharani	Krittika
Mrigasira	Rohini	Ashlesha
Punarvasu	Ardra	Magha
Pushya	P Phalguni	Chitra
Hasta	U Phalguni	Vishakha
Swati	P Ashadha	Jyeshta
Anuradha	U Ashadha	Mula
Shravana	P Bhadra	Dhanishta
Revati	U Bhadra	Shatabhishak

Nakshatras are classified into three groups of gods, humans, and demons. The main aspect of gana is usually studied to understand the nature of an individual.

Knowing the nature of the nakshatra allows us to understand the basic quality, so that we can develop from there. They are used primarily in relationship compatibility.

Varna – Caste

Varna are the spiritual divisions of man. They are often called castes but that is social divisions and not in harmony with the real meaning of these spiritual divisions. In the vedic age it was understood from the birth chart what was the true inclination and temperament of a person and his life was guided towards it. Each planet, sign and nakshatra had a particular spiritual quality, which moved them towards that path of self expression in the material life.

There are four primary varna, different directions available to the soul to express its karma in its journey through life:

- **Brahman** – the seeker and teacher of knowledge of a spiritual nature is Sattvic in quality.
- **Kshatriya** – the defenders, rulers, commanders, leaders of the nation are Rajasic quality.
- **Vaishya** – Those who are attracted to the material life where self interest and ambition dominate. The professional person, industrialists, and wealth creators are of rajasic and tamasic quality.
- **Shudra** – the workers, who are tamasic in nature.

The nakshatras add three more to the original varna. At present we may represent many different varna which have their origin in the first four.

Outcast: the outcast planets are usually Rahu and Ketu. Those who belong to the outcast nakshatras may not follow the law of the land, or they may do things in a different way. They may feel as outsiders in the world they live in. People who do unusual jobs or are immigrants can feel like outcasts in the society they live in.

Butcher: can be studied also for those who have expertise in cutting, dissecting, and surgery.

Farmers: are those who produce something. It can be linked to land and production but also to other kinds of production.

Brahmin	Kshatriya	Vaishya	Shudra
Krittika	Pushya	Ashwini	Rohini
P Phalguni	U Phalguni	Punarvasu	Magha
P Ashadha	U Ashadha	Hasta	Anuradha
P Bhadra	Dhanishta		Revati
	U Bhadra		

Farmer	Butcher	Outcast
Mrigasira	Ardra	Bharani
Chitra	Swati	Ashlesha
Jyeshta	Mula	Vishakha
	Shatabhi	Shravana

Each nakshatra belongs to a caste, therefore they are suited to performing those tasks. Try to look beyond negative qualities of these castes. If a nakshatra has a butcher quality, they could also be good at dissecting, surgery and research. The nakshatras reflect the outcast, those who do not fit into the above categories.

Directions of the Nakshatras

South	West	North	East
Ashwini	Bharani	Krittika	Rohini
Mrigasira	Ardra	Punarvasu	Pushya
Ashlesha	Magha	P Phalguni	U Phalguni
Hasta	Chitra	Swati	Vishakha
Anuradha	Jyeshta	Mula	P Ashadha
U Ashadha		Shravana	Dhanishta
Shatabhishak	P Bhadra	U Bhadra	Revati

Direction

This is usually used in prashna or for muhurta. If the Moon is in a particular nakshatra on the day you plan to travel, it signifies the auspiciousness of the direction of the nakshatra. However, if there are malefic planets placed in the nakshatra, then there can be trouble from that direction. Your best direction is given from the position of the nakshatra of your lagna, Sun and Moon and the dasha ruler. For example if Mercury dasha is running and Mercury is placed in Pushya nakshatra, Pushya's direction is east, so the eastern direction may become important for travel and living. Change the dasha to Ketu, which is in Krittika, whose direction is north – then the northern direction may have a greater influence. A change of home may be in the north part of the city or country too.

Nakshatra Panchamahabhutas

Pancha means five, *Maha* is great and *Bhuta* is element. *Bhuta* comes from the word *bhu* that means the earth. Bhuta is what is formed from the earth or experienced during the earthly birth. It has several other meanings: a primary substance, the true state of the soul, the real nature, or the way the worldly issues control the spiritual ones. The Pancha Maha Bhuta are the five primary elements that influence our physical body and also sheath the eternal consciousness. They are also known as the *Pancha Maha Tattvas*. Tattva is another name for bhuta specially when applied to the physical. The five great elements are:

Aakash	Ether
Vayu	Air
Agni	Fire
Apas	Water
Prithvi	Earth

Prithvi	Apas	Agni	Vayu	Aakash
Ashwini	Ardra	U Phalguni	Anuradha	Dhanishta
Bharani	Punarvasu	Hasta	Jyeshta	Shatabhishak
Krittika	Pushya	Chitra	Mula	P Bhadra
Rohini	Ashlesha	Swati	P Ashada	U Bhadra
Mrigasira	Magha	Vishakha	U Ashada	Revati
	P Phalguni		Shravana	

The knowledge of these five great elements is essential to understanding panchanga as well as the natal chart.

3
Strength and Weakness in the Nakshatras

The pada position of the planet is the key to its strength and weakness. In each chart we have the rashi and nakshatra position, but the secret lies in how these planets are in their pada/navamsha. Some are more obvious like exaltation, own sign and debilitation of planets by pada, but there are others that need to be understood. Vargottama, pushkara, ashtamamsha and gandanta are added qualities we need to know. Gandanta is discussed in Chapter 7. The pada shows the true quality of the planet placed within a sign and nakshatra. These positions will be discussed in the analysis of each nakshatra, so it is important to know them. They can create unexpected opportunities or blocks in the growth of the soul. Remember that navamsha and the nakshatra pada are one and the same thing.

Vargottama
Planets placed in the same sign in the rashi and navamsha chart are called *vargottama* and this gives added strength to the planets. *Varga* means division and *uttama* is supreme. It shows an integrated quality of the planet where the needs of the eternal soul and the individual soul are the same, the mind, body and spirit are in perfect harmony. It is a great position for planets to be in, even if planets become debilitated in vargottama.

Signs	Vargottama degrees
Aries, Cancer, Libra , Capricorn	0°00' to 3°20'
Taurus, Leo, Scorpio, Aquarius	13°20' to 16°40'
Gemini, Virgo, Sagittarius , Pisces	26°40' to 30°00'

Vargottama is linked to the modalities – cardinal, fixed and mutable. The planets are vargottama in the 1st navamsha of cardinal signs, the 5th navamsha of the fixed signs and the 9th navamsha of the mutable signs. The 1st, 5th and 9th houses and signs are linked to dharma, the ethical way of living. The vargottama navamsha makes the planets dharmic and pure, regardless of what the natural energy may be. It makes their energy whole again, despite being placed in enemy signs or difficult positions. Suppose Venus is debilitated but vargottama. Venus is the karaka of marriage, so its debilitation will indicate difficulty in that area. Being vargottama there can be an acceptance of difficulty in relationships and the individual tries to deal with it in the best way given the circumstances. Similarly the debilitation of the Sun can give lack of self confidence and a challenging relationship with the father. But its vargottama position will make peace with the father and learn to deal with the lack of self-confidence. Vargottama planets bring strength and steadiness and can give solid success.

Warren Buffett, 30 August 1930, 15:00 (+6.00 CST)
Omaha, Nebraska

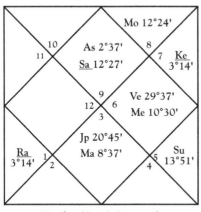

Rashi (D-1)General

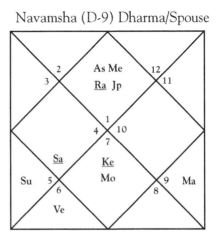

Navamsha (D-9) Dharma/Spouse

Warren Buffet is an American business magnate, investor, and philanthropist. He is widely considered the most successful investor of the 20th century (Wikipedia). There are four vargottama planets in his chart adding to his ability to succeed and to make the choices that have made him one of the richest men in the world.

Venus in Virgo and Chitra nakshatra and Virgo pada is debilitated yet vargottama. Venus in Virgo can give great business abilities, and being vargottama it is magnified. Venus is atmakaraka too.

The Sun is in Leo and Purva Phalguni nakshatra and Leo pada, which makes the 9th lord doubly powerful.

Rahu and Ketu are both vargottama. Rahu in Aries and Ashwini and Aries pada, Ketu in Libra and Chitra and Libra pada. Both bring karmic strength to the chart.

Pushkara Pada and Navamsha

Pushkara are special places in the zodiac that enhance the quality of the planet. *Push* means to nourish and *Kara* means 'who does' or 'what causes'. There is also a pushkara degree and navamsha. Both degree and navamsha show the ability of the planet to be strong. Obviously the closer to the exact degree of pushkara the planet is, the greater its strength in nourishing.

Pushkara degrees are:
21° Aries, 19° Leo,
23° Sagittarius
14° Taurus, 9° Virgo,
14° Capricorn
18° Gemini, 24° Libra,
19° Aquarius
8° Cancer, 11° Scorpio,
9° Pisces

Pushkara navamsha/pada nourishes the quality of the planet placed within it. This can take the quality of the planet from ordinary to extra-ordinary. Pushkara navamsha are not given in many texts. They form the secret part of vedic astrology in which when you dig deep you come up with gems of analysis. The mystery was essential to avoid disclosing the real essence of Jyotish to everyone.

There are two nourishing navamsha in every sign, 24 in all. Pushkara navamsha can be classified as follows:

> 4th pada of Rahu nakshatra – Ardra, Swati and Shatabhishak
> 2nd pada of Moon nakshatras – Rohini, Hasta, Shravana
> 1st pada and 4th pada of Sun nakshatras – Krittika, Uttara Phalguni, Uttara Ashadha

2nd pada and 4th pada of Jupiter nakshatras – Punarvasu, Vishakha, Purva Bhadra

2nd pada of Saturn nakshatra – Pushya, Anuradha, Uttara Bhadra

3rd pada of Venus nakshatras – Bharani, Purva Phalguni, Purva Ashadha

Pushkara Navamsha

Signs	Nakshatra	Degrees	Pushkara navamsha
Aries, Leo, Sagittarius	Bharani, P. Phalguni, P. Ashada	20°00' to 23°20'	Libra
	Krittika, U. Phalguni, U. Ashada	26°40' to 30°00'	Sagittarius
Taurus, Virgo, Capricorn	Krittika, U. Phalguni, U. Ashada	06°40' to 10°00'	Pisces
	Rohini, Hasta, Shravana	13°20' to 16°40'	Taurus
Gemini, Libra, Aquarius	Ardra, Swati, Shatabhishak	16°40' to 20°00'	Pisces
	Punarvasu, Vishakha, P. Bhadra	23°20' to 26°40'	Taurus
Cancer, Scorpio, Pisces	Punarvasu, Vishakha, P. Bhadra	0°00' to 03°20'	Cancer
	Pushya, Anuradha, U. Bhadra	06°40' to 10°00'	Virgo

Ketu (Ashwini, Magha, and Mula), Mercury (Ashlesha, Jyeshta, Revati) and Mars (Mrigasira, Chitra, Dhanishta) do not have any pushkara navamsha. Ketu nakshatras show the beginning of the soul's search and as there hasn't been time to collect any debris from this life they may be unwilling to let go of their past karmas. The soul has to search here without having the awareness of how to transform. The idealism is strong and as the soul is coming into contact with all that is new, it is not ready to change until it has a complete picture of its new life. Mars nakshatras are at a midpoint where the quality of the soul changes. Mercury nakshatras are areas of transformation where the debris of all the soul's negativity gets collected and we have to learn to transcend. The beginning, middle and last nakshatras do not have pushkara navamshas in each of the pariyayas or cycles. The pushkara navamshas throw up some interesting points:

- The rulerships of the navamshas are by benefic planets.
- Jupiter and Venus rule nine pushkara each. Jupiter and Venus are the great gurus of the Vedas as Brihaspati and Shukracharya. Both of them nourish and guide the cosmos to make the right choices. They help the planets placed in their padas to find the right direction.
- The Moon and Mercury rule three pushkara each. As the two planets of the mind they help to nourish it so the person is calm and ready to develop their spiritual self.

Planets in pushkara navamsha act like they are exalted. The main difference being while the exalted planet will follow in natural qualities, a planet in pushkara navamsha will need to cultivate its better qualities to find the best in itself. It will be strongly influenced by the ruler of its pushkara and therefore imbibe some of those qualities in a positive way only. Pushkara is auspicious, so the planets placed in them will also become so.

Ramana Maharishi 30 Dec 1879, 01:15 am (–5:30 IST) Tiruchizhi India

Rashi (D-1) General

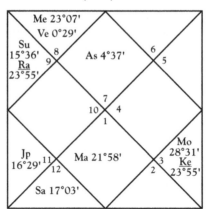

Planet Nakshatras and Pushkara Navamshas

Planet	Nakshatra	Lords	Pushkara
Ascendant	Chitra	Mars	
Sun	Purva Ashadha	Venus	
Moon	Punarvasu	Jupiter	
Mars	Bharani	Venus	Pushkara
Mercury	Jyestha	Mercury	
Jupiter	Shatabhishak	Rahu	
Venus	Vishakha	Jupiter	Pushkara
Saturn	Revati	Mercury	
Rahu	Purva Ashadha	Venus	
Ketu	Punarvasu	Jupiter	Pushkara

Sri Ramana Maharishi has three planets in pushkara. Mars at 21° 58' Aries is at the exact Pushkara degree and pada. Venus (0°29' Scorpio) and Ketu (23°56' Gemini) are both in pushkara navamsha/pada. His lagna is in Chitra nakshatra ruled by Mars and he has the Sun, Mars and Rahu placed in the nakshatras ruled by pushkara Venus.

Vimshottari			
Start Date		Age	Dashas
16/ 8/	1877	-2.4	Jp Ve
16/ 4/	1880	0.3	Jp Su
2/ 2/	1881	1.1	Jp Mo
4/ 6/	1882	2.4	Jp Ma
11/ 5/	1883	3.4	Jp Ra
4/ 10/	**1885**	**5.8**	**Sa Sa**
6/ 10/	1888	8.8	Sa Me
16/ 6/	1891	11.5	Sa Ke
25/ 7/	1892	12.6	Sa Ve
25/ 9/	1895	15.7	Sa Su
6/ 9/	1896	16.7	Sa Mo
7/ 4/	1898	18.3	Sa Ma

Sri Ramana Maharishi attained liberation at the age of 16 when he was running a Saturn Venus dasha. Venus is pushkara and his lagna lord. Sri Ramana Maharishi left home for Arunachala, a sacred mountain in the shape of a lingam at Tiruvannamalai, and lived there for the rest of his life. Arunachala temple is Shiva in the form of the Agni or fire element[4]. In this chart both the planets connected to fire, Mars and Ketu, are pushkara. Mars is at its exact pushkar degree and in Bharani nakshatra ruled by Venus. Mars exchanges nakshatra rulership with Venus as Venus in Chitra is in a Mars nakshatra.

---

4. More on elements in *Personal Panchanga*, Komilla Sutton. The Wessex Astrologer Ltd.

Sri Ramana maintained that the purest form of his teachings was the silence which radiated from his presence. He gave verbal teachings only for the benefit of those who could not understand his silence. Mars is the lord of the 2nd house of speech.

The influence of the pushkara gave him ability to purify himself and live an enlightened life whose teachings are still being followed.

Ashtamamsha

Ashtam means eight and *amsha* is division. This refers to the position when the planet is placed in the 8th sign in the navamsha/pada from its rashi sign. If the Sun is at 11° Virgo, it is in Aries pada, it is placed in the 8th sign in the navamsha from its position in the rashi. This creates an inner tension between the rashi, nakshatra and navamsha; a disconnection between what you want to achieve on a soul level and the physical one. Ashtamamsha is the most difficult position for the planet to be placed in. The individual soul does not understand what the universal soul wants. There is lack of integration. The mind is telling you something whereas your circumstances are giving other indications. This position of planets has to be handled with great sensitivity. Lack of cohesiveness, great inner conflict, being pulled in two different directions, causes problems. You must face transformation before you can understand the true message.

Ashtamamsha Grid

Degrees	Rashi	Navamsha	Pada
23°20'–26°40'	Aries	Scorpio	Bharani–4
10°00'–13°20'	Gemini	Capricorn	Ardra–2
23°20'–26°40'	Cancer	Aquarius	Ashlesha–3
10°00'–13°20'	Virgo	Aries	Hasta–1
23°20'–26°40'	Libra	Taurus	Vishakha–2
10°00'–13°20'	Sagittarius	Cancer	Mula–4
23°20'–26°40'	Capricorn	Leo	Dhanishta–1
10°00'–13°20'	Pisces	Libra	U Bhadra–3

To summarise:
8th navamsha of cardinal signs is Ashtamamsha – Aries (Scorpio navamsha), Cancer (Aquarius navamsha), Libra (Taurus navamsha) and Capricorn (Leo navamsha).

4th navamsha of mutable signs is ashtamamsha – Gemini (Capricorn navamsha), Virgo (Aries navamsha), Sagittarius (Cancer navamsha) and Pisces (Libra navamsha).

There are no ashtamamsha in the fixed signs of Taurus, Leo, Scorpio and Aquarius.

Certain planets may appear strong in their pada but can be in conflict:
Mars in Scorpio pada of Aries
Venus in Taurus pada of Libra
Jupiter exalted in Cancer pada of Sagittarius
Venus in Libra pada of Pisces.

There are only eight nakshatras that have ashtamamsha. They are Bharani, Ardra, Ashlesha, Hasta, Vishakha, Mula, Dhanishta and Uttara Bhadra. Each of these nakshatras show difficult aspects of soul growth where there are struggles to integrate the inner needs with the outer desires. The ashtamamsha challenges are:

- **Bharani** learns lessons in discipline; understands blocks in life and gains the knowledge of death and transformation.
- **Ardra** creates desire for perfection where we destroy what does not match up.
- **Ashlesha** is learning about the poisons of life, to embrace and to understand pain.
- **Hasta** gives mental distress, lack of peace of mind. Material aspirations create conflict with a more spiritual path.
- **Vishakha** shows you heaven but does not give it.
- **Mula** destroys materialism and security in search for moksha. Can separate you from those you love.
- **Dhanishta** makes you satisfy others' needs before your own. Unfulfilled personal ambitions can create frustrations.
- **Uttara Bhadra** faces the final struggles before they can embrace spirituality. It is a most profound position but can be the most difficult.

Michael Jackson 29 August 1958, 19:32 CDT, Gary , Indiana, USA

Rashi (D-1) General   Navamsha (D-9) Dharma/Spouse

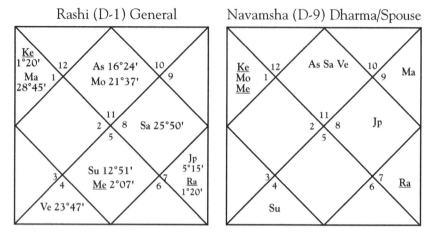

Planet Nakshatras and Pushkar Navamshas

Planet	Nakshatra	Rashi	Pada	Ashtamamsha
Asc	Shatabhishak	Aquarius	Aquarius	
Sun	Magha	Leo	Cancer	
Moon	Purva Bhadra	Aquarius	Aries	
Mars	Krittika	Aries	Sagittarius	
Mer	Magha	Leo	Aries	
Jup	Chitra	Libra	Scorpio	
Ven	Ashlesha	Cancer	Aquarius	Ashtamamsha
Sat	Jyeshta	Scorpio	Aquarius	
Rahu	Chitra	Libra	Libra	
Ketu	Ashwini	Aries	Aries	

Michael Jackson was the tragic superstar whose relationship with his father defined his life. He has Venus, the lord of the 9th house, in ashtamamsha. Venus goes from Cancer in rashi to Aquarius pada in the navamsha. Venus is also the rajayogakaraka, the best planet for Aquarius Ascendants and its position in ashtamamsha shows that he did not really enjoy his good fortune and luck. The 9th house deals with advisers. The quality of advice he received and the so-called advisers that crowded around him is reflected by Venus's ashtamamsha position.

4
The Nakshatras 1 to 27
1. Ashwini

0°00' to 13°20'
Padas: Aries, Taurus, Gemini, Cancer

Meaning

Ashwin means a cavalier or a horse tamer. The symbol of Ashwini is also the horse. Horses represent our senses, desires and creative energy. As cavaliers have the ability to ride horses they are connected to the ability to master our desires. *Ashwins* are the harbingers of *Usha* or dawn. Dawn brings with it a very special energy, the promise of a new tomorrow while still attached to the mysterious night. Ashwins are the link between the darkness

Ashwini
Devata: The Ashwini Kumara
Ruled by Ketu
Symbol: The Horse's Head
Animal sign: Male Horse
Motivation: Dharma
Guna Triplicity: Rajas, Rajas, Rajas
Ayurvedic Dosha: Kapha
Body Part: Upper Part of the Feet
Gana: Divine
Caste: Merchant
Quality: Light
Colour: Blood Red
Best Direction: South
Special Sounds: Choo, Che, Cho, La
Principal Star: Hamal and Sheratan
Other Names of Ashwini: Nasatya, Dasra, Ashwiyuka, Tutaga, Vaaji, Ashwa, Haya

of the night and the brightness of the day, and express the mysterious quality of the new morning, full of anticipation and uncertainty. The new day ends the darkness. Ashwins bring new light and awareness to the incarnating soul while being connected to the karma of old deeds. Indians believe that past lives fashion the present and the future, and Ashwini express this philosophy.

Devata – Ashwini Kumara

Ashwini Kumara are the twin sons of the Surya and the physicians to the gods. Their individual names are Nasatya and Dasra. The Sun represents the soul; the soul gives birth to its image through Ashwini. Ashwini Kumara are considered to be the deities of Ayurveda. They represent the duality of life by being the connection between heaven and earth, day and night, past and future. They are luminous in nature. They are beneficent and have great curative powers. They have the ability to restore youthfulness and rejuvenate the old.

They are the natural healers of the zodiac and Ashwini can be found in healing professions like doctors, healers, and spiritualists. At times they can be misunderstood as people do not sense the innocence and idealism under their strong exterior.

Planetary Ruler – Ketu

Ketu is a mystical planet which is headless and spiritual. It is hard to understand and has divine aspirations. Ketu is the past life planet and the significator for moksha. Moksha is spiritual liberation, letting go of our individual selves to merge with the eternal consciousness. The beginning of the nakshatra mandala ruled by Ketu nakshatra shows that the true reason of our manifestation on earth is to find moksha. This is the stage where the mind is pure and not yet entangled with the attachments and desires of this life, yet it brings past life issues that have to be resolved.

Ketu wants a state of absolute perfection where there is perpetual happiness and the soul is released from the cycles of unhappiness and pain. Very few people reach such a state or find such a perfect world. Therefore Ashwini can feel dissatisfied with the present as it never matches up to the idealism they crave.

Mesha Rashi

Ashwini is placed entirely in Mesha rashi (Aries). Warrior Aries has the courage to offer his life as the ultimate sacrifice for the protection of others. As Ashwini, these people have to sacrifice their senses and desires to search for the elusive self-realization. But they may swing from one extreme to the other, from ascetic to sensuous, spiritualist to materialistic.

Ashwini in Aries shows the living soul very much in touch with its roots in the past life. Aries has the courage to explore where others have not been; Ashwini brings idealism and honours the past. As Ketu acts like Mars, the combination of the dynamic and spiritual qualities of Mars works with all planets placed here. The purity of Martian action, courage and protection of humanity is powerfully indicated.

Symbol – The Head of the Horse

The *Brhad-aranyaka Upanishad*[1] begins with the description of the ceremony of the horse sacrifice. Horses are linked to unmanageable desires and the ability to control them is the key to happiness and moksha. The horse sacrifice metaphorically symbolises humans sacrificing their desires. Surya, the Sun, who rides the seven horses showing his mastery over desires is exalted in Ashwini.

Ashwa, or the horse, is connected with the number seven, which is a very auspicious number in Hindu philosophy; there are seven chakras - the creative energy which moves from the absolute within us, seven flames of eternal fire, seven states of wisdom and seven levels of consciousness.

Puranic Myth – The Birth of Ashwini Kumara

Skanda Purana[2] tells how Ashwini Kumara came to be born. Surya, the Sun, was married to Sanjana, the daughter of Vishwamitra. She loved him but Surya was very bright and hot, and his lustre was not easy to bear. Sanjana had three children, two sons and a daughter: Vaivasvart Manu, Yama and Yamuna. When his heat became unbearable Sanjana left Surya by creating a shadow wife Chhaya. She soon realized her mistake and wanted to come back but could not do so. (Read more in Bharani.)

Sanjana went away to a forest and disguised herself as a mare in order to keep herself safe. She only grazed on dry grass. She hoped that her tapas or austerity would bring back her husband and give her the strength to deal with the fire of the Surya.

When Surya discovered the truth, he went to find her. Surya transformed himself into a horse and re-established relations with his wife. The twins Ashwini Kumar were born through this relationship of Surya and Sanjana as horses.

The love of Surya and Sanjana overcame many hurdles and the conception and birth of Ashwini Kumar is from true love, forgiving and

---

1. Upanishads are ancient books of Vedic philosophy. *Brhad-aranyaka* is one of the most important and oldest of these Upanishads.
2. The Puranas came after the Upanishads. They tell mythological tales of deities, planets and talk philosophy. *Skanda Purana* is dedicated to Skanda who is a form of Kartikeya and a deity connected to the planet Mars.

all encompassing. This is the quality all Ashwini can seek, even when faced with challenges and deception.

Ashwini Aim is for Dharma

Ashwini expresses itself as dharmic. Dharma is the ethical use of religion, law, duty, and customs. Ashwini people are concerned about leading a moral life. They have a strong sense of destiny and uphold the ethics of their family, country and religion. They can have the tendency to be self-righteous. They will be deeply spiritual but do not necessarily openly express it.

Sacred Animal – The Seven Horses of Surya

Surya, the Sun, rides a chariot pulled by seven horses. Horses represent desires and Surya's ability to gain control of these desires is why he is exalted in Ashwini. At the stage of Ashwini, the soul wants to sacrifice its desires in order to control the lower nature. An exalted Sun wants to be in charge of its destiny. Planets in Ashwini tend to shine with the radiance of the Sun or look for some solar connection.

Venus and the Moon are shown riding horses. Kalki, the final avatara of Vishnu, is pictured as a riderless horse as he is yet to manifest. Kalki means the white horse and is seen as the destroyer of darkness. He is said to manifest at the end of the Kali yuga, the present age of darkness.

Ashwini people want to be masters of their desires and destiny. They are extremely idealistic and have not faced the challenges of life so still think they can manage it without obstacles.

Ayurvedic Dosha is Vata

Ashwini reflects the natural qualities of vata: action, sensation, inspiration, communication, exercise, action and dryness. Vata people tend to be of a nervous disposition; they are extremely active with lots of nervous energy to expend. They have short attention spans and generally live on their nerves, so have to watch out for stress.

Lagna and Planets in Ashwini

The person with lagna here is energetic and adventurous, yet knows how to be in control. Despite looking into the future there is a connection to the past, to history and tradition. They are natural healers with leadership qualities. They can be impatient and want to achieve things too quickly.

Study the strength of Mars and Ketu and their house positions to further understand the quality of the lagna.

The Sun enjoys the purity of this warrior impulse. He becomes exalted. Do not expect Sun in Ashwini people to be easy to get along with as they may be too powerful. They should learn to temper their power and understand their strengths. Leadership qualities abound but having a good advisor usually helps.

The Moon here shows a fiery mind and lots of ideas that need to be expressed now. Boredom can be a huge problem as these people forever need challenges. A sensual Moon can go down the path of passion and the wrong type of relationships. They can easily become selfish. A spiritual Moon will want to be a healer like the Ashwini Kumara. The first dasha is Ketu which can bring an unusual childhood. A person can experience issues of rejection or not being appreciated as a child.

Mars loves it here; it's his own sign and all the qualities are accentuated in the right way – idealism, leadership, courage. The soul feels ready to take on the world. The Mars in Aries soul feels free and has no fear.

Mercury brings a fiery intellect. The mind becomes impulsive, independent, militant and aggressive. Mercury is impressionable and can take on all the qualities of the Ashwini. As Mercury is not best placed in Aries, these people may not express themselves in the right way. Check the pada placement.

Jupiter brings new wisdom, good leadership quality and the feeling that these people were born to advise. They are embracing new ways of teaching, counselling and of being.

Venus is not considered well placed in Ashwini. These people can leave relationships just like Sanjana did and later regret their hasty action. This can lead to a period of austerity and tapas which ultimately brings balance into their relationships.

Saturn is debilitated as this nakshatra belongs to Surya and his sons Ashwini Kumara. Saturn was rejected by Surya and in this nakshatra anger can be prominent against the father or authority figures. These people may feel rejection from the father too. This is a new soul with a new set of problems and the inability to handle the old ones. The caution of experience is not there to guide Saturn, so it can go unchecked and repeat the same mistakes. Saturn can be angry, frustrated, impulsive and a risk taker instead of cautious and careful. One needs to embrace calmness and work on the anger and betrayal issues if present.

Special Quality of Rahu Ketu in Ashwini
Rahu Ketu's position in Ashwini is very interesting. As Rahu Ketu move in retrograde motion only, this nakshatra becomes the ending of their cycle rather than the beginning. Ashwini is the final block for Rahu Ketu to overcome as one cycle of soul development ends. They will repeat certain patterns of behavior that can keep them stuck in situations, but if they understand their patterns and the blocks to their growth it can lead to life altering changes.

There can be a poisonous edge to Rahu and Ketu as they are at the final knot. This is a truly karmic position. Both the planets are the root of their soul dilemma. If Ketu as the past life planet, in its own nakshatra, is placed here it is at the cause of their karmic journey – trying to unfold the last part of the conundrum but not necessarily understanding it, as it may require spiritual work to unravel Ketu's mysteries. Rahu is taking the soul to where it's meant to be yet it doesn't have all the answers. In my view, this is the most complex situation for the nodes to be as they feel they know everything yet all is hidden and secretive; it is a very developed soul that understands this message.

Amsha/Padas in Ashwini: Aries, Taurus, Gemini, Cancer
In these padas the Sun, Moon, Jupiter and Rahu can be exalted and Saturn and Mars debilitated. Ashwini helps the distribution of light by exalting the Sun, Moon and Jupiter. Rahu's exaltation in Ashwini pada suggests the highly spiritual role Rahu performs in life as it takes them finally to their spiritual destination. But Ashwini makes Mars realize its peaceful role by debilitating it in Cancer pada and weakens Saturn in its very first pada.

0°00' to 3°20' Aries – Aries pada
The 1st pada of Ashwini and the 1st navamsha of Aries is Aries. It is vargottama and this enhances the quality of planets placed in this division. They are what they are and there is no hidden agenda.

While being vargottama the planets can also be in their gandanta positions if they are within 0° to 48' of Aries. Gandanta shows the efforts of the soul to complete or begin a new cycle of soul growth. Planets can struggle with trying to open the spiritual knot regardless of whether they are strong or weak. The vargottama position emphasizes their strength in working with their new dilemmas. They are treading fresh grounds, making new initiatives yet striving to unblock the gandanta knot.

Lagna is vargottama and therefore strong. The Sun will be exalted in the rashi and pada. The Sun becomes a very powerful, idealistic leader. Despite the fact that Saturn is debilitated and weak, it gains strength due to vargottama, yet frustration can remain. Rahu Ketu travel backwards so they are going out of Aries into Pisces, out of Ashwini into Revati. They are seeing the end of the soul journey.

3°20' to 6°40' Aries – Taurus pada

Taurus is the 2nd pada of Ashwini and 2nd navamsha of Aries. The Moon and Rahu are exalted, Ketu is debilitated. The Moon is exalted by pada, so the sense of adventure and passion has an underlying balance and steadiness. Rahu is exalted and gets strength to understand its message as its leaves the cycle, whereas Ketu will feel confused and guilty about unfinished business and unresolved karma.

6°40' to 10°00' Aries – Gemini pada

The 3rd pada of Ashwini and 3rd navamsha of Aries is Gemini. Mithuna is connected to the sexuality, couples, and relationships. All planets emphasize the sexual aspect of Aries and question the spiritual one of Ashwini. No planets are exalted or debilitated by pada. Mercury is strong in its own pada and feels supported in a difficult sign.

10°00' to 13°20' Aries – Cancer pada

The 4th pada of Ashwini and fourth navamsha of Aries is Cancer. Mars gets depleted even though it is in its own rashi of Aries, as it is in its debilitated pada. The Ashwini impulse can get drowned in a sea of emotions for Mars. Jupiter gets special strength in these degrees as it is in its friendly house Aries and in an exalted pada. These people can use their wisdom to guide the soul in the right direction.

2. Bharani

13°20' to 26°40' Aries
Padas: Leo, Virgo, Libra, Scorpio

Meaning

Bharani means cherishing, supporting and nourishing. Bharani expresses feminine energy in its pure form. Its basic principle is *Shakti* – the passive female power. Female energy incubates the soul and transports it from one realm of existence to another. It goes from a spiritual manifestation to a more objective one. In a wider sense, Bharani people can be incubators of ideas and thoughts. They nourish creativity in any form: arts, ideas, thoughts and soul.

Bharani are the sensualists of the zodiac. They are forever searching for their spiritual self but are usually most happy expressing their sensual one.

Bharani
Ruled by Venus
Devata: Yama, The God of Death.
Symbol: Yoni. The Female Sexual Organ
Yoni: Elephant
Motivation: Artha
Guna Triplicity: Rajas, Rajas and Tamas
Dosha: Pitta
Body part: Lower Part of the Feet
Gana: Divine
Caste: Outcast
Quality: Fierce
Colour: Blood Red
Best Direction: West
Special Sounds: Li, Lu, Ley, Lo
Principal Star: Al Bhutain
Other Names of Bharani: Antaka, Yama, Tritanta

Bharani is the special nakshatra for goddesses. Their annual festival is celebrated when the full moon is in Bharani. In India, ancient monuments like Khajuraho honour the female sexuality in their immense sculptures. They personify fertility, harmony and growth. Sexuality for Bharani is an expression of divinity.

Devata – Yama

Yama is the god of dharma as well as the god of death. In Bharani, we recognize our own mortality and that life must come to an end. Those born on earth must learn to live with death. Not just physical death, but also of idealism, hopes and relationships.

As the god of death, Yama is also responsible for the seed of new life. He allows us to detach ourselves from previous lives so that we can look towards the future.

Yama has to do his dharma or duty. He has to take the souls away when their time is up and remain detached all the time as he cannot ignore death, whatever the pleas that are directed to him.

The other meaning of Yama is to do with yoga; in yoga yama (restraint) and niyama (practice or observation) these disciplines are used to channel the energies of the organs of action and the sense of perception in the right direction. This yama teaches us detachment from what life is going to throw at us.

Planetary Ruler – Venus

Venus brings creativity, sensuality and an essence of femininity to the nakshatra. Venus is also the guru in Jyotish, so these people can be very knowledgeable. Bharani people have the strength to handle their emotions and passions if they want to. This can emphasize sexuality and the need to connect with others, and this is not necessarily about commitment but relating on a basic level. If they misuse sexuality, promiscuity can become a problem and can deplete the inner resources. But they know how to do penance for this, to apologize for their sexual mistakes.

Venus brings beauty, femininity, elegance and the aspiration for the good things of life. Bharani can be stunning and magnetic, but not necessarily beautiful in the classical sense. It is not easy for everyone to understand the attraction of Bharani people, but the opposite sex is extremely drawn to them. As the nakshatra connected to the goddess, Venus brings this dignity and charm to people if they learn to move away from the earthy sensuality to the more spiritual self.

Mesha Rashi

Mars rules rashi, the outer energy and Venus rules the inner self. Venus likes the good things in life and Mars is passionate about life, wanting to explore all dimensions. Here the exploration of the sexual can be strong. The Venus and Mars combination emphasizes an overtly sensuous nature that can get out of control. There can be combustible relationships that may burn out as quickly as they began. Bharani emphasizes the passion and sensuality of Aries. These people do not always know how to control their passions, so making unwise choices in relationships can be a problem. Aries comes face to face with blatant sexuality. The idealism of Ashwini is absent. All planets placed in Bharani need to deal with its sexual quality in one way or the other.

Symbol – Yoni, Female Sexuality

Yoni is the vagina, female reproductive organ – this establishes Bharani as a channel for creation whether it is by a sexual act or incubation of other creative energies. The female sexual organ is very important if the soul has to be transported from one life to another. Bharani people act as the channel for moving the soul from the subjective to the objective; they are great at expressing obscure and divine messages in a practical and rational manner. They can be facilitators of creative expression, either their own or by encouraging others to do so too.

Puranic Myth – Yama and Saturn

The exact degree of Shani is debilitation at 20° Aries and this falls in Bharani, in a nakshatra ruled by his step brother. The myth explains why he is debilitated. Yama is the child of Surya and Sanjana. Later, when Sanjana became incapable of bearing the heat of the Sun, she generated Chhaya as her own form of illusion and asked her to be Surya's wife while she, Sanjana went back to her father's house. Three children were born to Chhaya. One of those children was Saturn.

Chhaya loved her sons and daughter but did not love the children of Sanjana. An angry Yama decided to confront Chhaya about her step-motherly attitude towards him and his siblings, and he tried to kick her. At this, Chhaya cursed him saying, "The feet you have raised to hit me may fall down at once."

Yama was taken aback by her curse and ran to complain to his father. Surya told Yama that a mother never curses her child despite his crimes. Yama's words removed the delusion that had been enveloping Surya and he understood the secret of Chhaya's behaviour. Surya confronted Chhaya who confessed the truth. Surya's anger burnt Chhaya. Saturn in turn was angry about his father's behaviour towards his mother as, according to him, his mother was only doing what was asked of her.

Yama and Saturn are step brothers. Saturn, being the child of Chhaya, has always felt the outsider and Bharani emphasizes that sense of alienation and anger that Saturn feels. (Read Ashwini nakshatra too.)

Bharani Aim is for Artha

Bharani is motivated by artha, which is activity on a material plain. Bharani people can be very materialistic unless they voluntarily decide to change. Their spiritual life is connected to the journey from the abstract to the real. They are still connected to the subtle energies but are aware that the real expression of their spirituality has to be in the physical and material world. They express it through creating and nurturing new ideas. Their spiritual side is often misunderstood as the outward expression is practical. They do not always want the wealth or Artha for their own needs but so they can use it to look after others.

Sacred Animal: the Elephant is linked to Ganesha, Laxmi, Indra and Brihaspati

Bharani's elephant connection brings respect and honour. There are many deities such as Brihaspati and Indra that have the elephant as their prime transport. Indra, a major vedic god, rode a white elephant called Airavat. Ganesha is the god with an elephant's head and Laxmi has a form known as Gaja Laxmi where she is accompanied by two elephants. In India, when people see an elephant in real life, they feel it is the living deity Ganesha. This is why elephants are part of all temple processions and celebrations.

Bharani can reflect the elephant characteristics by being larger than life, and respected by others. Despite his size the elephant is able to do many tasks; in India he is used for transport and hauling, in forestry and many other tasks. Bharani can multi-task. He is a gentle giant.

Ayurvedic Dosha is Pitta

Bharani reflects the dosha of pitta or the fiery quality. Bharani people are active, motivated and hot-tempered. They are creative, knowledgeable and intelligent, and are full of heat and passion. They have the tendency to burn out quickly. They need to calm their temperament with cool colours, food and places.

Lagna and Planets

People with planets in Bharani have primal sexual needs but they can develop feelings of guilt about these desires. They either learn to control these emotions or life brings up situations that forcibly control them. There is an ascetic side to their nature, which is symbolized by the god Yama. Planets placed here will face some type of loss or death according to their house rulerships and karakas. Venus in Bharani will have to deal with the loss of a partner, and if Venus rules the 10th house there may be a sudden transformation in the career.

People with a lagna in Bharani will like the good things in life. They admire beauty and the arts and love jewellery. They are aggressive and can at times seem selfish. They are a mix of sensuality and asceticism. Analyse the positions of Mars and Venus to get more information.

The Sun will know how to appreciate the feminine side. Despite their strengths these people will be creative and soft. They can also need support and comfort and can compromise their independence to be with someone.

The Bharani Moon sees sexuality as an expression of divinity and, as Venus is the first dasha, these people develop their sensual nature and love of good things from an early age. The Bharani Moon emphasizes the passion and sensuality of Aries but these people do not always know how to control their passions and can make unwise choices in relationships. With the Moon in Bharani they can initially live a life of excess and then as they learn to control their wayward emotions, develop their higher self. If they misuse their sexuality, or place an over-emphasis on sex and promiscuity, it can deplete their inner resources. Venus as the first dasha brings comfort and good things in childhood. It is a good dasha to have and shows a childhood full of fun and happiness. If Venus is negatively placed or weak the positive quality fails to materialize.

Mars is earthy, goal-orientated and always on the move. Mars the yogi can become apparent as they have courage to discipline themselves and be masters of their desires rather than slaves to it. They are not afraid of hard work. They can easily do hard manual labour as well as perform delicate tasks with great precision.

Mercury is flexible, moving from the asceticism of Yama to the sensuality of the Bharani. They will embrace life and it can lead them to experiment intellectually too.

Jupiter will try to practise temperance but can also be indulgent. These people will want to follow dharma. They will be creative with thinking and ideas and have a big vision. They can have a large appetite for life, food and sex.

Venus will admire beauty, arts, jewellery and luxury. They are aggressive and can at times seem selfish. They like good food.

Saturn is in its debilitated nakshatra and there can be frustrations and anger if a person allows their sense of injustice to take control. It is important to calm down and use the practice of austerities to keep the anger of Saturn in check. At times there is anger with their father over how he has been/is treating their mother – the Sun/ Saturn issues of the mythology.

Rahu will encourage excess, whether they are indulging in sex or doing Yoga they do not know when to stop. They are idealists. They want others to live up to their high expectations. As this is the penultimate nakshatra before the end of the Rahu journey, personalities will get very defined and powerful. Ketu will feel guilty of the excesses and can reject a way of being or indulge and then feel guilty. Again Ketu is coming to the end and Yama will bring a need for righteousness and correct behaviour.

Padas in Bharani: Leo, Virgo, Libra, Scorpio

The Sun, Moon, Venus and Rahu can become debilitated. Mercury, Saturn and Ketu can get exalted. Libra pada is Pushkara and Scorpio is Ashtamamsha.

13°20' to 16°40' Aries – Leo pada

The 1st pada of Bharani and 5th navamsha of Aries is Leo. Leo is the natural 5th house, the house of creativity, higher ideas and mantras. This position encourages all the best of Bharani: the fire of ideas, the urge to reproduce and the disciplined warrior.

16°40' to 20°00' Aries – Virgo pada

The 2nd pada of Bharani and 6th navamsha of Aries is Virgo. This is where the analysis starts – the questioning of excess. There can be a feeling that these people can spoil the purity of this divine experience. This is the pada where they finally realize that their contribution to life can pollute it too.

Mercury is in exalted pada; it learns to deal with its fiery mind and impulsive behavior through right thinking. Venus is never considered strong in Aries and here it is debilitated by pada. There are two minuses for Venus, a difficult rashi and a difficult pada. Venus can be obsessive about relationships, analysing, wanting, yet feeling the inability to get the ideal it is seeking.

20°00' to 23°20' Aries – Libra pada
The 3rd pada of Bharani and 7th navamsha of Aries is Libra. This is a Pushkara navamsha. It will enhance all the planets and give them an opportunity to heal their woes. There is secret strength even for planets which are otherwise weak. The Sun is debilitated by pada and indicates weakness and lack of confidence in going it alone. Yet the Pushkara nature of this pada gives indications that this debilitation is part of the process of evolution. A person can rule more justly, be aware of the other person's point of view and re-build a loss of confidence.

Saturn has its exact debilitation point at 20° Aries, but in the pada it is exalted. This brings forward an interesting point about the debilitation of Saturn; its weakness in rashi is being reinforced by the strength in pada. This is a pushkara nakshatra and therefore has a special capacity to heal. These contrary indications show that Saturn's weakness can also be its strength. Saturn is the lord of time and the significator of unhappiness. Saturn has to dole out its share of unhappiness to the world as it forces the soul to account for its karma; Saturn's strength or weakness does not stop this behaviour.

23°20' to 26°40' Aries – Scorpio pada
The 4th pada of Bharani and 8th navamsha of Aries is ruled by Scorpio. This is an ashtamamsha, the 8th pada from the rashi sign and is about facing mortality. But remember that the soul is eternal and death is an illusion. Planets in this placement can develop a more spiritual attitude and learn about detachment. This is where the recognition of differences between the living and the eternal soul is at its most acute. Aries promotes the birth of the soul and Bharani the death, while this ashtamamsha tells of mortality. Yama, the deity, is strong here. There will be an unexpected transformation brought on by sudden endings – not always through physical death. All the planets face sudden change or death-like circumstances at least once in life. Planets face crisis in this position and their dasha or bhuktis will be the time to experience the turning points. Unexpected is the key here. We cannot plan for the outcome of ashtamamsha planets, we can only understand that they will express themselves in unexpected ways.

3. Krittika

26°40' Aries to 10°00' Taurus
Padas: Sagittarius, Capricorn, Aquarius, Pisces

Meaning

Krit means to cut or divide and *tika* means to challenge. These people are never afraid to challenge and cut through oppositions. Krittika is considered fierce and destructive; it consists of 6 visible stars and one invisible star.

Krittika
Ruled by The Sun
Devata: Agni - The God of Fire
Symbol: Razor
Yoni: Goat/Sheep
Motivation: Kama
Guna Triplicity: Rajas, Rajas and Sattva
Ayurvedic Dosha: Kapha
Body Part: Head
Gana: Demon
Caste: Brahmin
Quality: Mixed
Colours: White
Best Direction: North
Principal Star: Pleiades
Special Sounds: Aa, I, U, Ae
Other Names of Krittika: Agni, Vahini, Anala, Krashanu, Dahana

As the first hymn of *Rig Veda* begins with Agni, and the deity is the Sun, Krittika is at times considered the first nakshatra – the nakshatras are mentioned from Krittika onwards ending in Bharani. I feel both Ashwini and Krittika can have relevance as first nakshatras as in Ashwini the Sun is exalted. The first three nakshatras are connected to Surya. Ashwini is named after the twin sons of Surya, Bharani's deity is the Yama, another son of Surya, and Krittika is Agni, a form of the Sun, and the Sun is the planetary ruler.

Devata – Agni

Agni is the god of fire and the acceptor of sacrifices. The sacrifices made to Agni go to the gods because Agni is a messenger from and to the Devata. The first hymn of *Rig Veda*[3] begins with Agni:

> *agnimilie purohitm yajnasya devam rtvijam*
> *hotaram ratna dhatamam RV 1.1.1*

---

3. *Rig Veda* is an ancient collection of sacred vedic sanskrit hymns. *RigVeda Samhita*, Ancient Rishis, trans. by Swami Satya Praksha Sarasvati and Satyakam Vidyalankar. New Delhi: Veda Pratishthana, 1977. Vol. 2:12.

> I worship Agni, the divine priest who holds the fire ritual, bright, shining
> and radiant, one who summons the deities and gets all the rewards of the
> rituals – the inner nectar, the soma, the wealth.

Agni is ever-young. In many temples the fire burns perpetually, and in
others it is re-lit daily. He has seven fiery tongues and is represented as red
and two-faced, suggesting both his destructive and beneficent qualities,
and has black eyes and hair, three legs and seven arms. He rides a ram.
He can be proud and this creates ego problems to Krittika people.

Agni is the sacred fire, representing the fire of the mind, the flames
of aspiration, and the blaze of intellect. Agni represents the seven flames,
which allow the seven levels of consciousness to operate.

How Agni behaves depends on your karma, your personal spiritual
growth and on how you connect with this divine force. Agni is volatile
and unless properly harnessed it can easily get out of control.

Krittika people must always be aware of the volatility and unstable
nature of their fire. Keep it well-managed so that it does not get out of
control. All planets in Krittika must be conscious of this quality and how
Krittika can bring an aspect to light, but it should not be allowed to be
overly dominating.

Planetary Ruler – The Sun

The Sun rules Krittika. The Sun signifies authority, power, vitality and
strength. It is warm, fierce, supportive as well as destructive. The Sun is
important for survival but get too close to it and you can get burnt. This
fire can be expressed as fire of intelligence, ideas, passions, emotions, anger,
and jealousy. Those who have experienced Krittika passion unchecked
will testify to its powerful devastating force. The problem with fire is that
whenever you take it out of its container you are not sure which direction
it will take. It can burn everything.

Krittika people have to temper their energy or it can become a
self-destructive force.

Mesha and Vrishibha Rashi

Krittika spans two Rashis, Aries and Taurus. Krittika Aries is the true
expression of the Sun. It is warm, fierce and supportive. This is about
controlled and wise use of power, the ability to love and be warm. There

can still be aggressiveness and cruelty – the quality of Mars and the Sun – but it is so measured that you do not see it fully. It can be relentless in cutting out the dross from its life. The fire burns brightly here.

The Taurus Krittika is more complex. From a fire that is allowed to develop its own strength in Aries, Taurus does not let it develop by itself. The result is that either the creative mind can over-develop and burn everything in sight, or at its best Taurus creates a positive container for the fire. The difficulty of Krittika in Taurus is the relationship between the Sun and Venus. There is outer sensuality and inner purity. The Sun needs to be a loner while Venus wants to enjoy the pleasures of the world. There is lustiness and guilt, both aspects of a personality that become over emphasized in Taurus, whereas in Aries, Krittika people may overindulge their passions but know how to keep them in check.

Symbol – Flaming Spear

Agni carried with it an axe, torch, prayer beads and a flaming spear in its seven arms. All these can be treated as symbols of Krittika. With the exception of the prayer beads, all these aspects can be used for positive or negative means. It depends entirely on the users and how spiritually developed they are. The flaming spear can cut through everything and bring about the destruction of tamas. The light can burn or enlighten.

The seven arms of Agni represent the swastika, a divine symbol which has become damaged in western eyes by the Nazis. The swastika represents inner growth, spiritual development and progress. The prayer beads show the power of prayer and regular spiritual practice.

Planets in Krittika have to take responsibility for themselves as to how they develop their qualities. All aspects of nature are present within Krittika according to the planets placed there, but the one they choose to nurture is the important factor.

Puranic Myth – The Birth of Kartikeya

The myth of Krittika is connected to the demon Taraka and the birth of Kartikeya, the warrior god Mars. Taraka had the blessing of Brahma, the creator of the universe, that only a seven-day old son of Shiva could kill him.

Shiva was meditating in the Himalayas and had no intention of producing a son. So the gods plotted to get the semen of Shiva through Kamadeva, the god of love. When they got his seed, Agni carried it to earth and the six Krittikas incubated it. Six babies were born and when Parvati, Shiva's wife embraced them, they became one person with six heads and twelve arms known as Kartikeya. Kartikeya, the warrior god, destroyed Taraka when he was 7 days old. This myth indicates the immense power of Krittika; Mars as the warrior god was born to defend, not to create wars. Krittika incubates power and all planets can incubate their potential, depending on the individual nature of the planet.

Krittika Aim is for Kama

Kama motivates Krittika. Kama is desires and needs on a very practical level. Under Krittika the passion is for courage and for fulfilling a very difficult responsibility. Krittika is a virile nakshatra and therefore there is passion for sexual relationships as well. Its deity is Agni who has a voracious appetite and he manipulated the wives of Sapta Rishi, the seven great sages, into having sex with him. Only Arundhati, the wife of Vashishta, withstood his fire and was recognised as a symbol of chastity. President Bill Clinton has his Moon in Krittika and much has been written about his affairs.

The linking of Krittika to the kundalini and yoga shows a person aware of their latent power. Krittika have the ability to purify themselves and take their body through a 'trial by fire' to find their inner core. There is always a search connected to Krittika. An invisible self is what they're seeking. There is a part of themselves they do not understand.

Sacred Animal – The Goat and Daksha Prajapati

The goat is the animal on which Agni rides but Daksha Prajapati, the father-in-law of the Moon god and creator, was also given the head of the goat by Shiva. This story illustrates important qualities of Krittika – anger, sacrifice, alienation from society and consequences of our actions. According to the *Skanda Purana*, Daksha Prajapati organised a great Yagya where he did not invite Shiva, who was married to his daughter's Sati. He felt his son-in law was not up to the standard of the other gods. Shiva was always an outsider and did not bother with convention. Sati was slighted by her father's behaviour. She went to the Yagya and threw herself into the holy fire and died. Shiva was extremely upset and in his anger threw a lock of his matted hair from the Mount Kailas. From this lock emerged Virabhadra, a formidable person of three eyes and a thousand arms. He, along with other Shiva followers, created havoc to the Yagya. Daksha was beheaded. Brahma, who was Daksha's father, intervened and asked Shiva to give Daksha back his life, but Virabhadra had thrown Daksha's head into the fire. So a goat's head was given to Daksha.

Krittika people can get angry quickly or face anger directed at them. They dislike any form of injustice but society can often treat them as outsiders. Anger and frustration can have consequences too. In the end there is forgiveness as Lord Shiva gave a different head to Daksha and forgave him. Krittika can take a new form after the anger is spent and must learn to forgive themselves too.

Ayurvedic Dosha is Kapha
The Krittika dosha is kapha. These people are philosophical, calm and patient. Krittika can be calm in the face of the greatest adversity. This makes them good commanders and leaders.

Lagna and Planets in Krittika
Planets in Krittika can be fiery, destructive or constructive depending on the padas and the quality of the lagna lord and the Moon.

Lagna in Krittika will be dynamic, creative and yet practical. How the Krittika personality develops depends on the strength of the lagna lord, Mars or Venus, and the ruler of the nakshatra, the Sun. Any weakness or negative position to these can exaggerate the weaknesses of Agni and Krittika.

The Sun will have immense courage and confidence. Krittika has the capacity to create powerful people who are not afraid to confront difficult situations; it is important to remember that Krittika represents the ability to challenge difficulties and oppositions. It is warm, fierce and supportive. These people use their power wisely.

People with the Moon in Krittika can become healers or warriors as they are not afraid to confront their demons or to fight causes. They can remove any negativity through right thinking. Krittika brings healing through the intense purification of the fire. The control of the mind is strong here because the Moon is exalted in Krittika, yet these people must watch their destructive tendencies. The first dasha of the Sun makes the Krittika Moon come face to face with their strengths and weaknesses from a young age. It gives them a sense of identity and purpose. This can help in later years.

Mars in Krittika people are calm, dedicated, and extremely intelligent. They are natural warriors. Their instinct is to defend, but they stay calm in a crisis. They can anger easily and need to watch this carefully. They do not necessarily like confrontations but if they are faced into a difficult position, they will not shy away from it.

Venus can have many admirers. There is a showbiz type persona. They can have two sides to their personality, an outgoing one and a puritan type. You will find both priests and entertainers among the Krittika.

Mercury people attract attention, not just for their striking looks but also for their intelligence and brightness.

Saturn people know that the fire that burns within them can be destructive if allowed to rage uncontrolled, so they learn early on how to harness this fire. They can be attracted to yoga and other disciplines.

Rahu can disturb the fire of Krittika and allow it to overpower them through desires and sensuality. Taurus Krittika is easier for them to handle whereas Aries can bring a sudden spurt of energy which can consume them. Ketu feels troubled by all the fire of Krittika; it will create huge issues that need to be addressed, but the headless Ketu does not always understand how to. These people need to work with their intuition and channel this power into positive, more spiritual areas, or use it to burn away the residual karma. The problem happens when not all karma is ready to be destroyed; only what is matured. Ketu may not know how to discriminate as it is debilitated in the Taurus part of Krittika.

Padas in Krittika: Sagittarius, Capricorn, Aquarius, Pisces

Krittika ends the first cycle of soul development as its padas are the last four of the zodiac. Knowledge is developed and a link is created to the next cycle. Krittika has two pushkara padas. There is only one pada in Krittika Aries and it is pushkara. All planets do well here specially the Sun and Mars. The Taurus Krittika can nurture the Agni of Krittika. Mars and Venus will get exalted by pada and Jupiter and Mercury debilitated by pada. Pisces pada is pushkara.

26°40' to 30°00' Aries – Sagittarius pada

The 1st pada of Krittika and 9th navamsha of Aries is Sagittarius. It is a healing zone for all planets. This is the true representation of the Aries impulse. This is the 9th navamsha from the rashi and sign, the position of dharma, the spiritual duty. Planets in Sagittarius pada in Aries are always willing to fight their battles. They will not sit back and be cowardly. No planets are debilitated or exalted here. Being Pushkara, all planets are enhanced by this placement.

0° to 3°20' Taurus – Capricorn pada

The 2nd pada of Krittika and 1st navamsha of Taurus is Capricorn, where Mars is exalted and Jupiter is debilitated. The Moon's exact exaltation point of 3° falls in this pada. Capricorn pada shows the Moon how to control its mind and be realistic. The mind is nurtured and feels secure; Krittika burns away all the dross and this aids the right type of mental development while Capricorn makes the individual more realistic.

Mars, also known as *Bhumi putra*, the son of earth, is strengthened by being in the first navamsha of Taurus where he is exalted. Mars again comes into strength when he is in a difficult situation. The godly Jupiter does not feel happy with the economic constraints of Taurus. Jupiter does not like practical application of its qualities but in the debilitated Capricorn pada there is no choice. These people have to be careful not to use their wisdom too commercially.

3°20' to 6°40' Taurus – Aquarius pada

The 3rd pada of Krittika and 2nd navamsha of Taurus is Aquarius. The air element of Aquarius can make the fires of Krittika burn too brightly and all planets placed here need to be aware of it. No planet is debilitated or exalted here.

6°40' to 10°00' Taurus – Pisces pada

The 4th pada of Krittika and 3rd navamsha of Taurus is Pisces. The advantage of being pushkara navamsha is that regardless of the weaknesses, the soul copes and makes for positive energy. Pushkara navamsha brings out the best qualities of Krittika. Venus is exalted, Jupiter is in its own sign and Mercury is debilitated here. This is the last pada of the 1st cycle of soul development.

Mercury is in Taurus, its friend's sign, but is debilitated in navamsha. There is a weakness in thinking but due to the pushkara nature there is an ability to deal with this weakness. Venus is exalted by pada and in its own sign. It brings the holy fire on earth through the birth of new souls. Venus creates something positive for the future.

4. Rohini

10°00' to 23°20' Taurus
Padas: Aries, Taurus, Gemini, Cancer

Meaning

Rohini in sanskrit means red, which relates to passion and sensuality. Rohini is emotional, romantic, loves grandly and is considered the favourite wife of the Moon. According to mythology the nakshatras are the wives of the male Moon god, Soma, who stayed one day a month with each one. The 28 symbolic wives of the Moon reflect the differing moods and ability of the mind to constantly love different things. Rohini is the first realisation of love, possessiveness, passion and

Rohini
Ruled by The Moon
Devata: Brahma
Symbol: Chariot
Yoni: Serpent
Motivation: Moksha
Guna Triplicity: Rajas, Tamas and Rajas
Ayurvedic Dosha: Kapha
Body Part: Forehead
Gana: Human
Caste: Shudra
Quality: Fixed
Colour: White
Best Direction: East
Principal Star: Aldebaran
Special Sounds: Au, Va, Vi, Vo
Other Names of Rohini: Dhata, Vishata, Brahma, Vidhi, Druhina, Viranchi, Prajapati

ecstasy, but it is also the start of making yourself emotionally weak as one person or one ideology does not satisfy. Rohini can suffer from jealousy of others as the wives of the Moon were jealous of Rohini.

Devata – Brahma

The ruling deity is Brahma. Brahma is the creator of the universe and is one of the main vedic gods. The belief is that we are all children of Brahma. Brahma represents infinity and we as individuals are supposed to be part of Brahma, connected to the universal soul through the Sapta Rishi who are the progenitors of all humanity. Rohini's link with Brahma indicates the desire for merging with the absolute. Rohini is stuck in material realms and expresses this through its desire for merging completely with another so that they become one.

Brahma was cursed for falling in love with his creation. Rohini's link with Brahma and with Chandra and his many wives can see these people becoming involved in inappropriate relationships that can get them into trouble with society. Rohini can be very creative, full of ideas, and artistic. They desire children who can be their creative legacy.

Planetary Ruler – Moon

Rohini is ruled by the Moon, which also signifies the mind, both the emotional and the intellectual. The Moon is the physical embodiment of our soul, the ebb and flow of our feelings, and the need for change on a daily basis. Just as the Moon roams the night skies in a perpetual search, so the mind remains unsettled in its restless search for peace and happiness. The start of the restlessness of the mind begins in Rohini. Planets in Rohini are forever seeking, restless, with many interests, emotional and intuitive.

Vrishibha Rashi

Rohini is entirely in Taurus which establishes itself through creativity. Within Rohini the mind begins to roam, the living soul is not satisfied by the steadiness of Taurus. While it feels comfortable and happy here, it questions – is that all? Maybe there should be more? This unleashes huge passions and desires. Rohini's passions and Taurus's lustfulness find the same voice. Although the search can be for true love, initially its expression can be many sexual relationships and the inability to find real love. This can also be considered the journey to find sexual satisfaction. While Rohini's motivation remains idealistic its expression can sometimes be very earthy.

Symbol – Ratha

Ratha means a chariot, the preferred mode of transport for all the gods. Chariots signify power, respect, honour and luxury. Rohini enjoys and wants all kinds of comforts and luxuries. Rohini like to live in style and enjoy the sensual side of nature. On a spiritual level, the chariot transports the soul to the material realm in comfort, and protects it while it gets ready to face its earthly responsibilities.

Puranic Myth – Birth of Krishna in Rohini Nakshatra

Rohini is the birth nakshatra of Krishna. Lord Vishnu manifested as Krishna on earth to deal with King Kansa, a cruel oppressor whose tyranny was out of control. The gods couldn't tolerate Kansa's atrocities against their devotees, so in a dream Kansa was told that his evil reign would be brought to an end by his sister Devaki's eighth child, Krishna, who would kill him. Kansa's solution was to imprison Devaki and her husband Vasudeva.

Devaki bore seven sons, six of whom were promptly killed by Kansa. The 7th child was transferred to the womb of Rohini, another wife of Vasudeva and was named Balarama. On the night that the eighth child Krishna was due to be born, the prison guards fell into a deep sleep and the doors magically unlocked. Vasudeva slipped out of the prison and whisked away the Vishnu Avatara Krishna to the safety of a neighbouring kingdom called Gokul. The Yamuna river parted her waters making a channel for Vasudeva to pass. The Gokul King Nanda and his wife Yashoda adopted Krishna.

Annually the birth of Lord Krishna is celebrated on Ashtami tithi when the Sun is in Leo and Moon in Rohini nakshatra.

Rohini can deal with adoption and other issues too and the need to fight the wrong caused by others.

Rohini Aim is for Moksha

Rohini motivation is moksha, spiritual realization, but at this stage that realization has to come from intense involvement in earthly passion.

Rohini people find enlightenment through devotion – to a lover, spouse, or god. This can lead to them feeling incomplete within themselves. The devotion has to be such that they lose any barriers between themselves and the object of their love. The love here is pure and idealistic. There is the feeling of sacrifice for the benefit of others. This sacrifice and devotion will finally make them reach their goal of eternal happiness; they just have to be careful they do not love the wrong people who do not appreciate their sacrifices.

Sacred animal – Snake – Adishesha, Rohini and Balarama

The animal of Rohini is the snake. Snakes are the guardians of treasure and represent silent wisdom. Rohini people can be wealthy financially and have much knowledge. The sarpa nature can at times make them angry and vicious too and this needs to be controlled. Rahu usually does well in Taurus and Rohini and this is his abode.

Kadru was the wife of Sage Kashyapa and gave birth to a race of snakes. His other wife Aditi gave birth to Surya. Kadru gave birth to one thousand great, powerful, invincible jewel-decorated and very poisonous snakes including Adishesha, Kaliya and Vasuki. Adishesha holds the world on his hood and is the bed for Vishnu, and Vasuki is worn by Shiva in his neck. Kaliya is the snake that Krishna fought with in the river Yamuna.

The great gods' association with these snakes shows their ability to control the negative qualities of the animals. Snakes represent mortality and re-incarnation. Planets in Rohini need to be forever aware of their Sarpa qualities and need to invoke their higher more godly nature to keep them in check. The negative Sarpa tendencies have to be abandoned in order to achieve self-realisation.

Ayurvedic Dosha is Kapha
The Rohini dosha is kapha, which signifies the water quality. Water is necessary for sustenance. These people are emotional and soft. They can become too attached to their emotions and this can create difficulties for them. Gaining weight can be a problem.

Lagna and Planets
Lagna in Rohini people will have to learn to control their passions and wayward desires. They appear secure and sure of their ideas yet internally they lack confidence. They will find it difficult to stay true to one person, one idea or one place. The position of Venus and the Moon will give further indications.

The Sun in Rohini gives into its desires. The Sun is usually considered weak in Venus signs as the free soul becomes entangled in matter. Rohini is the first stage of desires. Here the soul needs them if they are to remain true to enjoying every facet of life. These people can be interested in physical pursuits if they get good mentorship otherwise they can give in to laziness.

The Moon is in its exalted sign, but is after its exact degree of exaltation, so these people need to be careful that their dissatisfactions are not disturbing their good life. The mind is strong and bright. They will think long-term and are committed to their projects. The Moon in Rohini can suffer from multiple partners in keeping with the myth of the

28 wives. The Moon is not satisfied by the steadiness of Taurus and at Rohini the Moon is beginning its search. There can be thinking based on fun and pleasure and the consequences of perpetual indulgences are not always recognized. This is a good placement and will therefore give positive results in the end. The first dasha is of the Moon and shows that the restlessness of the mind begins at a young age and remains throughout life unless one channels it towards creativity, ideas and a variety of interests. Usually the Moon dasha at a young age should be fun unless the Moon is weak by tithi or in negative houses.

Mars struggles as it desires security, passions and luxury, all aspects that stop the flow of Mars. There will be interest in agriculture and farming. They can be body builders or have great physical prowess if disciplined.

Mercury is happy and the mind will flourish under these conditions. Mercury as the child of the Moon will thrive under its guidance (Mercury does better in Moon nakshatras than the Moon does in Mercury's. Mercury is the enemy of the Moon while the Moon loves Mercury). Intellect hates intuition but intuition knows that intellect is part of its energy. These people will be sensitive and get hurt easily. They are emotional, changeable, mysterious, and charming. They have much love to give and need devotion in return.

Venus can become very pleasure seeking and happy. These people will be comfortable, creative in a practical way, and seek an idealistic life, but this position does not promise fidelity in marriage. They can be known for beauty, perfection, and the striving towards feminine essence, but if placed in a difficult pada, they can feel unsure as they think life is not perfect.

Saturn is powerful in Taurus, but when it is placed in Rohini its ascetic nature baulks at all the excesses, emotions and the need for passions. Saturn tries to bring order and restriction within the given environment. There is a sense of insecurity for Saturn in Rohini as the underlying Moon rulership does not support it. (Read Rohini Bheda below.)

Rahu people enjoy all the pleasures of Rohini but they can go too far. There is a lack of commitment and the enjoyment of a hedonistic life style. They have to be careful not to allow sexual desires to overwhelm their lives. There can be the possibility of being involved in multiple relationships. Ketu does not like being in Rohini as it feels guilty of the desires and needs that Rohini unleashes. Its debilitation can create guilt regarding wealth, success and of being caught in the web of materialism. While Rahu revels in all that Rohini has to offer, Ketu feels disenchanted. It blames itself for having complicated emotional desires. These people should come to terms with their desires or they will become a huge psychological barrier in their personal development.

Rohini Bheda and Saturn

Bheda means piercing. Saturn's transit through Rohini nakshatra is not considered good as it is supposed to pierce the heart of Rohini, which is connected to growth and prosperity and is responsible for growth dependent on water. When Rohini is free of afflictions, crops grow well. When Saturn transits Rohini, crops can fail. Some consider this transit specifically negative for India.

In King Dashratha's times, when Saturn transited Rohini, there was a great famine. King Dashratha could not bear the pain of his subjects, so he prayed endlessly to Saturn to relieve their suffering. This pacified Saturn who changed his course and did not cross Rohini.

Saturn was at 20°52' Taurus, in Rohini nakshatra and Cancer pada, when the terrorist planes crashed into the twin towers in New York on Sept 11, 2001.

Padas in Rohini – Aries, Taurus, Gemini, Cancer

The padas in Rohini are on the second cycle of the soul's journey. They want freedom, youthfulness and no restrictions. This can lead to innovation and the opening of new horizons. The similar padas in Ashwini had very little emotional baggage. As the padas are repeated in Rohini, the soul memories and unresolved issues can weigh them down and the entanglement into materialism is slowly taking hold.

The Sun, Moon, Jupiter and Rahu are exalted by pada; Saturn, Mars and Ketu are debilitated. Taurus pada is both vargottama and pushkara.

10°00' to 13°20' Taurus – Aries pada

The 1st pada of Rohini and 4th navamsha of Taurus is Aries. This is the best position for Mars and the Sun in Rohini. Mars is in own sign, the Sun is exalted and Saturn is debilitated. The Sun is exalted by pada. These people will need to find their inner strengths. Partners came make them understand their power.

Saturn is extremely uncomfortable with the passions of Rohini and this is reflected by the first pada. This appears an impossible task for Saturn as it becomes involved in impulsiveness, desires, passion – many things it cannot control. Saturn has to struggle to keep its values of patience, detachment and hard work. This is one of the two positions of Shani bheda as the underlying conditions are weak. The other is Cancer pada.

13°20' to 16°40' Taurus – Taurus pada
The 2nd pada of Rohini and 5th navamsha of Taurus is Taurus, this is vargottama and pushkara. Taurus is a nurturing sign and no planet is debilitated here. Taurus makes everything productive and all planets, with the exception of Ketu, gain power. Even Ketu finds a solution to its dilemmas. Venus, the Moon and Rahu are specially energised. All planets reach a stable zone, the acceptance of Rohini's desires, which in fact means acceptance of their own desires. The idealism, the need to find self-realisation while still desiring luxury does appear as a conflict as this is a vargottama position. Pushkara adds to the auspiciousness.

The Moon gives a stable mind. It is creative and practical. These people have clear ideas of what they want from life. Rahu is well adjusted and secure in what is there. They will be more materialistic and full of desires, but they are not disturbed by it. Ketu will benefit from vargottama and pushkara. They will feel guilty of enjoying life and at times can lash out at themselves for exploring their material desires.

16°40' to 20°00' Taurus – Gemini pada
The 3rd pada of Rohini and 6th navamsha of Taurus is Gemini. Mercury in its own pada and the sign of its friend gets the most benefit here. All planets will think a lot about their options.

20°00' to 23°20' Taurus – Cancer pada
The 4th pada of Rohini and 7th navamsha of Taurus is Cancer, a great place for Jupiter and the Moon but difficult for Mars. Jupiter can keep its godliness while being involved in the practical pursuits of Taurus.

Mars can lose its warrior-like qualities by being in the dual comfort zones of Taurus and Cancer. This position makes Mars forsake its dynamic quality for laziness and selfishness. Passion and desires can stop courage and single-mindedness from flourishing. Jupiter is exalted by pada and therefore loses the practicality of Taurus and the indulgence of Rohini. It will use the experience to teach others and can show the path of light to those who are lost. Saturn is unstable in this pada, specially during transit, as the water sign Cancer can bring instability.

5. Mrigasira

23°20' Taurus to 6°40' Gemini
Padas: Leo, Virgo, Libra, Scorpio

Meaning

Mriga means a deer and *Sira* means head. The head of the deer is also a symbol of the Moon. Mrigasira is about the mind and intellect. In Indian mythology, the head of the deer is the representation of the Moon. The lunar energy that is reflected in Mrigasira makes these people restless, sensitive and emotional. Mrigasira essentially shows the search in the world of illusions.

Mrigasira
Ruled by Mars
Devata: Soma, The Moon God
Symbol: The Head of the Deer
Yoni: The Serpent
Motivation: Moksha
Guna Triplicity: Rajas, Tamas and Tamas
Ayurvedic Dosha: Pitta
Body Part: Eyebrow
Gana: Divine
Caste: Farmer
Quality: Soft
Colours: Silver
Best Direction: South
Principal Star: Orion
Special Sounds: Ke, Ko, Ha, Hi
Other Names for Mrigasira: Shashabrat, Shashi, Shashanka, Mriganka, Vidhu, Sudhanshu

The deer here is the golden deer that we all search for but can never find. Mrigasira's spirit does not accept the status quo and in doing so, it tends to get pulled more and more into life experiences. This leads to dissatisfaction with the given circumstances.

Dr. B.V. Raman, the great 20th century vedic astrologer and author of hundreds of books, had his Moon in Mrigasira. His prodigious writings and great intellect are hallmarks of Mrigasira.

Devata – Soma

Mrigasira's ruling deity is Soma, which is another name for the Moon. Soma is the mystical nectar that enhances the mind and its faculties; it is the nectar of immortality which the soul collects through its dharmic deeds. The gods consume it freely whereas humans do not have access to it. Indra and Agni used to consume great amounts of Soma nectar to keep their power.

Shiva is known as Somnath, the lord of the Moon. He wears the Moon in his hair and it shows his ability to control the mind. He rescued the Moon from the curse of Daksha Prajapati for favouring Rohini and therefore the Moon is eternally grateful Every time he was meant to die according to the curse, Shiva resurrected Soma. This was one of the reasons that Daksha did not like Shiva as he did not follow the rules. Monday, Moon's day is also the day of worshipping Shiva.

In the Vedas, there is a story known as *Tara's Rahasya* meaning Tara's secret. Tara was the wife of Brihaspati (Jupiter) who became involved in an affair with Soma (the Moon). She eloped with Soma. Brihaspati wanted her back but she refused. A Great War ensued in the heavens, the gods sided with Brihaspati and Venus and the demons sided with Soma. Finally Brahma intervened and Tara returned to Brihaspati. But Tara was pregnant and the child from her union from the Moon was Buddha (Mercury).

Mrigasira indicates the birth of Buddhi or intellect. For intellect to be born there had to be the merging of the godly impulses of Jupiter's wife with the earthly impulses of the Moon. The Moon represents the total mind and Mercury as the son of the Moon shows he is a fragment of the whole mind, the intellect.

The mind is active and can reflect differing qualities of high spiritual knowledge and good practical information too. Planets in Mrigasira will try to straddle both the godly and earthly impulses.

Planetary Ruler – Mars

Mars gives immense courage to move into new areas intellectually. Mars was born to defend and Mrigasira can only live in a negative situation for so long. If things become unbearable these people will fight their corner and take the right action. Mrigasira can get very angry unless it finds an outlet for Mars by learning to speak out against injustice and not storing everything within. Mars allows Mrigasira to actively use its intellect – all planets will be urged to make use of their capabilities.

The Mars deity Murughan is married to Devayani and Valli. Murughan represents Gnana shakti, the power of knowledge, Devayani represents Kriya Shakti, the power of action and Valli represents Iccha Shakti, the power of desire. Mars is the master of shakti and in Mrigasira he brings his knowledge to bear.

These qualities of Mars are evident in Mrigasira, where wars are won through superior knowledge, debate and wise action.

Vrishibha and Mithuna Rashi

Mrigasira spans two rashis and is equally divided between Taurus and Gemini. One of the important aspects of Mrigasira is the dichotomy of its active/passive nature. These people want to be something yet will not act on it. Taurus Mrigasira expresses this more as Taurus enjoys the comforts of life and Mrigasira will not let the present life be disrupted, even when they feel issues acutely and take the easy way out. Gemini Mrigasira tends to talk about injustices but not take any positive action. The quality of Mrigasira that emerges in Gemini, the thinking nakshatra in the thinking sign, can create great progress but inner conflicts too.

Taurus gives the ability to create, and to be comfortable. In Gemini the intellect becomes like the deer – overly active and not so easy to control. Gemini Mrigasira will think faster than it can act and will be forever seeking answers and think that they are different from others. The mind is constantly going from one place to another – swift, changeable and always on the move.

Symbol – The Head of the Deer

The symbol for Mrigasira is the head of the deer. The deer is symbolic of the Moon as according to Indian mythology the shadows on the lunar surface are supposed to represent the head of the deer. This makes birth in Mrigasira auspicious. It gives special sensitivity.

In certain forms, Shiva is seen with a deer in his hand. This represents the yogic powers of Shiva that have the ability to control the wayward mind which is fast, swift and never at one place.

Puranic Myth – Yagya becomes Mrigasira

Mrigasira is the nakshatra where the first Yagya or fire sacrifice was performed. Yagya is an act of ritual worship where Agni, the fire god, is evoked with many oblations to send message to the gods. Yagya also has a deity form. The gods used the Yagya all the time to gain power over manifestation. Daksha Prajapati had a grand Yagya where Shiva's wife Sati killed herself (read Krittika nakshatra for more) and Shiva vowed to destroy the Yagya. What ensued was great destruction and Yagya (the holy fire) was extinguished by Shiva's third eye. In order to avoid the further wrath of Shiva, Yagya took the form of a deer and flew into the sky. Shiva as Kala, or the lord of time, pursued the Yagya in the sky and killed him. After his death, Yagya's deer head was established among the stars as Mrigasira nakshatra and became the emblem for sacrifice. Yagyas performed when the Moon is in Mrigasira nakshatra have special significance and have the power to bring many spiritual rewards too.

Mrigasira Aim is for Moksha

Mrigasira's motivation is moksha or spiritual realisation, but at this stage that realisation has to come from intense involvement in earthly passion. There is an underlying sense of mission. The involvement is with earthly matters but the final destination is eternal happiness. Mrigasira people are at the beginning of the search. To truly find themselves, they need to look for answers in the outer world first. They may feel dissatisfied with the present circumstances of their life. There is a strong sense of individuality that could hamper the search for their spiritual self. They tend to look at the outer world and cannot find moksha there as it exists within. Their thinking shifts so quickly that it makes a kind of noise that drowns out the silence and real knowledge of moksha.

Sacred Animal – Sarpa and Parasurama

Snake worship forms an important part of ritual. Snakes represent secret knowledge and the concept of renewal and regeneration. Parasurama, an incarnation of Vishnu, defeated and killed over 21 Kshatriya tribes. He gave away the land he annexed from them to the Brahmins, then he had no place to call his home. Varuna, the lord of the Oceans, allowed him land where his Parasu weapon fell. This land is Kerala, the Konkan and Malabar region, the area on the west coast of India below Mumbai. When Parasurama inhabited this land, the Sarpa lost their homes so he granted them this boon – that people will worship them in all temples. There are many important temples of snake worship in this area. Mannarasala Shree Nagaraja Temple in Kerala and Nagarkoil, the city of Sarpa and its temple, are ancient pilgrimages for the devotees of serpent gods.

Mrigasira's connection to the divine Sarpa make these people interested in secret knowledge; they are wise and know much information. Others will admire Mrigasira but find it difficult to be totally close to them sensing a deeper more secretive nature within. Mrigasira people need to be careful, like their snake partner Rohini, of their more vicious poisonous side that can suddenly erupt.

Ayurvedic Dosha is Pitta

Mrigasira reflects the dosha of pitta or the fiery quality. These people are intelligent, perceptive and discriminating. They are natural leaders. Mrigasira can get angry very easily. Mrigasira people are active, and motivated. They tend to be creative, knowledgeable and intelligent. They have a fiery intellect. They have the tendency to burn out quickly.

Lagna and Planets

Lagna in Mrigasira wants to go out of the comfort zone of Taurus and expand its horizons. In Taurus security is essential, but Gemini will be more adventurous. Sometimes these people don't explore but the mind takes the journey and expands. There is dissatisfaction with the given conditions and this can be frustrating if they do not knowingly improve themselves.

The Sun will aspire for comfort and intellectual exploration; these people will also be ready to take on issues and fight the right battles. In Gemini Mrigasira, the thinking becomes more pronounced as does the need to explore. Mars nakshatra helps them feel at home and at peace.

The Moon continues its journey into finding new areas to explore. In Taurus Mrigasira, the Moon is happier, the mind is settled. It creates a very bright mind, not afraid to explore while also steady and calm. In Gemini Mrigasira it appears split in what direction to take and can at times be too stressed and unable to decide. The Moon in Mrigasira makes for restlessness, sensitivity and emotions. The self-image is usually a problem for Mrigasira; the more security these people seek, the less secure they feel. Mrigasira should learn to use their Mars and explore the new. Mars being the first dasha brings lots of energy at a young age. The Mrigasira mind needs to be occupied from the beginning otherwise it can lead to impatience, going from one idea to another, exploring many facets of the world even at a young age.

Mars is strong in its own nakshatra but the passive quality of Mars can be more evident here. These people may take the easy way out. Remember the choice is yours. Mrigasira encourages the mental strength and this is a thinking Mars.

Mercury becomes fiery and active in its search. It is a good position for writing.

Jupiter is helped by being in its friend's nakshatra. The excesses of Rohini give way to the search and expansion of Mrigasira. These people can understand beyond the normal way of thinking. Their world is never limited and they can be great advisors.

Venus wants to have all the comforts but reject them as well. The Mrigasira arouses an intellectual passion where search for pure comfort, pure love and desires have no meaning. Venus in the Taurus part is more comfort-loving where Gemini arouses the mind. Mrigasira can bring the best and worst out of Venus: creative, diplomatic and happy, or negative, critical, possessive and manipulative. It depends on the pada on how Venus develops.

Saturn is in conflict being in a Mars nakshatra. The frustration can be acute. Although Saturn appears to be in control in Taurus, the underlying energy of Mrigasira can highlight frustrations and make Saturn feel blocked by all this youthful exhuberance.

Rahu will be happy to explore the journey promised by Mrigasira. These people have to be careful not to use mind-enhancing techniques in this search especially if in Scorpio pada. Mrigasira can highlight the dissatisfaction of Rahu, but it can use this discontent to progress more in life. Ketu acts like Mars but its journey is not in the material world, therefore it feels uncomfortable. It tries to seek more and more spiritual alternatives. Ketu can help itself by accepting this journey and using these experiences to satisfy the emptiness. It should avoid giving into guilt.

Padas in Mrigasira: Leo, Virgo, Libra, Scorpio

The padas in Mrigasira want to expand into new horizons yet that the thirst for freedom can create attachments too and lead to changes. Sun, Moon and Venus are debilitated by pada. Saturn, Mercury and Ketu are exalted.

23°20' to 26°40' Taurus – Leo pada

The 1st pada of Mrigasira and 8th navamsha of Taurus is Leo. No planets are exalted or debilitated in this placement. As Leo is a fixed sign, the planets do become inflexible. They tend to follow just one dream or cause.

26°40' to 30°00' Taurus – Virgo pada

The 2nd pada of Mrigasira and 9th navamsha of Taurus is Virgo. This is a great position for Mercury as it is exalted here. The intellect is supposed to be born in Mrigasira, there is a sense of being an individual, and Mercury becomes comfortable in its search, its questioning nature. Mars gives Mercury its power and Taurus brings with it the earthly wisdom.

Venus loses out, as despite being in its own sign it becomes debilitated here. Venus starts to question why it is enjoying all the luxury. It will want to have all the comforts of Taurus but reject them as well. These people start looking for perfection yet everything they get involved in stops being perfect.

0°00' to 3°20' Gemini – Libra pada

The 3rd pada of Mrigasira and 1st navamsha of Gemini is Libra where Saturn is exalted, the Sun is debilitated and Venus is in its own house.

The Sun is weak here by being in its debilitated pada, and it brings on low self-esteem and lack of confidence. This is one of the most difficult positions for the Sun in Gemini. Mrigasira's search and Gemini's duality unsettle the Sun.

Saturn is in its friend Gemini's sign and exalted pada. The frustrations and blocks that Mrigasira represents bring out the best in Saturn. People are hard-working, responsible, and able to make the right adjustments in making their life strong. This is the first exaltation of Saturn in a good sign. In Aries Bharani, the exaltation by pada was much more troublesome.

3°20' to 6°40' Gemini – Scorpio pada

The 4th pada of Mrigasira and 2nd navamsha of Gemini is Scorpio and very difficult for the Moon, in its enemy sign and debilitated pada. Scorpio pada within Gemini is challenging as Gemini and Scorpio are such different energies. Lagna in this pada shows a person who must control their jealousy. If they are not careful, they can bring out the worst qualities of Gemini. All planets suffer in this pada and must learn to develop the good qualities and avoid the frictions.

The Moon can feel stuck in a position from where there appear no answers. It is important to be flexible and not allow the intensity to have an effect. On the positive side, Moon people can listen to their instinct and bring in a spiritual way of thinking.

Rahu is debilitated and it can lead to difficult places. These people will need to be careful not to get too obsessive or involved in drugs or secret societies. While this position is good for politics, it can manipulative the personality. Ketu exalted means that at last it feels right to use its intuition and bring the best out of this world of Gemini and Mrigasira. Ketu will combine intellect and intuition, and past life knowledge to the present circumstances.

6. Ardra

6°40' to 20°00' Gemini
Padas: Sagittarius, Capricorn, Aquarius, Pisces

Meaning

At the cosmic stage of Ardra, dissatisfaction with the present begins a search for answers. The ability to be both confused and enlightened at the same time is possible. *Ardra* means green, moist or like a teardrop. The moistness of the eyes can blur the picture yet we feel renewed and refreshed after tears have been shed.

Ardra is connected to intellectual fertility, the ability of the mind to create. Ardra people are both enhanced by their sharp thinking but also limited by their intellectual barriers. The limitations of intellect can confuse the mind or give great intelligence and connect to the sub-conscious to create rich grounds for new growth.

Ardra
Ruled by Rahu
Devata: Rudra - A Form of Shiva
Its Symbol: The Head, Teardrop or the Jewel
Yoni: Dog
Motivation: Kama
Guna Triplicity: Rajas, Tamas and Sattva
Ayurvedic Dosha: Vata
Body Part: Eyes
Gana: Human
Caste: Butcher
Quality: Sharp
Colour: Green
Best Direction: West
Special Sounds for Ardra: Koo, Kha, Ang, Chha
Principal Star: Al Han'ah
Other Names for Ardra: Rudra, Shiva, Isha, Trinetra

Devata – Rudra

Rudra, the god of storms, is the presiding deity; he can have a destructive and fierce side to his nature. Rudra is a form of Shiva, whose mission is to destroy ignorance; therefore he directs the consciousness towards knowledge and finding answers about this manifestation. At Ardra we start to study or learn the Law of Nature. The first time we do this we become dissatisfied with the nature of our lives and start expanding toward differing horizons.

People with planets in Ardra need to be careful of the fierceness of their nature and not to follow the destructive path.

Planetary Ruler – Rahu
Rahu drank the nectar which made him immortal, therefore as Ardra's ruler he wants to achieve the highest ambitions. Rahu needs to achieve the impossible, he reaches for the highest aspirations then makes us realise the futility of achievement. Achievement in itself does not bring satisfaction. Ardra searches for intellectual perfection but also makes us dissatisfied as perfection is an illusion and impossible to achieve. Rahu can feel isolated. As the demon who drank the amrita, his own people find him different and the planetary gods do not accept him as their own.

Mithuna Rashi
Ardra is entirely in Mithuna, Gemini. *Mithuna* means a couple, not an individual; a junction point, living together, cohabiting, twins, and union. The union between man and woman.

At Gemini, the third stage in the cosmic cycle of the signs, the intellect flourishes. Gemini's symbol is a couple (not twins), symbolising the meeting of universal consciousness and material reality. The union between man and woman and the duality of existence is part of the Gemini impulse and Gemini needs to relate and find its soul mate more than any other sign. This is the problem for Gemini. On an eternal level the soul is complete within itself, a whole, but the Gemini soul is not mature enough to realise it. They have to find this out through life experiences. Gemini people go from relationship to relationship, one idea to another, trying to find the missing puzzle of their lives. As their journey is usually outward, in the material realm, the dissatisfaction grows as the answers in the outer world cannot satisfy.

Symbols – the Head, the Teardrop or Jewel
Ardra has three important symbols – the head, teardrop and jewel. The symbol of the head is linked to the 5th head of Brahma that Shiva cut off in anger. There was an argument as to who was the greatest – Shiva or Brahma. Brahma felt he was and started to insult Shiva. Shiva incarnated in the form of Bhairava to punish Brahma and in anger Bhairava cut off one of Brahma's five heads. Since then Brahma has only four heads. Cutting off Brahma's fifth head made Bhairava guilty of Brahmanahatya, the killing of a Brahma. The head got stuck to his hand and he could not

get rid of it. When he asked Shiva how he, Bhairava, would get rid of this sin, Shiva said he would have to wander aimlessly till he found the right place. Bhairava wandered for many years till he finally came to Varanasi and then the head just fell off. This linking of Bhairava with the head of Brahma shows a powerful but destructive side to Ardra. Ardra people can get angry easily and then do something wrong that can take years of searching to absolve themselves. There is a seeking of redemption in Ardra. This shows devotion to a guru, people or causes for which Ardra are willing to do anything, and like Bhairava's devotion to Lord Shiva, this can be easily manipulated.

The teardrop indicates that Ardra people have to understand sorrow. After they have fallen tears clear the eyes. Ardra people need to understand their emotions while identifying with the intellect. The symbol of the jewel means the ability to absorb the kinetic, mystical and spiritual energies from the Sun. The jewels absorb energies around them and transmit them to the wearer. Ardra has the capacity to absorb these powers and can use them for good or bad.

Puranic Myth – Ardha Nareshwara

Brahma's first children were the four rishis called Sananda, Sanaka, Sanatana and Sanat Kumara. He wanted them to procreate the world but they preferred to be ascetics. Brahma was angry and this anger escaped from his eyebrows and took the form of Rudra. Rudra's form was of Ardha–Nareshwara, half woman and half man. Brahma commanded him to split his male and female forms. Rudra divided himself into Rudra the male and Rudrani the female. The word Rudra originated from the Sanskrit *rud* which means to cry or crying, thus *Rudra* means one who cries. Rudra and Rudrani further split into eleven parts. The Rudras were Ajan, Ekaath, Ahirbudhnya, Twashtar, Rudra, Hara, Shambhu, Tryambaka, Aparajita, Isana and Tribhuvana. Eleven Rudranis were also created who became consorts to the eleven Rudras. The eleven Rudranis are Dhee, Dhritti, Ushna, Uma, Neeyut, Sarpi, Ella, Ambika, Ieravati, Sudha and Deeksha.

There is duality. Male and female elements are within Ardra; there is anger and many facets to the same truth. Ardra people need to understand the multiple qualities that they are blessed with. Weak or malefic planets placed here can easily misuse this quality.

Ardra Aim is for Kama

Kama motivates Ardra. Kama is desires and needs on a very practical level. When we are born on this earth we have desires. Kama is passion – sexual, religious, for life, for a cause. Under Ardra the passion is for achievement, fulfilling impossible dreams, externalising inherent potentials and heightened perception. Gemini is the sign for coupling and Ardra's aim for kama creates great interest in sex and a variety of sexual partners.

Sacred Animal – The Dog of Bhairava

Bhairava has a dog as his divine vehicle. Bhairava means frightening, formidable or terrifying. He is the angry manifestation of Shiva and is associated with annihilation. He is depicted wearing snakes as his ornaments. Often people mistake his idol for Saturn as Saturn is also depicted with a black dog. Saturn worships Shiva and is a particular devotee of Bhairava. Bhairava is so fierce that he can take away sins or weaknesses, so people take alcohol, meat and other toxic things as Prasad to his temple.

The energy in a Bhairava temple is very divine. I have visited a Bhairava temple near Chandigarh many times and the fierceness of the deity means he can take away your negativity. He is powerful enough to deal with any weaknesses.

Ayurvedic Dosha is Vata

Ardra people reflect the natural vata qualities of action, agility, and conflict. They are perceptive and inspirational. They are extremely active with lots of nervous energy to expend. They have short attention spans and generally live on their nerves. They have to watch out for stress. They are unrealistic and need to keep themselves grounded. Ardra people are very social and talkative.

Lagna and Planets

Lagna in Ardra is looking for a different way of life. It is a soul that thinks it has all the answers itself, and should therefore be free to explore or find them. These people are bright, intelligent and clever. They can be also dissatisfied so are perpetually desiring change. They can destroy one lifestyle and move into another on a regular basis. It is important that

Ardra lagnas keep good company as this is a lagna that can be easily influenced and absorb all influences around them, good or bad.

The Sun in Ardra is unsettled, these people are unsure of what they want in life and where to go from here. The grass always seems greener on the other side.

The Moon is in its enemy sign and a difficult nakshatra. The nature can be tempestuous and there can be many emotional storms raging within. Lack of clarity can be a problem yet sometimes the storms can bring new shoots of growth, so if these people can control their stormy nature and learn to recognise their strengths and weaknesses, it can be a good place for mental fertility. As the first dasha Rahu is never easy, delivering a childhood (up to 18 years) that struggles with shadows it is not yet able to deal with. There can be ups and downs, great ambitions and great disappointments, all coming as part of the package. Even when Rahu is well placed in the chart, as the first dasha it is not easy to handle, leaving emotional scars that we need to work with in adult life. Rahu makes you feel like the outsider and as a child you never really fit in with your family or school. This can make you feel either a maverick or unloved.

Mars can be in its most destructive position but usually works well with turmoil as it finds its innate courage to deal with all change. Change will happen under this impulse but Mars finds wisdom as long it keeps disciplined. It can be unsure about where it wants to go, as Rahu creates fear and disturbs the courageous quality of Mars. Ambition, manipulation and fear guides the actions if they allow indecision and lack of control to take over. Self-destructive behaviour can spoil their life.

Mercury is strong and bright. The only negativity with these people is their ability to be influenced by others, and how they use this intelligence. Study the aspects and conjunctions to Mercury.

Jupiter wants to use its wisdom and strength but the darker forces of Ardra can cause problems. It is important for these people not to be too ambitious, but to build on what they have and try not to ruin the present for a rosy future. Jupiter can guide you to expand too far. Its quality depends on the pada it is placed in.

Venus can bring out its best here and create something profound for the next stage of soul growth. This is not a good position for relationships, as the urge to destroy love and create havoc within relationships is strong.

Multiple relationships, as well as destructive patterns and inability to see relationships and marriage for what it is, can be the big issues. Study the position in the pada, for this can also be a wise Venus which learns its lessons.

Saturn is steady but can destroy a way of being. It teaches emotional control but it does bring storms into your life so that Ardra can learn and grow from them. Saturn in Ardra shows the end of one way of life and the start of another. Usually these people have two strong careers and two ways of living.

Rahu is strong in its friends' signs and its own nakshatra. The search, the intellect and the mental strengths are all dominant. Rahu can be manipulative and political. There needs to be control over what can be achieved. The only problem is that Rahu wants to achieve everything and that can make Rahu unsettled and dissatisfied. The pada will decide how Rahu will act. Ketu is uncomfortable here. A Rahu nakshatra is a time for people to face the future and disconnect with the past and the intense turmoil of confusing the past with the present is highlighted. They must find reconciliation and not be afraid to move forward. Do not ignore instinct as Ketu is made truly uncomfortable by the ego of Ardra.

Padas in Ardra: Sagittarius, Capricorn, Aquarius, Pisces
Ardra ends the second cycle of soul growth. Great development takes places but there is also destruction of the old way of thinking.

6°40' to 10°00' Gemini – Sagittarius pada
The 1st pada of Ardra and 3rd navamsha of Gemini is Sagittarius. Jupiter gets strength in its own pada and learns to deal with the duality of Gemini and the destructive capabilities of Ardra and this creates wisdom and guidance. No planet is debilitated or exalted.

10°00' to 13°20' Gemini – Capricorn pada
The 2nd pada of Ardra and 4th navamsha of Gemini is Capricorn. Mars is exalted by pada and Jupiter debilitated. This is the ashtamamsha so all the planets are in an aggrieved position being in the 8th house from the rashi. Ashtamamsha makes planets dysfunctional, it is as if you know the other side of the argument but find it difficult to reconcile with it.

Unexpected events usually occur according to signification of the planet that leads to major transformation.

Lagna in ashtamamsha always struggles in life but with the uncertainty and unexpected quality of their rashi and navamsha lagna it is difficult to reconcile and understand.

Mars, despite being in its enemy's house, is strengthened by its exalted position in the pada. Mars usually knows how to deal with the ashtamamsha position as it thrives on challenges. Capricorn is about being realistic and planets have to learn to be realistic. Mars gets stronger after unplanned changes in life.

Jupiter is debilitated and ashtamamsha. Jupiter feels the inability to use its wisdom under the conditions promoted by Ardra and Gemini – the ego, the destructiveness, the lack of happiness. Jupiter can create ego issues, mercenary advisors and a feeling of lack of blessings. As a karaka of men and children, women can struggle with men/ husbands and both sexes may have challenges with children.

13°20' to 16°40' Gemini – Aquarius pada

The 3rd pada of Ardra and 5th navamsha of Gemini is Aquarius which strengthens Saturn and Rahu. Both like being in Gemini and their position is further strengthened by their own pada. Ambitious, aspiring to work hard for themselves and creating a better world for others, the highest qualities of Saturn and Rahu are evident here. No planet is exalted or debilitated. Most planets have to learn to deal with the high Vayu energy and these winds (vayu) can bring volatility and sudden changes to the planets according to their signification and house rulership in the chart.

16°40' to 20°00' Gemini – Pisces pada

The 4th pada of Ardra and 6th navamsha of Gemini is Pisces. Pisces shows the end of a way of thinking so the Ardra destructiveness can be present, but also the ability for fertility to survive and bring about new ideas. This pada signals the end of the second level of soul development. This is a pushkara navamsha. Pushkara gives a blessing to this moment of soul growth. All planets are coming to an important junction point of their personal development and therefore are looking beyond their limited visions. The pushkara nature of this pada is such that even weakness is rewarded. All planets are in a state of flux, but an important unrest, as it leads to key spiritual changes. Venus is exalted and Mercury debilitated in this pada.

The thinking principle represented by Mercury has no place in this pada as it becomes debilitated. Yet the pushkara gives it its blessing and Mercury begins to look beyond the limitations it had constructed by its rational/practical thinking and expands.

Exalted Venus shows the strength of wisdom, creativity and good relationships. Venus is extremely imaginative and fertile, full of ideas for the future.

7. Punarvasu

20°00' Gemini to 3°20' Cancer
Padas: Aries, Taurus, Gemini, Cancer

Meaning

Punah means again and *Vasu* means 'brilliant like the rays of the light'. Vasu is the home of the soul. Punarvasu relates to the Vasu who are solar deities that appear at different stages of the soul's birth to guide it towards its true direction. Vasu are like the rays of light from the Sun, which bring the divine message to earth. Punarvasu is connected to the transmigration of the soul where the soul lives in different bodies in search for its true home. In doing so, it transforms the ideas from higher planes of existence and brings them into earthly life.

Punarvasu
Ruled by Jupiter
Devata: Aditi, the Goddess of Infinity
Symbol: The Bow
Yoni: Cat
Motivation: Artha
Guna Triplicity: Rajas, Sattva, and Rajas
Ayurvedic Dosha: Vata
Body Part: Nose
Gana: Divine
Caste: Merchant
Quality: Mutable
Colour: Lead or Steel Grey
Best Direction: North
Special Sounds: Ke, Ko, Ha, Hi
Principal Star: Geminorium
Other Names for Punarvasu: Aditi, Aditya

One of the translations of their name is 'another home'. The soul finds another home to express itself through birth on earth. These people enjoy travel, whether it is from country to country or on different levels of consciousness. They are searching for the Truth and their true identity.

Devata – Aditi

Rig-Veda says of Aditi:

> *Aditi is sky, Aditi is air, Aditi is all gods, Aditi is Mother, father and son, Aditi is whatever shall be born.*

Punarvasu's ruling deity Aditi is the female principle as well as the representation of infinity. Aditi is the Mother Goddess of the Vedas and the mother of the twelve Adityas or Sun gods. She was married to Sage Kashyapa, the son of Marichi. Aditya is the name of the Sun and Aditya collectively is the name of all the planets. She is identified with both the heaven and the earth, hence infinity.

Aditi is a free-spirited goddess and the goddess of the past and future, the life cycle, the seven dimensions of the cosmos, the celestial light which permeates all things, and the consciousness of all living things. She is symbolized through the form of a cow as well.

Aditi is the Mother of the Universe, Life-Giving Force of Nature and the Divine Feminine Principle. The headless representation in sculpture is to take away the attention from her individuality and focus on sexual vigor, life, and nourishment, and her ability to love without intellectual reasoning. As the creative mother, she must love all she creates, and not differentiate. (Aditi is personified as a cow as well. The cow is considered the mother.)

Planetary Ruler – Jupiter

Jupiter is the celestial Guru, there to guide us on the righteous path. Punarvasu deals with the transfer of knowledge from the spiritual to the earthly, Jupiter as the true teacher has the responsibility to guide this process. Punarvasu deals with the wandering mind in search of its true identity.

Jupiter guides us towards a new way of life from out of the spiritual world to the more material world. Making a temporary home in the material world is not an easy choice. Punarvasu gives the individual this ability to be an advisor that others rely on and trust. This connection to guidance and trust is important for Punarvasu.

Mithuna and Karka Rashi

Punarvasu is mostly in Gemini and one pada is in Cancer. The search in Gemini Punarvasu may not always be in the right direction. There are dissatisfactions, too many questions asked and not so much use of instinct. Those who know how to ask the right questions will find this journey inspirational and full of joy.

Punarvasu in Cancer gives new vitality, a new home for the soul and the recognition of this new identity – multi-layered, multidimensional, different yet the same. While Punarvasu Cancer gets the best possible conditions, the main difference between Cancer and Gemini Punarvasu is that in Gemini, Punarvasu thinks analytically and is only looking for answers in the outer world. They see the world around them and recognise this as their new reality, but in Cancer, Punarvasu gets in touch with their soul, with their intuitive self.

Symbol – The Bow

The bow is identified with Sri Rama, an incarnation of Vishnu. This association of Rama and Punarvasu shows the extraordinary power this nakshatra has to make an individual strive for idealism while living in this world. Rama had to face many trials and tribulations, yet followed his dharma and was the representation of an ideal man, son, husband and father.

The symbol of the bow indicates that this nakshatra is the link between the archer and his objective. The archer is a man and to reach his object he needs to link to the bow/Punarvasu to give it a passage towards achieving his ambitions. Whether they are on a spiritual level or a material one, Punarvasu people create the facilities where they can prepare themselves for their goals. Punarvasu people must have an objective that they are aiming for. All planets need an objective to focus on and Punarvasu gives the wisdom to do it right.

Puranic Myth – Rama and Sita

Rama was the Prince of the Sun dynasty, son of King Dashratha. His story is told in the epic Ramayana. Sage Vishwamitra takes Rama to the Swayambara for Sita. *Swayam* in Sanskrit means self and *vara* means choice or desire. *Vara* can also mean groom. During Rama's time, women chose their own husbands. Sita said she would only marry a man who was strong enough to lift Shiva's Dhanus (Bow) and string it. Shiva's Dhanus was given to Sita's father for safekeeping by Parasurama who in turn had received it from Shiva himself for his discipleship. Rama picked up the bow easily and broke it in half. This won him the hand of Sita in marriage. Rama is the incarnation of the perfect man and Sita is the perfect woman.

Rama and Sita – marriage, fidelity, the hardships we go through together as a couple – all can be themes of this nakshatra. Planets can be powerful enough to break the bow(ego) and to face obstacles in order to follow their path. Difficult planets obviously do not use the power properly. Sri Rama was born on the waxing ninth tithi when the Sun was in Aries and Moon in Punarvasu nakshatra in Karka Rashi. Sri Rama had his Moon in Punarvasu so he upheld all its highest ideals.

Punarvasu aims for Artha

Artha motivates Punarvasu. Artha is practical expression of life. Artha is goal-orientated. These people want to create wealth of knowledge, of spirituality or of loving.

Punarvasu people are trying to find the correct surroundings in which their soul can express itself properly. The Punarvasu spiritual life path is connected to material life.

Punarvasu's connections to the eight vasus that rule different levels of manifestation give them the ability to connect to different levels of consciousness, but these levels have to find expression in the here and now. Their conflict is with their inner wisdom and outer search – how to make the inner vision productive and supportive.

Sacred Animal – Shasti Devi rides the Cat

The cat is the vehicle of Shasti devi, the goddess of the 6th tithi. She is one of the sixteen Matrikas (little mothers). Shasti Devi is the daughter of Indra. Shasti Devi was married to Kartikeya, the second son of Shiva and Parvati. She is also known as Devayani.

She protects the children with motherly affection and always remains near to every child in the form of aged Yogini. The 6th day after the birth of a child is very important and puja is done to gain the blessing of the goddess. She is specially prayed to when children suffer from serious diseases. Punarvasu planets want to protect their children and guard creativity.

Ayurvedic Dosha is Vata

Punarvasu people are active, perceptive, enthusiastic and inspirational. They are extremely active with lots of nervous energy to expend. They have short attention spans and generally live on their nerves. They have less resistance to disease. They need constant mental stimulation and activity.

Lagna and Planets

The lagna Punarvasu is on a lifelong journey. These people need to explore and find their soul, to express their inner feeling to the outer world. But what they must realise is that this is a journey and not the destination, so they should enjoy its many colours. In fact when Punarvasu finds a destination, they get bored and move on or feel frustrated. Lagna in Punarvasu Cancer's main need is to have a good home.

The Sun in Punarvasu is searching and this can make them feel unsettled, always working on many dimensions. Cancer Punarvasu brings steadiness to life and confidence for the Sun to settle down and make a home.

The Moon can be restless in Punarvasu. It is intuitive and changeable. Punarvasu is multidimensional and this can give too many ideas and directions for these people to explore, hence they remain unsettled despite the wisdom of Jupiter. There is a strong connection with the mother. Punarvasu needs a large family. If Punarvasu do not have a birth family, they will be naturally attracted to groups and associations where they can fulfil their mothering instincts. The first dasha lord, Jupiter, is one of the best to have. Unless Jupiter is badly afflicted, this should give an easy start to life.

Mars can find strength in the journey of Punarvasu. Its courage is defined, although the expression may not be in a traditional way. There can be a lack of focus and a wastage of energy in trying to find answers. Punarvasu Cancer debilitates Mars as desires and comforts get emphasised and that takes away the discipline of Mars. On the positive side, this is a peace-loving Mars devoted to home.

Mercury will take Punarvasu towards the intellectual search, wanting facts backed by data and research. But it has the ability to absorb all kinds of information.

Jupiter is in its element. It understands the need to move on spiritually. There is wisdom on many levels that Punarvasu can give to others. Jupiter is exalted in Punarvasu Cancer. Where the world of spirituality merges with the world of materialism, the eternal soul blends with the living soul and Jupiter can advise both sides.

People with Venus here can be very troubled. Relationships are uncertain as is the ability to fall for the right person. Creatively this can be a great position, especially if these people trust their instincts and expand their horizons, but it is not a world of comfort as new and different energies are coming in and creating the urge to be someone different.

Saturn finds the youthful energy and enthusiasm difficult to take but it soon finds its balance. Saturn is cautious about what it does.

People with Rahu in Punarvasu are forever searching at different levels of life. Once they find the answer to one level of manifestation – for example a material one – they will start a new search on the spiritual level, and so on. It is best to appreciate this restlessness for what it is or it could lead to a disappointment at not finding the final answer. Ketu is full of wisdom from past journeys. There is knowledge and subtle perception. Ketu must not try to ignore its instincts. When Gemini asks for proof and then questions it, ignoring your inner voice can lead to restlessness and lack of confidence. The outer world cannot supply the answers that are within. Cancer Punarvasu helps Ketu with their intuition.

Padas in Gemini Punarvasu: Aries, Taurus, Gemini
Punarvasu is the beginning of third cycle in the padas that will lead to major changes at the end of Cancer. Two padas are vargottama and pushkara. Therefore there is real support for planets on this journey.

20°00' to 23°20' Gemini – Aries pada
The 1st pada of Punarvasu and 7th navamsha of Gemini is Aries. This is the only challenging pada of Punarvasu as it is neither vargottama nor pushkara. Mars, the Sun and Jupiter do well in this pada. Saturn is debilitated.

The Sun moves into exaltation and finds idealism and the renewed search for the essence of the soul. Saturn goes from being in a friend's sign to an enemy and debilitated pada. The youthful enthusiasm and the new ideas and concepts that Punarvasu brings in do not sit comfortably with Saturn in its first pada. Saturn's weakness means that discipline is not the strong point and risk-taking is the norm; caution is not used. Watch for anger and frustration.

23°20' to 26°40' Gemini
The 2nd pada of Punarvasu and 8th navamsha of Gemini is Taurus, assimilating the ideas of the Punarvasu search. This is pushkara, a healing pada. The ideas are fertile, the ability to use them is there and the pushkara quality helps with the fruitfulness and development of the Punarvasu and Gemini impulses. The Moon and Rahu are exalted and Ketu debilitated.

The Moon finds peace of mind in its exaltation pada and develops the power of the mind, assimilating the analysis of Gemini and the wisdom of Punarvasu. The Moon will desire motherhood and express the qualities of Aditi.

Rahu is exalted by pada and can make the right choices. This is a Rahu that finds the journey exciting, and the search of Punarvasu can be used for good practical purposes. Rahu learns to limit itself yet fulfil and experience all that Gemini Punarvasu has to offer. The pushkara brings calmness and constructive behaviour. Ketu is unhappy here, being in a debilitated pada and a difficult sign. He does not want the commercial practicality of Taurus or the Gemini intellect. Punarvasu's need is to go and search in the outer world. Where is the subtlety and intuition? Ketu can feel guilty at enjoying the pleasures of the world but there can be reconciliation if they stop rejecting what is on offer. The pushkara quality of this pada helps Ketu settle.

26°40' to 30°00' Gemini – Gemini pada
The 3rd pada of Punarvasu and 9th navamsha of Gemini is Gemini. No planets are debilitated or exalted here. It is vargottama. All planets are empowered. This is the pure nature of Gemini, where the intellectual search is at its best. These people are able to move in different levels of consciousness without conflict. All planets become thinkers and analysts. They also want to be like universal mothers even if they are men.

00°00' to 03°20' Cancer – Cancer pada
The last pada of Punarvasu and 1st navamsha of Cancer is Cancer, which is pushkara and vargottama navamsha. Jupiter and the Moon become extra strong here. Mars is debilitated. There is new vitality, a new home for the soul and the recognition of this new identity as multi-layered, multi-dimensional, and different yet the same. Punarvasu gives the best possible conditions for the planets to deal with their issues.

A debilitated Mars in its debilitated pada changes warrior Mars into a peace-loving mode. These people may not know how to conserve their energy. They will need to focus to get things done. Physical weakness and lack of vitality can be a problem. They will aspire for comforts and may not have the toughness of a Martian personality. The pushkara and vargottama helps Mars to go from weakness to strength but physical issues can remain.

Jupiter is extremely powerful – exalted sign, own nakshatra, exalted pada, vargottama and pushkara. There are lots of blessings and the ability to give good advice as well as receive it. For women, it means good relationships/marriage and intelligent bright men to come into their life. This shows a past life where many good deeds were done and whose blessings you are receiving now. Do not take financial success to be the blessings of Jupiter, though it may include those as well. This is a good thinker, a dharmic person, wise and just; someone with spiritual wealth.

8. Pushya

3°20' to 16°40' Cancer
Padas: Leo, Virgo, Libra, Scorpio

Meaning

Pushya means to nourish or thrive. Pushya people work to nourish others and create conditions so the world can thrive. Pushya is considered a very auspicious nakshatra. Pushya's presiding deity is Brihaspati, another name for Jupiter. It is an expansive planet which increases everything it touches. Saturn, the planet that brings forth karmic restrictions, is the ruler of the nakshatra. These dual influences on Pushya are what make it so special. A

Pushya
Ruled by Saturn
Devata: Brihaspati
Symbols: A Flower, an Arrow and a Circle
Yoni: Goat/Sheep
Motivation: Dharma
Guna Triplicity: Rajas, Sattva and Tamas
Ayurvedic Dosha: Pitta
Body Part: Face
Gana: Divine
Caste: Warrior
Quality: Light
Colour: Red and Black
Best Direction: East
Special Sounds: Hoo, He, Ho, Da
Principal Star: An-Natharah
Other Names for Pushya: Ijya, Guru, Jiva, Tishya, Deva Purohita

balance between expansion and constraints is achieved under Pushya. The soul's restrictions as well as the knowledge of its limitlessness are fully expressed here.

Devata – Brihaspati

Brihaspati is the primary priest in the Vedas and the advisor to the gods. He teaches wisdom and love of truth, and his work is for the good of humanity. Brihaspati advised the gods on their religious duties and purification rituals needed for a sattvic life. He is considered to be the founder of vedic religion. Shiva bestowed him the title of being Dev Guru.

The Vedas portray him as bestowing good fortune, wealth and children, for giving the correct advice to kings and teaching them to respect learned people. Brihaspati brings happiness at home. As the divine teacher, he makes and follows the eternal laws. He has a continuing rivalry with Shukracharya (Venus) who is the guru to the Daityas – Demons.

Brihaspati is part of the establishment and does not always work for the average person. Planets in Pushya tend to be drawn to advising, teaching and learning.

Planetary Ruler – Saturn

The ruler of the Pushya is Saturn. Saturn teaches us about responsibility, death, and transformations, so that we can search for our true light. Saturn makes us aware of karma that has to be faced on earth. Facing this karma leads to personal development and strength within. Saturn brings the balance to the otherwise expansive quality of Pushya.

Karka Rashi

Pushya is entirely placed in Cancer. *Karka* means white, good, excellent, mirror, water jar and small cucumber. It also means the root of the lotus (that is the attachment to the spirituality; in other words the conduit from the mud to the flowering of the spiritual personality, or the aspiration to higher knowledge). It also means a kind of coitus – ratibandha, a poisonous root and a crab. These various meanings of Kartaka suggest the different aspects of Cancer. They are conductors for the soul to transform from spiritual to material.

The connection with a sexual act shows an interest in sexuality. *Rati* means pleasures and *bandha* means to tie, block or control. Rati bandha is a special yogic technique that is used to enhance and prolong the pleasure of the sexual union. Planets in Pushya can be very sexual especially the Moon, Mars and Venus.

Symbol – Flower, Arrow and Circle

The symbols of Pushya are a flower, arrow and circle. A flower is usually the expression of latent faculties, the outward expression of inner ideas. A flower blooms for others and may not recognise its own beauty. The flower if plucked wilts quickly, and Pushya if taken out of its natural environment can easily lose power and energy. The arrow shows ambition and directed activity. The circle is complete in itself, it focuses on this life, which is complete in itself, not the ending or the beginning.

Puranic Myth – Brihaspati refuses Shani

Jupiter and Saturn are the two major influences of Pushya and they have an uncomfortable relationship in the myths, yet they combine together and make for an auspicious nakshatra.

The myth explains their hostility to each other. Brihaspati, the guru of the gods and representative of Jupiter, refused to educate Saturn until he took a human incarnation. When Saturn came down to earth in the form of Sauri, he enrolled in Brihaspati's ashram and became a devoted student. At first Brihaspati taught him well but as soon as he realized that Saturn was the son of Surya and Chayya he asked Saturn to leave and did not take guru Dakshina from him. Guru Dakshina is given by a student to his guru at the end of the education and for a guru to refuse this means that he has not recognized the student and his efforts towards the education.

Saturn begged Brihaspati for Dakshina as a student's education is unfinished without the blessings of his guru. Later Saturn met Shukracharya (Venus) and studied under him. Then he realized that Brihaspati had kept many secrets from him and not given the key to the subjects Saturn had studied.

Saturn's anger with Brihaspati means that when Jupiter comes into Saturn's sign Capricorn, it becomes debilitated. When Saturn transits into Pushya it is a difficult transit. In turn Saturn affects the gurus, advisors and teachers by encouraging them to give wrong advice.

Pushya Aim for Dharma

Dharma motivates Pushya. Duty, responsibility, doing the right thing, acting out the duty to your self, your family, world and spirit, all dominate the thoughts of Pushya people. They will aim to do what is correct. They will never be shy in facing up to their responsibilities however hard they may be.

Pushya is spiritually connected to doing the right thing. These people have to express it through work, responsibility and duty. Pushya need to understand duty to themselves as well as to others. The spiritual path they adopt is to work within their given karma. They need religion and philosophy to help them overcome their inner conflicts.

Ayurvedic Dosha is Pitta

Pushya reflects the dosha of Pitta or the fiery quality. Pushya people are intelligent, spirited and warm. They are decisive and action orientated. They are creative, knowledgeable and intelligent, but have the tendency to burn out quickly.

Lagna and Planets

Pushya nurture the planets to make them ready for issues ahead. There is comfort and support for most of them.

Lagna in Pushya can be wise and caring. They desire home and comforts while trying to balance between their emotional needs and practical needs. There is calmness under an emotional exterior. The positions of the Moon and Saturn will give further clues.

The Sun has the full realisation of the materialisation process. The Saturn-ruled nakshatra can be challenging but Brihaspati is the devata and guides. There is no knowledge of how to deal with the materialistic desires that are erupting within the consciousness. The Sun is no longer happy to go it alone, it desires relationships and comforts. There is an underlying knowledge that the path you are taking is going to lead you away from the soul's mission and towards darkness. The Sun in Pushya is on its southerly course (Dakshinayana) away from the earth, therefore it is losing some of its brilliance.

The Moon will be comfortable in Pushya unless it is in its debilitated pada. It desires comfort, happiness and a home, but will also be wise and intuitive. The first dasha of Saturn can be restrictive; it shows an early life with Saturn limitations and rules – a child who feels old and responsible.

Mars always deals well with challenges and Mars becomes energised to make something of itself, to live in a new world. This Mars is mentally strong while still having physical weaknesses due to its debilitation. These people can be comfort loving which can take away some of their edge.

Mercury learns to combine both spirituality and materialism and form a new way of being. These are innovative thinkers who can create something fresh by merging two diverse ideas together.

Jupiter gets its exact exaltation degree in 5° Cancer in Pushya and therefore expresses its best quality – the ability to share knowledge, to develop the wisdom for others and be a great guide. Jupiter thrives. It progresses and allows ideas to flourish and guides though the maze of new dynamics. It shows a higher self to the individual.

Venus can feel frustrations about love and passions. Marriage can bring responsibilities. Pushya will not help the excesses of Venus as the devata Brihaspati is the rival to Venus devata Shukracharya. These people need to learn to be unselfish and less indulgent. To be a flower that is beautiful for others.

Saturn is in its own nakshatra, and is often considered strong. What is forgotten is the relationship between Saturn and the deity Brihaspati. Even though it rules the nakshatra, Saturn is never comfortable in Pushya, it does not know everything it needs to know, and it feels an outsider among the wise. This can lead to frustrations and bitterness.

Rahu takes on the challenge of Pushya, to be ready for the different experiences of the soul. While Rahu hates any form of restrictions, in Pushya it will accept them voluntarily. This gives the ability to control any phobias and fears. Ketu brings struggles to accept material responsibilities. Ketu wants to give up material responsibilities but here in Pushya it needs to be ready to embrace them. There is a huge struggle within – to live the life materially or reject it. Ketu should get over the guilt of enjoying the material life. This is also part of the soul's struggle.

Padas in Pushya: Leo, Virgo, Libra, Scorpio
The Sun, Moon, and Venus have debilitated padas in Pushya. Saturn feels frustrated in Scorpio pada and Mars gains. Mercury and Saturn have exalted padas. With planets here, we have to cross the barrier of weakness, recognise our own failings before we can find our strengths. There is pushkara pada.

03°20' to 06°40' Cancer – Leo pada
The 1st pada of Pushya and 2nd navamsha of Cancer is Leo. No planet is exalted or debilitated here. Saturn will struggle in Leo's house. The royal quality of Leo will encourage people to enjoy the fruits of Pushya and there can be indulgences especially by Venus. Mars gains strength.

06°40' to 10°00' Cancer – Virgo pada

The 2nd pada of Pushya and 3rd navamsha of Cancer is Virgo. This is also a pushkara navamsha therefore all planets flourish. Their problems can be healed and their dasha brings good luck. Mercury is exalted and Venus debilitated by pada.

Mercury will combine the intuition of Cancer, the wisdom of Pushya and the analytical power of Virgo, to make this a bright and intellectual position.

Venus is in its enemy sign and debilitated pada and in rival guru Brihaspati's nakshatra – not an easy position to be in. This does not mean lack of relationships but the need to question relationships relentlessly. These people will always try to analyse whether they are getting enough from their partners. It is a good position for a critic of the arts. Venus being debilitated in this pushkara navamsha shows this debilitation is an essential part of Venus' development, therefore whatever the circumstance Venus will find the best way to deal with relationships and its questioning nature.

10°00' to 13°20' Cancer – Libra pada

The 3rd pada of Pushya and 4th navamsha of Cancer is Libra. Saturn is exalted and the Sun, the significator of the soul, is debilitated here.

This is a most difficult pada for the Sun to be in as it is here it faces the full realisation of the materialisation process. The Saturn nakshatra and Libra pada makes for real weakness. The Sun desires relationships and comforts; its need for others can take people away from their singular path. This may be an easier Sun to deal with as its power is less obvious. Saturn gets strength from being in its exalted pada; it can face responsibility and take on the burden that the soul presents. It feels in charge and able to deal with the dictates of Brihaspati.

13°20' to 16°40' Cancer – Scorpio pada

The 4th pada of Pushya and 5th navamsha of Cancer is Scorpio. This is a difficult position for the Moon and Rahu while Ketu finds strength in its exalted pada.

The Moon becomes weak in debilitation. There is little flexibility for the Moon as the Saturn restriction means that it can become fixed both in thinking and the way of living. The Moon is learning to deal with all the poisons and there is a possibility of an addictive personality. They struggle for their freedom and the choices they do not have. They can use the potential of Scorpio and dig deep within their resources and elevate their mind.

Rahu's debilitation finds the negativity of Scorpio: the emotional possessiveness, the jealousy, the fear of not being able to love again – these obsessive needs can all come to the fore. This can also bring out addictive tendencies regarding food and alcohol. When Rahu is in Scorpio, whether by rashi or pada, be careful to set boundaries and not go into areas where the soul is not ready to go. Rahu in debilitation always needs to be managed, you cannot give it full freedom. Ketu is especially energised as it is in its exaltation pada. What Ketu cannot deal with in other parts of Pushya, here it finds itself. Ketu will work on a higher dimension, attracted to spiritual words and sound vibrations, working with its potential and making the most of what life is about.

9. Ashlesha

16°40' to 30°00' Cancer
Padas: Sagittarius, Capricorn, Aquarius, Pisces

Meaning

Ashlesha means to embrace. It indicates the soul embracing life so that it can act out its karma. This nakshatra is extremely powerful on a spiritual level. As soon as the soul embraces life, it becomes subject to the rules and regulations of the earth, in the process of life and death, happiness and unhappiness. Destiny, born from its own actions from previous lives (karma), influences the life today.

Never underestimate the power of Ashlesha, nor the poisons it carries within it. This is the struggle between strengths and weaknesses. Knowing the weaknesses and dealing with them is the greatest strength for Ashlesha. Ignoring the failings or giving in to them creates the karmic knot that is not easily untangled.

Ashlesha
Ruled by Mercury
Devata: Nagas
Symbol: The Serpent
Yoni: Cat
Motivation: Dharma
Guna Triplicity: Rajas, Sattva and Sattva
Ayurvedic Dosha: Kapha
Body Part: Ears
Gana: Demon
Caste: Outcast
Quality: Sharp
Colour: Red and Black
Best Direction: South
Special Sounds: De, Doo, Day, Do
Principal Star: Hydarae
Other Names of Ashlesha: Sarpa, Ugra, Bhogi, Bhujanga

Devata – Nagas

The presiding deities of Ashlesha are the Nagas. The Nagas are snakes who have great occult powers. Shesha is said to hold all the planets of the universe on his hoods and to constantly sing the glories of Vishnu from all his mouths. He is sometimes referred to as 'Ananta–Shesha' which means 'Endless Shesha' and as 'Adishesha', which means First Snake.

Patanjali, the great yogic sage and the author of Yoga Sutras, is considered an incarnation of Ananta, the source of all wisdom (Jnana) and of Shesha, the thousand-headed ruler of the serpent race, which is thought to guard the hidden treasures of the earth. Patanjali came down to earth to see the Dance of Shiva and learnt the knowledge of yoga from Shiva. He passed on this knowledge with the strict instructions that people can only receive his teaching as long as they followed his instructions fully. Patanjali did not want his students to see him so he hid behind a curtain. One day, his students wanting to see their great guru opened the curtain but Patanjali's eyes had so much power that like a laser they burned a thousand students with one look. Only one was left who had got delayed that day. The belief is that this student alone passed on the knowledge of Patanjali. The tale warns us about not obeying one's guru. Knowledge comes to those who follow their guru's words. The knowledge of Ashlesha is so powerful that it needs to be guarded and only those who follow the righteous path can be privy to it.

Ashlesha people can have hypnotic eyes that mesmerize people around them. This is why people often respect Ashlesha and can be a little wary of them at the same time.

All planets in Ashlesha are full of knowledge and can be custodians of secret wisdom.

Planetary Ruler – Mercury

The ruler of Ashlesha is Mercury who is the intellect that makes us different from other animals. Mercury is the ego, which identifies an individual from the universal soul. Mercury guides our rational thinking. This concentrates Ashlesha on the development of the human mind and the change in psyche that takes place when we give birth.

Mercury-ruled nakshatras are at the ending cycles of the nakshatras, where the psychology of an individual changes. Before Mercury helps an individual give up their attachment to the eternal soul and make a life on earth, he needs to know why. These people remain intellectually detached as they search into the inner core to find the deeper reasons. What they do not realise is that the more they search and analyse the truth, the more they get sucked into worldliness and lose their free spirit.

At the stage of Ashlesha, the commitment to living on earth has to be made. Mercury has to go beyond intellect to accept the inevitably of this changeover.

Planets in Ashlesha will question, yet be willing to go beyond the ideas and thinking of the times they live in.

Karka Rashi

Karka means white, good, excellent, mirror, water jar, small cucumber, the root of the lotus, a kind of coitus – ratibandha, a poisonous root, a crab. Ashlesha is where the actual realisation happens that you need to embrace a new way of being. This makes for tough situations and intellectual struggles before the mind finally accepts this new way.

This is the nakshatra where most of the toxins and poisons of Cancer are collected. At the end of Ashlesha and Cancer is the poisonous root. Therefore the soul struggles here in increasing frequency as it reaches the end. Planets placed in Ashlesha always need to be aware of the poisonous root of collected karma that is there even if they are not placed at the end of Cancer and Ashlesha. The poisons can come out in behaviour patterns, sexual excesses and other types of weaknesses.

Symbol – The Serpent

Serpents signify wisdom in the vedas. All gods pay homage to the serpents. Shiva wears the serpent Vasuki in his neck, Vishnu reclines on Adishesha and Lord Ganesha wears a belt of serpents. All temples in South India have a shrine to the serpents.

This shows the ability of the Devas to control the venom and negativity of the nagas. There will always be a serpent symbol with the gods. They are to remind the humans of their mortality. The serpents shed their skins and are symbols of re-birth and transformation. The process of the shedding of the old skin is always a painful one. It relates to a change of the mind, emotional and intellectual, the evolving of the human consciousness.

The snake carries his poison in a pouch and its body is not filled with poison. The poison can be used for healing or for killing. The serpents have the capacity for both good and bad.

Ashlesha can lead people to knowledge, wisdom, wealth and prosperity but it can also take them down the path of danger, self destruction, sexual adventure and unexpected happenings.

Puranic Myth – Birth of Serpents

Nagas are serpents. Originally the Nagas were poisonous, violent and deadly and they were indiscriminately killing humans with their venom. Humans begged Brahma to save them. He promised protection and cursed the serpents so they would face a serious decline. The serpents in turn pleaded with Brahma and reminded him that he had created them as they were – so how could he complain? They asked for a separate abode. Brahma relented and gave them the underworld (Patala, Vitala and Sutala) and a boon that if they bit those who troubled them they would not be punished.

The Nagas came to symbolise all that is secret and hidden, the possessors of great occult powers. Ashlesha can have venomous qualities as well as divine vision. These people must control one and develop the other.

Ashlesha Aim for Dharma

Ashlesha is connected to acting out its destiny and dharma plays an important part of acting out the given karma. Ashlesha will always try to do the right thing. These people understand the importance of their spiritual responsibilities and expressing them through right actions. Patanjali demanded dharma from his students and strict adherence to the guru/student relationship, and this is a quality that Ashlesha should conform to as getting off this path has potential dangers.

Ashlesha people need to accept that they are responsible for what they experience. Ashlesha will always feel a strong connection with doing the right thing. They are ending the search into outer realities and need to be prepared to express their knowledge through work in this life. Their spiritual path is connected to change and transformation.

Sacred Animals – The Deceptive Cat of the Panchatantras

The cat is the animal of Shasti Devi who protects and cares for children (read about her in Punarvasu). Here I am focusing on another aspect of Ashlesha. Ashlesha with all its mystical power has a flip side which can by hypocritical, deceptive and poisonous. These people should be wary of expressing it and always try to control their lower nature. The cat, pretending to meditate from the Panchtantra fables, shows this negative side. Panchtantra tells of a hypocrite cat who pretended to be a priest when a partridge and a hare come to it to solve their dispute. The cat invited them to come near and ate them. The meditating cat is a warning to the unaware that one should be wary of hypocrites pretending to be highly spiritual as they can take advantage.

Ashlesha has many pitfalls, and planets placed here should always be cautious and try to remain on the path of dharma and truth.

Ayurvedic Dosha is Kapha

Ashlesha people are philosophical, calm and of a patient nature. They are emotional and soft, able to retain knowledge, and practical in outlook. Under Ashlesha, they can learn to be calm in mind. At times this can lead to mental inertia.

Lagna and Planets in Ashlesha

Ashlesha lagnas have to face some complex energies in life and must take precautions at every stage. They can be intuitive, intelligent, wise, aware of spiritual responsibility and have the ability to understand deep philosophical issues. On the negative side these people have to watch their irrational possessiveness, jealousy and vicious nature. The position of the Moon and Mercury will give further information.

The Sun in Ashlesha can bring issues with the father but this is a struggle of the soul coming to terms with the person's own fallibility. There are human weaknesses here. Papering over them will not make them stronger. Recognising them will. People will always admire those who have the Sun in Ashlesha but may not make friends easily with them. They can be independent and not very ready to settle down. They are visionaries and can literally see the future (good in astrology).

In India astrologers do not like the Moon in Ashlesha and relate it only to the poisonous aspect. They name jealousy, possessiveness, vindictiveness... but forget the inspirational qualities of Ashlesha, the knowledge, profundity and mysticism. The Moon remains troubled regardless of the path chosen as Ashlesha is all about transformation. While they may not be able to change the past, Ashlesha Moon people can use the positive energy and wisdom to transform the 'now'. The first dasha will be Mercury which can be a good experience unless an individual is born with the Moon in the gandanta. Then this can be a painful or traumatic start to life, with unexpected events or experiences that bring unhappiness. Watch out for the end of Mercury dasha, where the poisons of Cancer and Ashlesha accumulate.

Mars is not afraid to face its demons so it gets special strength in parts of Ashlesha where it uses its powers and courage. But it can make foolhardy choices as well as this is the nakshatra where it has its greatest debilitation degree as well as its exaltation pada.

Mercury is unsure in Ashlesha unless you take special steps to nurture it. But be careful not to go into the negativity voluntarily as this Mercury can make the situation worse than it was thought possible. George W. Bush has Mercury in Ashlesha, and his voluntary war in Iraq opened a well of poisonous hatred against him. He will be dealing with this poison for years to come, especially as he is now in Mercury dasha.

Jupiter gets its debilitated pada in Ashlesha and rules two of the padas. There is an urge to use knowledge for practical purposes in Capricorn but otherwise the huge instinct and wisdom of Ashlesha is what Jupiter works with. There are no easy answers and Jupiter must try to follow the path of dharma, the right way.

Venus suffers in Ashlesha. Relationships can be negative or vicious or controlling. Venus makes you explore more and more and break horizons but Ashlesha also exalts Venus by pada so this search turns spiritual and brings out the best quality of Venus. Venus as the sage Bhrighu knows how to deal with toxins and is the only guru who can bring the dead to life. So Venus is very powerful in Ashlesha if it nurtures its healing quality. Shiva drank the poison of the world and saved the world from the venom of Vasuki. Venus has this quality, but there has to be selflessness involved.

Saturn owns two of the padas in Ashlesha so he finds his work rewarded. This will be a realistic Saturn who takes his medicine.

Rahu has to tread carefully in Ashlesha as it can bring out the worst qualities. Bitterness and unscrupulous behaviour can become its signatures. Ketu can see all the past life trauma. It can either live in pain of the subconscious or it can use the subtle memories to transcend.

Padas in Ashlesha – Sagittarius, Capricorn, Aquarius, Pisces

The padas of Ashlesha – Sagittarius, Capricorn, Aquarius and Pisces – are the last signs of the zodiac, and this is where spirituality flourishes. The rashi and nakshatras both end at Ashlesha together, making this an important point of spiritual development. The third pada of Ashlesha is Ashtamamsha and the 4th pada ends in gandanta, the karmic knot.

16°40' to 20°00' Cancer – Sagittarius pada

The 1st pada of Ashlesha and 6th navamsha of Cancer is Sagittarius. No planets are exalted or debilitated here. As Sagittarius is the sixth sign from Cancer, all planets may face some obstacles in their path as they aspire for the knowledge of Ashlesha.

20°00' to 23°20' Cancer – Capricorn pada

The 2nd pada of Ashlesha and 7th navamsha of Cancer is Capricorn. Exalted Jupiter becomes debilitated in the navamsha – outer strength, inner weakness. It is the reverse for Mars, a debilitated Mars becomes exalted.

Mars finds strength in its exalted pada. The key to understanding Mars lies here. Give Mars challenges (Capricorn) and it reacts well but give it comfort and emotional satisfaction (Cancer) and it does not know what to do. In this pada Mars people go from the emotional weakness of Cancer to the empowering discipline of Capricorn, so they can have the best of both the worlds.

The mysticism and the poisonous qualities of Ashlesha get to Jupiter in its debilitated pada. There is a hidden weakness and possible misuse of the Jupiterian qualities of wisdom, sharing of knowledge and giving the right advice. There can be commercial use of knowledge or susceptibility to giving the wrong advice that needs to be curbed. In a woman's chart it shows hidden dissatisfaction with the man in her life.

23°20' to 26°40' Cancer – Aquarius pada

The 3rd pada of Ashlesha and 8th navamsha of Cancer is Aquarius. No planet is debilitated or exalted. It is ashtamamsha, all planetary significations suffer. The planets feel unsupported and events happen unexpectedly to spoil the houses that are ruled by the planet placed here. Ashlesha is a difficult nakshatra and this is a complex pada, every planet undergoes major transformations. They come face to face with difficult situations that can create havoc. Selfless work and learning to come to terms with the personal demons is one way of dealing with this.

26°40' to 30°00' Cancer – Pisces pada

The 4th pada of Ashlesha and 9th navamsha of Cancer is Pisces. This is a karmic position for all planets to be placed in. At the end of this pada there is a gandanta where the sign and nakshatra ends. The planets placed in gandanta are linked to karmic development and spiritual awakening. Mercury is debilitated and Venus is exalted in this pada. Mars has its exact debilitation degree in this pada.

Mars' degree of debilitation, 28° Cancer, is in this karmic pada indicating that we have to let go of our aggression and fight completely before we are able to develop spiritually. While fighting and courage is good up to certain level, you have to go in peace to really find strength.

Mercury is debilitated in this pada, again showing that spiritual development has to go beyond intellectual debate. It cannot question what is happening as there are no practical answers.

Venus will be exalted in this navamsha but it can teach karmic lessons about love and relationships, about making commitments and being bound by certain rules and conditions because of that. This is a position of great ideas for the future. Venus will be using occult knowledge in its highest form. Exalted Venus in pada gives purity and clarity, a soul ready to leave the outer person behind and work with their inner purity.

Planets in Cancer Ashlesha Gandanta – 29°12 to 30°00 Cancer

The end of Ashlesha is gandanta, the karmic knot where most of the toxins and poisons are collected. It is the end of the sign, nakshatra and pada. This is one of the three important places where the soul has to confront its past karma and try to untangle the knot that has been created.

Ashlesha is where people have to come to terms with where they are, and to deal with all the accumulated debris of previous lives.

All planets placed in gandanta will be troubled according to their karaka and house rulerships. It is a complex situation and much suffering can come with this placement. Often developing a higher self and doing spiritual remedies of selfless work and giving back to society are some of the ways to work with gandanta planets.

10. Magha

00°00' to 13°20' Leo
Padas: Aries, Taurus, Gemini, Cancer

Meaning

Magha means 'mighty' or 'great'. People born in this nakshatra aspire towards eminence and are usually prominent in their chosen field. The abilities of Magha are linked to their past life karma. The enjoyment of worldly pleasures is strong here. Magha is the beginning of the fourth cycle in the soul's journey. This is the involvement into the world of tamas which is illusion, darkness and attachment. The signs Leo to

Magha
Ruled by Ketu
Devata: Pitris – The Forefathers
Symbol: A Palanquin
Yoni: Rat
Motivation: Artha
Guna Triplicity: Tamasic, Rajas and Rajas
Ayurvedic Dosha: Kapha
Body Part: Lips and chin
Gana: Demon
Caste: Shudra
Quality: Fierce
Colour: Ivory or Cream
Best Direction: West
Special Sounds: Ma, Me, Moo, May
Principal Stars: Regulas
Other Names for Magha: Pitra, Pitar

Scorpio bring the soul's full involvement into the pleasures and pains of the earthly life. Magha people are idealistic even if their mission is to fulfill their materialistic needs. This does create misunderstandings at times. Others can suspect their honour and sincerity.

Devata – Pitris

Magha's ruling deity is Pitris, the fore-fathers of humanity whose mission is to guide their children to the right course of life. The fathers only interfere if you are going off the right path. Pitris as the deity for Magha makes the sign very special. It always has a power greater than itself to guide it at difficult times of life when the going gets tough. It needs to ask for inner advice, for only then will the Pitris oblige. As long as Magha thinks it can do things its own way, the Pitris will not interfere.

The Pitris need to be kept happy in order to receive their support There are many ways to do so: a good time to remember the fore-fathers is Shraddha, which occurs annually. The belief is that the Pitris are waiting at all pilgrimage places for their family to remember them and to do special rituals so that the Pitris are kept happy and they give blessings from their world to their descendants. Unhappy Pitris can cause emotional, mental and other problems to their descendants, who get the benefit in the afterlife.

Every amavasya (dark Moon night) tithi is also a good time to remember the Pitris.

Planetary Ruler – Ketu

The shadow planet Ketu rules Magha. Ketu is the tail of the celestial snake. The tail carries with it the past life karmas or the potential of man. It has no head, therefore it reacts instinctively and emotionally. Ketu's role in a birth chart is to look at the bigger picture. Once you stop being restricted by the conscious mind, you make the fusion between the consciousness and the subconscious; your world is open to all sorts of mysteries. The real struggle for people born in Magha is how to create a reality from their many visionary ideas.

Ketu, the significator of spiritual realisation ruling the commencing point of the materialistic journey, shows that enjoyment of life is part of the soul's divine mission. Here Ketu encourages you to get involved in family life, relationships and putting the stamp of your soul on this earth. Within Ketu is the seed of creation and Ketu nakshatras always carry the story of an individual life through many incarnations. People born in Magha are more likely to be connected to their previous lives, if they want to. It can give many talents and qualities that manifest now, but which have their roots in past life experiences.

Simha Rashi

Magha is in Simha, Leo. *Simha* means a lion. Its other meanings are the best in the class and powerful, as it roams the jungle and is free. Leo allows the inner being to express itself but still have a need for freedom. In Magha the soul has a very difficult choice to make. The dharma is to follow their path in the material, more tamasic world, yet the soul desires to connect to the eternal and the idealistic. This conflict can lead to the excesses of the material world and too many desires, which can create attachments to this new life.

Symbol – The Palanquin

The symbol of Magha is a palanquin. The palanquin is a transport which is carried by humans for a very special person. It brings eminence to Magha, above other human beings. The palanquin has a central rod made from a bamboo pole representing the spinal cord, with the knots in the pole as the points of chakras which we need to open to activate the kundalini or our latent power. Magha people have a divine connection; both an outer power that makes them special among their own and an ability to harness their divinity to become even greater human beings.

Puranic Myth – Pitris Loka

> They who through sacrifices, charity and penance have conquered the worlds, pass into the smoke (funeral pyre) and move into the world of Pitri Loka. From there they go to the Moon and become food for the Devas. Once their dharmic merit is exhausted, they are reborn again into this earth and re-start the cycle of existence.
>
> *Paraphrased from Brihad Aranyaka 6.2.16*

The Pitris are our forefathers who are no longer alive. The verse of Brihad Aranyaka says that they are nothing but our soul from previous lifetimes stuck in the cycle of birth and death.

The annual celebration where forefathers are honoured is called Shraddha, which means faith and reverence. Shraddha is mainly performed for three generations of Pitris, namely the father, the grandfather and the great grandfather who have passed away. In a philosophical context, we are our own creators, so we are honouring our own journey through many lifetimes. Shraddha ceremonies are performed in the Krishna paksha (waning Moon fortnight) before the New Moon in Virgo. The fifteen tithis from Krishna pratipada to amavasya when the Sun is in Virgo is dedicated to remembering the dead, and rituals performed during this time give great religious merit. The final day is the Mahalaya amavasya, which starts when the Moon is 12° away from the Sun in Virgo. All the ancestors are prayed to at this time, and the belief is that they come down to Earth from their abode and join the world of the living for a day.

Magha is an inner voice we could call intuition, that comes from walking the path of the fore-fathers. This can give Magha people special intuitive powers if they listen to it but can remain blocked if they do not honour their ancestral legacy.

Magha Aim for Artha

Artha or practical expression of life motivates Magha. The material expression of life, being successful and happy and rich, is as important for an individual as the spiritual one.

They need to externalise their inherent capabilities; their other qualities have to come out so that they can do good for the community and guide other souls towards their right path while remembering their own humility. Much wisdom has been gathered through actions of past life. Now they are being given an opportunity to bring forth its results. The spiritual path is connected to doing the right thing, here and now. They use their powers to become pillars of society and support others through the artha activities.

Sacred Animal – Ganesha Vahana is the Rat

Rat is the Vahana (transport) of Ganesha. The ability for us to worship even the smallest creatures and respect their role in ecology is the message. The rat is a small animal yet it can be destructive for its size, and Ganesha riding one indicates the ability to control them. The rat is connected to tamas and darkness and Ganesha brings light by his ability to control them.

There was a demon called Gaja Mukha who was out of control, but no one could destroy him. Ganesha threw his tusk at him and killed him, then Ganesha made Gaja Mukha into the rat, his Vahana. This further indicates Ganesha's ability to restrain the demonic energies within us.

Magha have both the weaknesses as well as the restraint to be able to deal with what all the world of tamas will throw at them, and master their demonic forces if the divine grace is invoked.

Ayurvedic Dosha is Kapha

Magha is kapha. These people are emotional, calm and philosophical. Their kapha dosha makes them appear calmer than they really are. They have large frames and the tendency for putting on weight. Comfort eating can be the main problem. When Magha feel under extreme stress they resort to food.

Planets and Lagna

All planets in Magha need to ask for divine guidance from within. If they truly want to know their life direction, their soul will bring them the answers. This is the quality of Pitris. Planets within the first 48' of Leo will be in gandanta and therefore in a challenging position.

The lagna is strong in Magha. These people have leadership qualities that show idealistic power. They are needy for attention and will feel that the usual rules do not apply to them. The position of Sun and Ketu need to be studied.

The Sun placed here gives supreme leadership ability. Former US President Bill Clinton has his Sun in Magha. He was popular and is loved even today, years after his presidency. The Sun in Magha is warm, giving and idealistic. These people tend to uphold the law and want to use their ideas and strength to help others and make the world a better place. The idealism to make a good world to live in can be often misunderstood. They have to dig deep within and a strong desire for sex can hinder personal growth.

The Magha Moon can be a visionary, one who has the ability to change the way the world thinks. As yet these people are idealistic and not fully influenced by the materialistic world. The mind can sometimes face rejection and shy away from expressing their true self so it is important to trust their intuition and judgement. The way to do this is to connect to the inner pitris and ask for advice. Ketu as the first dasha is never easy. The conflict between idealism and practicality, mundane and spiritual, desires and moksha, can make them feel torn in two and never sure where their loyalty lies. As a child they may feel different from the others and lead an unusual life. Their merits may not be recognized and they may be slow learners. Ketu dasha can last a maximum of seven years.

Mars will be usually strong and always ready to take on the world and its challenges. Mars can still leave some unfulfilled desires but usually these people will be leaders, and shoulder responsibility.

Mercury is in a hurry to explore ideas, so people with Mercury in Magha try to make sense of the deeper vision. But this can confuse them as there are no direct answers. The thirst to establish themselves in this new world can make them cut corners and take impulsive actions which can create complications in the future.

Jupiter is in a most difficult position having just come out of its exaltation sign of Cancer. Usually Magha is not the best nakshatra for these people as the voice of forefathers drowns out the Guru in this life. Sometimes Jupiter can want to take the power for itself and not be in an advisory capacity. The ego has to be watched.

Venus can create too many desires and a greater fire that can ultimately make these people feel totally depleted and dissatisfied.

Saturn feels uncomfortable in the power of Leo and Magha. These people want to be powerful themselves but feel disempowered, which can create frustrations and anger against the establishment and those in power. Saturn in Magha can be in great crisis or create major problems during its transit. The sub-prime mortgage crisis which led to the worldwide financial meltdown started the moment Saturn transited into Magha on 15th July, 2007.

Rahu creates the karma and adds to the fear of not achieving desires. This can make the desires complicated, but Ketu is very concerned with past karma and certain weaknesses surface from past lives that have to be dealt with in the here and now.

Padas in Magha: Aries, Taurus, Gemini, Cancer

This is the start of the 4th cycle of soul development. A new set of padas begin. There are no vargottama, ashtamamsha and pushkara in these padas.

00°00' to 03°20' Leo – Aries pada

The 1st pada and 1st navamsha of Leo is Aries. This is also a gandanta where planets have special karmic issues; this is the start of a spiritual journey in a material world. Sign, nakshatra and navamsha all begin again. The first 48' of this pada is gandanta. The Sun is exalted and Saturn debilitated.

The Sun becomes powerful in its own sign and exalted pada. This is a powerful personality: dominant, strong and sometimes selfish too. It has good leadership qualities and a strong character but it is not an easy personality as the light of the Sun is very bright and can obscure those that come too near.

Saturn is debilitated. This is a difficult position for Saturn as it is in its enemy sign and debilitated pada. Saturn does not feel responsible in Aries; these people do not know how to face the karma of past lives.

The impulsiveness of Saturn brings more problems yet they have to go towards this path.

03°20' to 06°40' Leo – Taurus pada

The 2nd pada of Magha and the 2nd navamsha of Leo is Taurus. The planets start feeling more secure. The sense of creating and establishing their earthly identity is strong. The Moon and Rahu are exalted and as no planet is debilitated, except Ketu, they all flourish.

The Moon is exalted and feels very happy; all the blocks are sorted out and the mind can feel settled and secure.

Rahu and Ketu have a difficult relationship with Leo but the pada exalts Rahu and debilitates Ketu, so Rahu's placement here is easier to deal with. Ketu struggles to find its identity and becomes aware that its instinct being blocked. Ketu struggles with the overtly materialistic and creative message. Where is the self realisation? Ketu can feel guilty of the pleasures on offer and has to learn to not feel guilty about the material path in this life.

06°40' to 10°00' Leo – Gemini pada

The 3rd pada of Magha and 3rd navamsha of Leo is Gemini. It gives added strength to Mercury. No planets are debilitated or exalted here. The planets start to think about what is in store for them. There is the need to understand what materialism is about and how to intellectually accept the path life is taking them towards. Gemini pada brings uncertainty in the world of Leo.

10°00' to 13°20' Leo – Cancer pada

The 4th pada of Magha and 4th navamsha of Leo is Cancer. It is good for both the Moon and Jupiter as they are in their friend's sign, plus the Moon is in its own pada and Jupiter is in an exalted pada. Mars is debilitated.

Mars' strength in Leo is greatly reduced by being in its debilitated pada. Mars cannot accept the past wisdom; it has to go where others have not been. The knowledge that lots of their present wisdom comes from the forefathers does not sit well. These people can either abdicate responsibility or allow the qualities of Magha with its developing materialism to envelop them, which takes away their sharpness.

The first three padas of Magha are not good for Jupiter, especially by transit, as these are just after its exaltation in Cancer. But the 4th navamsha brings Jupiter back to normal. This is a wise, generous and expansive Jupiter.

Leo Magha Gandanta – 00°00' to 00°48' Leo

The gandanta at the start of Leo differs from the Cancer Ashlesha gandanta where issues had accumulated and the soul was stuck. Magha beings a new journey, the soul was caught in the past but is now making transition into a whole new way of living and thinking.

Planets placed in Magha gandanta will feel insecure and are troubled. The soul is finally getting ready to experience life at a material level. This is a junction point and the intellectual changes which it has already experienced at the Cancer/Ashlesha level are still strong. The will to dominate and create in this new world is hampered by the mind that remains idealistic and tied to the past.

All planets placed here will experience challenges. These gandanta degrees throw up many complex situations which are mostly psychological and are challenges for the soul to overcome.

11. Purva Phalguni

13°20' to 26°40' Leo
Padas: Leo, Virgo, Libra, Scorpio

Meaning

Purva and Uttara Phalguni are two parts of a whole nakshatra of four stars, which looks like a bed. They indicate a similar purpose with very specific differences. Venus rules Purva Phalguni.

Phal means fruit and *Guni* connected to gunas or good qualities. Phalguni is the nakshatra which gives the fruit of our good deeds. Purva means east, indicating it is the eastern part of the Phalguni nakshatras. This nakshatra has the capacity to fulfil our desires on a materialistic level. The luck depends on the gunas or personal good qualities a person has accumulated by doing good karma. The fruits of past karmas allow the soul to rest and enjoy the comfort of a satisfactory relationship, great children and general happiness.

Purva Phalguni takes a break from the soul's journey towards self-realisation by fulfilling its material commitments.

Purva Phalguni
Ruled by Venus
Devata: Bhaga– The Vedic God of Luck
Symbols: Fireplace, Bed, Platform
Yoni : Rat
Motivation: Kama
Guna Triplicity: Tamas, Rajas and Tamas
Ayurvedic Dosha: Pitta
Body Part: Right Hand
Gana: Human
Caste: Brahmin
Quality: Fierce
Colour: Pale Brown
Best Direction: North
Special Sounds: Mo, Ta, Tee, Too
Principal Star: Az– Zubrah
Other Names for Purva Phalguni: Bhaga, Bhagya, Yoni

Devata – Bhaga

Bhaga, the presiding deity of Purva Phalguni, is another name for the Sun. He is one of the 12 sons of Aditi, the universal mother. This adds the solar beneficence to this nakshatra and magnifies its results for the good. This is the nakshatra for achievement, getting the results of past actions, but on the material level.

Bhaga, the god of good fortune and luck, indicates that the fruits promised by Purva Phalguni are usually highly auspicious. The Indian belief is that good luck shines on you due to the actions of your past life.

Bhaga also represents the inherited share we receive when we come of age; the share in the tribal spoils or the share of our karma. An individual can gain either in this nakshatra.

Bhaga also stands for a woman's womb and procreation. It is considered a woman's good luck if she bears children. Naturally, Purva Phalguni is the nakshatra where the children or creativity is pronounced.

Planetary Ruler – Venus

The sanskrit name for Venus is *shukra* or semen. Shukra directly relates to procreation. Both sexes of Purva Phalguni are fond of children and are good parents; children were considered to represent divine creativity and their birth gave a human the ability to harness this natural power. The establishment of the family unit and perpetuating humanity are important. Purva Phalguni people establish relationships to marry and start a family, express their creativity in artistic areas like drama, films, TV, music, show business, design and paintings. Venus brings out their appreciation of fine things and beauty.

Simha Rashi

Purva Phalguni is in Leo. The soul now wants to procreate in its own image, not realising that the creation will also lead to the restrictions as the quality of what it creates depends on past karmas. Creation can be in the form of higher ideas, artistic nature, and writing ability. On an even higher level, it can give interest in Mantra Shastra and Bhakti (sacred sounds and worship).

Symbol – The Fireplace and Bed

The symbol of Purva Phalguni, the fireplace, is where we take time off from the initial purpose of life. We gather around the fire with family and friends to relax and let go of our daily problems. In the Upanishads, the sages assembled people around the fireplace to tell the people of the philosophies of life, to enlighten their thoughts. Higher thoughts and pleasures of life are all intermingled in Purva Phalguni.

The bed of Purva Phalguni is a luxurious one, where the soul takes rest from its trials and tribulations to enjoy life. This is a marital bed and it supports relationships.

The platform is a place made for leaders to address their public, for the soul to address its future needs, and for an individual to plan how they are going to deal with their material desires.

Puranic Myth – Prajapati, Creation and Bhaga

Prajapati is viewed as the ultimate creator. Prajapati is another name for Brahma. He is said to have made the heavens and the earth, and the creatures that live within the universe including humans and animals. Prajapati was alone in the world and to ease his loneliness he split himself into two: a man and a woman. They then procreated and the race of man was born. Taittiriya Brahmana says that Prajapati was continually creating living creatures out of the sacrifices to the gods.

When Prajapati saw the goddess Sarawati, he desired her. It is to be remembered that everybody is Prajapati's child. This was a sin in the eyes of the gods, who felt that Saraswati was Prajapati's daughter as he was the creator. This puts Prajapati in an impossible situation as every living person is his child. So the gods told Lord Shiva that Prajapati was committing a sin, and he should be punished. Lord Shiva threw his trident and pierced him. Half the semen fell to the ground. When the anger of the gods subsided, they decided to save Prajapati as without him creation would end. They decided to use the semen in the sacrifice and gave it to Bhaga to eat. The light of semen was so strong that when Bhaga looked at it it burnt his eyes immediately. Then they gave it to Pusan, but it knocked out his teeth. Brihaspati advised the gods to give it to Savitr (the Sun), who could cause the semen to be born and therefore would not have the power to harm him.

Venus, the ruling planet, signifies semen, and Bhaga may have some connection with Bhrigu who is also supposed to be blind in one eye. So the myth of Prajapti shows that creation is not an easy task. Prajapati was cursed for loving his own creation and Bhaga inadvertently got involved with the curse and lost his eyes. Eyes can symbolically refer to our ability to be rational – Purva Phalguni may love what they create and may not be able to see life or children in balance and with detachment as they are blind to their faults.

Purva Phalguni Aim for Kama

Under Purva Phalguni, the passion is for children, creativity, enjoying life, friends, and family. The desire for a close family unit and the success of their children motivate Purva Phalguni. Those who do not have children will focus their passion on their creativity and ideas.

The spiritual path is connected to the enjoyments of the fruits of their labour, creating karma through children, being involved in every which way in life. Purva Phalguni people should enjoy life and its many attachments, while remembering there is a higher calling to experience at a later date.

Sacred Animal – Lord Ganesha and the Rat

The sacred animal is the rat which is the transport of Lord Ganesha. I wrote about the importance of the rat in Magha which shares the same animal. The rat is considered vermin, which is always eating away at things and hoarding them. The rat's relentlessness is the symbol of the senses which are never satisfied, the need to hoard everything, always being slaves to desires. The link to lord Ganesha and Purva Phalguni shows that desire can be controlled – the wise person will learn to ride their desires rather than be ridden by them. The rat represents the demon Gaja Mukha, a wild elephant-shaped demon that Ganesha killed and made into a form of transport. This further shows our ability to master the demonic qualities within us.

Purva Phalguni people can become masters of their desires and their demons if they endeavor to control them. When the planets are strong here, these people will be able to control themselves, whereas others may find their desires running away with them. Venus, Saturn, Rahu and Ketu usually need to be careful.

Ayurvedic Dosha is Pitta

Purva Phalguni reflects the dosha of pitta or the fiery quality. Purva Phalguni people are warm and loving. They are creative, knowledgeable and intelligent. They are passionate and sensuous. They are ambitious and work hard to achieve their desires. They need to watch the tendency to burn out quickly. They are vital and aggressive. The fire quality burns brightly in them.

Lagna and Planets

Lagna in Purva Phalguni needs to share in the wealth of the world they live in. These people need to make their mark on society, to relate with everyone and enjoy the pleasures of life. This is the material coming of age of the soul and they can no longer ignore the need to be part of this world, to enjoy the blessings of past karma and to create in their own image. The struggle is to be all things to all people. The placement of Sun and Venus will further clarify the analysis.

The Sun is strong as it can embody the qualities of the perfect soul and have the splendour and valour, yet be detached from all involvement. These people will be generous, giving and supportive but the Sun can sometimes be blind to its weaknesses.

The Moon is happy to be involved in the worldliness, to create and find security within the family. This also shows a happy childhood spent enjoying the Venus dasha. Venus has to be extremely negative to take away the comforts and joy of Purva Phalguni. Venus dasha can last up to 20 years and is usually a contented time.

Mars will enjoy the absolute might. These people are very conscious of their rights. They need to avoid being too egoistic. There can be disputes regarding property.

Mercury appreciates the glory and the knowledge. These people will also enjoy the company of friends and debates regarding philosophical ideas. There can be some rigidity in their thinking but they can be full of creative ideas.

Jupiter brings the righteousness and dharma. There is wisdom and power but they cannot always enjoy glory and beauty.

Venus finds this nakshatra pleasurable. Purva Phalguni can give them too many desires and they can lose their objectivity. Obsessiveness with beauty and desires can be the downfall.

Saturn can become wise after the experience, not before. Saturn does not like the comfort and the prosperity of Purva Phalguni; he feels guilty enjoying it and he may therefore disrupt a seemingly comfortable life. This nakshatra carries Saturn's exalted pada, so he will eventually find a balance between enjoyment and responsibility.

Rahu and Ketu, as both the planets of karma, bring an uncertain view of what their share of this life should be. Rahu wants everyone's share and can secretly try for more than they need or deserve. This can create distrust. Care should be taken to follow the ethical path. Ketu remains detached and not wanting all this material stuff. There can be rejection of the pleasure and guilt if they enjoy what Purva Phalguni offers. Ketu needs to understand what they are getting is only the fruits of their past labours.

Padas in Purva Phalguni: Leo, Virgo, Libra, Scorpio
There is vargottama and pushkara pada. The Sun, Moon and Venus become debilitated, Saturn and Mercury are exalted.

13°20' to 16°40' Leo – Leo pada
The 1st pada of Purva Phalguni and 5th navamsha of Leo is Leo. This is a vargottama pada so planets placed here will become strengthened and have deep foundations of power, except Saturn which is very aggravated in Leo.

People with the lagna aim for dharma, the absolute power that can be used well, the aspiration for love, beauty and glory without becoming attached to them. This is a glorious position for the Sun as it is in its own house, own pada and vargotamma.

16°40' to 20°00' Leo – Virgo pada
The 2nd pada of Purva Phalguni and 6th navamsha of Leo is Virgo. It is a place of strength for Mercury as it is exalted but a weakness for Venus in debilitation.

The fiery intellect of Mercury becomes very evident. These people learn to plan and enjoy their life. They have many ideas which shine and can be used productively.

Venus in Leo can become indulgent and there is the added critical quality of Venus in Virgo pada which can create major problems. On one hand these people want to enjoy the warmth and comfort of Leo, on the other they want to analyse all the pleasures and therefore find them wanting. Men with Venus in this position should be careful not to be involved in inappropriate relationships.

20°00' to 23°20' Leo – Libra pada

The 3rd pada of Purva Phalguni and 7th navamsha of Leo is Libra, the debilitation sign for the Sun. This is a pushkara navamsha that helps all the planets.

The weakness of the Sun is an essential part of its growth. A strong vibrant Sun develops the need for support. These people cannot be alone and want relationships. While this may give a softer quality to the Sun, it weakens the natural power of it, hence the debilitation. Lack of confidence, problems with ethics – all can be rectified through positive effort.

Saturn is exalted. A troubled Saturn in Leo gains strength in its exalted pada. Libra brings about the right sense of non-attachment to rewards, desires and ability to control the demons within. Saturn may be struggling in the autocratic power of Leo but in this pada it develops its democratic skills and shows its strength.

23°20' to 26°40' Leo – Scorpio pada

The 4th pada of Purva Phalguni and 8th navamsha of Leo is Scorpio. Scorpio can bring out the best or the worst as it is the depository of all our karmas and desires, good and bad. We can either wallow in their negativity or gain inspiration from our past mistakes and use our inherited skills to get the best. This is a difficult position for the Moon and Rahu as both can find the worst in Purva Phalguni and Leo. Ketu is in exaltation.

The Moon can be possessive, obsessive or totally involved in being bent on fulfilling all the desires. The good aspects of Jupiter can calm this quality and guide these people towards their spiritual path. Usually they will struggle to leave materialism behind.

Rahu placed here can become addicted to power, desires and sexual fulfillment. Wanting too much, not sharing and being too greedy. Ketu can deal with Leo in its exalted pada by going back to its roots. It will work with the past and develop the ability to let go of the guilt.

12. Uttara Phalguni

26°40' Leo to 10°00' Virgo
Padas: Sagittarius, Capricorn, Aquarius, Pisces

Meaning

Purva and Uttara Phalguni are two parts of a whole nakshatra of four stars, which looks like a bed. They indicate a similar purpose with very specific differences. Uttara Phalguni is the male energy to Purva's female. *Phal* means fruit and *Guni* is connected to gunas or good qualities. Uttara means north, indicating it is the northern part of the Phalguni nakshatras. This nakshatra has the capacity to fulfil our desires on a materialistic level. Uttara Phaguni vibrates on a higher vibration as it is getting ready to develop its spiritual nature.

Uttara Phalguni
Ruled by The Sun
Devata: Aryaman
Symbol: Four Legs of the Cot
Animal Sign: Bull
Motivation: Moksha
Guna Triplicity: Tamas, Rajas and Sattva
Ayurvedic Dosha: Vata
Body Part: Left Hand
Gana: Human
Caste: Warrior
Quality: Fixed
Colour: Bright Blue
Best Direction: East
Special Sounds: Tay, Too, Pa, Pe
Principal Star: Al Sarfah
Other Names for Purva Phalguni: Aryaman, Pubba, Purva

Devata – Aryaman

Aryaman is another solar god who is the son of Aditi. Aryaman is famous for his leadership qualities: chivalry, honour, nobility, and rules of society. He maintains traditions, custom and religion and rules over matrimonial alliances and the performance of social rituals. So Uttara Phalguni is concerned about a good quality of material life and living according to spiritual principles in a material world.

Uttara Phalguni people recognise that their ambitions are limited by the vastness of the task ahead. Uttara Phalguni gives courage in the face of adversity, individual effort against all odds.

Aryaman represents the eye; the quality of insight, the ability to see beyond the practical realities of life. He wants to live this life in the right way. This is most obvious in Uttara Phalguni Leo.

Planetary Ruler – The Sun

The Sun rules Uttara Phalguni. The Sun signifies creation and carries within it the knowledge of individual Karma. The Sun represents authority, power, vitality and strength.

Uttara Phalguni allows the soul to recognise its own failings as well as the restriction imposed on it by its limited destiny in this life. These people work for perfection, for maturity of the soul, the ripening of their 'fruit' so that it can break away from its purely material role. But their happiness lies in reconciling with their material goal not struggling with it.

Simha and Kanya Rashi

Uttara Phalguni spans two signs, Leo and Virgo. In Leo, there is a sense of achievement, of comforts that are yours by right, while Virgo starts to question these desires. There is only one pada of this nakshatra in Leo, the rest of the pada belongs to Virgo. In my view there is a sense of perfection in this nakshatra in Leo. Uttara Phalguni in Leo gives the sense of divine right, the need to be and experience the good qualities in a socially acceptable manner, to forge alliances and to enjoy life.

Kanya means a virgin or a young girl. The main thing about young girls is that they grow up. The moment a young girl becomes involved in life, she matures into a woman. This is the great complexity of the Virgo impulse. Virgo Uttara Phalguni always feels it is not living up to its own exacting standards. The discussions and analysis of how this is best to be done can sometimes totally obscure their larger vision.

The special quality of Virgo Uttara Phalguni is that the rulers Mercury and the Sun are always close together by transit. Mercury never goes further than 45° from the Sun and it is governed by the gravitational pull of the Sun. This celestial relationship, where the soul's divine message is being continuously received, is only in Virgo Uttara Phalguni.

Symbol – The Four Legs of a Bed

The four legs of the cots represent the sexual energy of the soul, the downward flow of the power. Each of the legs represents the sheaths in which the soul becomes entangled: the physical, the ethereal, the astral and the mental. These sheaths surround the evolving soul during its stay in the Phalguni nakshatras. The number four represents the four heads of Brahma, the four cardinal directions and the four Vedas.

Puranic Myth – Halahala, the drinking of poison by Shiva and Nandi
Nandi is the bull upon which Lord Shiva rides, so thus has a protective relationship to him. This is explained by the following myth. When the ocean of milk was being churned during creation, the snake Vasuki was the rope that was pulled by gods on one side and demons on the other and Vasuki got agitated and threw up the Halahala poison. All the gods thought that creation was finished and everything would be destroyed but Shiva removed the poison by drinking it. While he was drinking this poison, some of it fell on the ground and Nandi the ever-devoted disciple, drank it. The gods thought this would kill Nandi but he was so pure at heart that he was able to drink the poison and save the world.

Purva Phalguni has both devotion as well as the ability to take poisons so that the society/world can prosper.

Uttara Phalguni Aim for Moksha
Uttara Phalguni is the nakshatra that reflects complete involvement in the material aspects of life. Its motivation of Moksha shows that this involvement is not enough for Uttara Phalguni, who recognise the bigger picture. Their ruler, the Sun, represents the eternal connection and it helps Uttara Phalguni to move towards Moksha even while reaping the rewards of its karma on earth.

Uttara Phalguni directs the soul to its earth-bound role. The individual becomes a conduit through which the soul can express its earthly karma, and the spiritual path connects to fulfilling this responsibility properly. These people need immense courage and a warrior spirit to express this karma, as the experience of the trials and tribulations of life is never easy. But the end result is good. The experiences of life allow the soul to mature and be ready for the next level of spiritual growth.

Sacred Animal – Nandikeshwara, the Bull of Shiva
Nandi is the trusted guardian of Shiva and he is always in front of the Shiva temples. Nandi means joy, delight, happiness. Devotees will first pray to Nandi and ask his permission to visit Shiva; his devotion is such that he will do anything for his master. He is depicted either as a human body with the head of the bull or as bull that Shiva rides. After visiting the inner Sanctum, devotees will go to the Nandikeshwara shrine inside and clap. This is a way of registering their presence at the temple.

Nandi, as the sacred animal for Uttara Phalguni, suggests that these people are always ready to serve the higher cause. Their hearts are clear and their motivation is pure. They will do anything to promote their causes and support those whom they honour.

Ayurvedic Dosha is Vata

In Uttara Phalguni, this nervousness may not be immediately apparent. These people appear quite in control of their lives, placid, and calm from the outside, but they will become vata when things do not work out in the way they want them to. They can live on their nerves and can get stressed quickly. Uttara Phalguni needs to have a well-planned schedule. These people need security and stability. Sudden changes in life can make them ill and the vata energy can get out of control.

Lagna and Planets

Lagna in Uttara Phalguni suggests a person who has many social graces. They leave large footprints that others follow. They will never be the ones who go against the grain but it doesn't mean that they cannot achieve unique distinctions with what they do. Tiger Woods, Doris Day, Harrison Ford, Winston Churchill and Franklin D Roosevelt are some of the famous people who have their Ascendant in Uttara Phalguni. Winston Churchill and Roosevelt both had the leadership qualities of Aryaman while Tiger Woods has created new footprints for others to follow. Doris Day and Harrison Ford brought forth the perfection, social graces and different qualities.

The Sun is strong where leadership qualities are called for. Uttara Phalguni goes down an untrodden worldly path, and creates rules to live in a harmonious world. This requires physical courage and mental analysis.

The Moon is the follower not the leader, so the many questions it has to answer emotionally do not make for happiness. These people adapt to the more worldly path of Uttara Phalguni – the social graces, critics, analyses, why, how they or others feel. What the Uttara Phalguni Moon people must understand is that they can make their world a much better place if they make realistic rules with which they can live their life. The Moon in Virgo Uttara Phalguni can be self-critical and forget to trust its intuition. The first dasha of the Sun can be good as these people learn about social rules and interaction early in life.

Mars as a leader will be very happy in Leo Uttara Phalguni but developing diplomacy and social skills in Virgo are tougher. The first two padas of Uttara Phalguni are excellent for Mars but soon it loses its steam like a warrior/leader bogged down by small details.

Mercury comes into its exaltation sign in Virgo. It is ready to take the challenges, to analyse the laws, to follow the rules. But the last pada of Uttara Phalguni can also bring out its weaknesses and the need to trust intuition.

Jupiter is the advisor to the Leaders. In Virgo, the thinking and wisdom allows Jupiter to guide others in how to lead their lives. They can be perfectionists. Jupiter in Uttara Phalguni can develop practical skills in a way to distribute wisdom. Jupiter may be too critical and self-analytical but often this can develop into a skill for analysing the finer points of nature's laws.

Venus suffers in both parts of Uttara Phalguni. It can be over indulgent in Leo and Virgo is its debilitation sign and an unfriendly nakshatra. Usually Venus in Virgo is the beautiful perfectionist. If the Uttara Phalguni person wants further social graces and nobility as the planet is debilitated, then these ideas become extreme and the needs are not easily fulfilled. The concepts of Uttara Phalguni are great, but Venus cannot be of benefit to these people as it does not work idealistically; there is a need for a purity that doesn't exist. This is the issue that blights relationships for these people as they can be too demanding, they seek divine qualities that humans cannot fulfill. They try to find answers by becoming someone who they not truly are. Rigid in their ideas, over-burdened by responsibility, making a practical marriage – most bring some sense of unhappiness. The last pada of Uttara Phalguni brings exaltation and help with combining the outer demands with inner purity.

Saturn is the envoy of the Sun and it gives its difficult message to the earth. As Saturn moves from Leo to Virgo in Uttara Phalguni, it comes into its comfort zone, so usually it works well in Virgo and rules two of the padas of Uttara Phalguni. Saturn is not comfortable in the Leo part of Uttara Phalguni where the power of Leo opposes his democratic nature. While in Virgo, Saturn finds its strength as the dispenser of divine law (the fruits of karma), which he likes to uphold it and encourage others to do the same.

Rahu revels in Uttara Phalguni. There is the power and discernment. Although these people may know that they cannot match up to what they aspire, they have no problem in aspiring to be the greatest. This can create many worldly needs as they want more and more. But there is also an understanding of a greater purpose which only comes once the disappointment of consumerism raises its head. Ketu does not like being in Uttara Phalguni, where he cannot be a leader as he has no head. Leadership needs an ego, Ketu has none – so how best to deal with it? On one level it suggests a past life where it has already experienced all these issues but now can ignore society. These people will not follow the rules and should enjoy being different.

Padas in Uttara Phalguni – Sagittarius Capricorn, Aquarius, Pisces
These padas end the 4th cycle of the soul's development. There is a debilitation of Jupiter and Mercury and an exaltation of Venus and Mars. Two padas are pushkara so there is a lot of protection for the planets.

26°40' to 30°00' Leo – Sagittarius pada
The 1st pada of Utara Phalguni and 9th navamsha of Leo is Sagittarius. This is a great place for Jupiter, Mars and the Sun. Being a pushkara navamsha, all the planets become positive by being placed here. Lagna embodies the principles of Uttara Phalguni. Even any weakness of the lagna lord who also is the nakshatra lord is supported due to the lagna being pushkara. The Sun is very strong in its own nakshatra, as it understands the path suggested by these impulses. This is one of the most perfect positions for the Sun to be in.

00°00' to 03°20' Virgo – Capricorn pada
The 2nd pada of Uttara Phalguni and 1st navamsha of Virgo is Capricorn. The 1st navamsha of Capricorn debilitates Jupiter and exalts Mars, which being in its enemy sign and in an exalted navamsha becomes very strong. A thinking Mars is a planner and very logical. These people are not afraid to speak their mind. Many great strategists have Mars in this position.

Virgo is neutral for Jupiter and by being placed in its debilitation pada can be practical and less open to new ideas. Debilitated Jupiter can bring commercialism to the wisdom and this can make people utilise their knowledge profitably. This position will also give more female children as both Virgo and Capricorn are female signs.

03°20' to 06°40' Virgo – Aquarius pada

The 3rd pada of Uttara Phalguni and 2nd navamsha of Virgo is Aquarius bringing added strength to Saturn and Rahu. Aquarius and Virgo are such diverse emotions that all planets would struggle in establishing what is right. Virgo seeks a perfect world and tries to make a world in this vision; Uttara Phalguni sets rules and wants to experience the good karma through a life of enjoyment. Aquarius works for the good of humanity. In this pada, the soul goes from being concerned just about its immediate environment to a much bigger picture. These people learn not just to do right by their own society and family but also by the greater family. No planet is exalted or debilitated in this pada.

06°40' to 10°00' Virgo – Pisces pada

The 4th pada of Uttara Phalguni and 3rd navamsha of Virgo is Pisces, the end of the 4th cycle of spiritual development. This is also pushkara. All planets are boosted when placed here. Virgo and Pisces are combining the opposites. It is a life lived in two worlds. People will change drastically at some stage of their life. They remain happy in opposing views; this is a pushkara navamsha so all points of view are meant to add strength and allow the soul to develop from worldly to spiritual, to be a person living in the world of matter but totally in tune with the more spiritual world within. Venus is exalted and Mercury debilitated in this pada.

Although exalted by rashi, Mercury is debilitated by pada. This can create a visionary person, who can see beyond the restrictions the mind brings. They may not always make good worldly decisions but can take themselves beyond the barriers that the mind erects.

Venus goes from a debilitated rashi to an exalted pada and finds extra help from the pushkara. Venus represents true creativity and drives the next process of soul evolution; it sows the seeds to move on to the fifth level of soul development.

The nodal axis reverses in the pada so Rahu goes into Pisces and Ketu into Virgo, this pada is the bridge from past life. The past and the present are playing a cosmic dance. What karma these people create now can only move forward if they reconcile with the past. Rahu has to learn to respect the past and recognise it and then reconcile with it. It cannot remain in denial. Ketu must accept the present. Not easy, lots of churning but there are answers out there.

13. Hasta

10°00' to 23°20' Virgo
Padas: Aries, Taurus, Gemini, Cancer

Meaning

Hasta means 'the hand'. Hasta is connected to the elephant and it is in fact another name for the elephant. The elephant's trunk is its extra hand and he uses it to do all its jobs. Hasta nakshatra is where we think we can achieve whatever we desire and therefore can concentrate on our own efforts and forget the divine blessings that come with it.

The elephant is an important animal as it is the link to Lord Ganesha and Brihaspati.

Hasta
Ruled by the Moon
Devata: Savitar, the Sun God
Symbol: Palm of the Hand
Yoni: Buffalo
Motivation: Moksha
Guna Triplicity: Tamas, Tamas and Rajas
Ayurvedic Dosha: Vata
Body Part: Fingers
Gana: Divine
Caste: Merchant
Quality: Light
Colour: Green
Best Direction: South
Special Sounds: Pu, Sha, Naa, Tha
Principal Star: Al- Auwa
Other Names of Hasta: Ravi, Kara, Surya, Vraghna, Arka, Tarni, Tapan

It is domesticated in India and therefore Hasta can train themselves, develop their higher thinking and use the power and ability to achieve whatever they want. These people can be respected as well as honoured, yet if the ego gets out of control they can be brought down to earth by collective karmic forces.

Devata – Savitar

Savitar is a form of Surya and one of the Adityas, the twelve sons of Aditi. Aditi represents infinity, and her 12 sons the zodiac signs are different expressions of this eternal energy. *Svetasavatara Upanishad* says that:

> Savitar, by guiding us to control the mind, brought the light
> of Agni down to earth. Agni deals with the fire of intellect.
> With that we can obtain heaven and inspire them to shine
> their great light on us.

Savitar is the deity invoked in the Gayatri Mantra, the most important chant connected to the Vedas. In the mantra the devotee asks the Savitar to show the inner most spiritual light.

Hasta people, through the blessing of Savitar, are able to bring ancient wisdom to earth and explain it to ordinary individuals. This ancient knowledge can only come down once they have learnt control of the mind, and this also allows them to find the divine light. Both the Moon and Mercury are the influences on Hasta and they both represent the mind. Words inspire thought, and thoughts can create mental disturbances if the mind is not under control. Mantras, sacred sounds, help us to have power over the mind. The sacred words direct us towards the higher self. By being able to control the power of thought, and developing the ability to blank the mind at will, it becomes peaceful and calm and open to higher areas of thought and consciousness.

Planetary Ruler – The Moon

Hasta develops potential through self-effort and understanding the laws of nature. The Moon rulership of this nakshatra makes for changing perspectives and moving realities. Hasta has the quality for the individual to change, and to grow in different directions.

These people can be moody and they reflect the waxing and waning phases of the Moon. Although they appear confident and in control, the inner self is vulnerable, insecure and in conflict, as they are always questioning themselves.

Kanya Rashi

Hasta is entirely in Virgo. Hasta people can know everything or at least think that they know it all. But this is the aspect that can either give them immense power or restrict their personal growth. They feel by controlling the flow of their destiny, they can become what the soul wants them to be. But they can sometimes limit themselves to more material desires and try to control the limited vision. The real vision of Hasta should be limitless and universal, but as Virgo needs to express the perfection and purity of the new world, Hasta can struggle to achieve that perfection within their own world and in doing so compromise many of their bigger principles. These people genuinely believe that they can change their relationships to suit their way and this can lead them into partnerships that are inherently flawed.

Symbol – The Hand

Its symbol is the hand. The hand reflects the destiny of an individual and their individual effort. The right and the left hands are positive and negative, male and female energies, past and future lives. The four fingers of the hand show the four motivations: *Artha*, *Kama*, *Dharma* and *Moksha*, and the four directions: North, South, East and West. The three digits on the fingers are the three gunas or psychological qualities: *Rajas*, *Tamas* and *Sattva*; and the three Ayurvedic doshas: *Vata*, *Pitta* and *Kapha*. The fingers and thumbs show the five senses (sight, hearing, taste, smell and touch) and the five elements (earth, water, fire, air and ether). The joints on the four fingers show the twelve zodiac signs, and the joints of the thumbs and fingers together number 30, or the thirty days of the solar month. The hand also reflects the solar system and its planets. To write about all we can see from the hand is to contemplate an entire field of knowledge, a knowledge which is reflected in the Hasta nakshatra. They are masters of knowledge.

Puranic Myth – Gayatri Mantra

The Gayatri Mantra is found in the *Rig-Veda* (*Rig-Veda III/62/10*) and in three other Vedas too. It is chanted to invoke Savitar, the spiritual Sun, and through him Parabrahman (Eternity). While we can all see the physical Sun, the spiritual aspirant wants the Sun to reveal its inner light and bring enlightenment. It is chanted three times a day at times known as the three sandhyas: morning, midday and evening.

The main function of Gayatri is to free the souls from the bondage of Maya (illusion). At the Hasta stage the soul is stuck in materialism and needs to invoke the higher power and see the inner world, so regular chanting of Gayatri Mantra will help Hasta people develop their higher selves and free them from their material ties.

Hasta Aim for Moksha

Hasta craves a degree of perfection where they sublimate their ego to the purest of experiences, but their outward karma is in the material field. Hasta people realise that they need to harness their qualities in pursuit of spiritual enlightenment. They turn to yoga, which teaches them to balance their physical life with the spiritual direction. There is conflict to begin with as they learn the lessons of letting go, but they achieve peace and harmony.

Hasta represents the dawn of spiritual consciousness so Hasta people will be happy leading their mundane lives, but within them will be an emptiness and feeling of incompleteness. As consciousness of the higher truths dawns on them, it will fill the void.

Sacred Animal – Buffalo and Durga as Mahishasura Mardani

The animal of Hasta is the buffalo. The story of Durga and Mahisha Asura is the triumph over our lower desires. In Hasta, this is an important battle.

Mahisha was an *asura* (demon). *Mahisha* means a Buffalo. Mahisha became so powerful that he controlled the gods and disallowed worship to them. He could change his form between man and buffalo at will. Indra lost his war against him. The gods decided to create Durga and each god gave her their powers. She was beautiful and extremely powerful and single-handedly fought the demon Mahisha and killed him. This is why she is known as Mahisha Mardani – the destroyed of Mahisha. This battle is celebrated annually during Navaratri when the new Moon and Sun are in Virgo and the 10th tithi is celebrated as Vijaya dashami – the day Durga was victorious over Mahisha.

Hasta people have to be careful they do not develop an ego like Mahisha and think themselves all powerful. Hasta can also indicate the fight to defeat one's inner demons. It takes a long time to do so but if there is the blessing of the goddess, then victory is guaranteed.

Ayurvedic Dosha is Vata

Hasta reflects the natural qualities of action, agility, and conflict. In Hasta, this nervousness is apparent beneath a calm persona. Hasta people are always trying to control their tensions and they can stress out easily. Hasta try to find answers to calm their nature and are drawn to yoga. Any kind of physical discipline that addresses both the mind and the body will be good for Hasta as they need to express yet harness their vata energy.

Lagna and Planets

Hasta always shows a person who thinks too much, which is both their strength and their weakness. The deity Savitar says that they should seek inspiration from the sacred sound to show them the bright heavens, but most Hasta people want only material inspiration and this keeps their mind unsteady. They can be great thinkers and good at words but troubled if their mind is not at peace.

Lagna in Hasta people feel that whatever they desire, they can achieve. But they can feel frustrated by this as it does not always bring inner peace. They must link the higher notes of Hasta, then the world opens up. They will have a strong connection with words and self-effort. The position of Mercury and the Moon decides how they are going to work the Hasta energy.

The Sun is strong as it finds a way to inspire. Words matter. John Lennon with his Hasta Sun used the power of words to influence a whole generation, first in a purely material way, and then by inspiring people with higher knowledge.

The Moon is more troubled as the mind tries for control and is mostly unsuccessful. The Moon is fickle and does not remain focused. The mind is very bright and inspirational yet the lack of peace makes these people feel unsure and indecisive, which further adds to their troubles. The Moon as the first dasha can be fun. These people develop their intellect early but must learn to control their wayward minds. There can be many changes and an unsettled life. The Moon dasha can last up to ten years.

Mars is not at his best here, and these people can be overly critical or unsure about their direction. Hasta gives power but not of combative skills, more of planning and thinking. If Mars can use this energy and become a thinking leader or warrior, they can become great leaders. Bill Clinton, Nelson Mandela, Yasser Arafat, Bill Gates, Winston Churchill – all have their Mars in Hasta. They learned to talk the war, and use the words as weapons in their success as leaders and warriors.

Mercury is exalted in Hasta, its exact degree falls here. It is at its best. It understands words and their power to encourage and inspire; it can change the way people think and help them to connect with the sacred sounds.

Jupiter usually finds it difficult to deal with the ambitions of Hasta, but can feel the divine power. These people know about the destiny that binds us, but they can be proactive about learning to harness and change it. They will use their wisdom through their words, but the weakness can be of individuals who use their words to control the people around them.

Jupiter in Hasta has the power to influence and make others feel their wisdom is the right one, even if it isn't.

Venus in Hasta promotes talking about relationships rather than experiencing them. In Hasta, Venus is weak so this talk disturbs the relationships that it was meant to help.

Saturn does not fare well in the Moon's nakshatra but it is strong in Virgo. Saturn will use the power of Hasta to inspire discipline and try to control the wayward mind. The words spoken will be few and well thought out. These people will do rather than speak – walk the talk – this is their strength.

Rahu emphasises the attempts of man to try to control his destiny through his own efforts. The intuitive Moon allows a look beyond the ties of the material world, but Rahu's placement in the intellectual part of Hasta can restrict spiritual growth through fear and mistrust. The essence of Rahu in Hasta lies in the karmic relationship between the Moon and Rahu; at the time of a lunar eclipse Rahu's shadow becomes visible, indicating that the Moon-ruled nakshatras can expose the truth about the node. If Rahu allows itself to look beyond the inner darkness, it can see the light that leads to the path of enlightenment. Ketu in Hasta brings a lot of frustrations into this life but the essence of this placement is the ability to recognise life beyond its present restrictions. Ketu has no head so it cannot articulate the words that Hasta wants it to speak. Here the intuitive words and the powers of the mantras will bring out the hidden issues of Ketu.

Padas in Hasta: Aries, Taurus, Gemini, Cancer

This is the beginning of the fifth cycle of spiritual development which begins with an Ashtamamsha pada. This is the only nakshatra where the first pada is Ashtamamsha and therefore there must be changes, unexpected and unplanned, to reveal the Hasta message.

10°00' to 13°20' Virgo – Aries pada

The 1st pada of Hasta and 4th navamsha of Virgo is Aries and ashtamamsha. This is a place of struggle for all planets. Ashtamamsha means unexpected changes when least expected. New rules are coming in Hasta which are in conflict with the outer aspects of the chart. The fifth cycle of soul development begins with transformation and planets placed here are continuously experiencing that.

The person with a lagna in this pada is troubled as there are the opposites of Mars and Mercury to deal with. A major transformation is experienced. The Sun and Mars gain in strength by being in their good pada, but the ashtamamsha does not give them an easy ride. Both of them want to focus more on their martial strengths than their mental ones.

Saturn becomes debilitated. The impulsiveness of Aries does not allow for control and this creates problems in facing up to reality, and how to use the power of Hasta in a productive way.

13°20' to 16°40' Virgo – Taurus pada

The 2nd pada of Hasta and 5th navamsha of Virgo is Taurus which is also pushkara. All planets benefit here, even Ketu. Taurus is the natural second sign and therefore reflects the quality of voice and the spoken word. It gives the stability of mind that Hasta seeks.

The Moon goes from an enemy rashi to an exalted sign here and it finds peace; this is where the mind is calm and can know the great picture that is promised by Hasta.

Mercury's exact exaltation degree is in this pada at 15°00' Virgo and it receives the support of Virgo, Hasta and Taurus. Mercury is the karaka of speech, which makes this the place where the word and speech rule supreme. The path of self-realisation is make clearer by the divine word.

Rahu revels in this position. These people want all the knowledge and will be willing to talk about it to everyone. Whether the talk is totally for their ends or for the good of others depends usually on how it relates to the Moon and Mercury. Ketu the planet of instinct, cannot deal with the analytical qualities of Virgo and the materialism of Taurus pada. This is a tough position for Ketu but the pushkara allows it to understand on a subliminal level that this path is essential for it. These people can find their inner soul through the practice of mantras.

16°40' to 20°00' Virgo – Gemini pada

The 3rd pada of Hasta and 6th navamsha of Virgo is Gemini. This pada promotes the analytical mind. Gemini pada people can be overtly intellectual and this is not good for a calm and peaceful mind. Too many questions can create mental storms. No planets are exalted or debilitated – all the planets become intensely mercurial.

20°00' to 23°40' Virgo – Cancer pada

The 4th pada of Hasta and 7th navamsha of Virgo is Cancer. Here the instinct and emotions dominate and the planets learn to trust their instinct. There is intellect, emotions and the search for power. Words get a special resonance as these people learn to recognise their roots. Jupiter is exalted and Mars debilitated.

Mars is in a debilitated pada and an enemy sign and so is in a weak position. The person may be too analytical, not willing to fight for their rights and have a tendency to shy away from hardships. They need to be more disciplined and learn to face up to the matters rather than avoid them.

Jupiter gets exalted in this pada and becomes wise; it uses the power of words both for writing and speaking but also as a way of life. This is a strong Jupiter which explores purity of thought and these people learn to trust their instincts.

14. Chitra

23°40' Virgo to 6°40' Libra
Padas: Leo, Virgo, Libra, Scorpio

Meaning

Chitra means a reflection or a beautiful picture. Chitra people are usually very attractive. The reflection also includes the soul as Chitra reflects the potential of the soul. It is connected to Chitra Gupta. *Gupta* means secret and *Chitra Gupta* was the assistant of Lord Yama and the keeper of the Akashik records. On a deeper level Chitra can know the deep secrets of human life. To get to this position they need to unveil their true self from the grip of the tamasic world.

> **Chitra**
> Ruled by Mars
> Devata: Tvashtar, The Celestial Architect
> Symbol: Pearl
> Yoni: Tiger
> Motivation: Kama
> Guna Triplicity: Tamas, Tamas and Tamas
> Ayurvedic Dosha: Pitta
> Body Part: Neck
> Gana: Demon
> Caste: Farmer
> Quality: Soft
> Colour: Black
> Best Direction: West
> Special Sounds: Pay, Po, Raa, Ree
> Principal Star: Spica
> Other Names for Chitra: Twashtri, Twashtra, Taksha

Chitra have two types of life experience: one where they are totally immersed in the material world, almost unaware of their spiritual potential, and the other when circumstances and situations force them to recognise their higher nature. When the personality is reformed, this process is painful. The ego has to be cut away so that the inner soul can emerge.

Devata

Tvashtar, the ruling deity of Chitra, is the celestial architect. His responsibility is to fashion the outer persona of the individual. Symbolically Tvashtar takes an uncut stone and makes it into a beautiful statue. The uncut stone is the human being encased in the world of matter. Chitra bound in tamas. Their true beauty is hidden. Tvashtar begins to cut away at the life of matter. This process is extremely painful for Chitra. They feel torn apart, but slowly their inner light comes through.

Tvatshar is the divine artisan, a vedic deity considered in the *Rig Veda* as the ideal artist. It is also a name for Brahma Prajapati and

Vishwakarma, the celestial architect. He wields the great axe and forged the thunderbolt of Indra. He is the bestower of long life, imparting generative power and offspring. He created Brihaspati (Jupiter), generated fire along with heaven and earth, the waters and the Bhrigus, who were the ancestors of Venus.

This gives Chitra great creative ability on many levels. Ideas, artists, architects and actors can all have a link with Chitra. Amitabh Bachchan, the great Bollywood actor has his Sun in Chitra.

Planetary Ruler – Mars
Mars is a dynamic planet which has plenty of courage. The Chitra personality depends on whether they have discovered their potential or not. Their inner beauty can be well hidden and if controlled by desires they can be lazy and selfish. From an early stage these people are aware there is more to life than meets the eye. Mars gives them courage and confidence to externalise potential regardless of the personal cost. They are not fearful of what the next part of life will bring, or the obstacles they have to face. As they externalise their latent talents, the second type of Chitra emerges, who is selfless and truly beautiful.

Kanya and Tula Rashi
Chitra spans Virgo and Libra. Virgo represents the perfectionist stage and Libra is where it strives for balance. This is where the soul starts seeing the reflection of its self. There are usually two types of Chitra, one where they do not recognise anything beyond this world as a reality, and another where they suddenly come face to face with their soul and start to develop to re-establish the connection. Virgo is puritanical and Chitra is immersed in material pursuits, especially in Virgo. There is an intellectual understanding of the soul, but not any deep connection. Chitra in Libra tries to balance its needs and reaches a point of harmony where the questing of Virgo stops; now it needs to find the truth which brings the harmony.

Symbol – The Pearl
The symbol of Chitra is the pearl. The pearl is found in a hard shell, and the lustrous pearl doesn't emerge until the shell is broken. It takes a long time to make a pearl, in the same way for the pearl within a person to

appear takes many cycles of life and death. This breaking of the shell is a difficult process and usually means an individual has to make immense changes before their true personality can shine through.

The pearl is called *mukta* which in Sanskrit means spiritual enlightenment. Chitra focuses on this highest form of personal ambition while still being involved in discharging its mundane responsibilities.

Puranic Myth – Chitragupta, Keeper of Akashik records

Chitragupta was the assistant of Lord Yama and the keeper of the Akashik records. *Chitragupta* means secret pictures; it could refer to the records of the lives of all people. It is believed that Chitragupta examines the good and bad karma a person has created during their life and keeps a record of it. When a person dies, his soul first goes to Lord Yama, where Chitragupta tallies the deeds and reports them to Yama. This decides where the soul is heading after death.

Chitra Purnima is observed when the full Moon is in Chitra (April–May). Special worship is done to Chitragupta to appeal for forgiveness for our karmic shortcomings.

Chitragupta's link shows an interest in history, past life and the actions (karma and its rewards) that can develop for Chitra people.

Chitra Aim for Kama

Kama is desires and needs on a very practical level. Under Chitra the passion is for expressing life at the fullest. Chitra lives life on two polarities, the intensely material and the completely spiritual. Kama deals with creative expression and Chitra can be extremely creative in art, cinema, writing, thinking and other areas where craft or art is essential.

Sacred Animal – Tiger: Ayyappa and the Milk of the Tigress

Ayyappa, the ascetic god, is the child of Shiva and Mohini. Mohini was the form Vishnu took when he had to wrest the amrita, the nectar of immortality, from the demons.

Ayyappa took human incarnation as Manikantan. He was a child alone in the forest and Raja Rajasekhara of Pandalam adopted him. When his coronation was taking place as Yuva Raja (Heir Apparent), the queen was against it as by then there was another child. So she manufactured an illness and told the king that only the milk of a tigress would cure her. Manikantan volunteered to get the tigress's milk for his mother. Everyone thought he would be killed in this endeavour, but soon he came back riding a tigress with her cubs trailing behind. Then both the king and queen realized that this was no ordinary son and the king built a Temple at Sabrimala where ascetics go to worship annually around Makar Sankranti in January.

The Chitra link to Lord Ayyappa shows that Chitra can embody the qualities of both Shiva and Vishnu, yet Ayyappa was abandoned by them and there are issues regarding parenting that Chitra may have to deal with. Their personality becomes very strong if they develop spiritually. Ayyappa rides the tigress, a very difficult animal to tame. Chitra can tame the tiger within them if they so decide, and become masters of their destiny.

Ayurvedic Dosha is Pitta

Chitra people are leaders. They are dynamic and full of energy. They are generous, creative, knowledgeable and intelligent. They are passionate and sensuous. Chitra are ambitious and driven to make a mark in society; they do not recognise their fallibility. They can be short tempered. Chitra people have the capacity to burn out if they do not pace themselves properly.

Lagna and Planets

Lagna in Chitra people will be creative, and talented with many skills. In Virgo Chitra we find the perfectionist craftsman who thinks a lot. The position of Mars and its relationship with Mercury will reveal more. In Libra Chitra these people hope to find harmony between material and spiritual. They can be good at making judgements and can take the role of an advisor. The natal positions of Mars and Venus will give the complete picture.

The Sun is learning to interact with others and sometimes these people have to lessen their fiery nature. This takes away some of its absolute strength. They question their perfection and try to find the answer of who they are. The Sun must remain confident but this position does not allow it.

The Moon is creative here and can be too involved in outer pursuits. The Moon usually represents the soma or our collection of good karmas. These people need to keep their karma creative and try not to squander the good qualities through indecision or too much analysis. The Chitra Moon does not give an easy childhood, although Mars is the first dasha (maximum seven years), which can be positive. It is followed by Rahu which can be uncertain. Mars can make a person dynamic, active and full of energy. The Rahu dasha following it while still in childhood is never easy as Rahu can increase the negative qualities of Chitra and immerse these people in a world of illusion.

Mars is in its own nakshatra. It develops leadership qualities here, so these people may be a thinking politician or leader. There can be a special interest in weapons. Mars will try for balance but it can develop a taste for comfort and luxury that deflects from the true warrior quality.

Mercury is extremely creative and uses the mind to originate new ideas and is a good position for writers, commentators and artists who continuously refashion their work.

Jupiter was created by Tvatshar, indicating that wisdom is fashioned here. Jupiter will do some pioneering work with writing, words and giving knowledge.

This is the nakshatra where Venus gets its exact debilitation. Venus desires perfection, the perfect partner, a perfect relationship, which is not easy to get.

Saturn learns to find perfection. Saturn is strong in parts of Chitra. It gives the ability to withstand challenges. Saturn can keep the potential covered up but when the time is right, it is able to face up to the hardest tasks in the search for the lost soul.

Rahu in Chitra reinforces its deceptions. The illusions and shadows that Rahu represents are so strong that these people can easily live in a false or unrealistic world. This can still allow success yet dissatisfactions remain until the soul connection is made. Ketu is associated with Chitra Gupta, the keeper of the Akashik records and can have a profound inner world and knowledge only if it allows itself to go deep. Ketu indicates the past life in a world of darkness, yet some experiences show the true reflection of its soul. But it does not know how to express this.

Padas in Chitra – Leo, Virgo, Libra, Scorpio

Chitra has two vargottama padas one each in Virgo and Libra. Venus gets its exact debilitation degree, and Mercury and Saturn get exalted. The Scorpio pada is where the message of Chitra is at its most acute; the need to dominate, to control, to be the greatest leader, to be possessive, to be the right partner. In fact the illusion is at its greatest, therefore the revelation of the soul gives maximum pain and then the greatest insight. The Sun (soul) and Moon (mind) are debilitated by the pada. The reason is that the Sun has to learn to relate whereas the Moon has to learn to move away from desires and towards spirituality.

23°20' to 16°40' Virgo – Leo pada
The 1st pada of Chitra and 8th navamsha of Virgo is Leo. No planet is exalted or debilitated in this navamsha, indicating the harmonious nature of this pada; the planets are left to follow their own instincts. Leo brings power and the will to succeed to all planets. Saturn usually struggles with Leo. Rahu wants to dominate.

26°40' to 30°00' Virgo – Virgo pada
The 2nd pada of Chitra and 9th navamsha of Virgo is the vargottama Virgo. Mercury is in exalted navamsha and rashi while Venus is in debilitated navamsha and rashi.

Mercury is exalted and Vargottama shows a great mind, the ability to analyse, to create something special. There is a strong sense of being, of understanding the purpose of life and being comfortable with it.

Venus is exactly debilitated at 27° Virgo in this pada. Venus forgets to enjoy and these people want to know the exact meaning of every gesture, feeling, and thought. This super-critical Venus is especially difficult for relationships. This does not show a lack of relationships but emphasises the quality of relationships. These people tend analyse their relationships too much and this can take away much of its pleasure. Being vargottama, Venus has the ability to overcome these issues and can rise to be creative. There is a lack of felicity and enjoyment of love as these people are always trying to gain perfection while forgetting to enjoy the world as it is. This can give an ability to be good at business. Warren Buffet, the great tycoon and investor has his Venus placed in this pada.

00°00' to 03°20' Libra – Libra pada
The 3rd pada of Chitra and 1st navamsha of Libra is vargottama Libra. In my view this is the strongest position for Saturn in the chart, and the

weakest position for the Sun. Saturn is in an exalted pada and sign while the Sun is in a debilitated pada and sign.

The Sun, as the giver of light to the solar system, can never be totally weak. The soul can become enmeshed in its material pursuits but the inner quality remains pure and perfect. These people have a great healing force behind them that allows them to get out of the lack of vitality and confidence that the debilitated Sun brings. But this Sun will need the support of partners and cannot stand alone.

Saturn slowly reveals the soul, so they have the ability to face pain, to be truly detached and re-fashion their life.

03°20' to 06°40' Libra – Scorpio pada

The 4th pada of Chitra and 2nd navamsha of Libra is Scorpio, a difficult position for the Moon and Rahu. Ketu enjoys its exaltation and Mars is strengthened in its own navamsha. This is a difficult pada for the planets to be in, as the material illusion is at its strongest. Personal habits and involvement in the material aspects of life can also become fixed, yet this is the pada that creates the maximum transformation.

The Moon is debilitated in this pada. Scorpio usually brings turmoil and pulls the person in two directions. The soul is encased in the covering of materialism. This is where the hard shell can break and reveal the soul. It holds the true secret of what Chitra Gupta has recorded of your karmic deeds and therefore gives an opportunity to atone for them. Rahu can become obsessed with finding inner secrets. A word of warning, the soul should reveal itself when the time is right, but Rahu's obsessions can open you up to your soul secrets before you are able to cope with them. This can create inner turmoil and the vulnerability can be masked by attraction to intoxicating substances or intense involvement in relationships. Ketu is in a very special place; here it can face the shadows of the past which are obscuring the true picture of the soul. Ketu helps in cutting through the veils and exposing the true soul. Old habits and patterns of behaviour have to be modified and changed and then the revelation of the inner being takes place. This is the true place of the secret knowledge of Chitra Gupta that flourishes in Ketu.

15. Swati

6°40' to 20°00' Libra
Padas: Sagittarius, Capricorn, Aquarius, Pisces

Meaning

Swati means sword. The sword can be used for both negative and positive reasons. Swati people carry the sword as a tool for self-advancement, cutting through competition and obstacles in their path. Swati is the name of the wife of the Sun. In Swati, the Sun forgets its spiritual purpose, and gets involved with the pleasures and pains of relationship so it becomes debilitated. For a moment it is not bothered about Moksha or enlightenment, which is its primary motivation.

Swati
Ruled by Rahu
Ruling Deity: Vayu, The God of Wind and Life Breath
Symbol: Coral
Yoni: Buffalo
Motivation: Artha
Guna Triplicity: Tamas, Tamas and Sattva
Ayurvedic Dosha: Kapha
Body Part: Chest
Gana: Divine
Caste: Butcher
Quality: Mutable
Shakti: Transforming
Colour: Black
Best Direction: North
Special Sounds: Ru, Ray, Ra, Ta
Principal Star: Arcturus
Other Names for Swati: Vayu, Vaat, Sameer, Anil, Marut

Devata – Vayu

Vayu (Wind) rules the material world along with Agni (Fire) and Surya (the Sun). Vayu controls the intellect. It is the prana, the breath or the life force within the human that connects him to the eternal energy. Vayu is the essence of speech, the purifier.

Kubera, the god of wealth is a manifestation of Vayu. Vayu arose out of the mouth of Brahma and was blowing hard, disturbing the peace and showering hailstones. Brahma calmed it down by making it the guardian of wealth, Kubera. It indicates that when the individual gets to preserve what they create, they make even more of it as their energy gets used properly. Otherwise they can become agitated and revel in destructive behaviour. Bill Gates has his Sun in Swati, and as the richest man in the world it seems appropriate.

Vayu can have a gentle form and a very destructive form – the gentle breeze that calms us or the destructive winds that annihilate everything in its path. Vayu has drunk the soma or the nectar of self-realisation and therefore lends Swati people the real motivation to find themselves. But Swati can make the mistake of searching in the material world.

Planetary Ruler – Rahu

Rahu creates a desire for success, wealth, finance and the ability to take risks. Swati are 'ideas' people, disciplined with the ability to make these ideas into good commercial and profitable realities. Rahu gives these people the ability to go where others have not been. Many millionaires are born in Swati.

Rahu forms just the head of the snake; it has no body. It thinks and forgets to feel. Swati people initially project the subconscious through the strong identification with their personality. Self-reliance and personal ego are strong where people lose touch with their soul. Their dissatisfaction with what they have achieved leads them to look inward. Often Swati people think too much and do not use their intuition; always doing things while not enjoying the rewards of all this action.

Tula Rashi

Swati is entirely in Tula, Libra. Swati is where the Sun reaches its exact debilitation point at 10° Libra, it appears weak and this is when the Sun is furthest away from the earth. It seems that the Sun has forgotten the real purpose of the soul. Yet fulfilling worldly desires is an important step as part of spiritual growth. This is the debt one has to pay for being born on earth. Swati Sun wants relationship, to be connected to the world and take support from partners. To be a true Swati, they should live their life fully but also try to remain detached from it and find the balance that Libra seeks. Yet, the experience of full involvement into earthy, materialistic pleasures brings dissatisfaction as the scales will be too biased to one side, and get out of balance.

Symbol – Coral

The symbol is coral, which has a hard outer sheath but is self-propagating. It lives in a marine environment that it both affects and is affected by. This symbolises the human being; he lives in the world which influences his life but in turn makes an impact on the world around him. Swati people influence those around them, and in turn they use the influence of the society to improve themselves.

Puranic Myth – Hanuman, the son of Vayu
Hanuman was the son of Vayu. He was an ideal devotee giving his life in devotion to Shri Rama. He represents courage and devotion, qualities that can be seen in Swati.

According to the epic Ramayana, Anjana was worshipping Lord Shiva and asking him for a child. At the same time Dashratha, the King of Ayodhya, was performing the Putrakama Yagya in order to have children. As a Prasad he received kheer (rice pudding) which was to be eaten by the three wives of King Dashratha. This led to the births of his four children Shri Rama, Lakshmana, Bharata and Shatrughna. A bird snatched a bit of the Prasad and dropped it where Anjana was worshipping. Vayu carried the falling Prasad to the hands of Anjana, who consumed it. Hanuman was born to her as a result and he is known as Pawanputra, the son of Vayu.

Swati can reflect qualities of Hanuman – devoted, caring, brave and flexible. Hanuman represents the ideal devotee, and if people who are linked to this energy get passionate about something they can give all their life to it. This can lead to success too as it gives them the ability to focus.

Swati Aim for Artha
Swati is motivated by artha, which is activity on a material plain. Swati are very materialistic and will take practical steps to make their dreams come true. These dreams are initially about achieving success in this world and making their mark. Artha is important if they are to achieve their ambitions.

Swati are practical. Creating wealth and being good at business is part of their spiritual makeup. They should try not to feel inadequate if they are unable to express their spirituality fully. They can use their practical skills to make the world a better place for others. Artha is very important, as these people support all others who cannot do it for themselves. Artha pays taxes and runs community initiatives.

Sacred animal – Buffalo of Yama and Shani

The buffalo is associated with Yama but often it is Saturn that will be seen riding the buffalo. Saturn is the brother of Yama, who is in charge of weighing the karma of the individuals at the time of death while Shani asks people to pay for their karma during the life time. Both are referred to as Mahakal along with Shiva whose devotees they are. Both Yama and Shani are doing an essential duty even if those impacted by their influence do not like it. We all have to deal with our karma so it's best to be cautious today of what we create. There's no point blaming Yama or Shani for it.

In Swati Saturn is strong, and at the end of it he becomes exalted. It is difficult to judge whether 20° Libra is the end of Swati or the beginning of Vishakha. As Swati debilitates the Sun, usually this makes Saturn strong.

Buffalo people can show great willpower but also anger in Swati. Their lower energies are fierce and need to be controlled, yet if they become masters of their buffalo nature they can be forever giving, supporting others without receiving any appreciation in return. People respect them yet remain wary of them.

Ayurvedic Dosha is Kapha

Swati's kapha nature makes them calm and philosophical. Swati can be very placid in the competitive world. This makes them good industrialists and business people; they will stay calm whatever the crisis.

The Secret of the Sun Debilitation in Swati

Why is the Sun is debilitated in Swati Libra? This is due to Swati's connection with Parashurama, the Venus incarnation of Vishnu.

Parasurama was a pupil of Shiva and his father was Sage Jamdaghni. In the time of Parashurama there was great persecution of the sages by those in royal power. Kartavirya had a thousand hands and was an extremely powerful king. He stole the Kamdhenu cow from the Sage Jamdagni for which Parashurama killed him. In turn Kartavirya's sons killed Sage Jamdagni. Parashurama took revenge for his father's death by killing 21 clans of Kshatriyas.

Sun is a Kshatriya or warrior and when it comes to the sign of Libra and Swati nakshatra, it becomes debilitated. This can indicate that the Sun can misuse his powers. Swati Sun people need to be cautious about how they use their powers; they can lack confidence and therefore may try to over express it to others, which can lead to all types of excess if left unchecked.

Lagna and Planets

Lagna in Swati people are creative with many new ideas. They must remember the destructive side of Swati and tread carefully in arousing their inner storms. The positions of Rahu and Venus and their relationships to each will give clearer guidance of how to use this energy.

The Sun is debilitated and will not therefore work well in Swati. These people feel weak and insecure within so they try to dominate and impose their will but are not always successful; they do not want to be alone and will need support of relationships.. The Sun must recognise the need for others and try to be more democratic in its views.

Swati Moon people live in their own world and have the ability to influence those around them, but they shouldn't forget that others can influence their well-made environment too. Swati Moons can be very refined with an underlying rough edge. As the first dasha ruler, Rahu will encourage a person towards ambition and success, yet not much will satisfy them. Rahu dasha at a young age is never easy, as a person can chase many shadows and not catch any of them. A Rahu childhood can be very uncertain, where one leads an unconventional life with many ups and downs.

Mars finds it difficult, as this is a world where ideas are king, communication is essential, and there appears to be no direct role for Mars in Swati people who then have to establish a new way to use their energy. There can be a huge attachment to relationships and support which can scupper individual effort and personal strength. Mars can work in helping others to realize their dreams.

Mercury loves being in Swati, as it likes to communicate and to connect with others. This is a thinking planet in a thinking nakshatra. But he must not ignore traditions and the more subtle and spiritual concepts.

Jupiter does not feel at home in Swati, an enemy sign and a difficult nakshatra. Jupiter teaches profound wisdom, but in the realm of Swati sometimes the knowledge is what is available to all and too much focus is given to success and relationships. These people have to learn the art of give and take. Jupiter knows how to give but is not always comfortable taking. The commercialisation of wisdom which Swati can create is against the natural Jupiterian impulse.

Venus is strong, in its own sign, and in a friend's nakshatra. The emphasis is on relationships and understanding the ways of the world. There are many new ideas, and the ability to communicate them easily.

Saturn is moving towards its exaltation degree at 20° Libra. This is at the end of Swati and the beginning of Vishakha. Saturn deals with wisdom imparted through personal work and life experience. In Swati it can remain detached. Saturn represents Vayu and communicates a higher message to Earthlings of taking responsibility for their karma. A strong Saturn takes them on happily in Swati. Saturn teaches the notion of divine relationships and to love with true detachment. It tells us of the illusion of earthly love and shows us the higher, more spiritual love where we learn to take the good and bad within a relationship in the same vein.

Rahu people are interested in politics and strategy and they know how to plan, maneuver, beguile and play power games. Business and mental creativity all come to the fore. Ketu cannot deal with all the material desires, the need to create a world in its own image. It struggles, usually rejects this world and brings up the storms of Swati that can be destructive. Ketu needs to learn detachment and balance. Ketu in Swati people may not like the life they have but destruction is not the answer. They need to take a more spiritual view of life and this will bring harmony.

Padas in Swati: Sagittarius, Capricorn, Aquarius, Pisces
This is the ending of the 5th cycle of spiritual development. The ending cycles of the padas usually represent that one way of thinking is becoming more acute so that the soul will transform itself at the end. Swati shows dependence on material life coming to an end.

06°40' to 10°00' Libra – Sagittarius pada
The 1st pada of Swati and 3rd navamsha of Libra is Sagittarius. It shows the beginning of a spiritual search within the material world Swati establishes. No planet is exalted or debilitated here.

10°00' to 13°20' Libra – Capricorn pada

The 2nd pada of Swati and 4th navamsha of Libra is Capricorn, which aids practical development of the soul. To accept the responsibilities that are imposed by life on earth. Planets that learn to deal with these responsibilities thrive but for others the burden can be immense. Jupiter loses by being in a debilitated pada while Mars gains.

Mars can take on the quality of Hanuman – devotion and courage. Mars finds the ability to make the best. Do not be mistaken by the soft message on the outside. These people are determined to succeed.

Jupiter can become too commercial and works well in the worldly pursuits. I find Jupiter debilitated makes a person feel that they lack good luck, but that is not really true. If they take their responsibilities seriously and try not to be too business-like, they can prosper. It is a good position for law, politics and accountants.

13°20' to 16°40' Libra – Aquarius pada

The 3rd pada of Swati and the 5th navamsha is Aquarius, good for Saturn and Rahu. Here Rahu is in its own nakshatra. All planets develop a keen sense of worldly responsibility and common justice. In a rashi and nakshatra that is developing in materialism, this inner core surprises people. People with planets placed here will think of others, and do socially conscious work. The vayu element is strong in this pada as the sign, nakshatra and pada are all vayu, but this can make for volatility. The mind needs to be directed in the right direction otherwise the winds of Swati and pada Aquarius can blow everything away and create problems with the rulership and significations of the planets placed here.

16°40' to 20°00' Libra – Pisces pada

The 4th pada of Swati and 6th navamsha of Libra is Pisces. This is an unusual navamsha, the last in the 5th cycle. Here the destruction of Vayu can be present. It is pushkara so all the planets benefit from this change. The outer aspect is of Libra and Swati still keeping their feet firmly on the material plane, but the internal ground has shifted and if people do not recognise the shift, they will feel extremely unsettled. Pisces pada can be sexual or spiritual. In fact sacred sex can be a divine inspiration, where sex is used to procreate, but there can be hidden aspects where a person becomes entangled by the outer attractions.

Mercury is profound. The analytical nature of Mercury cannot work, making practical decisions difficult, but Mercury sees beyond what man has imposed. These people understand that mind has to change, that the old ways and structures are crumbling. Like the wind that takes away the old leaves, vayu will rid the mind of its old beliefs and props so that new shoots of intellect will come out later.

Even an exalted Venus will not promise smooth relationships. The soul has to detach from others before it can find its purity. As the soul moves back towards its roots, life cannot remain the same. Venus has the major role in sowing the seed that will flourish in a new incarnation.

16. Vishakha

20°00' Libra to 3°20' Scorpio
Padas: Aries, Taurus, Gemini, Cancer

Meaning

Vishakha have several meanings. *Visha* means to enter and *Kha* means the heavens. Vishakha stands for transformation and the aspiration to enter the heavens to connect with the eternal self. Vishakha people are standing at the threshold of a new life. The change is yet to take place, as this is the soul looking from outward to within. It has reached that place in life where there is a great attraction to go towards the inner sanctum, the great unknown. It can throw out both negative and positive issues. There is no guarantee of the experience inside. *Vish* means poison, excrement and feces. 'Akha' means the manifestation. This is the nakshatra where the poisons of past life, of unfulfilled emotional desires and negative aspects of past karma can be stored. Vishakha shows knowledge of toxins of the mind, and of what has been collected through the experiences of many lifetimes.

> **Vishakha**
> Ruler is Jupiter
> Devata: Agni, the God of Fire and Indra, the God of Gods
> Symbol: The Potter's Wheel, Archway
> Yoni: Male Tiger
> Motivation: Dharma
> Guna Triplicity: Tamas, Sattva and Rajas
> Dosha: Kapha
> Body Part: Breast
> Gana: Demon
> Caste: Outcast
> Quality: Mixed
> Colour: Golden
> Best Direction: East
> Special Sounds: Te, Tu, Tay, To
> Principal Star: Az Zubanan - the Two Claws of Scorpio.
> Other Names for Vishakha: Shakragni, Vrashagni, Indragni, Dweesha, Radha

Devata – Indra and Agni

Vishakha is the only nakshatra with two deities. Agni and Indra are the two power deities of the Vedas. Both deal with excesses of power and its ability to transform for more spiritual gains. Both enjoy Soma, the nectar of immortality. Agni is offered that as part of the yagya (see Krittika) and Indra is a great consumer of it. Soma gives them both immense strengths.

Agni is the god of fire and the acceptor of sacrifices. The sacrifices made to Agni during Vedic rituals go directly to the gods because Agni is a messenger from and to the gods. He is ever-young, because the fire is re-lit every day, and immortal. Agni is volatile as fire is difficult to control.

Indra is the King of the Devas (gods), Lord of Heaven, and God of War, Storms, and Rainfall. Vritrá, a demon serpent, stole all the water in the world and Indra slew the monster and brought water back to Earth.

Indira is the lord of the senses too, and therefore enjoys sensuality and luxury. He gets into trouble by having an affair with the Rishi Gautama's wife, Ahilya, and he gets cursed into having a thousand vaginas. Realizing what has happened, he makes many sacrifices and practices austerities which allow him to overcome the curse and get a 1000 eyes instead.

For Vishakha people, this great sensuality can lead them to unwise sexual alliances, but they also have the ability to learn about tapasya and self-control. Vishakha represents both the sensuous and ascetic within us.

Planetary Ruler – Jupiter

Jupiter brings the wisdom that eases the way on a new journey towards change and the ability to expand horizons, to go beyond the present. Vishakha people aspire to touch the heavens, therefore they can achieve a lot materially but this leaves a residual sense of dissatisfaction within. Jupiter guides Vishakha through this important stage where the soul is willing and able to take on board its lessons and change its outlook. This change does not take place without great churning of emotions.

Tula and Vrishchika Rashi

Vishakha spans two signs; it is mostly in Libra, with one pada in Scorpio. This is the start of the 6th level in the soul's development. At the stage of Vishakha the life is still totally immersed in materialism and it takes time for individuals to realise that they want more and this makes them look inward and dig deeper. The main difference between Libra Vishakha and Scorpio Vishakha is that in Libra, they struggle to juggle the material and the spiritual, trying to find meaning in the two differing realities that are now present for the soul; Scorpio Vishakha finds it impossible to achieve a balance. Libra allows an individual to live a life materially while recognising the spiritual soul; Scorpio needs change and transformation.

The Scorpio Vishakha has many toxic qualities especially for the Moon. This can lead to secret knowledge which people can use, the knowledge to transform the present life. It can attract weaknesses like obsessive behaviour and addictions.

Symbol – Potter's Wheel and the Archway

The symbol of the potter's wheel shows the static inner core, which is steeped in the tamas of worldly illusions and the outer full of energy and vitality. The clay fashioned by the potter is likened to life, which is shaped in different ways by the hands of destiny; the experiences of life help it to mature.

The archway shows a soul at the threshold of spiritual development, looking from their material world into a more spiritual one. They can remain spectators or decide to cross under the archway, but usually for Vishakha, the moment they cross a threshold, another comes on the horizon. The archway is symbolic of their thirst for spiritual development. They have reached that place in life where there is a great attraction to go towards the inner sanctum, the great unknown.

The gateway here can at first be the sexual achievement, or the woman's vagina that is the first gateway to find orgasmic experience. In ancient tradition, sex was a ritualistic practice that was sacred, and a woman's vagina was considered a gateway to heavenly experiences (temples in Khajuraho are testament). Be careful not to abuse your sexual powers.

Puranic Myth – Indra and the Brahmin Boy

The story of the Devata Indra explains some of the qualities that Vishakha can inherit. Indra's defeat of the demon Vritra elevated to him to the rank of King of the Gods. To celebrate this, Indra orders the celestial architect, Vishwakarma, to build him a grand palace. Full of pride, Indra becomes very demanding. Vishwakarma could not satisfy Indra's ever increasing demands so he asks for divine help. In order to teach Indra a lesson, Vishnu visits Indra's palace in the form of a Brahmin boy. Vishnu praises Indra's palace, adding that no former Indra had succeeded in building such a place. Indira admires the Brahmin boy's knowledge; he claims to know former Indras and much more. During the boy's speech, a procession of ants had entered the hall. The boy saw the ants and laughed. Indra asks the boy why he laughed. The boy revealed that the ants are all former Indras. They are so many that you can't even count them and there will be so many more to come in future lifetimes. They were all equally brave, or more. So there is no need to take so much pride in defeating the Vritra Asura. A humbled Indra realized the wisdom of the Brahmin boy and intuitively understood that it was none other than great Vishnu.

Vishkha people have grand plans for their life but must always watch their ego and that their pride is not hindering their progress. Their successes can make them proud and develop a large ego. Vishkha people can be very attached to having a grand residence just like Indra.

Vishakha aim for Dharma

Dharma motivates Vishakha. Doing the right thing is important. These people aim for correct behaviour. They face up to their responsibilities socially and spiritually and are keen to do their duty; at times going beyond the call of duty. Vishakha people can be dogmatic about their views.

Vishakha's spiritual life path is connected to facing up to change. This is an important nakshatra of transformation, about understanding the two polarities of life. These people have to learn detachment while still being involved in their material life. This is a time for preparation, for what is to come ahead.

Sacred Animal – Vyaghrapada, the Sage with Tiger's Feet

Vyaghra means tiger and *pada* is feet. Vyaghrapada was a rishi and a devotee of Shiva. Every day he prayed to a self-generated form of Shiva and picked fresh flowers from the forest. He wanted them so pure that even the bees had not been on them. His feet were troubled by thorns and rough surfaces from the daily excursions, and he would pray to Shiva, "please give me feet like a tiger so that I could fulfill this duty easily". So Shiva granted him the wish. There are many carvings for Sage Vyaghrapada in Chidambaram temple where he would go daily with his offerings along with Patanjali (see Ashlesha). Shiva blessed both his devotees Patanjali and Vyaghrapada by showing them Ananda Tandava, the dance of Bliss.

The tiger's ability to go where others cannot reach and Vyaghrapada's devotion are two aspects of Vishakha. They are willing to change in whatever way necessary if their devotion can be fulfilled. Also the desire for purity – of the untouched flowers – remains within Vishakha people.

Ayurvedic Dosha is Kapha

Vishakha are calm and patient in a life that can be at times full of turmoil. So much is changing around them, but their kapha nature helps them to come to terms with it.

Lagna and Planets

Lagna in Vishakha people want to achieve heaven, so first they try to build an empire or create a perfect world. There is a huge need to fulfill all their desires but this can lead to dissatisfaction. If they understand what their soul is telling them, then they will learn to control their desires and remain satisfied with their world regardless of unfulfilled ambitions. They need to control their sexual urges and avoid unsuitable relationships.

The Sun in Vishakha has moved on from its debilitation nakshatra, so this is a Sun that is revealing itself. There is a need for material props still, the fire that burns within these people has to be of material achievements to start with but becomes transformed into more spiritual fire.

The Vishakha Moon person is aspiring to cross the threshold into heaven, striving to break away from the layers of materialism. These people can be willing and able to take on board new lessons that change their outlook on life, but the change does not take place without great churning of emotions. The feeling that heaven is always somewhere else creates dissatisfaction with current circumstances. Scorpio Vishakha Moon is more complex, it needs to transform but can remain stuck in its old ways. The Moon is debilitated here so is very troubled especially if there is a refusal to change and transform. These people have to be careful that they are not dominated by their weaknesses (jealousy, possessiveness, bitterness, envy etc.). They need to find inspiration from their darkness and discover the divinity within. The first dasha for Vishakha is Jupiter, which is usually comfortable and happy. The dasha that follows Jupiter is Saturn and depending on the length of the Jupiter dasha, Saturn can suddenly bring childhood to an end.

Mars will go from strength to weakness. It does not know how to keep its balance. Mars in Vishakha must exercise discipline otherwise its direction can become overtly sensuous.

Mercury loves to explore the new realms of Vishakha. There is an intellectual journey for these people. They are exposed to desires both sexual and material and try to balance the burgeoning interest in spirituality. Mercury is innately curious and thinks about moving into the more spiritual direction and there are many interesting travels for these people as each threshold reveals another and Mercury remains captivated.

Jupiter placed here brings out the advisor. These people can guide, help others and understand the revelations that each layer of Vishakha experience brings. This makes them very wise in worldly and spiritual matters.

Venus experiences a similar effect as it understands how to guide humanity but also develops further wisdom that takes them to a more spiritual path.

Saturn is exalted in Vishakha but it also finds its greatest weakness. It promotes the ascetic side of Vishakha only after committing the maximum excesses. Saturn is usually about teaching lessons. Those who have Saturn placed here will find themselves attracted to the excessive nature of Vishakha, only to develop the more ascetic and disciplined life.

Rahu has to be careful that it does not become too overtly sexual. Rahu always promotes dissatisfaction and a nakshatra that creates this feeling can be damaging to happiness. It is essential to curb those feelings and develop philosophically and guide the Rahu desires to discover the inner world, the soul. Scorpio Vishakha can encourage Rahu's weaknesses. Ketu can bring out past life issues with sexuality and the need to achieve impossible targets. Ketu cannot find heaven in this life but it has to let go of the negative feelings and work on dealing with its excessive sexual desires. Scorpio Vishakha helps Ketu find its higher nature.

Padas in Vishakha: Aries, Taurus, Gemini, Cancer

The sixth cycle of soul development begins. There are new impulses, further developments within the concept of relationships, and developments in how we view life and embrace the changes needed to control the poisons that our karma or lifestyles have created for us. The Sun and Moon debilitation padas in Vishakha are pushkara, showing the potential for the luminaries to sort out problems that would usually weaken the others.

20°00' to 23°20' Libra – Aries pada

The 1st pada of Vishakha and 7th navamsha of Libra is Aries; the pada is opposite to the rashi and therefore life can completely transform. Aries is a new way of life, the shift of balance. The soul is looking to a new world so excess can be the norm as it initially doesn't know how to use this new energy properly. Being placed in its exalted pada energises the debilitated Sun, but Saturn loses power by being debilitated.

The Sun finds its strength at last. The exalted pada guides the Sun back to its confidence, to self-reliance and absolute power. There is less involvement in relationships.

20° Libra is the exaltation degree of Saturn and again like its debilitation degree (see Bharani), the extreme exaltation of Saturn has a karmic weakness within it. Saturn weak or strong always brings some major lessons. Saturn will encourage the excess of Vishakha; there can be an overtly sexual agenda, the wrong type of relationships that finally teach a lesson.

23°20' to 26°40' Libra – Taurus pada

The 2nd pada of Vishakha and 8th navamsha of Libra is Taurus. This is an unusual navamsha, it is pushkara and Ashtamamsha. There is a major transformation taking place here although it may not always appear so from the outside. This transformation is auspicious in nature as the soul establishes ground from which it will launch its start back to purity. The ideas or creativity that were sown in Swati and Pisces pada are now bearing fruit. These people are learning to deal with the poisons of their lifestyle after unexpected events have forced them into recognition. They are all fulfilling a major responsibility to their soul and whether the planets are strong or weak, this experience changes them and makes them aware of their burgeoning spirituality. The need to transform is essential but if they remain struck in worldly ways, it can continue to unsettle. The Moon and Rahu are exalted and Ketu is debilitated.

Even the Moon in its exalted pada can experience difficulties. The Moon can feel unsettled but if it allows the change, it will develop a profound nature.

Rahu will aim for balance and it is through transformation that it nurtures the soul. There can be a fear that the soul will not find its voice, but if Rahu is placed here, you should have no doubts. Ketu can create bonds with people and to sex that is difficult to let go. This could be a past life problem. There are unfinished matters that can hinder the path of spiritual growth.

26°40' to 30°00' Libra – Gemini pada
The 3rd pada of Vishakha and 9th navamsha of Libra is Gemini. Mercury is well placed here. This is where the dual deities of Vishakha become prominent. The pull between the passions of Indra and Agni against their more divine natures can trouble the planets. The sanskrit for Gemini is Mithuna, which is linked to coupling or the sexual act, so sexuality can play an important part. The need to find answers through a partner, or the other half of the soul, can become paramount. No planet is exalted or debilitated in this pada.

00°00' to 03°20' Scorpio – Cancer pada
The 4th pada and 1st pada of Scorpio is Cancer. Being a pushkara pada, it helps all planets to improve and heal their problems. The divine bliss that this pada promises needs recognition that the world may be less than perfect, and it is up to the individual to make it better. Mars is debilitated and Jupiter is exalted.

The Moon is in its own pada but this is also its exact debilitation degree (3° Scorpio). Why does the Moon become debilitated in its own pada? Both are water signs and the emotions overwhelm the Moon; these people cannot look beyond their own emotional needs. There can be an overwhelming need to satisfy every emotion. As the water gets more and more fixed, it can lose its ability to detoxify so the poisonous elements start multiplying like in a pond of still waters. If the emotions are not allowed to flow, they become putrid and can take on the worst habits of Scorpio and Vishakha. This is also an addictive position for the Moon, so avoid alcohol and drugs. Do not think you can indulge and remain unaffected.

Mars becomes debilitated, showing his weakness. Although strong by rashi, this Mars indicates that it has not yet found the strength to deal with its weakness. These people will find that their weaknesses keep them emotionally involved and sexually active, sometimes in the wrong ways.

Jupiter becomes exalted here and he has the wisdom to navigate the dark waters of Scorpio. He gives insight on how to use these poisons, to heal and make something wonderful from it.

17. Anuradha

3°20 to 16°40 Scorpio
Padas: Leo, Virgo, Libra, Scorpio

Meaning

Anuradha means a 'small flash of lightning' or 'a tiny spark'. Here it suggests that it takes only a small flash of intuition or a tiny spark of consciousness to make us aware of our connection with the divine. *Anu* also means small and *Radha* is the name of the beloved of Lord Krishna. Radha was a separate entity to Krishna, but desired to merge with him. Again the meaning of Anuradha is connecting the individual to the universal. The soul immersed in the world of materialism forgets its divine heritage. Anuradha unveils

Anuradha
Ruled by Saturn
Devata: Mitra, the God of Light
Symbol: The Lotus
Yoni: Deer
Motivation: Dharma
Guna Triplicity: Tamas, Sattva and Tamas
Ayurvedic Dosha: Pitta
Body Part: Stomach
Gana: Divine
Caste: Shudra
Quality: Soft
Shakti: Abundance
Colour: Red Brown
Best Direction: South
Special Sounds: Na, Nee, Nu, Nay
Principal Stars: Three stars at the Head of Scorpionis.
Other Names of Anuradha: Mitra

the hidden purity and opens our mind to the kundalini – the mysterious power within us, which we need to activate to go towards a path of higher consciousness. The knowledge of our secret faculties has to be handled carefully as it can create turmoil within our normal life.

Devata – Mitra

Mitra, the ruling deity of Anuradha is a personification of the Sun. Mitra is one of the sons of Aditi, the universal mother. Mitra rules daylight. 'Mitra' means friends, which unite opposites. It unveils the experiences of the night, the time spent by an individual in harnessing his power. In Anuradha, it exposes the latent potential that has become hidden by a life engulfed in materialism. Mitra helps us to get rid of our darkness by giving us light.

Mitra refers to the Sage Vishwamitra who had a difficult path to enlightenment. He went from being a king to a rishi. There were many occasions that he fell from his path of purity. He was enticed by Apsara Menaka on the orders of Indra and Vishwamitra lost years of his tapasya (austerities and spiritual focus). *Apsara* means celestial nymphs who live in the kingdom of Indra. Many times his weaknesses were tested, yet each time he came back to his path of righteousness and finally the Sage Vashishta made him a Maharishi. Sage Vashishta touched Vishwamitra's third eye and he heard the rhythm of the world in seven differing sounds of the most sacred Gayatri Mantra.

Anuradha people can also be tested by their weaknesses but they can come back again and again to the spiritual path. Their soul can be indomitable and their resolve strong.

Planetary Ruler – Saturn
Saturn, the great teacher of cosmic truths, rules Anuradha. His influence is tough to deal with as he teaches responsibility, restriction, and the ability to endure life in the hope of finding the light that will guide to self-realisation Anuradha people learn about restrictions early on. Saturn gives the ability to endure what life has to offer in the hope of finding the elusive truth that will transform and bring happiness beyond imagination. They have tremendous capacity to face pain and can stay in an unhappy situation far longer than seems possible.

Vrishchika Rashi
Anuradha is a beautiful nakshatra living within the dark complexity of Scorpio, showing that light can shine anywhere. People can aspire to their divinity in whatever situation they are in. They should never lose hope or consider their life hopeless; all it takes is a little spark that ignites the fire of spirituality and personal progress towards the soul in all of us.

Symbol – Lotus
The symbol of Anuradha is the Lotus, which flourishes in stagnant waters. The Lotus flower seeds in the mud and flowers towards the solar energy. Once it has flowered, it withers away and goes back to the mud, where it will root again to repeat the whole process. The lotus is said to flower so that it can be laid at the feet of the gods, just as the soul is born to experience life and death so that it can break away from it to find enlightenment.

The Lotus flowers under the most difficult conditions and similarly the beauty of Anuradha can emerge wherever they are – they do not need to be in a special place or condition in order to prosper.

Puranic Myth – Love of Radha

Radha's unconditional love for Krishna and their relationship is often interpreted as the quest for union with the divine. This kind of love is of the highest form of devotion. Radha, daughter of Vrishabhanu, was the devotee of Krishna. Since childhood they were close to each other but the world pulled them apart. She loved him unconditionally and so great was Radha's love for Krishna that even today her name is uttered whenever Krishna is referred to, and Krishna worship is thought to be incomplete without the deification of Radha.

Anuradha is about getting in touch with the divine, and human love can be mistaken for the divine. Anuradha people have great capacity to love but if they fall in love with an inappropriate person they will still keep loving them. They must learn to discriminate.

Anuradha Aim for Dharma

Dharma motivates Anuradha. They recognise their duty to the divine and to the world. Anuradha people will be equally concerned about doing their dharma or right action in the world they live in and expressing their dharmic tendencies in search for the higher truths. This can make them self-righteous at times, as if they are the only ones who have uncovered the new realities. Anuradha's spiritual life path is being on earth while aspiring towards the divine. Here they must relate to the tree that has its roots firmly in the ground, but its branches spread towards the sky.

Sacred Animal – The Deer and Shiva

Anuradha's animal is the deer. The deer is the ride of the Moon but he is often pictured with Lord Shiva as he is the master of the Moon (mind). The deer usually represents the Moon or the Mind as it is swift, fast and always on the run just like the mind. Shiva had the ability to control the wayward mind through his yogic ability and he would sit on the skin of a spotted deer. The important factor was that the deer died a natural death. If you sit on a deer skin which has been killed, it will further disturb the mind as you take on its negative energies.

The deer plays an important part in two epics: Ramayana and Mahabharata. In Ramayana, Sita asks Rama to get the golden deer, which turns out to be a demon in disguise. Sita's desire for the golden deer leads her to be abducted by Ravana. In Mahabharata, the King Pandu kills a stag who was copulating with a deer and he gets cursed that next time he makes love, he will die. This killing started the whole series of events that lead to the Mahabharata.

Anuradha people can chase illusions like the deer of Ramayana. Their minds can be unsettled but the blessings of Shiva can lead them to yoga which helps them to calm the mind and find mental stability.

Ayurvedic Dosha is Pitta

Anuradha people are charitable, aesthetic, learned and bright. They are also hotheaded and stimulating and can be short tempered. They are energetic, forceful and charismatic. They are leaders and innovators, being ambitious and willing to work hard to achieve. Their pitta energy usually makes it hard for them to delegate so they take on far too much responsibility.

Lagna and Planets

Planets can feel bound by their material role and it is essential that they learn to be philosophical about that otherwise they will feel they are never getting what they want regardless of their achievements.

Lagna in Anuradha aims for idealism yet the life never matches that idealism. It is always important to accept the constraints of life while retaining the aspirations. These people can be driven, yet a sense of frustration at not getting there dogs them. They should adjust to the life they are living or they can feel bitter and frustrated, always living in the future when the circumstances will be better. If they can appreciate that life is good, however imperfect it is, it rewards. The quality of the present improves and with that the prospect of the future. The relationships between Saturn and Mars in the birth chart will tell the complete story.

The Sun can be strong and weak depending on the pada, but as the nakshatra reveals the source and is linked to Mitra, the Sun makes the connection back to its spiritual path. Anuradha people are never totally comfortable in their material life but it is important for them to remember they still have to live it.

The Moon in Anuradha is always auspicious as it is coming out of its debilitation point. The immense churning in Vishakha makes room for a greater vision and peacefulness. The Anuradha Moon must keep aspiring for the best. The Moon can feel blocked until it learns to restrain its natural desires. Its greatest weakness is idealism and unrealistic expectations of love and relationships, the ability to love for the sake of love can bring disappointments. The first dasha is ruled by Saturn, which makes for a disciplined life as a child and the child tends to live a more adult life. Saturn at the beginning of life gives Anuradha Moon the ability to bear pain, and these people tend to take on burdens from a young age. The Saturn dasha can run up to nineteen years, affecting childhood and the teens.

Mars wants to act but Saturn keeps restricting it. This causes a great deal of friction until these contrary energies are harnessed and used properly. Mars has to learn to trust its instinct but not lose its logic. At times it does extremely well but at others it struggles. Jealousy and mental obsessions can spoil but inspiration towards self improvement can help these people get out of their negativity.

Jupiter can guide towards the higher self and is therefore in a strong position. Saturn and Jupiter restore the balance in life. Jupiter will inspire and Saturn as the nakshatra lord will promote realism. Usually the idealism triumphs and this Jupiter becomes very potent as a guiding light. I have noticed Jupiter in Anuradha can be too idealistic and can sometimes neglect the present in lieu of future expectations.

Venus will bring out the love and the relationship aspect. People with Venus in Anuradha have unrealistic expectations about love and relationships; whether they achieve it or not depends on the pada it is placed in. As Venus becomes debilitated by pada in Anuradha, this nakshatra shows ups its weakness of loving in an unwise way.

Saturn is stronger in its own nakshatra, so it will force Anuradha to remain realistic. The work ethic dominates; this can be frustrating for Saturn as the aspiration for the future means that not much attention is being placed on the present. But this can become a fertile ground for Saturn to teach lessons. These can be painful, but that is the role of Saturn, to demand payment for karmic debts to the material world.

Rahu is debilitated in Scorpio but Anuradha controls the more negative aspects. It focuses on paying the karmic debts, which usually remains a struggle. There can be obsessions regarding relationships and unwise patterns of complex love entanglements. The sense that the future is better than the present can create problems with feeling happy now. Ketu shows that many karmic debts were paid, the divine spark lit and now is the time to truly inspire for self-realisation. This is an excellent position for Ketu – divine, inspired and in its element.

Padas in Anuradha: Leo, Virgo, Libra, Scorpio
The amsha padas of Anuradha show that the strong involvement of material issues still dominate while the inner aspect of the personality is moving towards spiritual change. Scorpio brings the realisation of the spiritual path while established in the material realm, Anuradha wants divinity but cannot always get it. The padas are showing the dominance of the tamasic way of life, where the soul is still controlled by the material self. This is the reason that Anuradha can be so frustrating and the planets struggle between extremes of spiritualism and materialism. They need to find the goal but also accept the reality of their present situation. One pada is pushkara and one pada is vargottama. The Sun, Moon, Venus and Rahu have debilitated pada and Mercury, Saturn and Ketu have exalted pada.

03°20' to 06°40' Scorpio – Leo pada
The 1st pada of Anuradha and 2nd navamsha of Scorpio is Leo, which gives power to the Sun. No planets are debilitated or exalted. Usually most planets do well here. Saturn may struggle.

06°40' to 10°00' Scorpio – Virgo pada
The 2nd pada of Anuradha and 3rd navamsha of Scorpio is Virgo. It also is a pushkara navamsha, indicating that even the weakest of planets have strength and are part of an important unfolding of consciousness. Mercury is exalted and Venus debilitated in this pada.

Mercury goes from enemy sign to exaltation improving its quality. This is the position where the mind has clarity of thought and these people can analyse their position and add instinct to their rational thinking. They will be able to deal with jealousy and sexual obsessions as they have a special talent in analysing them for others or writing about them. Pushkara gives a healing quality.

Venus goes from enemy sign to debilitation, an ineffective position. All Anuradha's hopes and aspirations of finding the light, the divine relationships, the one-sided love can become spoilt. Scorpio adds jealousy, possessiveness and the craving for sexual happiness. There is the need for analysis, the search for perfection that doesn't really exist, the lack of happiness from relationships. The pushkara nature allows these issues to get resolved.

10°00' to 13°20' Scorpio – Libra pada

The 3rd pada of Anuradha and 4th navamsha of Scorpio is Libra, the debilitation pada for the Sun. Saturn goes from being aggravated in Scorpio to its exaltation, a quantum improvement. Libra pada is the final balancing act as the soul prepares to detach from its materialistic role.

The Sun can be very relationship and sexually orientated before it finally breaks away from the material role. Involvement in relationships can stop the spiritual progress. In this debilitation there is no pushkara for the Sun so it indicates some genuine weaknesses.

Saturn in its exaltation pada finds the strength in the turbulent waters of Scorpio. This is where he also detaches from the more materialistic role. There can be pain but also awareness of the rightness of the experience. Control over life is the great gift, where regardless of the cost, the individual works for a higher aim.

13°20' to 16°40' Scorpio – Scorpio pada

The 4th pada of Anuradha and 5th navamsha of Scorpio is the vargottama Scorpio. All the planets become empowered. In my view they cannot lose the intensity of Scorpio. The push and pull of Scorpio will also be at its strongest and the soul is tugged powerfully in both directions. There is no balance but the vargottama makes them realise their strength and the rightness of both sides of their needs. Moon and Rahu are debilitated and Ketu is exalted.

The Moon is debilitated in vargottama, as this is one of the most intense positions for it. The double influence of Scorpio can empower the Moon but these people have to be careful not to use these powers unethically. The mind can be churned up and possessiveness, sexual intensity, and the inability to move emotionally can create issues that are hard to resolve.

Rahu is vargottama and debilitated. This is the most complex position for Rahu to be placed in as there is lack of understanding of the soul direction and possibility of it being guided in all the wrong ways. Do not dig a hole too deep from where it is impossible to climb out. Ketu is in a perfect position where it is aware of the need to transform for moksha. It is able to use past knowledge positively.

18. Jyeshta

16°40' to 30°00' Scorpio
Padas: Sagittarius, Capricorn, Aquarius, Pisces

Meaning

Jyeshta means elder sister, and the middle finger or the holy river Ganges. It has esteem attached to it. In India, the elder sister is looked upon with great respect as she is like one's mother. The river Ganges is said to wash away all our negative karma. The middle finger is the finger of destiny. It is used in yoga during pranayama to control the flow of breath. Pranayama is performed so that we are able to activate the kundalini and the seven chakras. At Jyeshta, the guidance is given to begin activating the kundalini.

Jyeshta
Ruled by Mercury
Devata: Indra, the God of Gods
Symbol: An Earring
Yoni: Male Deer
Motivation: Artha
Guna Triplicity: Tamas, Sattva and Sattva
Ayurvedic Dosha: Vata
Body Part: Right Side
Gana: Demon
Caste: Farmer
Quality: Sharp
Shakti: Heroic
Colour: Cream
Best Direction: West
Special Sounds: No, Ya, and Ye, Yo
The Principal Star: Antares
Other names for Jyeshta: Indra, Shakra, Vasava, Akhandal, Purandhara

Jyeshta Devi is a goddess whose power has been dimmed in Kali Yuga. Worshipping her can take away misfortune. She is the elder sister of Goddess Laxmi who sacrificed herself for the sake of her family, but her sacrifice is not recognised. Her true energy is obscured and people started to shun her instead of worshipping her, thereby increasing their misfortune. Jyeshta Devi needs to be understood and her blessing sought.

Jyeshta has a darker meaning; she is considered the goddess of bad luck, Alaxmi. It does not mean that those born in Jyeshta are unlucky but they must not be the creators of their own misfortune. It indicates their ability to overcome their bad fortune, fight their inner demons.

The Key of Jyeshta

Here the soul tries to break away from its materialistic course of life and moves towards the spiritual journey. The end of Jyeshta is the end of

Scorpio – the gandanta. It is the place of immense transformation where the soul tries to unknot its spiritual blocks. It is never an easy journey.

Devata – Indra

Indra, the ruling deity, is considered the King of the Gods. Indra controls our senses or 'indirayas'. Indra has the power to control our senses. This power he achieved after hard toils, penance and difficult lessons. He can enjoy the sensuality and pleasures of life, as he is privy to the secret of how to master them.

Jyeshta people can learn to control their senses with the practice of yoga. Yoga is a system of unfolding of consciousness that unites the spiritual with the tangible. Indra is considered one of the gods of yoga as well.

Planetary Ruler – Mercury

The ruler of Jyeshta is Mercury, who is the celestial link between materialism and spiritualism. At Jyeshta the change starts happening towards spiritualism. If the soul is not ready, it struggles to give up its material desires and attachments and this creates unhappiness. Jyeshta represents the struggle of the mind to adapt to the new reality of life and these people can find that their intellect can limit their perception when they want to widen the scope of their understanding of the occult and the mysteries of the world. They question everything and this can create blocks.

Mercury's curiosity encourages people with planets in Jyeshta to look beyond man-made barriers and intellectually accept the spiritual path.

Vrishchika Rashi

Scorpio always shows a soul split into two; the material desires run rampant and the spiritual desires are strong as well. Desires can rule at the stage of Jyeshta, where they enjoy the sensuality and pleasures of life to the full. At Jyeshta, these become even more polarised as it is the last nakshatra of materialistic tendencies, so they have the greatest desires but also the inner need for change. This deep need for change makes them want to master their desires and their hidden demons. They instinctively know that they will not need or desire in the same way so this gives them a voracious appetite for life, this becomes their weakness. But sometimes taking their weakness to the extreme leads to the change too.

Symbol – An Earring and Chattri
The Jyeshta earring is in the form of a ring and a coil, similar to how the kundalini is pictured. The sages would wear it in their ears as they were master of their kundalini. The earring is an occult status symbol, given to the divine kings who had conquered their lower nature and gained occult powers and mastered their kundalini. Once they had completed their discipline properly, they had powers with which they could rule the world, communicate with the spirits and have the knowledge of past and future lives. Jyeshta can be masters of their lower nature too and like the war of Indra with the demon Vritra they can be victorious if they set their mind to it.

Chattri is like a parasol that used to protect the gods. This shows the ability for Jyeshta to be important and respected.

Jyeshta people command respect – both their symbols are only given to people with status which has been earned.

Puranic Myth – The Curse of Indra
Indra was cursed by the Guru Gautama for having an affair with his wife Ahilya, and his body pasted with 1000 vaginas. Indra, the King of Gods overstepped his mark and therefore had to do tapas (penance) for 1000 years before this curse could be modified into a thousand eyes. Indra did this tapasya at Suchindram Temple, in Tamil Nadu. The belief is that he still comes there every night to do Ardhajama puja. Ardhajama is the night-time prayer ceremony.

Jyeshta people feel very powerful; they think they can control themselves and that different rules apply to them. This arrogance makes them generate their own bad luck, their own demons and it can create baggage throughout their life until they make amends and turn towards a more spiritual journey. Sexual issues can be one of the challenges.

Jyeshta aim for Artha
Artha or practical expression of life motivates Jyeshta people who are still involved in making a success on the material plain. Financial success is important as that enables them to pursue their spiritual interests. They

like a luxurious life, therefore they work hard and have practical goals to achieve it.

Jyeshta's life path is connected to yoga and pranayama. Once they bring this discipline into their life, they are able to realise their immense potential. They have to learn about nature's finer forces.

Sacred Animal – The Deer of Soma

The deer is connected to Soma and he is also the vahana (transport) of Soma, the Moon. This reflects the activity of uncertainty of mind. Soma riding the deer means that a good Moon can control it but the Moon in Jyeshta is always complex and represents the unpredictability of the deer.

Deer often change their habitat due to fires, earthquakes etc. but they are extremely adaptable to new environments. Jyeshta people will also emerge after major disasters or obstacles and re-establish their roots with ease.

An important feature of the deer's characteristics is the growing and shedding of antlers and then re-growing them again. This shows the continuity of nature and in a way it represents the shedding of old karmic patterns and creating them in a similar, yet different forms. The deer as an animal of the gandanta point reinforces the concept of transformation that individuals have to go through where one persona is shed and a new one develops. The deer shed their antlers after their mating season, so individuals may decide to make major transformations after important relationships form.

Ayurvedic Dosha is Vata

Jyeshta reflects the natural qualities of vata. They are active and always on the go. These people tend to live on their nervous energies. They can experience allergies and breathing problems. Jyeshta people need lots of comforting food and surroundings. They will appear to be calm and self-assured but within they are a mass of nerves. They can get stressed easily.

Lagna and Planets

Planets in Jyeshta are in transition. Their feet are firmly rooted in the worldly desires so the transition is not always easy to accept. Planets placed at the end of Jyeshta especially, face major transformation in life due to circumstances beyond their control. The end of Jyeshta is the most important gandanta.

People with a lagna in Jyeshta want everything. They want to be spiritual but usually their material desires dominate and this does not allow them to benefit from their spiritual work. Unless they control their desires, they will remain dissatisfied. The position of Mars, Ketu and Mercury should give indication how they learn the lessons of Jyeshta.

The Sun is strong and will try to burn away the hold of desires. They will follow an essentially sensuous path to start with but then they will learn about themselves and develop spiritually.

People with the Moon placed here are usually troubled, unsure about what to do, and this troubled mind can get them involved in inappropriate sexual relationships. But this is a Moon learning about spirituality and more able to adapt to the greater spiritual force. It is important that they do not go further than they are mentally able to deal with, especially with occult practices. The ruler of Jyeshta is Mercury and Jyeshta represents the struggle of the mind to adapt to the new reality of life. The first dasha of Mercury in early childhood may not show the angst of Jyeshta but there can be issues connected to the mother or the relationship with the mother that influences the whole life. The end of Mercury dasha always carries negativity or karmic poisons within and to face these issues in childhood is usually difficult. The Moon placed in the last degrees of Jyeshta, in gandanta, is in a very difficult position. Here the storms of transformation are intense and life will transform at a very young age as the dasha changes from Mercury to Ketu almost immediately after birth.

Mars is strong and these individuals will find the ability to be greatly spiritual. People can always accuse them of being sexual beings, but their inner being is satisfied with spirituality, asceticism and deep spiritual work. They will also aspire towards awakening their kundalini.

Mercury in its own nakshatra will try to create boundaries for the intellect, so these people want to remain in the sensuous, material world. This will bring mental agitation as if this world is no longer enough. The art of Jyeshta is to look beyond, the more these people attach to materialism, the greater their inner turmoil and lack of clarity.

Jupiter will bring spiritual wisdom and the ability to move in this transition; the guidance to make the right decisions, to honour the material life, while exploring the occult, the spiritual life direction and aspiring towards the higher modes.

Venus usually shows its sexual nature most in Jyeshta except the last pada. It wants to explore sexuality and can think that is the only answer to life. Unwise relationships can lead to being mired in negativity and unhappy situations.

Saturn will create attachments to material things in life and stop the flow towards the spiritual at first. It can give immense material success but create dissatisfactions. Learning to say no, and controlling the desires will bring so much positive energy and allow happiness to flow. But most people with Saturn in Jyeshta do not trust this choice and therefore remain architects of their own unhappiness and distress.

Rahu is very agitated and usually wants to explore sexuality, the occult and mind-enhancing drugs or substances. It can get addicted to power control. But it is all for the wrong reasons. This Rahu needs control as it is debilitated and naturally takes the wrong options. Ketu is in bliss. It will enjoy the turmoil and remain calm as this is about changing and letting go of the past. The transformation leads to deep understanding of the soul path. It will develop the ascetic skill of giving up desires rather than creating more.

Padas in Jyeshta: Sagittarius, Capricorn, Aquarius, Pisces

Jyeshta is the end of the 6th cycle of personal development. There is no vargottama, pushkara or ashtamamsha. The end of Jyeshta is gandanta.
 It is the wrapping up of one way of being. The Scorpio ending is the most difficult gandanta as it is about giving up your possessions, desires and wants. The mind plays tricks on the individual, the more there is the need to give up, the mind tells us to acquire. Herein lies the pain of Jyeshta, the more people try to cling and to own, the greater the struggle. It does not mean that Jyeshta should not enjoy life but the real meaning is that they must recognise that this is not the real thing.

A Jyeshta Lagna client of mine said 'it is not what I need but what I want that motivates me'. This 'want' keeps her eternally dissatisfied. Jyeshta should aspire to only fulfil their needs and enjoy what life has to offer, not pile on more and more desires.

16°40' to 20°00' Scorpio – Sagittarius pada

The 1st pada of Jyeshta and 6th navamsha of Scorpio is Sagittarius, which is good for Jupiter and Mars. No planet is exalted or debilitated. This aids search for the divine within.

20°00' to 23°20' Scorpio – Capricorn pada

The 2nd pada of Jyeshta and 7th navamsha of Scorpio is Capricorn, excellent for Mars as it is exalted but weak for Jupiter in a debilitated pada.

Mars is exalted by pada. The awareness of the tough path ahead brings the best out of these people. They are disciplined, ascetic and will usually take a solo path. They have to be careful that they do not use sexuality to enhance their own strength through negative tantric practices.

Jupiter is debilitated and wisdom is not always at its best here. People can be moving towards spirituality but there is danger of using their knowledge in unethical ways. They are endowed with practical wisdom. Instead of fighting against this, they should remember to take the practical responsibilities with a smile. There is no need to show others their spirituality. Women can make unwise choices regarding relationships or meet partners who appear spiritual but turn out not to be so. They can be let down by the men in their lives.

23°20' to 26°40' Scorpio – Aquarius pada

The 3rd pada of Jyeshta and 8th navamsha of Scorpio is Aquarius. Saturn gains strength but Rahu also feels more comfortable here. The process of separating from the material world is now firmly in place, but the soul struggles to make this change. Many issues become obvious and the soul has to deal with them. This leads to the sudden breaking of the ego and the revelation of the inner person. But if the person becomes totally fixed about who they are and what they want from life, they can struggle as life chokes them and their true soul remains shrouded. The windy quality of Aquarius can take away old structures too.

26°40' to 30°00' Scorpio – Pisces pada and Gandanta

The 4th pada of Jyeshta and 9th navamsha of Scorpio is Pisces. This is the most karmic pada of all. It is the gandanta pada where sign, pada and nakshatra ends. The last 48' of this pada represents the gandanta position and only planets placed in those degrees will face the maximum strain. The planets placed here whether strong or weak are linked to karmic development and spiritual awakening. Pay special attention to the karaka of the planets as they can have the ability to teach a karmic lesson. Venus is exalted, Mercury debilitated and Jupiter is in its own sign. The knowledge and wisdom of Jupiter and Venus triumph while the analytical prowess of Mercury has no place in this pada.

Mercury is debilitated. People can make bad decisions in a practical sense whereas their mind is very spiritually aware. They have to be careful about allowing others to influence them in a wrong way.

Venus is exalted, is strong in sowing the seeds of spirituality and will bring luck and good fortune. This is a placement of karmic endings and in this life time the unsettled nature and lack of support creates insecurity.

Abhukta Mula – Jyeshta and Mula Gandanta
29°12' to 30°00' Scorpio and 00°00' to 00°48' Sagittarius

The gandanta at the end of Scorpio and the beginning of Sagittarius is known as Abhukta Mula. *Abhukta* means uneaten, not enjoyed, unused, unexpended. *Mula* means the root. Abhukta Mula has been wrongly given as bad luck. This indicates a soul who is unable to enjoy the blessings of life due to karmic circumstances. It can also indicate the inability to gain stability or get to the roots of our existence.

Ganda means knot and *anta* is ending. These are knots that block spiritual growth by giving some difficult issues that the soul tries to unravel. Abhukta Mula is the most difficult gandanta as it moves the inner soul towards its final direction of merging with the universal consciousness. This is the stage where the material ties are being shattered and the soul realises its true spiritual direction. This is where the maximum churning of the inner emotions takes place. Even when the soul recognises its path towards its true nature, it fights against it. It creates many psychological or physical blocks that need to be tackled with great maturity.

At the Scorpio/Jyeshta stage, there is immense churning of the inner emotions; this is where material sheaths break up and lead to inner change. If there is a resistance to a change it becomes very difficult for the person.

At the Mula/Sagittarius stage, the soul recognises it has to change and in many ways it already has. But there remain ties to its past life and its earthly needs, which Mula meaning 'root' suggests. These roots are buried in the ground or in deep material realms and it needs to break the outer crust of earth to reach towards its higher potential.

All planets in gandanta points face difficulties in expressing themselves as they are at the point of two opposing energies. If planets are placed there it gives much instability and lack of support during life, even when the key supporting people (father, mother) are living and present. The Sun placed in the gandanta point forces the soul to change its direction. But the main connection is with the Moon and the Ascendant. The first dasha will be difficult to deal with if the Moon is in gandanta. There is a quick change of dasha from Mercury to Ketu or an individual born at the start of Ketu dasha.

19. Mula

00°00' to 13°20' Sagittarius
Padas: Aries, Taurus, Gemini, Cancer

Meaning

Mula is the start of the final part of the soul's mission towards finding moksha or self-realisation. *Mula* means root and it is connected to the *Muladhara Chakra* (the repository of latent spiritual energy). Mula suggests that we are the root of all our problems as well as the blessings of all our good fortunes. We are rooted in the physical, the objective and the material while our aspirations may be for the subtle and psychic.

The dissatisfaction with life will lessen if we realize that a tree needs strong roots to grow upwards. A soul cannot let go of their material responsibilities in their search for spiritual ones.

Mula
Ruled by Ketu
Devata: Niritti
Symbol: The Tail of a Lion or an Elephant's Goad.
Yoni: Male Dog
Motivation: Kama
Guna Triplicity: Sattva, Rajas and Rajas
Ayurvedic Dosha: Vata
Body Part: Left Side
Gana: Demon
Caste: Butcher
Quality: Sharp
Colours: Mustard
Best Direction: North
Special Sounds: Yay, Yo, Ba, Be
The Principal Stars: Vicrtau or Two Releasers
Other Names for Mula: Nirriti, Rakshasha, Asarpa

Mula people need to be practical and build strong foundations in their lives before they can move towards their higher aspirations. Mula is an intense experience and at least once in their lifetime they will cut away from their roots and try to create new ones. There is a self-destructive tendency in Mula that needs to be controlled.

Devata – Niritti

The deity that rules Mula is Niritti, the goddess of death and destruction. This personifies the destruction of the material sheaths and the foundation on which the spiritual enfoldment can be undertaken. The pain experienced by the influence of Mula changes the personality. The destructive nature of Niritti means that Mula people can be self-destructive and spoil things for themselves. They need to remember the importance of roots, tradition and security. Their lives need pruning so that the spiritual tree is ready for new growth, but if they cut down the tree completely their spirituality may die and take a long time to recover. The vedic thinking is that we must burn the root of karma in order to find self-realisation, but only a few are ready to take this extreme step. Most need to keep their roots and progress from there.

Niritti is connected to Goddess Kali. The name Kali comes from Kāla which means black, time, death, and Shiva. Kali is represented as dark and violent, but she is worshipped as a mother goddess. Kali is the main tantric goddess of the highest reality; she is the love that exists at the heart of life, which is the immortal soul that endures through both life and death. Kali grants us eternal life, yet the eternal life has a price. Only that which is immortal can be immortal, as nothing can change its own nature. The mortal and the transient must pass away. To gain the eternity that is Kali, our mortal nature must be sacrificed. Hence Kali appears frightening and destructive to the ordinary vision.

Mula demands that we sacrifice our human desires to move on the path of divine. This experience can be fearsome for those who are not ready for this sacrifice, but enlightening for those who are.

Planetary ruler – Ketu
Mula is the third nakshatra ruled by Ketu, which fulfills its role as a moksha planet by arousing the soul towards its ultimate destination. Ketu is the significator for *moksha* or self-realisation. According to Indian philosophy a soul is born to earth to enjoy life but not get attached to it. Its final aim is moksha, the final liberation from the cycles of life and death. It aspires to freedom, release and the break from the burden of responsibilities and is usually careless about practical responsibilities. Ketu can make you reject your roots, but how can the tree grow or prosper without its roots? Jupiter, the sign ruler, brings spiritual wisdom and Ketu is the past. If only we would reconcile with the past, that true wisdom can flourish. If we accept today, then we can be happy with tomorrow. Mula is never an easy message but Jupiter guides though knowledge, wisdom and following the right path, however difficult it is to help make this transition easy.

Dhanus Rashi

Mula is entirely in Dhanus, Sagittarius. Sagittarius is where man is striving to control the lower impulses so that the soul can move towards moksha. Mula moves toward the path of self-discovery and the conflict with the sexual and spiritual self emerges. Mula Sagittarius can become overtly sexual or totally spiritual, struggling to settle in one direction.

Symbol – Ankush

Ankush is the elephant's goad, which is used to guide the elephant in the correct direction. In people, this symbol represents the constant prodding or pain we have to suffer in search for the spiritual pathway. Ganesha carries an ankush in one of his hands. It symbolizes his ability to guide the elephant. As the elephant is such a large and unwieldy animal it needs a little prodding to go in the right direction. Similarly the Mula soul is large and stuck in its ways and the prodding helps us go on the right course.

Puranic Myth – Worship of the Ten Divine Mother Goddesses

Mula is connected to tantra and the worship of the divine mother. The Dasa Maha Vidya are ten aspects of the Divine Mother. *Dasa* is ten, *Maha* means great and *Vidya* is knowledge. The Ten Mahavidyas are wisdom goddesses, who represent various forms of feminine divinity and are known collectively as Shakti. The ten divine mothers are:

1. Kali the Eternal Night "Devourer of Time"
2. Tara the Goddess who gives self realisation
3. Lalita Tripurasundari – the Goddess who is Beautiful in the Three Worlds
4. Bhuvaneshvari the world mother
5. Chinnamasta who cuts off her Own Head and encourages us to be in pure awareness
6. Bhairavi the Fierce Goddess, who represents Divine anger and wrath
7. Dhumawati the widow Goddess who gives knowledge about life and death
8. Bagalamukhi the Goddess who possesses the truth
9. Matangi the Goddess of Tantric knowledge
10. Kamala is the divine Laxmi

The central aim of the ten goddesses is to stretch one's consciousness beyond the conventional, to break away from approved social norms, roles and expectations. By rejecting the conventional, the adept seeks to liberate their consciousness from the inherited or imposed restrictions.

People with planets in Mula, through understanding tantra and expanding their consciousness beyond the restrictions of life, can truly aspire towards the spiritual path.

Mula aim is for Kama

Kama is passion – sexual, religious, for life, for a cause. At Mula, the passion can be for sex and worldly cravings as the nakshatra is rooted into the lower desires. Once it learns to transcend the immediate needs, the passion can be for the divine. Worshipping the divine in its purest form can uplift the energy of Mula.

The important thing Mula people must remember is that they are the root so they should remain rooted in the physical, objective and the material. Their aspirations are for the subtle and psychic. Their dissatisfaction with life will lessen if they realise that a tree needs strong roots to grow upwards.

Sacred Animal – Dog of Bhairava

The dog is the transport for Bhairava – the fierce companion of Lord Shiva. Bhairava is worshipped along with Kali and he guards all the 52 Shakti temples. The dog in the wild is vicious, but as the transport of Bhairava it shows the ability to control its ferocious nature. A black dog is sometimes the transport for Saturn (read more on Bhairava in Ardra).

The dog in the wild is fierce and aggressive and very dangerous, but it can be trained and become a working dog or household pet. If Mula allow their natural instinct to take over, they can be wild and aggressive, but if they develop some self-discipline they can be hard working, charming, loyal, and loving.

Ayurvedic Dosha is Vata

Mula reflects the natural qualities of Vata. There is so much change in the psychology of Mula, these people tend to live on their nerves. They have a lot to experience and new realities to understand. Their minds are greatly activated so they find it difficult to relax.

Lagna and Planets

People with the lagna in Mula are spiritual warriors ready to move to their higher selves. They will be interested in gaining knowledge and passing it on. They should not reject tradition, the past, friends and relatives as they form an important part of the personal support system. Don't confuse support as possessiveness. The Mula journey has to be alone, but the approval and help of family and friends makes it easier. Mula people must always be conscious of their self-destructive tendencies. Jupiter and Ketu in the natal chart will show more.

The Sun is well placed in Mula although there may be some karmic issues with the father. The Sun-Mula person is committed to the higher path and during this lifetime they will develop into a better person. They should be careful not to be too dogmatic about ideas. There are natural guru qualities that people will admire and follow.

The Mula Moon needs to be practical and build strong foundations before it can move towards the spiritual journey, but it may feel lack of emotional support from the mother. If the Moon is in gandanta then the soul will struggle to find itself throughout the life. The first dasha is Ketu, which will be complex, unconventional and unusual. They can have a childhood where they were not appreciated, their talents not recognised, and there will be karmic events that shape the later life. There has to be a transforming experience early in life that colours their personality. The relationship with the mother is never easy. They can be either too attached to their mother or suffer from total rejection. Either way they lack the ability to connect emotionally with others. The turmoil between the personal development and strong attachments to the roots is constantly troubling them. Gandanta Mula Moon usually has the hardest struggles which as a child are difficult to comprehend.

Mars starts strong in Mula but it becomes unsure and indecisive. Only the first pada promotes Mars, then it becomes embroiled in self-doubt and will not have the courage to break away from the material realms. The desire to do so is strong but the will is not established as yet. These people need to avoid fighting with siblings and work at keeping their relationships strong.

Mercury can embrace the new spiritual instincts and totally reject the old. Therefore these people have many new ideas but are unwilling to take advice or trust. They will block out their past and move to a new tomorrow and this can create insecurity and uncertainty as they feel unsupported.

Jupiter is strong in Mula, but these people may not follow their own advice as they can have issues with their guru from a past life and that can create mistrust. The relationship with husband and children, specially boys, can be difficult as they may have a strong need to develop spiritually and in doing so avoid domestic responsibilities.

Venus is in transition, so there is a new dawn and new rules apply. As yet Venus does not know how to deal with them. People with Venus here will reject relationships but also get involved in relationships with their gurus or advisors, which will not be easy. There can be painful lessons regarding relationships that appear to destroy everything they stood for.

Saturn in Mula will not let people escape from the past; it will insist that they take responsibility for their karma and only then can they flourish. Saturn can make them face the negative aspects of their personality again and again before it finally decides that the karma is paid for. This is a wisdom learnt from personal action. These people will feel rootless and are perpetually learning how to reconcile the wisdom learnt in previous lives.

Rahu in Mula is ruled by Ketu, making this is power point of the nakshatra system. Mula is the root from which all spirituality flowers and Rahu has to learn to let go of the more basic human needs and start to reach upwards. If these people feel disillusioned, maybe they are looking for happiness in the wrong place. Rahu in Mula will only be truly fulfilled when it starts to look upward. The moment these people shift their attention, the Rahu in Mula will prosper and be very profound. Ketu can keep them mired in the roots of their lives, not allowing the individual to grow upward. Ketu in its own nakshatra suggests that the past life was spent aspiring towards spirituality which led to a change in the psychology of the individual. It now fulfils its role as the moksha planet by arousing the soul. This is a very important incarnation for the individual with heavy soul responsibility to use the past lessons to sprout shoots for a further spiritual growth.

Padas in Mula: Aries, Taurus, Gemini, Cancer
Mula starts from Aries, showing a beginning of the 7th level of spiritual development. The start of the spiritual inspiration means that they have to start from scratch. Unlike the padas in Aries Ashwini, here the soul is not just beginning a new cycle but a new way of being. They have to let go of the structures, the sureties of materialism and things that they had become fond of. Unless this situation is handled sensitively, it can be very destructive. The planets are now working on very high vibrations.

There is no pushkara and vargottama in Mula. Cancer pada is ashtamamsha.

Abhukta Mula: 00°00' to 00°48' Sagittarius
The first 48' of Mula is known as Abhukta Mula and shared with Jyeshta as a gandanta. *Abhukta* means uneaten; not enjoyed, unused, unexpended. *Mula* means the root. Abhukta Mula has been wrongly described as bad luck. This indicates a soul who is unable to enjoy the blessings of life due to karmic circumstances. It can also indicate the inability to have stability or enjoy the roots of their existence. (Read Jyeshta nakshatra too).

This is not as dire as it first appears. The social and emotional support from family and worldly issues may not be there, so the individual needs to find their own strength to develop their inner awareness, to be able to fight their spiritual battles alone. But as I had stated earlier, it is important that they should not press the self-destruct button and be their own worst enemy.

Abhukta Mula is very tough where the individual is living a life of turmoil and many situations come into life that they have no control over. As the soul detaches from the material path, the experience can be painful. All planets will suffer by being placed in these degrees.

00°00' to 03°20' Sagittarius – Aries pada
The 1st pada of Mula and 1st navamsha of Sagittarius is Aries. This is the most karmic pada as it is gandanta as well as Abhukta Mula (see above). The Sun is exalted, Saturn debilitated and Mars in its own sign. This is reminder from the lord of time, Saturn, that time does not matter to those who are on a spiritual path. They are able to override the restrictions of time and welcome the pain inflicted by Saturn as it allows

them to confront their karma and let it go. All planets experience karmic situations placed here.

The Sun is exalted and strong. The relationship with the father may be difficult, but the soul exposes its inner light and the need to follow dharma and the right way of living is intense.

Saturn is debilitated in Aries pada. All the fire energy can seriously disturb Saturn and its air energy. These people can be impulsive and in a rush. Often this position for Saturn shows people do not have much capacity for endurance – they can get sidetracked by everything that happens, so they need to develop some focus.

03°20' to 06°40' Sagittarius – Taurus pada

The 2nd pada of Mula and 2nd navamsha of Sagittarius is Taurus. This pada is less destructive where the planets care for their roots. That may not allow immediate spiritual gains but helps them to use their previous strengths to build for a proper and sustained spiritual growth. It should be a strong one for the Moon and Rahu who are exalted, and weak for Ketu due to its debilitation.

The Moon still suffers from being in Mula. The insecurity of this new spiritual terrain is tempered by the security of Taurus, but social structures are no longer necessary for further development and the Moon finds security in the spiritual endeavour.

Both Rahu and Ketu are in a complex nakshatra and this pada improves the situation for Rahu and makes it more difficult for Ketu as it is forced to consider the practicality of Taurus before it can try aspire for moksha. Rahu will find steadiness in the Taurus pada and start to make a positive contribution to the search for spirituality. Ketu will feel remorseful about not making faster progress spiritually. There can be some obstacles in the psyche that do not promote inner growth.

06°40' to 10°00' Sagittarius – Gemini pada

The 3rd pada of Mula and the 3rd navamsha of Sagittarius is Gemini. No planets are exalted or debilitated here. The planets think and can be doing many things, trying to analyse this role. Too much analysis can be counter-productive to development but it is an important part of the process.

10°00' to 13°20' Sagittarius – Cancer pada

The 4th pada of Mula and the 4th navamsha of Sagittarius is Cancer; it is the exaltation pada of Jupiter, debilitation of Mars but also the ashtamamsha. Cancer wants to create a home where the spirituality can live but the ashtamamsha suggests that this home is fragile at its best and subject to the vagaries of karma and past desires. Ashtamamsha in Mula indicates that from now on it is all change, life cannot remain the same. So people with planets placed here will undergo a profound transformation at some point in their lives. Those with the lagna will feel insecure. The Moon remains stressed even though it is in its own house. Sudden unexpected events will take place that separate the soul from its material entanglements.

Mars is debilitated. These people can opt for comforts and emotional support and forget about their wars and the need to fight for their causes. This is not a good position for Mars. Physical and spiritual weakness stops them from letting go of their emotional dependence. They need to break away from their entanglements. Like Arjuna, not wanting to fight his friends and enemies, here Mars may also not want to fight for the sake of dharma or may fight for the wrong causes.

Only Jupiter (wisdom, the right path of dharma) has the capacity to survive the negativity of the ashtamamsha and become strong. Jupiter is in own rashi sign and exalted by pada, so it will use the secret codes of Mula and develop itself and help others with this knowledge. There can be interest in tantra.

20. Purva Ashadha

13°20' to 26°40' Sagittarius
Padas: Leo, Virgo, Libra, Scorpio

Meaning

Purva means first and *Ashadha* means 'not subdued'. It indicates that which cannot be suppressed. The true nature of man comes out regardless of what opposition they have to face. It is linked to the following nakshatra, Uttara Ashadha, and together they represent the common principle of unfolding new talents. In Purva Ashadha, there are still some blockages to expressing their nature fully; Uttara Ashadha embraces the changes. The true personality and nature reveal themselves however hard they try to suppress them. These people will express karmic qualities and in the end reach their goals regardless of the hindrances they face.

Purva Ashadha
Ruled by Venus
Deity: Apas, the Water God
Symbol: The Elephant's Tusk
Yoni: Male Monkey
Motivation: Moksha
Guna Triplicity: Sattva, Rajas and Tamas
Ayurvedic Dosha: Pitta
Body Part: Back
Gana: Human
Caste: Brahmin
Quality: Fierce
Colours: Black
Best Direction: East
Special Sounds: Bu, Dha, Bha, Dhha
The Principal Stars: An- Naaim
Other Names for Purva Ashadha: Jala, Neer, Udaka, Ambu, Toya

Purva Ashadha indicates the discovery of new possibilities, externalisation of latent faculties and the uncovering of one's most valuable qualities. The meaning of life can be suddenly revealed, hidden knowledge uncovered, and intuitive faculties sharpened. Purva Ashadha develops knowledge and wisdom that can never be taken away; these people can be highly creative with many talents.

Devata – Apas

Apas, the god of water indicates the transforming nature of this nakshatra. Apas deals with water in a container, emotions that are restrained or suppressed and are unable to be free. Apas differs from Varuna, the god of the oceans, in that Apas, being water in a container, is spirituality caught in the world of materialism, while Varuna is free flowing. This water while being pure in essence can easily become contaminated. Planets placed can be easily influenced.

Apas is one of the Panchamahabhuta, the five great elements.[1] Apas is the water element and connects to Swadhisthana chakra.[2] Venus is the lord of apas. In Purva Ashadha the Devata and the ruling planet both deal with water and Swadhisthana. As the body is over 85% water, this is the most important element. Keeping it pure and flowing goes a long way to creating emotional harmony. Water is kept pure by right thoughts, actions and correct diet.

Water is always used in rituals to cleanse and rejuvenate the inner soul. Water represents purity and is sattvic. Ganga Jal, or the water of the river Ganges, is used at all auspicious occasions. At Purva Ashadha, the soul wants to cleanse its past sins to prepare itself for its final journey in understanding the purpose of life, in being fulfilled.

Planetary Ruler – Venus

Purva Ashadha's ruler is Venus. Purva Ashadha will lead us towards externalising our inner strengths and finding our own light. There will be difficulties on the way, but Venus eases the path and creates situations where wisdom flourishes.

Venus, the planetary ruler, bestows talent for the arts, crafts, music and drama. These people can be plagued by self-doubt as they aspire for perfection, the ultimate happiness and the greatest expression of their talents, but their life is as yet limited by their humanness.

Life on earth does not grant self-realization and at the stage of Purva Ashadha, the revelation of talents and latent spirituality takes place but these people must also be concerned about living the material path.

---

1. The Panchmahabhutas are: *akash* (ether), *vayu* (air), *agni* (fire), *apas* (water), prithvi (earth).
2. There are seven main chakras: 1. Sahasrara – crown chakra 2. Ajna- third eye 3. Vishuddhi – throat chakra 4. Anahata – heart chakra 5. Manipura – solar plexus chakra 6. Swadhisthana – sacral chakra 7. Muladhara – base chakra. The two higher chakras, Sahasrara and Ajna are beyond the control of the elements, while Vishuddhi, Anahata, Manipura, Swadhisthana and Muladhara come under the influence of the elements.

Dhanus Rashi

Purva Ashadha is entirely in Dhanus, Sagittarius. Planets in Dhanus rashi will aspire to be spiritual warriors, wanting to conquer their inner and outer worlds, be knowledgeable and wise. People will want to learn from them, they can be leaders, but mostly they want to teach their wisdom to others. Many creative geniuses are born under this sign. Jupiter and Venus, the two gurus of the zodiac, influence this nakshatra, making this position wise both in the worldly and spiritual sense.

Dhanus means a bow. The Avatara of Lord Vishnu, Sri Rama is always depicted with the bow. Sri Rama was an ideal man, a great warrior and he fought the dharmic war. Another great warrior Arjuna is linked to the bow as he was the greatest archer. The dilemma of Arjuna which is solved through the teachings of Bhagawad Geeta by Lord Krishna, explain the dilemma facing many with Sagittarius planets.

Symbol – The Elephant's Tusk

The symbol of the elephant's tusk shows the revelation of the inner faculties. The tusk is the most expensive part of the elephant and is valued for its beauty and elephants are killed for it. Others value the knowledge that Purva Ashadha uncovers but it can lead demonic forces to try to take away this new power of their talents. Often Purva Ashadha suffers from jealousy and envy.

The tusk, if cut off will grow again, showing wisdom once gained cannot be taken away. A person seeking his higher self has to face dangers from the world around him in pursuit for his chosen path. Elvis Presley had his Sun in Purva Ashadha and he was surrounded by negative people who desired his talents (metaphorically the tusk of the elephant).

Puranic Myth – Rivalry of the Gurus

Purva Ashadha is ruled by the two gurus of the Vedas – Jupiter and Venus. Jupiter represents Brihaspati who was the son of Sage Angiras and Venus represents Sage Shukracharya who is the son of Sage Bhrigu. Both the gurus have a major disagreement between each other and will usually support the opposite view to each other.

Brihaspati is the advisor of the devas or gods and Shukracharya is the advisors of the asura or demons. Shukracharya has the ability to rejuvenate the dead from his knowledge of the Sanjeevani mantra and he has supported the demons in order to defy the gods.

This rivalry has a great influence on those with planets in Purva Ashadha who may be drawn to differing ideas which may either confuse them or allow them to see both sides of the argument. In order to develop the higher self they must know how to suppress the demons, and this knowledge is available to Shukracharya. The demonic energies will bow down to the message of Venus whereas they may not be ready to listen to Jupiter's advice. My guru Dr Ajit Sinha used to say that to be a great teacher, we must imbibe a bit of both the gurus, and the Purva Ashadha planets will have this gift.

Purva Ashadha aim for Moksha

Purva Ashadha people are now moving towards moksha. They will voluntarily take this path and understand the great responsibility resting on their shoulders. They find enlightenment by using their own experiences to uncover their potential.

Their spiritual path is connected to understanding the final blocks that stop their spiritual flowering. These can be relationships, career, family or friends. They have to learn to deal with them and use the experiences of life to unravel their spiritual knots.

Sacred Animal – Monkey as the divine Hanuman

Purva Ashadha's animal is the monkey. Monkeys are revered as the god Hanuman who exemplifies the ideal devotee. Hanuman is connected to both Vishnu and Shiva (see Swati nakshatra). Hanuman was the devotee of Rama, the incarnation of Vishnu, and his mother Anjana was a devotee of Shiva. According to Ramayana, vanara or monkeys are created by Brahma to help Rama in battle against Ravana. Vanaras are powerful monkeys who have many godly traits. After the vanaras were created they began to organize into armies and spread across the forests. They helped Rama in his search for his wife, Sita, who had been abducted by Ravana. Later when Rama needed to cross over to Sri Lanka, the monkeys made a bridge of stones that magically floated to the surface and enabled Rama to cross the sea, defeat Ravana and rescue Sita.

Purva Ashadha can develop loyalty and give great support to those they admire. They are forever in a fight against injustice. They will be organised and have the capacity to plan. Purva Ashadha deals with the valour of heroes who defeat all odds to conquer their enemies.

The monkey animal in the form of Vanara Hanuman and Sugreeva show support to those on the righteous path. Vanaras are amusing, childish, mildly irritating, badgering, hyperactive, adventurous, bluntly honest, loyal, courageous, and kind.

Ayurvedic Dosha is Pitta

Purva Ashadha are active, forceful and charismatic. These people are creative, intuitive and inspirational, and are good at leading. They are ambitious and hardworking, fiery in temperament and very motivated. The fire quality is why many creative people are born under this nakshatra, Elvis Presley and David Bowie being two of them.

Lagna and Planets

Planets in Purva Ashadha must try to maintain their purity because they can get easily influenced by others and their purity spoilt. They need to keep their environment, friends, diet, thinking and aspirations unpolluted as far as they can help it and periodically cleanse their surroundings. This will help them to maintain their integrity. They must practice inner cleansing as well through mantras, rituals and spiritual practices. Jupiter and Venus will influence the lagna, making them great advisors, having worldly and spiritual wisdom. They will be talented in whichever direction they choose , which could be business, law, writing, etc. as well as spiritual abilities. The position of Jupiter and Venus and their relationship with each other will define this.

The Sun shines brightly, giving these people a deep sense of understanding of their spiritual path. They will be idealistic, creative and have influence on those around them. This is a position where the Sun can be profound or weak depending on the pada it is placed in. These people must always keep themselves surrounded by good influences and advisors.

The Moon tries to understand this new energy. As the Moon stands for water and purity, the mind can become polluted if these people are not careful. The mind is usually unsettled in Sagittarius as the Moon rules the 8th sign from it; it is subject to change through the life experience. These people need to be particular of what influences they allow into their life. As water can change colour, their emotions can change according to the company they keep. The first dasha is Venus;

usually a good dasha. It can inspire them to be creative right from the beginning. Knowledge and education is important for them and children born with this Moon should be encouraged to follow yoga and develop a steady mind from a young age.

Mars will find both weakness and strength in Purva Ashadha. The lack of direction and change that signifies Purva Ashadha can make Mars uncertain and unsure regarding what direction to take. There are underlying passions and strong desires that hamper progress towards spirituality, but also unfolding knowledge that will change the way they want to act during their lifetime.

People with Mercury placed here will enjoy creativity and intelligence. They will feel at home both materially and spiritually but have a limited sense of what they are. As this sense changes (which is inevitable) they will embrace many new ideas and ways of being.

Jupiter will develop as a great advisor who guides people over troubled waters. These people will be interested in rituals, philosophy and mantras. They will try to keep their purity and develop further talents during their life.

Venus is both strong and weak. It can be inspirational and creative or it can question everything and spoil it. The talents are there but the way they are used is important. Venus people should try to know the complete picture and not allow their old patterns of thinking to influence the good ideas that come now.

Saturn will help to hone the talents. It can be strong in this time of change but it can get wisdom from life experiences too.

Rahu can create difficulties. It can pollute the spiritual waters, making these people use the knowledge in a negative way or become attracted to the wrong kind of philosophies. Rahu will be attracted to foreign philosophies and can create something profound out of very negative situations. Ketu has dealt with troubled waters in the past but has collected wisdom and experienced the growth of spirituality. This is the message these people need to pass on to the world. They must trust their instinct and not deny it. They should help others to understand the trials and tribulations of the spiritual path. But it also gives some unusual talents and the ability to understand philosophy and ideas in very different ways.

Padas in Purva Ashadha: Leo, Virgo, Libra, Sagittarius
These people are developing their spirituality but are also facing ingrained desires that are difficult to give up. The philosophy and spiritual development is idealistic and young so the inner struggles are not always recognised for what they are. The soul has made the transition but there is a residue of materialism and still work to be done before these people can call themselves enlightened. So in these padas holding onto the past delays the development, but the soul is also discovering roots in this new age, and new spiritual ways. There is pushkara pada in Purva Ashadha.

13°20' to 16°40' Sagittarius – Leo pada
The 1st pada of Purva Ashadha and 5th navamsha of Sagittarius is Leo. This is where the confidence about spirituality develops. These people have a strong sense of being on the right path, trusting their judgment and developing spiritual strength. No planets is exalted or debilitated in this pada.

16°40' to 20°00' Sagittarius – Virgo pada
The 2nd pada of Purva Ashadha and 6th navamsha of Sagittarius is Virgo. Virgo weakens Venus and strengthens Mercury. Virgo is the sign of dissatisfaction and involvement with materialism, so here the spiritual path can be obstructed by perceived reality, the need to analyse and find answers before accepting the need to change.

Mercury becomes exalted. How can any spiritual quest go forward unless all the questions are answered? This position keeps the mind attached to the material aspects of life and the development towards spirituality only takes place once the intellect is satisfied.

Venus is debilitated and therefore the person questions their relationships and their role in the life of spiritual aspirants. This can lead to unsettled partnerships.

20°00' to 23°20' Sagittarius – Libra pada
The 3rd pada of Purva Ashadha and 7th navamsha of Sagittarius is Libra. Saturn is exalted, the Sun debilitated and Venus is in its own sign. Libra brings balance between materialism and the spiritual quest. Remember that the Apas of Purva Ashadha is water that is contained and not free flowing. Therefore spirituality cannot take over the life. Materialism has

a role here and Libra can bring balance. Pushkara suggests that this is an auspicious balance that benefits all planets.

The Sun, from a strong position in the rashi, goes into debilitation. Notice how the Sun benefits by the pushkara status of its debilitated padas in its good signs (Aries, Leo and Sagittarius). It has to learn about self-esteem which brings lack of confidence in finding an inner light. This may have dimmed a bit as the soul appears to be crowded by desires for love, relationship and support. The pushkara suggests that this weakness brings strength as this may be the last time that this individual will seek materialism; soon the spiritual light will be too powerful to ignore.

Saturn is exalted and therefore it allows individuals to pay their karmic debts and carry less of the karma that hinders them from reaching their higher goals. Saturn people will make an effort towards spirituality by paying their debts to the society they live in, taking responsibility for their own karma.

23°20' to 26°40' Sagittarius

The 4th pada of Purva Ashadha and 8th navamsha of Sagittarius is Scorpio. Both the Moon and Rahu suffer due to debilitation, Ketu is exalted and happy. This is one of the most difficult positions for spiritual aspirants as Scorpio is where the debris of all our past desires settles. It can bring the worst out of the personality, but as the soul is changing spiritually, our past knowledge has to be used. We have to learn discipline so that the soul does not go back or wallow in old habits, desires and negative personality traits. While this pada digs deep to find the hidden potential, it will make all planets struggle with their weaknesses. The water (Apas) of Purva Ashadha can get too muddy. The emotions need to be filtered and cleansed periodically so they don't become stagnant, otherwise the path towards transformation that is so desired by Scorpio will be blocked.

The Moon is emotionally troubled here. There is a lack of security, and these people have to let go of emotional neediness as that can create a troubled mind. They must learn to change and grow. Stagnation can lead to spiritual confusion and lack of stability.

Rahu can focus on the dark sexuality of Scorpio, the possessiveness and control, and these aspects put a block to any growth of Purva Ashadha and Sagittarius. These individuals have to start disciplining themselves and aspiring towards the higher quality. Whatever the darkness, Purva Ashadha should bring out the positive qualities and create the transformation. Ketu understands the karma, the deepness and the spirituality of Scorpio. It will allow the individual to be comfortable with their karma and make for a positive move to let go of their karmic baggage.

21. Uttara Ashadha

26°40' Sagittarius to 10°00' Capricorn
Padas: Sagittarius, Capricorn, Aquarius, Pisces

Meaning

Uttara means higher and *Ashadha* means 'not subdued'. It indicates what cannot be suppressed. The true nature of man comes out regardless of what opposition they have to face – the victory over the lower nature and expression of the higher one. It links to the previous nakshatra Purva Ashadha, and together they represent the common principle of unfolding new talents. In Purva Ashadha, there was a dawning of how the new reality may affect it psychologically, but the assimilation into the psyche takes place in Uttara Ashadha.

Uttara Ashadha
Ruled by The Sun
Devata: Vishwadevas - The Universal Gods
Symbol: Planks of a bed
Yoni: Mongoose
Motivation: Moksha
Guna Triplicity: Sattva, Rajas and Sattva
Dosha: Kapha
Body Part: Waist
Gana: Human
Caste: Warrior
Quality: Fixed
Colour: Copper
Best Direction: South
Special Sounds: Be, Bo, Ja, Je
The Principal Stars: Al- Baldah
Other Names for Uttara Ashadha: Vishwe, Vishwadeva

Uttara Ashadha people are creative and talented like their cosmic other half, but they have moved on spiritually so their journey is more internal. Their creativity is not always expressed through artistic expression but a philosophical one.

Uttara Ashadha is a lonely nakshatra. All its symbolism is connected to being alone. The planks of the bed are the symbol of Uttara Ashadha. This is an austere bed, not made for comfort. These people are moving away from sensuality and adopting a simple life even when they are materially wealthy.

Devata – Vishwadeva

Vishwadeva means the god of the world. In India there are 33 core Devata (330 million) and all bless this nakshatra. Vishwadeva delivers their worshippers across the choppy waters of human life to a more spiritual place. Uttara Ashadha is the start of personal sacrifice in the quest of spirituality. The other nakshatras of Sagittarius, Mula and Purva Ashadha, become aware of the path and try to cut themselves away from materialism. It is in Uttara Ashadha that the individual takes voluntary steps to control life around them, to cross over from one threshold to another. The Vishwadevas guide them, help them over this difficult path.

Vishwadevas are the gods controlling the brain cells. Uttara Ashadha concentrates on the mind of the individual and its intellectual development. Vishwadevas promote social interaction and give harmonious physical conditions so that the inner person can develop. It shows a life lived in public with an inner desire to be alone.

In Sagittarius, the outer/inner connection is more harmonious. It is as it was meant to be. Uttara Ashadha struggles more in its Capricorn portion.

Planetary ruler – Sun

The Sun signifies authority, power, vitality and strength and these people easily achieve leadership positions. The reason for this is that they learn to control their own needs in pursuit of their higher goals. This gives them skills to command others. It is a natural progression. The Sun gives them the authority, as it is about influence and power in the community. They are dynamic and intellectually gifted. They are leaders who doggedly pursue their ambitions. They can be composed and stoical. They tend to keep an emotional distance from others. The Sun in Capricorn Uttara Ashadha becomes more of a loner as they aspire for change and make it happen. They may be wealthy or powerful but tend to live simply.

Dhanus and Makar Rashi

Sagittarius and Capricorn are two differing experiences of Uttara Ashadha. In Sagittarius, there is still the need to be the spiritual warrior, to teach, to advise and to express knowledge in each and every way. Uttara Ashadha Sagittarius is a sweet spot as the pada reflects the fire energy and is warm and all embracing. All the planets work well here.

Capricorn Uttara Ashadha learns to express its nature by controlling its desires. This is more ascetic than its Sagittarian counterpart. The Saturn-Sun rulership is not the easiest to deal with.

It struggles with the outer Capricorn impulse. These people have a complicated relationship with the power, authority and success that the Uttara Ashadha in Sagittarius has. They will be distant or cool leaders who do not inspire love in those who work for them but awe at their ability to take responsibility and face even the most difficult tasks.

Uttara Ashadha is ruled by the Sun. The consciousness is signified by the Sun and the influence of Sagittarius and Capricorn creates a bridge to develop the spirituality that moves it towards a wholly different direction.

Symbol – The Planks of the Bed

The planks of the bed, the symbol of Uttara Ashadha are an austere bed, not one of comfort. This is where there is voluntary embracing of asceticism, as sleeping in a hard bed indicates the giving up of desires and needs and living simply.

Sleep is a necessary requirement to open our minds to its higher connections. Rest is used in yoga to relax the muscles so that the next asana can be taken slightly further. In the same way, Uttara Ashadha creates conditions so that the mind can relax and open itself to further wisdom and look beyond perception.

Puranic Myth – Lord Venkateshwara and his Debt to Kubera

Vishnu incarnated as the supreme form of Venkateshwara and married Padmavathi to whom he had promised marriage in a previous lifetime. To commemorate this eternal love and marriage, the temple of Tirupati was built. The belief is that the Lord Venkateshwara did not have money to pay for his marriage to Padmavathi and therefore took a loan from Kubera. Devotees in their millions still come to this sacred place, returning the loan of Kubera and paying off the debt of Lord Venkateshwara. Even today at the temple there is a special daily celebration called Kalyanotsavam that celebrates the divine union. Kalyanotsavam is a marriage ritual and it is held every day (except on certain festivals and eclipse days) and devotees can participate in it.

One of the most spiritually powerful and wealthiest temples in India is the Tirumala Venkateshwara Temple. Wealth and spirituality – both themes of Uttara Ashadha – are present here. Often Uttara Ashadha people use their wealth to pay back their old karmic debts too.

The dichotomy of Uttara Ashadha is that they can be very rich at the same time as aspiring towards a higher being. The combination of asceticism and wealth is personified by Steve Jobs, the founder of Apple, who had his Atmakaraka Venus in Uttara Ashadha.

Uttara Ashadha Aim for Moksha

Uttara Ashadha makes the real psychological adjustment towards moksha. For these people letting go of their ego and merging with universal consciousness becomes paramount. The change and the inner need to leave the cycle of unhappiness behind is so profound, that Uttara Ashadha sometimes lose their knack of relating to this world.

Uttara Ashadha's spiritual life path is connected with working practically towards their life ambitions. They have to work to fulfill their own ambitions first so that they are in a position to work beyond that. This will make them selfish to start with, but their mind will change and from the selfishness a selfless individual emerges who will give and sacrifice their own needs for the good of others.

Sacred Animal – Kubera and Mongoose

The mongoose is the animal connected to the god of wealth, Kubera. He is described as a dwarf and he holds a mongoose in his hands. Kubera's early descriptions are negative and ugly. I think his image represented the ugliness of karma we all carry within us. Kubera holding the mongoose suggests a victory over the *naga* or the snakes. The snakes were guardians of treasures but also represent karma and mortality. Uttara Ashadha wants to kill the Sarpa (poisons) within and allow the higher self to develop. Metaphorically, the killing of the snake is killing of old karma and breaking away from mortality to become immortal. Uttara Ashadha wants to remove all poisons from their personality and past lives so that they are purified to move ahead on their spiritual path.

Ayurvedic Dosha is Kapha

Kapha is philosophical, spiritual and emotional. Kapha can also be lazy, and blocked by emotions. These people can eat for comfort and feed their emotions through shopping, eating and indulgences. Uttara Ashadha individuals are bright, but they need to be careful for if they give into their indulgences too much they can dull their mind. This will create problems for them in other areas of their life.

Makar Sankranti and Uttara Ashadha

The day the Sun moves into Capricorn (from pada 1 to pada 2 of Uttara Ashadha) is celebrated as Makara Sankranti. Sankranti means to go from one place to another (to change). Makara is the sign of Capricorn. This is when the Sun stops moving away from the earth and begins Uttarayana or the northerly course, coming closer to the earth and promising longer and warmer days. Makara Sankranti3 is the day the Sun dies and is reborn.

The symbolic rebirth of the Sun celebrates the Sun coming back towards the earth on its northerly route. The ancients felt that the Sun on its southerly route was going away from them and they were getting less of its energy. This is a major celebration, prayers are said to welcome the Sun back. The Sun is divine light and we welcome its intensity back to the earth to help light our path.

The rebirth of the Sun suggests that people with planets placed at this junction point in Uttara Ashadha will have a major rebirth during their time, especially if the Sun is placed in Uttara Ashadha.

Lagna and Planets

Lagna in Uttara Ashadha moves from philosophy to responsibility. In Sagittarius they will be the spiritual warriors, while in Capricorn they look at life practically, hiding their spiritual ambitions. Deep within they thirst for spirituality. Sagittarius Uttara Ashadha lagna is a great place to be and it is vargottama and pushkara. Many blessings are there. Depending on the rashi, the relative positions of Jupiter and the Sun plus Saturn and the Sun will show how they deal with this.

The Sun is in a state of flux. The ingress between Sagittarius and Capricorn is the position where the Sun is reborn every year, so it is important for people with the Sun in Uttara Ashadha to be aware of their light, and not allow the darkness of the Saturnine impulse to overshadow them. There can be an overwhelming desire to assert their

---

3. More details at http://www.komilla.com/pages/makarsankranti.html

authority while there can be a lack of confidence to do so. The soul is struggling to find itself. Letting go of the personal ego and taking on the right responsibility helps. Uttara Ashadha individuals work to do good for others. They are paying off their past karma so that they are lighter at the end of it.

The Moon has a hard time embracing the austere regime of Uttara Ashadha. In Sagittarius it can be easier than in Capricorn. The Moon is not at its best. Where are the pleasures of life? These people can feel depressed and lonely. They need to adapt to this life style otherwise their life can feel joyless. The Moon copes in two vargottama padas but feels unsettled in the last two. The Sun rules Uttara Ashadha and the first dasha of the Sun can give an uneasy relationship with the father. These people learn about power and democracy from an early age and it can give political ambitions when young. It is a good dasha to begin, as the solar blessings shine.

Mars enjoys the struggles of Uttara Ashadha as it has the courage to face difficult times. It is in a friends of Jupiter sign and then exalted in Capricorn and enjoys the nakshatra of its friend the Sun. A warrior's lot is to enjoy loneliness and struggle.

Mercury learns to rationalise and understand the spiritual desires. This is a dreamer who becomes a practical thinker. This is where the mind changes and the practical no longer satisfies but the spiritual desires are hidden deep. There can be a feeling of depression with so much responsibility on the mind. As the deity of Uttara Ashadha deals with the brain, mental activity is heightened.

Jupiter is extraordinarily strong in the Sagittarius portion of Uttara Ashadha and becomes equally weak and debilitated in Capricorn. The restriction imposed on Jupiter is part of the karmic process. Jupiter eases our life and when there is no Jupiter to shine its beneficence we have to learn to be our own support. Uttara Ashadha Jupiter feels this lack of support. The hard bed is not the usual domain of Jupiter, who enjoys the fruits of its good deeds by living a comfortable life. The person may have a materially comfortable life with this Jupiter but they do not find any pleasure in it. There is an underlying resentment at what life has given them.

Venus people will find the restrictions of Uttara Ashadha difficult to deal with. They can become overly fond of luxury as the soul demands sacrifice, but as they develop there is a giving up of desires which creates a dry personality despite the visual accompaniment of wealth.

Saturn is in his element and own sign but the Sun rulership shows these individuals are always looking for approval, searching for their light while feeling the world does not appreciate them. The light is there for them if they look away from their resentments and anger. They may have had a difficult relationship with their father.

Rahu feels immensely lonely and unfulfilled. Uttara Ashadha is a naturally lonely nakshatra so in trying to fill the emptiness in life people with Rahu in Uttara Ashadha can be relentlessly searching for love and emotions, yet intellectually reject them. They can also become unduly attached to financial or material security. The moment they stop identifying material security with happiness, they find their comfort level, their inner peace. Ketu shows a past life that was ascetic, and it can feel guilty trying to connect with material things now. Ketu in Uttara Ashadha adjust their mind towards moksha. The change and the inner need to leave the cycle of unhappiness behind is so profound that Ketu people sometimes lose their knack of relating to this world. The soul identifies with a lonely spiritual life.

Padas in Uttara Ashadha: Sagittarius, Capricorn, Aquarius, Pisces

Uttara Ashadha is the most complex and highly spiritual nakshatra. It has two vargottama positions and two pushkara ones. The exact degree of Jupiter's debilitation is here.

26°40' to 30°00' Sagittarius – Sagittarius pada

The 1st pada of Uttara Ashadha and 9th navamsha of Sagittarius is Sagittarius. It is vargottama and pushkara – a great position for all planets. They are all in harmony with their outer world and their need to develop their inner vision. Sagittarius does not debilitate any planet. Uttara Ashadha brings philosophy, new ways of thinking, development of talent and a great outer world. Pushkara allows the planets to heal themselves. Usually the vargottama position suggests that all planets are comfortable with what they need to achieve. They do not struggle with themselves, even if the issues are difficult.

Jupiter is in one of its best positions, in its own sign, a friend's nakshatra, vargottama, pushkara: what more could you want? There are high ideals, great thinking and beneficence. These people do not care about financial or material success but about being good followers of dharma. Yet they achieve material success and honour. When I was thinking of founding BAVA, the British Association for Vedic Astrology, in 1996 with Andrew Foss, we chose this position of Jupiter for BAVA birth muhurta (elected birth chart). Jupiter has allowed BAVA to follow a path of high idealism.

0°00' to 3°20' Capricorn – Capricorn pada

The 2nd pada of Uttara Ashadha and 1st navamsha of Capricorn is the vargottama Capricorn. All planets will be strong here, and even if their path appears difficult they will be reconciled to it. Mars is extremely strong here while Jupiter has a difficult journey.

The lagna is vargottama and will make these individuals strong and powerful, but they are happy to take on their responsibilities. It can make others take them for granted too.

The Sun in this pada means you are born around the Makar Sankranti. It can cause a complex in Sun people of not feeling strong, but this is a highly spiritual position.

Mars enjoys power and supremacy. It is able to deal with the hardship of Uttara Ashadha and triumph over it. It improves the quality of Mars and gives it the ability to focus, discipline and achieve whatever it sets it mind to.

A debilitated Jupiter in vargottama becomes practical and conscious of money. One needs to cultivate feelings of joy as Jupiter in Capricorn can be particularly dry and desolate. Health problems, especially with the liver, can happen. In a woman's chart, the owner may opt for a practical marriage or find their partners are too ascetic, boring or not much fun.

3°20' to 6°40' Capricorn – Aquarius pada

The 3rd pada of Uttara Ashadha and 2nd navamsha of Capricorn is Aquarius. No planet is exalted or debilitated in this pada. 5° Capricorn is the exact debilitation degree for Jupiter, so the light of knowledge can be obscured as the individual becomes obsessed with paying karmic debts. In order to do so there may be an attraction to professions that are practical, like accounting or financial services. It is the outer quality of Jupiter that remains shrouded, but if they decide to try to understand their nature, the true quality will emerge.

6°40' to 10°00' Capricorn – Pisces pada

The 4th pada of Uttara Ashadha and 3rd navamsha of Capricorn is Pisces. This is a pushkara navamsha. All planets prosper here. This pada belongs to Abhijit nakshatra. It is a power position in the zodiac. This is the ending of the 7th cycle of the soul's development which is the first cycle on the sattvic level. This is fertile ground for developing the principle of spirituality and its links with austerity and aloneness. Mercury is debilitated and Venus exalted.

Mercury will be debilitated by pada but it is also pushkara. This is a rather tough situation for Mercury, it goes from the restrictions and limitation that Capricorn and Uttara Ashadha impose to the expansive-ness of Pisces. From rational to spiritual thinking, where no restrictions are appreciated, a world of no boundaries that take the thinking into another realm entirely. On the positive side, this is not a Mercury that demands evidence, but one in harmony with the spiritual plan, making changes and shifting its axis with the help of pushkara.

Venus is exalted; it will also become fertile and brimming with ideas on spirituality and future growth. This can expose the true talents of the individual. This would create more harmonious relationships and the toll of spiritual development is no longer on the personal life.

Abhijit

6°40' to 11°13'20" Capricorn
Planetary Ruler: The Sun
Pada: Pisces and part of Aries overlaying the
nakshatras of Uttara Ashadha and Shravana
Devata – Vidhata
Star – Vega

Abhijit is the 28th nakshatra and there is very little information available on it. It is used in some techniques and not specifically used for natal interpretation.

Meaning

Abhijit means victorious, conquering completely. The nakshatra lord Vidhata refers to Brahma and the name Abhijit connects to Vishnu. Abhijit is connected to the great gods of the Vedas and therefore shows a lot of power and spiritual strength. Vishnu preserves and Brahma creates. Here the individual can write their own destiny and preserve all the dharma they have created so far. They are both preservers and creators due to the connection with Brahma and Vishnu. This can give these people the ability to preserve the old ways of life while creating new and innovative things. Preservation of the wealth of the ancestors, both materially and spiritually, is important.

Intercalary Nakshatra

Abhijit is an intercalary nakshatra, it is beyond the nakshatra mandala. It runs side by side with Uttara Ashadha and Shravana, so if you have planets placed in Abhijit, they usually give the effect of either Uttara Ashadha or Shravana. But you can add further special qualities of Abh ijit, like the striving for dharma, the spiritual drive and the ability to always want to win regardless of the circumstances.

Puranic Myth – why Abhijit was taken away from the nakshatras

According to a vedic myth, Abhijit was the most auspicious nakshatra. It was such a powerful nakshatra that to achieve success in every act, persons used to start their important activities on the day the Moon was positioned there. This usually happens when the Sun is in Capricorn from 14 Jan to 13 Feb annually, depending on the Ayanamsha (this may have been a different month during Sri Krishna's time).

During the Mahabharata, Lord Sri Krishna came to know that Duryodhana was planning to start the war with Pancha Pandavas on this auspicious day; combining with Amavasya and Abhijit nakshatra made it a potent force for being victorious over the enemy. On getting to know Duryodhana's plans, Sri Krishna knew that if the Kauravas and Duryodhana started Mahabharata on this day, the Pandavas would lose. Sri Krishna removed Abhijit nakshatra from the nakshatras Mandala as he wanted to avoid any misuse of it.

Devata – Vidhata
Vidhata is another name for Brahma, he is the god who writes the destiny of all the new born. Vidhata is the eighth son of Aditi and is another solar god. Those born during Abhijit have the capacity to write their own destiny and can be so strong that they can also guide others. They need to be careful not to become too confident.

Planetary Ruler – The Sun
The Sun shares the rulership with the Uttara Ashadha portion but continues to give added influence to the small portion in Shravana. The Sun's rulership shows the inner purity of the nakshatra and that it can purify any energy and make it auspicious.

The Sun is the atma, the soul, and here the individual aspires to connect back to its soul. But usually an important duty has to be done in this world, a dharma fulfilled before it can be fully revealed. The Sun gives form to the ideas and reveals the karma that has to be paid for now – only then can the soul truly get back to its source. Something important is revealed about the planets placed in Abhijit; this can be a burden or an opportunity depending on how they view the revelation and if the soul is prepared for the next essential step in soul growth.

Uses of Abhijit
Abhijit is used when the 28 scheme of nakshatras is employed. It is used for Gotra, Purushartha, Dina nakshatras[4] and Sarvatobhadra chakra. But even if you use the time when the Moon is in Abhijit for electing

time, the effect will not be as strong, as the nakshatra is now out of the Mandala and therefore its influence dimmed. We can observe Abhijit in the chart more as an added influence and not as the only one.

Barack Obama and Abhijit

Barack Obama, 4 August 1961, 19:24 (+10:00hrs) Hawaii Time, Honolulu, Hawaii

Rashi (D-1) General

Ke 4°34'

11
12

Sa 2°00'
Jp 7°32'
As 24°44'

9

8

10

1   7

4

Su 19°13'
Me 9°0'

Mo
0°02'

2
3

6

5

Ve 8°28'

Ra 4°34'
Ma 29°15'

Vimshottari

Start Date		Age	Dashas	
24/ 3/ 2001	39.6	Jp	Me
30/ 6/ 2003	41.9	Jp	Ke
5/ 6/ 2004	42.8	Jp	Ve
4/ 2/ 2007	45.5	Jp	Su
23/11/ 2007	46.3	Jp	Mo
24/ 3/ 2009	47.6	Jp	Ma
28/ 2/ 2010	48.6	Jp	Ra
24/ 7/ 2012	**51.0**	**Sa**	**Sa**
28/ 7/ 2015	54.0	Sa	Me
6/ 4/ 2018	56.7	Sa	Ke
16/ 5/ 2019	57.8	Sa	Ve
15/ 7/ 2022	60.9	Sa	Su

President Barack Obama has Jupiter placed in 7°32' Capricorn. At first glance it appears that Jupiter is debilitated, therefore lacking in power. So how could he become the first black President of United States in Jupiter's maha dasha? When you study it more deeply, the important factors change the quality to extraordinary. First, Jupiter is placed in the 1st house where it gets dik bala – directional strength. Second, a retrograde planet achieves cancellation of debilitation. And finally, while being in Utara Ashadha nakshatra, it is also in the degrees of Abhijit which gives exceptional power to Jupiter to achieve against all odds.

---

4. More on Dina nakshatras in *Personal Panchanga*, Komilla Sutton, The Wessex Astrologer Ltd.
5. The rules for cancellation of debilitation are given in most foundation books on Jyotish. You can also read about them in *The Essentials of Vedic Astrology*, Komilla Sutton, The Wessex Astrologer Ltd.

22. Shravana

10°00' to 23°20' Capricorn
Padas: Aries, Taurus, Gemini, Cancer

Meaning

Shravana means listening, especially to the scriptures. In ancient times the scriptures were handed down orally from teacher to student so Shravana was an important part of the spiritual seeker's discipline. Now reading scriptures is also part of Shravana. We can hear the true meaning of the scriptures when there is silence of the mind. It is then we begin to hear new sounds that we were not aware of before. To sit in silence we have to like ourselves, as it forces us to recognise the truths and not hide within the cacophony of life. Shravana is the nakshatra of total silence. This silence leads

Shravana
Ruled by The Moon
Devata: Vishnu - The Preserver of the Universe
Symbol: The Ear, The Three Footsteps Footprint
Yoni: Monkey
Motivation: Artha
Guna Triplicity: Sattva, Tamas and Rajas
Ayurvedic Dosha: Kapha
Body Part: Genitals
Gana: Divine
Caste: Outcast
Quality: Mutable
Colours: Light Blue
Best Direction: North
Special Sounds: Ju, Jay, Jo, Gha
The Principal Stars: Altair
Other Names for Shravana: Govind, Vishnu, Shruti, Karna,

to the perception of the manifestation and our ability to see through the illusions of life. This nakshatra indicates the need for quietness and reflection. The silence that total meditation brings in our heart will lead to a better understanding within. The need is to assimilate these ideas and listen to what others have to say as well as what our inner self is telling us.

Part of the first pada of Shravana belongs to Abhijit nakshatra as well, showing the power of this part of the spiritual journey.

Devata – Vishnu

Vishnu is the light beyond our perception. Vishnu is the personification of all the 12 Sun gods, therefore he represents the zodiac. Vishnu is considered one of the most important gods of the Vedas, forming the holy trinity with Shiva and Brahma. Vishnu means 'he who crosses heights'. He encourages his followers to scale the heights beyond their capabilities. He is responsible for preserving the world and supporting creation. Here he will preserve the new found spirituality and create the right conditions for development of higher knowledge. He gives Shravana individuals the ability to go beyond their present view of the worlds, and see their incarnation in a new way, if they are ready to do so. Not many people are willing to see their life from a new point of view, as they are usually afraid of what they will find. But if they are ready, then Vishnu will guide them to a new world, nurture their spirituality and give them the courage to explore this brave new world.

Planetary Ruler – Moon
The Moon rules Shravana. As well as signifying the mind, the Moon is the physical embodiment of your soul, the ebb and flow of your feelings, emotions and the need for change on a daily basis. The Moon is the controller of life on earth where nothing is certain. At Shravana, your mind has to learn the lesson of equilibrium and to be at peace. The Moon, with its waxing and waning cycle, represents the ever changing mind.

If sorrow and happiness are treated equally and with detachment, then the mind is ready to experience inner growth and move towards higher knowledge. Shravana can create conditions to make this possible through constant practice of managing the mind through meditation and silence.

Makara Rashi
Capricorn provides the bridge between Man and the Supreme and now the individual is consciously co-operating with the divine plan. It is an initiation into a different stage of life. At Shravana-Capricorn the soul initiates itself into higher learning to understand concepts of spirituality, responsibility to this world and how to realize itself.

Symbol – The Ear
The symbol of the ear assigned to Shravana is further enhancing its listening quality. In the Upanishad there is a prayer to grant the capacity to listen properly. This is listening in the true sense of the word. When we learn to listen properly, then the nuances of life become clear and we

gain the ability to understand what was left unsaid; to hear beyond the spoken word.

Puranic Myth – Trivikrama Vishnu and Vamana

Another symbol of Shravana is the three footsteps which are connected to Vamana, the 5th incarnation of Vishnu. Sri Bhagavatam[6] recounts that the Vamana avatar was taken by Vishnu to restore Indra's authority over the heavens, which was snatched by force by the demon king Mahabali in Dravida. Vamana in the disguise of a dwarf Brahmin, requested King Mahabali to grant him three steps of land to live in. Guru Shukracharya warned King Mahabali not to agree to this request, but the King was drunk with his ego and ignored his guru's advice and doubted how much land the dwarf could actually take – so he gave the promise of three steps of land to Vamana. It is then that Sri Vishnu showed his true form which turned Vamana from a dwarf to this huge person whose first step equalled the earth, the second, heaven and finally Vamana asked King Mahabali, "Where should I put the third"? The humbled king recognizing the miracle of Sri Vishnu, bowed his head and said, "You can put it on my head". Vishnu placing the third foot on the king's head and in so doing removed all ego from him. Vamana taught King Mahabali that arrogance and pride should be abandoned if any advancement in life is to be made, and that wealth should never be taken for granted since it can so easily be taken away. Jupiter is the planet connected with this incarnation of Lord Vishnu.

Vishnu took the three steps to dispel the ignorance, desires and past karma from Bali which block the path of an individual to true knowledge. By letting go of the ego Shravana allows the divine grace to flow and the true wisdom to dawn.

This myth teaches Shravana people about listening to their guru. Often when a person is drunk with ego they forget to listen and understand the message that is being given. Sage Shukracharya recognised the dwarf Brahmin to be something other that what he was portraying, whereas King Mahabali took him at face value.

---

6. Śrī Bhāgavatam is one of the Maha Puranas (great ancient scripture) of vedic literature. Its primary focus is devotion to the incarnations of Vishnu. Puranas are written later than the vedic literature.

Shravana Aim for Artha

Shravana individuals are goal orientated and they focus on achievement. Their goals are connected to business, building wealth (both spiritual and material) and making an impact on the world around them. They are pragmatic and will be disciplined in their approach to life. The artha for Shravana means practical ways of doing service for the good of humanity.

Shravana people have to let go of their selfish needs to work for others, preserving their rights, caring for their needs. They have to work in the world while they desire to move towards a more spiritual place. Shravana has the ability to look beyond what ordinary people aspire towards.

Sacred Animal – Hanuman and Saturn

The animal of Shravana is the monkey. Hanuman, the popular god, is in the form of a monkey. He was known for his devotion to Rama as well as his ability to withstand the challenges from Saturn. Once when Saturn threatened to trouble him by his transit, Hanuman carried him on his back and took him around the world a few times till Saturn begged him to put him back on the earth. Since then Saturn gave a special immunity to the worshippers of Hanuman that he will not trouble them by transit. This is why those who have difficult Saturn transits worship Hanuman.

Shravana people who are rooted in their spiritual practice are not afraid of challenging transits, just like Hanuman. They develop the ability to deal with testing times and take the good with the bad in the same vein. Hanuman was celibate and many Shravana people choose celibacy.

Ayurvedic Dosha is Kapha

Shravana people are philosophical, spiritual and emotional. Their emotions play an important role in their life as they are continually trying to control them. They have to beware of self-indulgence, in their emotions and with food. Kapha can make them calm in a crisis and also help in their meditations and yogic practices.

Lagna and Planets

People with lagna in Shravana will want to control their life. They may also feel that they are seeing life in a new way. They will be sensitive underneath although they may appear aloof and self-contained. The mind is still active, the emotions strong. It depends on the mutual position of Saturn and the Moon whether they can control their mind or not.

The Sun is strong, getting stronger by the day, finding its spiritual light. As Vishnu controls this nakshatra, the Sun will be quite dominant in spiritual pursuits and making transformations in life.

The Moon has to learn the lesson of equilibrium and be at peace with itself which is not easy as its nature is changeable. The Moon placed in its own nakshatra can emphasise emotions. Our earthly instincts have got to be regulated, which finally leads us to a deeper understanding of the essence of life. These people struggle with the dictates of Saturn, but the more they learn to control their emotions, to become detached, the better it is for them. Studying and learning scriptures, reading books of philosophy and working with yoga to still their mind will all be helpful. The first dasha is of the Moon, which makes for an easier childhood. This can be quite studious with a thirst for knowledge as this is a nakshatra that needs knowledge and silence. Even if they did not develop it earlier in life, Shravana Moon people will be forever studying and learning.

Mars remains exalted and shows both strength and weakness in Shravana. Mars is not always good at listening, yet it has strength and courage to enter the new world of Shravana. Shravana can expose the weakness of Mars.

Mercury is uncomfortable with the intuitiveness of Shravana. It will want to understand the scriptures, but before it can do so Mercury needs to develop steadiness of mind. These individuals love to read and understand life. They will appear practical on the outside but are intuitive as well and this allows them to think outside the box.

Jupiter remains debilitated by rashi but the underlying conditions change. Shravana is ruled by the Moon which exalts Jupiter. Shravana fosters the listening/studying of scriptures which is what Jupiter promotes. It is in Shravana that the soul now searches for lost wisdom, so Jupiter becomes empowered and slowly the good feeling and natural beneficence of Jupiter starts coming back. There is a great difference in the position of Jupiter in Capricorn. In Uttara Ashadha it is very weak but now it is on the journey back to finding its true strength and in Shravana connecting back to the eternal wisdom takes place and Jupiter finally finds itself.

Venus will struggle with desires and emotions but its higher vibration is connected to knowledge. As Shukracharya, he is one of the two gurus, so here the mantle of Venus will go from being connected with material comforts to one aspiring towards discipline and higher knowledge. It is not an easy nakshatra for marriage or relationships but it is helpful for spiritual development.

Saturn is unsettled in Shravana. This is the nakshatra where his weakness is exposed. The spiritual scriptures, the need to listen and the rulership of the Moon means that Saturn has to relax its rigidity. Saturn will find it an uneasy platform for his pursuits. Saturn is usually uncomfortable with the new path advocated by Shravana so there will be struggles with emotions and coldness, until they find an even plane.

Rahu can intensify the fear of the mind. Rahu has to make sense of the ever changing perspective and bring a steadiness and grounding to its search. Rahu in this nakshatra indicates the need for quietness and reflection yet Rahu will initially find it impossible to sit still for long enough to hear the sounds of silence. There will be total lack of peace of mind as the soul searches for this silence and peace. Rahu learns to experience the silence of the soul and to master its restlessness. Ketu indicates that the need for quietness and reflection was part of our previous life. The silence of this total meditation brought a better understanding within. The soul searches for this silence and peace in this life. In the past life they learnt to control the mind – it helps Ketu to focus.

Padas in Shravana: Aries, Taurus, Gemini, Cancer
Shravana is the start of 8th level of development, the vibrations are now getting higher and higher, the padas start from Aries again. This is a very high resonance of Aries, where courage to go into the world unknown or hidden from a material aspirant comes alive. There is ashtamamsha and pushkara, there is no vargottama pada.

10°00' to 13°20' Capricorn – Aries pada
The 1st pada of Shravana and 4th navamsha of Capricorn is Aries. The Sun is exalted while Saturn becomes weak in its own sign. Mars remain strong in an exalted rashi and its own pada.

The Sun is strong in exaltation pada. This is the first exaltation after the Sun has moved into Uttarayana, its northern direction. By paying homage to the rigidity of Saturn, through knowledge and understanding, the Sun soon finds its inner light. This pada exposes the weakness of Saturn. The pragmatic approach will suffer due to the philosophy of Shravana.

The need to control the mind will overshadow the mission of Saturn. The underlying emotions will throw Saturn off balance and the end result is not an easy one. The adventurous spirit of Aries, the need to nurture this new world does not see Saturn at its best. It struggles to find the right answers.

13°20' to 16°40' Capricorn – Taurus pada

The 2nd pada of Shravana and 5th navamsha of Capricorn is Taurus. This is a pushkara navamsha, so all planets gain. It is specially good for the Moon and Rahu as they are both exalted. Venus also gains by being in its own house. Ketu feels debilitated.

The Moon is a mind at peace, ready to adapt to the message of Shravana. This position promotes the right way of thinking and calmness of mind.

Rahu is exalted and it can understand that something concrete is going to come out of the future. It is suddenly not so afraid and therefore the agitation lessens. Ketu shows a past life where study and responsibility were strong, yet Taurus will make it guilty about wealth and comfort. The pushkara nature of this pada will help Ketu let go of remorse.

16°40' to 20°00' Capricorn – Gemini pada

The 3rd pada of Shravana and 6th navamsha of Capricorn is Gemini. Mercury gains by being in its own sign. Gemini navamsha shows that here the soul also wants to embark on a new way of thinking. The thoughts are similar to those of the Gemini rashi but here the vibration is higher. No planet is exalted or debilitated.

20°00' to 23°20' Capricorn – Cancer pada

The 4th pada of Shravana and 7th navamsha of Capricorn is Cancer. This pada provides the most dramatic change for all planets placed here as they replace the restrictions of Saturn with the emotions of Cancer. But both the signs are connected to living on the edges of spirituality and materialism. All planets need to work on both areas. They cannot give up one for the other. This is the pada where the opposites do rule and need to be understood but in the end it is the Cancer issues that dominate; emotions, comfort and home.

Mars is weak internally as it is in an exalted rashi and debilitated pada. Mars is a warrior planet and this position shows that within it is peace-loving. Mars in Shravana Cancer pada may talk the talk and appear brave and courageous, but when it comes to taking action, they are not able to walk the walk.

Jupiter is exalted. The pada usually gives the final strength. This portion of Capricorn and Shravana exalts Jupiter so what appears as weakness suddenly becomes strength. The right kind of knowledge is imbibed, the right path is taken. The power of Vamana can be evident in this pada of Shravana, where wisdom triumphs over ego and power.

23. Dhanishta

23°20' Capricorn to 6°40' Aquarius
Padas: Leo, Virgo, Libra, Scorpio

Meaning

Dhani means wealthy and *Ishta* means complete, so Dhanishta is wealthy in mind and spirit. In ancient texts when the sages alluded to a person being wealthy, they meant that they had the wealth of good character, thoughts and actions. This was considered far superior than mere material wealth. Their nature is more spiritually inclined.

Spiritual wealth does not come easily to Dhanishta, but they can achieve it through selfless work, letting go of their personal egos and working with compassion and high ideals for the universal good. They have to fight for their rights, but also do a lot of service for others.

Dhanishta
Ruled by Mars
Devata: The Eight Vasus
Symbol: Mridanga and Bansuri
Yoni: Lion
Motivation is Dharma
Guna Triplicity: Sattva, Tamas and Tamas
Ayurvedic Dosha: Pitta
Body Part: Anus
Gana: Demon
Caste: Warrior
Quality: Mutable
Colours: Silver
Best Direction: East
Special Sounds: Ga, Ge, Go, Gay
The Principal Stars: Sa'd-as-Suud
Other Names for Dhanishta: Vasu, Shravishta

Devata – Ashta Vasus

Their deity is Ashta Vasu. Vasus are personifications of the Sun. *Vasu* means dweller or dwelling and *Ashta* means eight. They are eight elemental gods representing aspects of nature and cosmic natural phenomenon. The Ashta Vasus are:

Apas	Water
Dhruva	Steady, the Polestar
Soma	The Moon, Nectar of Immortality
Dhara	Support, Prithvi, Earth
Anila	Vayu, Wind

Anala	Agni, Fire
Pratyusha	Pre-dawn
Prabhas	Dyaus, Sky, Ether

These deities have a strong connection with the Sun and appear at different stages of manifestation to guide the soul towards its true direction. Vasus are connected to the nakshatra Punarvasu as well, where they guide the soul from the divine to the human. Here their guidance is the opposite. They are guiding Dhanishta to finish its earthly journey and begin the journey towards the divine. They transform the ideas from life experiences and use that knowledge to move towards the higher planes of existence.

Planetary Ruler – Mars

The ruling planet Mars is the planet of courage and action. Mars allows single-minded pursuit of dharmic responsibility. Dhanishta people have to conquer their inner demons and outer enemies (material desires). Mars is a warrior who defends and here his main role is to defend against negative desires, the forces that do not allow the soul to grow. Mars will also show immense courage to guard the soul while it assimilates its new spiritual direction.

Makara and Kumbha Rashi

Dhanishta spans two signs – Capricorn and Aquarius – both are ruled by Saturn. Dhanishta is very different here in Capricorn than in Aquarius. Capricorn Dhanishta people will want to be responsible in life and do their duty, and it is easy for them to get so involved in what others want to do – family, friends, children, parents – that they lose sight of what they want themselves. Aquarius Dhanishta wants to take on the responsibility of the world, earth issues, environment, etc.

Mars rules Dhanishta. Saturn rules Capricorn, and Saturn and Rahu rule Aquarius. Mars and Saturn are opposing energies, one standing for bravery and action and the other for caution and restrictions. Saturn forces Dhanishta to harness the powerful Mars energy. Dhanishta in Aquarius gets the added rulership of Rahu. Saturn will create responsibility and the ability to face pain, whereas Rahu fears that it may not be able to reach its objective. In Aquarius Dhanishta, Mars, Rahu and Saturn are conflicting energies and the planets placed here find themselves caught in an internal conflict which is the catalyst for change and transformation.

Symbol – Mridanga and Bansuri

Dhanishta is connected to the symbols of Mridanga, the drum, and Bansuri, the flute – Shiva's drum or Krishna's flute. The symbol of the drum or the flute implies it is beating to the rhythm of someone else; others are to play their song through this drum. Dhanishta's connection to both Shiva and Krishna shows the ability to connect to divine music. It suggests a general talent with music too.

Both the drum and the flute are hollow. This means emptiness within the Dhanishta person unless he finds something to fill it. Sometimes this can be a fruitless chasing of dreams, chasing or fulfilling other people's dreams. These people must learn to write their own music and fill their life with love and joy, or they may feel very empty and frustrated within. There is a need for higher knowledge and spiritual works to fill this void otherwise the soul feels empty and compensates with purely material stuff.

Puranic Myth: Dyaus – Bhishma and the Curse of Vashishta

Bhishma, the great-grandfather personality of Mahabharata, is the incarnation of Dyaus, one of the Ashta Vasu. The eight Vasus stole Nandini, the wish-fulfilling cow who was the daughter of Kamdhenu from Sage Vashishta's ashram, on the behest of Dyaus's wife. All were cursed by Sage Vashishta to be born on earth. The Vasus appealed to Vashishta for mercy. The seven Vasus had their curse modified so that they would be liberated from their human birth as soon as they were born; however Dyaus would have to endure a longer human birth.

Dyaus was born as Bhishma, the youngest son of the illustrious King Shantanu and goddess Ganga. Only Bhishma had to live a life on earth due to the curse; the other Vasus were freed by Ganga as soon as they were born. Goddess Ganga left King Shantanu as he decided to keep Bhishma as his son.

Bhishma means 'He of the Terrible Oath', referring to his vow of life-long celibacy and to be of service to whoever sat on the throne of his father. He denied himself the kingdom and marital happiness and lived the life of a loner so that his father could be happy and re-marry when Goddess Ganga left him. As he had made such a sacrifice, his father granted him a boon. He could choose the day he will die. This is known as Ichcha Mrityu. Bhishma was injured during Mahabharata, but he wanted to die on Makar Sankranti day which is the most auspicious day to die. He waited many days before the Sun changed course into Uttarayana to die. Dhanishta people have a strong personality, and are fearless, duty bound and willing to atone for their transgressions. It can be the life of a loner but this is generally self-imposed.

Dhanishta Aim for Dharma

The motivation of dharma is at its most potent at this stage. Shri Krishna taught dharma to Arjuna in Bhagavad Gita, 'the Divine Song' that is the essence of the Vedas. The setting of Bhagawad Gita is a battlefield and the war is against his family. But on a spiritual level, the war between Arjuna and his relatives is the war we fight daily when we are trying to conquer our desires, feelings and temptations. Lord Krishna guides Arjuna towards his duty – dharma – that is his destiny. This is the essence of dharma for Dhanishta.

Dhanishta's spiritual path is connecting to selfless service to humanity. For this they have to empty their soul of its desires and make themselves pure within. This state usually comes after a painful experience where they learn to let go of their egos and become a conduit for the higher powers that can be used for the good of humanity.

In some cases they will choose to have a celibate life as they want to be of service to the higher cause. It may be some experience in their early life or in their sub-conscious that stops them from forming relationships.

Sacred Animal – Narasimhi, Half Lioness, Half Woman

The animal for Dhanishta is the lioness. Narasimhi is the wife of Narasimha, half-lion, half-man incarnation of Vishnu, who was born to kill the demon Hiranyakashipu. Brahma granted him the boon that he would be killed neither by man, nor by animal, neither at night, nor at day, and neither outside nor inside the house. This demon became out of control, and he wanted everyone to worship him as God. Finally Vishnu took an Avatara as Narasimha, half-man, half-lion and killed Hiranyakashipu at dusk and in the doorway. His wife is Narasimhi, one of the Matrikas (mother goddesses). She was born to calm down Narasimha after he killed Hiranyakashipu. Narasimha was so angry that the gods believed that he would destroy the world if he was not pacified. Hence a fierce goddess was created with the body of a beautiful woman and head of a lioness. She managed to calm him down.

This link shows the fierceness of Dhanishta people but also the ability for calm if they have the right partnership. Narasimhi is fierce herself – so they need partners of equal intensity to help in their journey who are not afraid of tough situations. The lioness is usually regarded as tougher than the lion himself.

Ayurvedic Dosha is Pitta

Pitta is the fire in the belly that provides the fuel for Dhanishta to operate. They are inspired, active and goal orientated. They want to burn away all the dross of their life so that they are able to move on the next level of development. Pitta people need to be careful they do not allow the fire to burn uncontrolled or they might burn away even what was useful to them.

Lagna and Planets

Individuals with Danishta in the Ascendant feel their duty to others acutely. People can dump their problems on Dhanishta's shoulders regularly, so they must be aware why they take on these responsibilities and should avoid taking on useless ones as this will not allow their soul to move ahead.

The Sun feels both strong and weak in Dhanishta. The problem is, as the soul recognises its spirit, it needs to sacrifice personal needs for the global good. The Sun is not good at being of service; it has to learn to give.

People with the Moon in Dhanishta will feel the emotional need to give and this will not be always easy, but as the Dhanishta experience takes effect, the mind will adapt to their new reality. They can be selfless and giving but must consider their own needs too otherwise they can get drowned in the demands of others. They will learn to be detached yet responsible from a young age. They are stubborn and once they have made up their minds, they will not give up. The first dasha is Mars and while Mars as a first dasha is good, Rahu immediately follows it so Dhanishta

Moon people usually have an unusual start to life. These people can feel that they are outsiders even if they are leading conventional lives.

Mars is strong in Dhanishta. This is where it is at its exact exaltation degree at 28° Capricorn. It will defend the spirituality, look after others, thinking it is its dharma. This is an excellent position for Mars.

Mercury flourishes in Dhanishta. The reality of Dhanishta is very powerful. Mercury will learn about discipline but also learn about different levels of consciousness.

Jupiter struggles with changes and usually has a very practical outlook to life. In Dhanishta it is said that the soul takes a break from its spiritual journey to pay off any residual karma. Jupiter is not always comfortable with this as it can forget the more spiritual reason it adapted to the material life. When transit Jupiter moves into Dhanishta Aquarius, it is celebrated as Jupiter ends its debilitation. This is considered the time when the nectar of immortality was found and the darkness that incased humans disappeared. The Kumbha mela, is a great festival that is celebrated every twelve years in Prayag to honour Jupiter's transit into Dhanishta Aquarius. People with Jupiter in Aquarius Dhanishta find a way to deal with their shadows positively and develop their higher self that connects them back to the light.

Venus is not strong in the Capricorn part of Dhanishta. It feels attached to earthly desires and is unable to let them go even though there are higher responsibilities to fulfil.

Saturn will do all the service to others but will struggle with ego, especially in the Leo pada. It will become more drawn to service and taking on other people's responsibilities.

Rahu in Dhanishta usually searches for material wealth, and when that does not bring happiness, they search for the higher wealth. Then the soul begins an inner cleansing, of sorting out the inner demons to prepare the ground for divine aspirations. Ketu needs to remember many of the deeds it has done in the past life, where the soul worked hard to acquire this wealth through self-less work, letting go of its personal ego and working with compassion and high ideals. Ketu in Dhanishta people represent the inner cleansing of the soul to get it ready to receive divine music.

Padas in Danishta: Leo, Virgo, Libra, Scorpio
There is no vargottama and pushkara in Dhanishta. Ashtamamsha in its first pada brings unexpected transformations. This ashtamamsha shakes up the quality of all planets. The beginning of Hasta and the beginning of Dhanishta are the only two ashtamamsha that start the nakshatra, therefore these are significant changes taking place.

23°20' to 26°40' Capricorn – Leo pada
The 1st pada of Dhanishta and 8th navamsha of Capricorn is Leo. This is also ashtamamsha, creating sudden changes. The ashtamamsha in Capricorn brings ego issues to the selfless giving of both Capricorn and Dhanishta. It promises a major change. The ego struggles with responsibility and this creates problems for all the planets. Even the Sun suffers from being in its pada of Leo. No planets are debilitated or exalted, all will experience change, conflict and unexpected life events due to the ashtamamsha. The struggle between ego and responsibility is emphasised.

26°40' to 30°00' Capricorn – Virgo pada
The 2nd pada of Dhanishta and 9th navamsha of Capricorn is Virgo. This is where the message of Dhanishta is at its purest. Virgo helps with the service, it shows Dhanishta the way to deal with what Capricorn orders. This is the exact exaltation degree for Mars, Mercury is exalted and Venus debilitated.

Mars at 28° degrees Capricorn is in its exaltation degree. When Mars is in its exaltation degree do not expect these people to have easy personalities; they are combative and always willing to fight their corner. What is most interesting about the exaltation degree of Mars is that it is in its enemy sign and pada. Usually Virgo is a very difficult placement for Mars but now this pada exalts it. The position of Mars in Mercury's signs always gives it the ability to think and plan its actions, allows the warrior Mars to become a commander who is good at war and at strategy, whether it is for spiritual development, suppressing of desires, or making the world a better place for others to live in.

Mercury is exalted by pada. The intellectual Mercury finally understands the message of Capricorn and Dhanishta. To use the intellect for the good of others, to appreciate that there are other worlds out there beyond the one we are living in; other ways to develop the mind. The ideas are good for both practical living and for the spiritual quest.

Venus goes from practical Capricorn to the analytical Virgo. Dhanishta Venus people have to take care that they do not lose all the natural pleasures and become constrained by all the negativity. Venus is not able to realize its role as the creative power here, it is too practical and analytical and will question everything. It remains stuck in whichever groove it finds itself in. These people can be fussy and critical about life, pleasures, and relationships. Venus in this position has to let go of this attitude, learn to enjoy giving to others and ignore the more selfish desires.

3°20' to 6°40' Aquarius – Libra pada
The 3rd pada of Dhanishta and 1st navamsha of Aquarius is Libra. The Sun is debilitated and Saturn is exalted. The Sun is in difficulty, lacking confidence through being in an enemy sign and debilitated pada. These people have to think of others, learn to depend on them, and not be a loner. This is also a time to learn balance between the self and the other. So the Sun is unsure as it starts this journey; its glory and warmth can become depleted.

Saturn is in its own sign and exalted pada so is very strong. The need to remain humble and to break the negativity of ego is how Saturn expresses itself.

6°40' to 10°00' Aquarius – Scorpio pada
The 4th pada of Dhanishta and 2nd navamsha of Aquarius is Scorpio. The Moon and Rahu are troubled here. Ketu is exalted. All the planets have challenges as Aquarius and Scorpio are considered two of the most complex rashis and they combine with Dhanishta. Old karma in the shape of poisonous Scorpio issues needs to be dealt with before they can move on.

The Moon is uncomfortable in Aquarius and then goes into the intense debilitation of Scorpio. The mind is unsettled, searching for peace of mind, sometimes being struck in difficult situations. People with the Moon here will need to work toward spirituality, try to let go of their personal attachments and be humanitarian and think of others. Letting go will help them, but hanging on will create mental tensions.

Rahu desires it all for himself and will explore the dark deep secrets; there can be weakness from addictive personality disorders. These people have to be careful that they do not expose themselves to the wrong type of dependency. Rahu will attach too much worth to personal possessions but then there can be a huge transformation that makes them re-think their strategy. Ketu is exalted and will thrive. This recalls a past life where they paid homage to others, gave a life in service and learnt to use the sacred knowledge for the good of others. Now Ketu brings with it deep occult knowledge and intuition that helps these individuals to work with life as it is now. There is a talent for doing humanitarian works too.

24. Shatabhishak

6°40' to 20°00' Aquarius
Padas: Sagittarius, Capricorn, Aquarius, Pisces

Meaning

Shatabhishak can have many meanings. *Shat* means hundred and *Bhishak* means demons. *Abhishak* means healers, so this nakshatra can be both demonic and godly. Shatabhishak highlights the good and evil, both sides of man. Shatabhishak people are perpetually fighting with the negative forces within, trying to control the inner demons so that they can aspire towards the divine. They seek higher guidance to lead them from the darkness to the light. These aspirations are idealistic and great, but not everyone can achieve them. Most struggle to control their inner demons.

Shatabhishak
Ruled by Rahu
Symbol: The Hundred Stars
Devata: Varuna, The God of the Sea
Yoni: Horse
Motivation: Dharma
Guna Triplicity: Sattva, Tamas and Sattva
Ayurvedic Dosha: Vata
Body Part: Right Thigh
Gana: Demon
Caste: Butcher
Quality: Mutable
Colour: Aquamarine
Best Direction: South
Special Sounds: Go, Sa, Se, So
The Principal Stars: Sa'd-al-Akhbi-yah
Other Names for Shatabhishak are: Varuna, Apanpati, Neeresha, Jalesha

Shatabhishak individuals will try to hide these struggles from other people: they feel that if others really knew their true nature, they would not love or respect them. But they should not hide their true natures as people will be much more understanding than expected. It is the Shatabhishak tendency to secrecy and attempts to hide parts of their true nature that causes the trouble.

Devata – Varuna

Varuna is an ancient vedic god who rules the ocean and directs the Sun and the wind. He represents the night as this is the celestial ocean. He is said to have extraordinary powers to heal and rejuvenate through physic herbs and medicine and can save you from death and destruction. As the god of the oceans he controls the emotions and has the ability to bestow wisdom and change the direction of the mind. He rules both the law and the underworld. There are two sides of his nature – a brighter more positive side and a darker secretive one.

Shatabhishak people can be healers with a special knowledge of herbs and medicine. Like Varuna, they can be comfortable in both worlds (the lawful and the lawless). The message of Shatabhishak is to try not to go to the hidden, darker areas, but to recognise them as an essential part of man and learn to manage them so that they can be used to develop the higher self.

Planetary Ruler – Rahu

Rahu is the mental projection of the past life issues into the present, so these individuals become obsessed with externalising unfulfilled past life wishes through present experiences. The effect of Shatabhishak is to try to dampen the demonic and expose the godly.

Most interpretations only focus on the negative side of Rahu and Shatabhishak, the one linked to the demonic personality. This is only seeing half the picture. Once Shatabhishak people train their energy to become a positive force, they learn to heal their inner poisons and awaken to a glorious new world where they have the capacity to defy gravity, convention and make immense changes to their way of thinking.

The fears of negative forces can be very real, so they have to learn control and become masters of their destiny. As long as their demons control them, they find it difficult to express themselves.

Kumbha Rashi

Kumbha means the pot or pitcher. The word Kumbha is associated with Kumbhaka, a yogic practice of breath control. Breath is prana, the life within us. If we are able to retain and control our breath, we are able to control life. Symbolically, we are able to understand the secret of life and death.

The Samudra Manthan, Churning of the Oceans, took place when Jupiter was in Aquarius. Vishnu took the form of Kurma Avatar to form a secure base for finding the Amrita. [7]

---

7. Read more about it in my book *The Lunar Nodes – Crisis and Redemption*.

Saturn and Rahu rule Aquarius. It is not an easy sign. There is work to be done. As the individual starts to break free from their ego and work in accordance with cosmic law, traditional ideas and worldly attachments are destroyed. Saturn is ruthless in forcing them to recognise the final goals. The Aquarius impulse is on a thinking level not an emotional one. Aquarius' pitcher can only pour forth its water of universal life if it is broken, symbolising the need for the final breaking down of the individual personality. People with Shatabhishak in Aquarius are forced to work for the good of all rather than for personal ambitions.

Symbol – The Hundred Stars

The Shatabhishak symbol is the hundred stars, which shows the deep connection of Shatabhishak with the cosmos and past karma. The stars are supposed to be silent watchers of the game of life; they resemble the lotus of thousand petals, the symbol of *Sahasara Chakra* (the Crown Chakra) which represents the highest power within our astral body. When you reach the highest understanding of your spiritual path, it flowers and gives the ability to transcend the restrictions that destiny and past karma have imposed. The flowering of the Sahasrara lotus indicates the complete flowering of the inner beauty when the trappings of material life are no longer required and the soul is fully connected to the divine.

Shatabhishak people can join completely with the divine, though most are on the path of trying to make the connection. The flower blooms for the joy of others so by working for the good of others the divine can flower within them too. The practice required for the Sahasrara chakra to open is not an easy one and usually shows an old soul who has been working towards it for many lifetimes.

Puranic Myth – Valmiki

The story of changing negative qualities to positive resonates with the story of Sage Valmiki. He was a robber before he found the true path. Valmiki is revered as the Adi Kavi, which means First Poet, for he discovered the first shloka (verse) of sanskrit which set the base and form of Sanskrit poetry. He is credited with writing the great epic Ramayana and Yoga Vashishta.

Maharishi Valmiki was born as Ratnakara to sage Prachetasa. He got lost as a child in the forest and was fostered by a hunter. Unable to look after his family, Ratnakara became a robber. One day he tried to rob the great sage Narada, who asked him this important question: "If you are robbing in the name of your family, have you ever asked them if they are happy to share this sin?" When Ratnakara's family refused to be part of his sins, he went back to sage Narada to ask for forgiveness. Narada told him that in order to get redemption Valmiki should do tapas (austerity) by chanting the name of Rama and sitting in meditation till the time Narada came back. Ratnakara kept doing tapas for many years, during which time his body became completely covered by an anthill. At last, when Narada came back, he told Ratnakara that his tapasya had paid off and he had gained divine blessings. Ratnakara was bestowed with the honour of a Brahma rishi and given the name of Valmiki, since he was reborn from the Valmika (the ant-hill).

Shatabhishak can sometimes make mistakes, and do wrong deeds but can find redemption and reach the highest pinnacle of spirituality.

Shatabhishak Aim for Dharma

The motivation of dharma is at its final intensity now as this is the last nakshatra to reflect it. Shatabhishak people know about doing the right thing; they have fought the battles with their desires and won, they have learnt the lesson of letting go of their ego, and the dharma here is to be connected to doing the right thing by themselves. They do not need to prove their dharmic self to others, they know what lies between their final realisation is only their mind.

The Shatabhishak spiritual life path is about letting the mind merge with the consciousness rather than allowing it to block the process; a clever and intelligent mind will at times become a block to understanding the infinite forces of nature as it tries to understand everything using logic rather than trusting the inner voice. Shatabhishak people should let go of their individuality, allow themselves to expand the mind and venture into the unknown.

Sacred Animal – Hayagriva

The animal for Shatabhishak is the horse. The story of Hayagriva is very interesting as in mythology he is both an avatar of Vishnu and a demon. He is worshipped as the god of knowledge and wisdom, with a human body and a horse's head, brilliant white in color, with white garments, and seated on a white lotus. Symbolically, the story represents the triumph of pure knowledge guided by the hand of God over the demonic forces of passion and darkness.

The Vedas had been stolen by the demons Madhu and Kaitabha – and in some stories Hayagriva rescues and returns them, while in others this role is given to Matsaya, Avatara of Lord Vishnu, and Hayagriva is the taker of the Vedas. Hayagriva tells the story of Shatabhishak showing both sides of man – demonic and godly. Often it generates confusion but for those who can learn to manage the demonic energy, the light can shine brightly.

Ayurvedic Dosha is Vata

Shatabhishak individuals can have nervous minds. Their restlessness creates lots of physical and mental stress. This sign is so connected to psychological blocks that vata further aggravates it. The mind is in such a hurry to find the answers, it sucks up all its energy to the crown. The vata energy needs to be calmed, otherwise there is a possibility of a mental overload.

Lagna and Planets

People with the ascendant placed here are very idealistic, yet if they are not careful they can be full of fear that they cannot achieve what they want to do. They need to stop considering themselves and start working for others. They can be very stormy and not easy to get along with.

The Sun placed in Shatabhishak can make for unreliable people. Their life is caught between shadow and light. At times they feel they live up to their standard and at others they detest their weaknesses. They will not be up front about who they are and this can cause problems. Those who take refuge in the coolness of their shade feel grateful but those who feel obscured by their shadowy presence can feel only fear.

The Moon in Shatabhishak struggles with darkness and light – these people have two sides to their personality that can perpetually frustrate them until they start to think of others and forget their own inner dilemma. They can be like a shadow, elusive and unreliable. As people try to chase shadows, they realise they are intangible, and consequently that they may never really know a Shatabhishak person. Thus Shatabhishak Moon individuals feel lonely and isolated, yet are responsible for this loneliness themselves. As they are unable to confide in others, they feel they are not as good as others think they are. Their need to hide makes them unreliable, so others do not trust them. They have special talents with herbs and healing. The first dasha of Rahu would be tough to deal with as it carries fears within the psyche of not being able to complete the divine mission. This is never an easy nakshatra to work with unless you understand its higher vibrations. As a child, it can make you feel like an outsider even among friends and family.

Mars will be strong in this nakshatra, as it always reacts to challenges, but there can be underlying passions to struggle with.

Mercury is troubled by this position; the mind is disturbed by the Shatabhishak energy. There can be fears and dilemmas; the world cannot be put in one rational equation. As long as these people try to be conventional thinkers the position is difficult but if they stretch themselves and work on higher levels of thought, the mind becomes productive.

Jupiter works on the higher self. The mind is encouraged to go towards spirituality, so that it can deal with the fear of its weaknesses. There is enough wisdom to recognise the failings and turn the person around.

Venus helps the lotus to bloom. A person will be wise, have the ability to give advice to others, be profound, with knowledge of herbs and healing.

Saturn will face the music and be realistic. It is naturally concerned with uplifting others, so it will control the less salubrious desires of Shatabhishak. Saturn rules Aquarius and Rahu acts like Saturn. This double saturnine influence is difficult to handle unless activities are directed towards serving humanity. The struggles of Shatabhishak can be acute but the reward can be the opening of the doorway to the cosmic connection.

Rahu can be both demonic and spiritual. It can be elusive, untrustworthy, fickle, and full of fear, but if it understands its fears and stops the play of shadows, it can reverse the trends, become highly spiritual and create a deep connection with the cosmos and be divine. Ketu is very spiritual. It is in Rahu's signs and nakshatra, so it can confuse the past with the present. Ketu can struggle to suppress the demons from past lives. Awareness of past lives is essential and effort needs to be made to try to disconnect the past troubles from the present. This position can churn up the emotions unless we learn to let go.

Padas in Shatabhishak: Sagittarius, Capricorn, Aquarius, Pisces

The padas of Shatabhishak represent the end of the pada cycle. This is the ending of the 8th cycle of spiritual growth and the 2nd one in the world of sattva. The soul destroys one way of thinking as it prepares for the final journey which will lead it back to merge with the source. The vibration of Shatabhishak is high. The third pada is vargottama and the fourth one is pushkara.

6°40' to 10°00' Aquarius – Sagittarius pada

The 1st pada of Shatabhishak and 3rd navamsha of Aquarius is Sagittarius. Whereas in Sagittarius rashi the soul is aspiring for the spiritual and learning to differentiate the man from the animal, in Sagittarius pada of Aquarius the spiritual path has been adopted and mankind has to reconcile with the residual demons that block its path to a new level of spiritual understanding. No planets are debilitated or exalted – everyone learns to fight their own wars.

6°40' to 10°00' Aquarius – Capricorn pada

The 2nd pada of Shatabhishak and 4th navamsha of Aquarius is Capricorn. This exalts Mars and debilitates Jupiter.

Mars is strong in its exalted pada. It will show immense courage to follow the path of its convictions. It will be able to control the demons that the other planets struggle to do.

Jupiter has a moment of pure darkness. It appears that old issues have come to haunt these individuals. There is an attachment to practical things as the soul tries to hang onto them. As the planet of spirituality, Jupiter is showing a deep underlying weakness and these are the demons that will haunt Jupiter. These individuals will feel unworthy within. They may pretend to be spiritual and practical, and this falseness can haunt them. Remember that this is a highly developed Jupiter that is facing some of its demons on the final path of moksha. The whole energy is not corrupted so the lower energy must not be allowed to gain control.

6°40' to 10°00' Aquarius – Aquarius pada
The 3rd pada of Shatabhishak and 5th navamsha of Aquarius is the vargottama Aquarius. People with Vargottama navamsha are always integrated with whatever their path is. Even if it is challenging, the fact that it is vargottama makes the planets feel comfortable in it. As this is Aquarius, the quality is spiritual, humanitarian, and working for the world. Therefore the planets have a good agenda. This can be the pada where the ocean was churned. No planet is exalted or debilitated in this pada.

16°40' to 20°00' Aquarius – Pisces pada
The 4th pada of Shatabhishak and 6th navamsha of Aquarius is in Pisces. This is a pushkara nakshatra, so all the planets will do well here. The dilemma of Shatabhishak gets its best possible outcome. The planets manage to conquer their demons and work to create new energy for the final steps towards moksha. The ego is broken and the waters of Aquarius flow freely. This can be the pada where the Amrita was found after the churning of the oceans. This is the exaltation pada for Venus, its own for Jupiter and debilitation for Mercury. Being Pushkara, even Mercury can deal with its debilitation.

Mercury's debilitation may see these people make silly choices on a material level. They may not be worldly wise but this is because they have surrendered their rational thinking to work with the world beyond their recognition. They know that they need to make the changes and they do. They know what is right for them spiritually so they have to learn to make proper decisions on a material level.

Venus is ready to co-operate with the grand plan of creation. It will submerge its identity into the cosmic emotions, the water will flow easily and the spirituality and good points of the individual will rise up. They will be in charge of their demons and the healing qualities surface.

25. Purva Bhadra

20°00'Aquarius to 3°20' Pisces
padas: Aries, Taurus, Gemini, Cancer

Meaning

Purva Bhadra is connected to Uttara Bhadra. While having distinct personalities, they form a singular principle that is split into two opposing forces. Jupiter rules Purva and Saturn rules Uttara. Together they represent the Sun and Moon, darkness and light, fire and water, heat and cold, masculine and feminine, the lion and the cow.

Purva means first and *Bhadra* has many meanings: beautiful, auspicious, blessed, gracious and happy. The blessings usually come from good deeds from past lives, which are now experienced as good luck. Indian good luck is not connected to financial wealth alone. Good fortune means having a good family, excellent relationships, wonderful children and a good life, where knowledge and wisdom guide us to find the true beauty. This is not physical beauty, but the loveliness of a good soul and spiritual inner being.

Purva Bhadra
Ruled by Jupiter
Devata: Aja Ekapada - The One Footed Goat
Symbol: The Sword
Yoni: Lion
Motivation: Artha
Guna Triplicity: Sattva, Sattva and Rajas
Ayurvedic Dosha: Vata
Body Part: Left Thigh
Gana: Human
Caste: Brahmin
Quality: Fierce
Colours: Silver
Best Direction: West
Special Sounds: Say, So, Da, De
The Principal Stars: Al-Fargh-Al-Mukdim
Other Names for Purva Bhadra: Ajpada, Acharna, Ajanghri

Purva Bhadra relates to the position where the true meaning of life has been understood and revealed. It teaches the lesson of being at peace within itself, to lead life with no expectation of personal rewards, glorification or ambitions.

Devata – Aja Ekapada

The ruling deity is Aja Ekapada – the one footed goat. *Aja* means the unborn, *Eka* one and pada, feet. Aja Ekapada is a form of Rudra, closely linked to Shiva. He is connected to Surya and Agni, the holy fire. Aja

Ekapada relates to infinity, where there is no sound or motion, where there is an outward stillness with creative energies bubbling underneath. It raises our spiritual aspiration in life. The Rudras battle with the demons in order to protect the Gods and humans.

The goat gives milk, lives alone and is silent or unborn. It cannot articulate its inner desires. It does not need any kind of nourishment from others, yet it sustains life. A goat may not be necessarily physically attractive, but it reveals its beauty by giving and supporting life.

The ugliness of the goat would be the residue karma that holds Purva Bhadra back. Purva Bhadra people can feel ugly because on a subtle level they are seeing the issues of their karma clearly and these are not appealing. This can make them suffer with image problems in the material world. Aja Ekapada are creating for the future, there are many hidden talents within Purva Bhadra too, some that are ripe to express now but others that may be of use in future lives.

Planetary Ruler – Jupiter

Jupiter is *Brihaspati*, the advisor/guru of the gods. Knowledge is the key. Jupiter stands for expansion, happiness and higher knowledge and it represents the positive fruits of past karma, which bring forth conditions in this life of affluence, comfort and happiness. Jupiter's main concern is to give a good material life so the individual can concentrate of the essential spiritual development.

Jupiter rules the nakshatras where guidance is required. He guides Purva Bhadra on a journey to the divine and can be a teacher who advises others in their path to self realisation.

Kumbha and Mina Rashi

Purva Bhadra is mostly in Aquarius with one pada in Pisces. In Aquarius, Saturn rules the sign and Jupiter the nakshatra. Saturn and Jupiter represent the duality of expansion and restriction, which finally makes for the eternal balance. In Aquarius, Saturn will still stop Purva Bhadra from achieving all its aims. There are still responsibilities to be fulfilled for humanity, the ego issues to be worked out. Material life still has a say here. The soul must be conscious of its karmic responsibilities. Jupiter becomes a guide during this tough balancing act.

In Pisces, Jupiter rules both sign and nakshatra. This is where the final push for self realisation takes place. The soul is extremely mature yet can make immature mistakes as it feels driven to be at one with the cosmic plan. Pisces only wants to merge with the eternal. As the nakshatras come towards their end, the soul becomes less attached to the material world and is more spiritually concerned; however these people need to recognise that they still have to live in the practical world too.

Symbol – The Sword
The symbol is the sword, an instrument which can be used to attack as well as to defend. The sword cuts through any restrictions and it symbolises a fight for universal causes; it was used for many religious and spiritual causes as well as nefarious reasons. People have been immensely cruel using the power of the sword as well as good in defending the weak so the sword represents an instrument for furthering an ideal. The quality of the ideal is in the hands of the users; the question is how they go about achieving that ideal. The pen has also been considered a verbal sword.

Purva Bhadra individuals can be dynamic in furthering their cause and will not hold back from fighting for it. They can cut through negativity and see the path clearly if they use their sword wisely.

Puranic Myth – The Story of Two Bhadra
The twinning of the Bhadra nakshatras shows a connection to the two Bhadra – Bhadra Kali, the auspicious and fortunate form of Kali, and Bhadra, the sister of Shani who has a much more fearsome energy. Bhadra Kali is considered the consort of Shiva in the form of Rudra. Kali is the Universal Power. She is both benign and terrible. She creates and nourishes as well as kills and destroys. Through her magic we see both good and bad, but in reality there is neither. The whole world is the play of Maya, the veiling power of the Divine Mother. God is neither good nor bad, nor both. God is beyond the pair of opposites which constitute this relative existence.

Purva Bhadra can relate to the great goddess and she showers blessings on the people who understand about the play of Maya or illusion. They learn to see beyond the weakness and strengths to the true vision of the divine with detachment.

The link to Purva Bhadra of the sword symbol and Bhadra Kali can make them very good at martial arts and always ready to right wrongs. Read more on Saturn's sister Bhadra in Uttara Bhadra.

Purva Bhadra Aim for Artha

Artha usually means work or wealth creating activities. On a subtle level Artha means 'the answer'. Purva Bhadra people look beyond the Artha of the practical life and search for answers in the cosmos, from being in harmony with creation. Purva Bhadra will also be good at practical expression of Artha by supporting those who need it and the desire to create support systems from which others can benefit.

Purva Bhadra people are spirituality itself. Their path is connected with giving. Their karma is compassion, kindness and fight for injustice. Their inner self is connected to the purity of the Sun, that reflects its beneficence for the good of all, to the selflessness of Jupiter that gives without expectation of return, and finally to Aja Ekapada, the silent one footed goat who sustains others while being totally self-reliant.

Animal Sign – Lion, The Vahana of Durga

The lion is the animal for goddess Durga, the embodiment of feminine power. She is the shakti of Shiva and was born to save the world from the demon Mahisha. (Read how she slayed the buffalo demon in Swati nakshatra.) She always rides the lion which is the fiercest animal, and her ability to ride it indicates that she can control the savagery of the lower urges. There are many forms of Durga and in north India she is called Sheranwali or the goddess with the lion. In this incarnation she is prayed to as Vaishno Devi and one of the most popular temples for Devi worship is in Jammu, Kashmir.

The lion is the king of the Jungle. Purva Bhadra people can be in positions of power. They may have a powerful inner personality. Having the lion as their animal can symbolise their strong urges and ego that must be mastered on the path of self realisation. Durga the deity fights a fierce war to protect the devas, and Bhadrakali joins in. The sword is also a symbol of war. This war needs to be thought of metaphorically as the war at the final stages of self-realisation that planets in Purva Bhadra fight to calm their lower self.

Ayurvedic Dosha is Vata

Vata is discontentment, inconsistency, and agitation. Purva Bhadra people keep their tensions and conflicts buried deep within themselves. They are worriers and can fret mostly about worldly issues: the world, environment, fair play, truth. They will hardly worry about themselves. This consumes their inner energy as everyday there can be a new issue to worry about. They use up their entire fund of resources for the good of humanity.

Lagna and Planets

All individuals with planets in Purva Bhadra are seeking answers, but the questions they ask are becoming more and more complex; there are no easy answers.

Someone with the lagna placed here is seeking within and is a very spiritual being. They need to know more, yet learning more and more does not satisfy as the answer is elusive. They have to stop asking questions and assimilate what they know so far as they are on a journey of self-discovery and their personality emerges as they develop.

People with the Sun here will be unsure if the path they are on is the right one. There is the other half of the conundrum they do not yet know. If they decide to undertake an internal journey and trust their acquired wisdom, all will be revealed. They can be strong like the lion, yet will lack confidence on how to express their strength.

Neither will the Moon know the entire picture. It will try to find the answers and be strong-minded about what it understands, but the duality of Purva Bhadra can make these people lack confidence. They are spiritual yet adventurous, seeking to find solutions with their new-found spirituality. This can be a problem for practical purposes as this is not a very materialistic Moon. The first dasha will be of Jupiter, which is usually good, but Saturn follows it. Depending on how long the Jupiter dasha is, Purva Bhadra can soon experience the restrictions of Saturn and learn about the two sides of its nature. There are still some worldly issues to resolve before it can totally submerge itself in being one with the divine.

Mars will bring out the aggression of Purva Bhadra and these people will be at their best fighting for the causes that are dear to them. They can feel acutely about spirituality and materialism. The duality of existence can frustrate them.

Mercury people will try to reason with the situation they find themselves in. This can create a fiery intellect that uses its knowledge to write, think and talk about fighting the causes dear to them. But they may not take any action.

Jupiter is in its own nakshatra. The soul has to understand how to use wisdom for higher matters. It can be a good guide, philosopher and mentor, but there can be a problem if these people ignore their own advice and lack confidence in what they are. They can unnecessarily restrict themselves to seeking answers in the material world, whereas they should try trusting their inner wisdom.

Venus people will develop a more alternative personality, they care for others but often do not know all the answers. Purva Bhadra shows that this life is a journey to purity and Venus can show many forms in this nakshatra, from the adventurous to the divine.

Saturn has no attraction for worldly things. The karma has been fulfilled and the new energy is about letting go of time, giving up the material responsibilities. Saturn must learn that its caution still has a role to play. The wisdom acquired through personal effort is still important.

Rahu always knows that his personality is not perfect, and through the shadows of its realm it strives to bring out its elusive beauty. Individuals with this placement can suffer from a poor self-image as they think of themselves in terms of the ugly goat and fail to recognise the purity of the intention hidden behind their fears. Rahu struggles with the crystallizing karma; the restrictions imposed by past life crises and mental blockages. Ketu suggests previous lives where the soul had almost reached its state of perfection when it chose to be re-born. The soul struggles to accept the material rewards, as it will create desires that can lead to pain and sorrow. Ketu in Purva Bhadra gives the soul courage to change the course of its life.

Padas in Purva Bhadra: Aries, Taurus, Gemini, Cancer

This is the beginning of the 9th and final cycle of soul development. Planets here are divine and working on deep spiritual energies even if they do not appear to be. There is no ashtamamsha and vargottama. Two padas are pushkara.

20°00' to 23°20' Aquarius – Aries pada

The 1st pada of Purva Bhadra and the 7th navamsha of Aquarius is Aries. The Sun is exalted and Saturn is debilitated by the pada.

The Sun is strong in its exalted pada. These people are able to work for others, yet remain true to themselves. They nurture this purity and idealism; they will fight for what is right and be confident, although their mission is to guard the spirit of humanity and protect people.

Saturn is unsure of what it needs to do due to its debilitation. It can make the wrong effort. There can be anger and frustration. The self-image is bad and these people can be unwilling to shoulder responsibility. They can regress from staid to childish in one breath. Aries is their testing ground as it gives a new way of looking at life and it will take Saturn time to adjust.

23°20' to 26°40' Aquarius – Taurus pada

The 2nd pada of Purva Bhadra and the 8th navamsha of Aquarius is Taurus. This is an exalted pada for the Moon and Rahu and debilitated for Ketu. It is also pushkara so it helps all the planets.

The Moon is happy, and these individuals will be settled on their spiritual path. This shows a mind that has accepted the new paths forged by Aquarius Purva Bhadra and is learning to detach.

Rahu placed here is exalted and will find peace. The person will be conscious of their duality but aware that both sides want the same thing. The desires will become less troublesome. Ketu people are not happy at the blocks of materialism that Taurus represents. They feel that they did not fulfill their mission in the past life. Ketu can feel uncomfortable here as Taurus pada debilitates. Usually pushkara suggests that they come to terms with it.

26°40 to 30°00 Aquarius – Gemini pada

The 3rd pada of Purva Bhadra and 9th navamsha of Aquarius is Gemini. Planets will be intellectually charged and thinking about how to assimilate the quality mentally. Thinking about the path they are on and where their spiritual direction is taking them is important for all planets. These are thoughts that can hinder spiritual progress yet they are essential for the growth process.

0°00' to 3°20' Pisces – Cancer pada

Only one pada of Purva Bhadra is in Pisces. The 4th pada of Purva Bhadra and 1st navamsha of Pisces is Cancer. This is the most auspicious place of the Bhadra where there is understanding and assimilation of its spiritual journey. Mars is debilitated, so decisive action has no place in spiritual thought. Jupiter is exalted. All planets benefit from the blessings of Jupiter and the pushkara navamsha.

Mars gets debilitated and emotion clouds the warrior's actions. Here the Purva Bhadra sword will only be for peaceful purposes. This is also a Pushkara navamsha so even Mars debilitation has a different kind of strength where there is courage to develop ideas and become the true defender who gives peace a chance.

Jupiter is in one of the best positions in the zodiac, in its own sign, nakshatra and exaltation. Higher knowledge, wisdom, right expansion, and the nurturing of the seed of creation will all be promoted by Jupiter.

26. Uttara Bhadra

3°20' to 16°40' Pisces
Padas: Leo, Virgo, Libra, Sagittarius

Meaning

Uttara Bhadra is an extension of the previous nakshatra, Purva Bhadra. While having distinct personalities, they form a singular principle that is split into two opposing forces. Jupiter rules Purva and Saturn rules Uttara so together they represent Sun and Moon, light and darkness, fire and water, heat and cold, masculine and feminine, the lion and the cow. Uttara represents the latter qualities. Jupiter bestows wisdom in Purva Bhadra and Saturn rewards all the trials and tribulations in Uttara Bhadra. *Uttara* means higher and *Bhadra* has many meanings. Beautiful, auspicious, blessed, gracious and happy. All aspects highlight the positive qualities that Uttara Bhadra are blessed with. The blessings usually come from good deeds in past lives, which are now being experienced as good luck. The blessings are on a higher, a more subtle plane, as the soul wants more than just the ordinary.

Uttara Bhadra
Ruled by Saturn
Devata: Ahir Budhyana
Symbol: The Twins
Yoni: Cow
Motivation: Kama
Guna Triplicity: Sattva, Sattva and Tamas
Ayurvedic Dosha: Pitta
Body Part: Shins
Gana: Human
Caste: Warrior
Quality: Fixed
Shakti: Stabalizing
Colours: Purple
Best Direction: North
Special Sounds: Du, Tha, Aa, Jna
The Principal Stars: Al-Fargh-Al-Mukdim
Other Names for Uttara Bhadra: Ahir Budhanaya

Uttara Bhadra people can remain passive and non-active until an event or happening makes them change their perception of life altogether. Then the journey of looking beyond their immediate circumstances begins and spirituality grows. Their need to transcend ordinary life makes it difficult for them to have traditional relationships.

Devata – Ahir Budhnya

Ahir Budhnya is linked to Soma (the Moon). He is one of the Eleven Rudras. It is associated with water and darkness. The passivity of darkness is the mysterious source from which all forms of creation have arisen. Ahir Budhnya is the deep ocean snake representing the merging of consciousness into the deep sea of eternity. The serpent represents wisdom. The water snake needs to come to the surface to breathe, therefore the soul of Uttara Bhadra cannot remain in water (spirituality) forever; it needs to periodically connect with the real world.

Ahir means a cowherd and *Ahi* means a snake and a cow. This nakshatra straddles the opposite aspects of human nature. The snake represents poisons, but can also show the ability to deal with them. The cow personifies an auspicious good nature, the need to care and nurture the world. The snake part of the nakshatra sheds its skin through painful life experiences and reveals its better nature, while Ahir as the cowherd shows the ability to shepherd the auspiciousness, to deal with the toxins.

Ahir Budhnya is the son of Vishwakarma, the celestial architect (see Chitra nakshatra). Here the architect is laying the foundations for the next life time by doing the deeds now. Recognizing the contribution of this life leads to the smooth running of future lives. Ahir Budhnya produced 80 million invincible trident-holding secondary Rudras who were spread in all directions to protect mankind.

Planetary Ruler – Saturn
Saturn is the great teacher of cosmic truths and his influence is tough to deal with. Uttara Bhadra has the blessing to use the lessons of Saturn in the best possible way.

Saturn is the planet of karmic retribution; it keeps an account of all the past acts and releases this karma unexpectedly. Faced with such powerful karmic forces Uttara Bhadra people have to dig deep into their inner resources. In childhood, teens and young adulthood, this causes frustration as Saturn restricts the natural energy from expanding. With maturity they learn to use the Saturn forces properly, and start on the path towards self-realisation. Saturn deals with karma on a very finite level. The karmic debts still to be paid or the unfulfilled desires may be blocking the final doorway to the higher self for Uttara Bhadra. If they understand and reconcile, they can move towards the final transformation of the soul.

Mina Rashi

The Pisces fish are not like the Cancer crab or the Capricorn crocodile – they cannot live out of water. Pisces wants only to be spiritual. The great ocean appears infinite and silent yet there are many under currents within it. Pisces people can appear calm yet their mind may be turbulent as they try to understand universal truth. They know we all have to bow to cosmic law. They have the strength to face the ups and downs of this life because they accept the restrictions of the material world and allow their minds to submerge themselves in the eternal.

Pisces is a highly spiritual sign. The padas within it create the final blocks in finding self realisation. This is not a sign where the material skills are good. They have to try hard to stay grounded or they can make wrong, even foolish choices in the material world.

Symbol – The Twins

Uttara Ashadha represent duality in every form. It is one of the Bhadras; it has found light so it must go into darkness, it is sattvic therefore it embraces tamas. Uttara Ashadha loses interest in life yet has to live successfully in this world. The twin reflects the splitting of the atom, the gravitational pull of the earth. All these polarities make this nakshatra extremely complex and full of intuitive energies.

Puranic Myth – Bhadra, Saturn's Sister

There are two Bhadras – Bhadra Kali and Bhadra, the daughter of the Sun and sister of Saturn. Both Kali and Bhadra have a fierce form and a spiritual energy. We have to go beyond the apparent fierceness of these deities in order to find the divine. Bhadra, the sister of Saturn is extremely ferocious. She is described as having a huge body, face of donkey, three legs, seven arms, is black in colour with a long tail and fire emerging from her mouth. She has eyes like cowrie shells and emanates a sound like thunder. She smears her body with ash, wears clothes made from shrouds and rides on dead bodies in the cremation ground. She forcefully attacked an army of demons and massacred them. The gods, happy with her ferocious protection, granted her the rulership of the eighth movable karana.[8] This karana is also called Vishti and reflects Saturn's energy.

---

8. Karana is one of the limbs of Panchanga. Panchanga is studied to analyse the quality of the day. Read more in *Personal Panchanga*.

This time is considered inauspicious to begin new projects as the fiery nature of Bhadra Devi consumes the good energy. Yet Bhadra is there to protect, just like Kali – her persona of negativity is just how we view the forces of nature. Read more on Bhadra Kali in Purva Bhadra.

Uttara Bhadra can have a fierce nature and in extreme cases have a persona similar to Bhadra, and this can appear as a weakness.

Uttara Bhadra Aim is for Kama

The motivation of kama or passion is not connected to sexual passion but to the intense passion to merge with the unconscious, to use the talents for the good of humanity. The passion and dynamism are all reflected on a spiritual mode.

The Uttara Bhadra spiritual path is connected to living life successfully on earth but remaining detached from it. The state of being is such that the attachment to material pleasures has ended, but there is still a distance to go to the end of the road to enlightenment.

Sacred Animal – the Five Cows of Shiva

The cow is the most sacred animal in India and its link to Uttara Bhadra suggests the honour and respect that these people can command. Uttara Bhadra is about transition and immortality. The connection to Shiva and his holy ash explains more about the mystical power of Uttara Bhadra. Kalagni Rudra is one of the eleven Rudras, a form of Shiva. He teaches the greatness of the sacred ash. Lord Shiva is depicted as having five faces that are linked to the five great elements. From each of these Shiva emanated a particular power and from that power a special holy cow was born and each produced a type of sacred ash. This is the ash that is worn by all Shiva devotees. Knowing the secret of the holy Ash and its use is to understand the key of Shiva, Shakti, Sun and Moon and transcending death.

Form of Shiva	Element	Power	Sacred Cow	Holy Ash
Sadhyojatha	Earth	Bliss	Nanda	Vibhuti
Vamadeva	Water	Awakening	Bhadra	Bhasitha
Aghora	Fire	Knowledge	Surabhi (Kamdhenu)	Bhasma
Tatpurusha	Air	Peace	Sushila	Kshara
Ishana	Ether	Protection	Suman	Raksha

Vibhuti, Bhasitha, Bhasma, Kshara and Raksha are five different names of the holy ash. Vibhuti gives wealth, Bhasma removes the sins, Bhasitha makes life glitter, Kshara protects from dangers and Raksha acts like a shield.

Uttara Bhadra represents the ability to gain this secret knowledge and with it to transcend its ties to the material world.

Ayurvedic Dosha is Pitta

Pitta people are adventurous and determined. Uttara Ashadha people use this dosha to take them into the sea of nothingness, which gives them the dynamism to make this difficult task a reality. There is no nervousness of vata or the philosophy and laid back approach of kapha. Pitta people use their grit and determination to make the impossible happen.

Lagna and Planets

All planets struggle with letting go of the deeper negative qualities in Uttara Bhadra. These are not immediately visible to the person as they have to work through them in this lifetime. Often certain weaknesses can erupt suddenly or come to light and they need to deal with these aspects before they are ready to move on spiritually.

The lagna placed shows a mind ready to submerge into the world of spirituality but material aspects keep getting in the way. These people need to work with their karmic responsibilities first and only then are able to advance further. The position of Saturn and Jupiter will give a clearer picture.

People with the Sun in Uttara Bhadra should try to sublimate their egos. They can be generous, giving and spiritual, yet ego and arrogance can get in the way. They are full of knowledge and unless they learn humility, they cannot experience the full advantage of their wisdom.

Moon people will be very bright but have to be particularly careful of their poisonous tendencies. They will be very spiritual but there are underlying ways of thinking that block future growth. So while they can be creative and idealistic, it is their own ways of thinking that limit their progress. Life will bring changes for them to truly find their way. The Uttara Bhadra Moon understands about blessings on a higher, more subtle plane. The soul wants more than just the ordinary. The first dasha of Saturn can cause frustration, even misery in childhood and teens, as it restricts the natural energy from expanding. These people may shoulder adult responsibilities as a child. With maturity, if these people learn to use the Saturn forces properly, they can start on the path towards self-realisation.

Mars people have the courage to swim these choppy waters which comes from an inner wisdom to face life. There can be turbulent emotions and anger issues that erupt like a volcano unless addressed. Sexual desires can be a problem too as Uttara Bhadra wants to be an ascetic while Mars wants passion.

Mercury is debilitated in Uttara Bhadra. Its rational intellect does not work well here. It can get swamped by emotional issues and not know how to deal with this sea of spirituality where the language is different. While this is an excellent position for writers and for working with your imagination, purely from practical point of view Mercury can feel a failure. These individuals need to work on the practical side of their nature or they can make mistakes and be susceptible to wrong judgements.

Jupiter will revel in the spirituality of Uttara Bhadra and enjoy the fruits of a life lived on spiritual terms. This is a great position for teachers and those with deep knowledge of esoteric wisdom. They have to be careful that they don't misuse this wisdom, but that can only happen if there are negative aspects to Jupiter.

Venus is working towards sowing the seed of creation and ideas for future generations. These people will want to experience good relationships, be giving and generous. There will be changes in life, and maybe some dissatisfaction with relationships, despite Venus being exalted. Material relationships can fail to satisfy them fully as they want to make a more divine connection, demanding perfection and purity. They need to recognise their partners are an expression of the divine and if they change their attitude to love it can be beautiful.

Saturn benefits from its own nakshatra, using the practical life to clear the final hurdles to spiritual evolution. These people must deal with their responsibilities and in this life they can never be totally immersed in spirituality.

Rahu-Uttara Bhadra indicates a journey to a beautiful place yet the steps Rahu takes to reach this place will initially be wrong. It is at a threshold of change that cannot be expressed through self-will or personal importance. Uttara Bhadra is the 2nd nakshatra Rahu retrogrades into, and it thinks it understands the intensity but actually it is floundering in this deep cosmic ocean, not mature enough to cope with it. Ketu in Uttara Bhadra shows a past life where the individual let go of their fears and moved towards the maturity of the soul. The soul will want to remain in the spiritual and this creates problems for them in totally honouring the practical and the here and now.

Padas in Uttara Bhadra: Leo, Virgo, Libra, Scorpio
All padas in Uttara Bhadra need to find stability in material life so that they can aspire to spiritual freedom. To pay the last debts to mankind so that life goes forward spiritually. There is pushkara and ashtamamsha pada and no vargottama.

3°20' to 6°40' Pisces – Leo pada
The 1st pada of Uttara Bhadra and 2nd navamsha of Pisces is Leo. In Leo, Pisces faces the reality of its material needs. Ego can be the big issue here. This is the final ego rearing its head and the soul must try to work it out. All planets need to reconcile with power, identity and creativity. No planet is exalted or debilitated here.

6°40' to 10°00' Pisces – Virgo pada
The 2nd pada of Uttara Bhadra and 3rd navamsha of Pisces is Virgo and is Pushkara. Pisces wants to immerse itself in spirituality. Uttara Bhadra promises a new world but Virgo questions the need and feels unsure of the promises. The mind has to organize itself and be more practical as that is the way even for those on the spiritual path. Exalted Venus gets debilitated, and debilitated Mercury becomes exalted; both benefit from the pushkara position. Pushkara usually shows the ability of the planet to thrive regardless of its position. Pada is opposite to the rashi and this can bring a complete change in the life of a person with lagna or any planets placed here.

Mercury finds a fertile ground for its practical vision. This placement is the marrying of the spiritual and the practical together and gives the message of Uttara Bhadra clearly. Sort out the practical to get to the spiritual.

Venus is debilitated by pada and the material desires keep it from expressing its full beauty. Venus will become fussier, more critical and unable to accept the path it is on naturally. There can be hidden weaknesses. Pushkara will help to heal these.

10°00' to 13°20' Pisces – Libra pada

The 3rd pada of Uttara Bhadra and 4th navamsha of Pisces is Libra and ashtamamsha. This is the pada where the main transformation takes place. The seas of Pisces are churned up, and the journey becomes more clouded as the soul tries to find answers in this turbulent world. How can Libra bring about balance where all has to change? There cannot be detachment when the soul has to face major transformations.

People with this lagna will feel the ashtamamsha acutely. Usually there is a major change in life that leads to a true understanding of their role.

The Sun is in a complex situation – weak in debilitation and ashtamamsha. It will want props for the ego while Pisces demands a letting go of dependency and individuality. The right thing to do here is to be true to the Libra impulse as this is the answer to the puzzle. Libra is demanding to remain balanced and detached while all is changing. Being ready for sudden transformation is the key.

Exalted Saturn is not in its best position from the rashi sign. It will try to be balanced and do the right thing but the material world and trying to live in it will produce huge turbulence. Saturn will try to remain detached. Old karma has to be dealt with and it will lead to a positive change.

13°20' to 16°40' Pisces – Scorpio pada

The 4th pada of Uttara Bhadra and 5th navamsha of Pisces is Scorpio. This is the highest vibration of Scorpio at work, transformational, intuitive and full of deep secret knowledge. This is difficult for both the Moon and Rahu. Ketu is exalted.

The Moon can go from an idealistic Pisces to an intense Scorpio, both signs creating emotional storms. Moon people try to cling to their desire-fueled nature and struggle against transformation being forced. Here the poisons of Uttara Bhadra can be in evidence.

Rahu in Pisces and in Scorpio pada gets lost and tries to find its answers by digging deep into its negativity. It needs understanding of its confusion to allow it to emerge unscathed. Ketu is in heaven, Scorpio gives it deep wisdom which has come from past lives to handle the difficulties of today. These people feel secure in their aspiration for moksha. They will sacrifice all to achieve this. They may need to let go of the final residue of negative thoughts but usually they are happy to do so.

27. Revati

16°40' to 30°00' Pisces
Padas: Sagittarius, Capricorn, Aquarius, Pisces

Meaning

Revati means abundant or wealthy. Revati's wealth is both spiritual and material wealth as the crops were usually harvested at the time when the Sun is in Revati nakshatra so the ancient sages felt the beneficence of Revati.

Revati
Ruled by Mercury
Devata: Pushan
Symbol: The Fish
Yoni: Elephant
Motivation: Moksha
Guna Triplicity: Sattva, Sattva and Sattva
Ayurvedic Dosha: Kapha
Body Part: Ankles
Gana: Divine
Caste: Shudra
Quality: Soft
Colours: Brown
Best Direction: East
Special Sounds: De, Do, Chaa, Chee
The Principal Stars: Batn-Al-Hut
Other Names for Revati: Pushan, Antya

It is in Revati where you sow the seed for fruition at a later date. Being the last nakshatra of the zodiac, Revati is powerful in realising the ultimate truths about ourselves, life, death, transformation and change. The experience of Revati changes our way of thinking towards a higher, deeper prospective. She provides nourishment to the soul while it struggles with the great implications of finding itself. Once we find the seed of creation within us, the divine, life cannot remain the same. We create major changes and transformations as this seed will grow into another future.

Not everyone is meant to be so highly spiritual. The average Revati individual aspires for the ideal, yet they remain stuck their everyday lives. They feel let down by society and the world as it fails to live up to their ideal.

Devata – Pushan

Its ruling deity is Pushan, an Aditya, which is one of the 12 forms of the Sun. Pushan is connected to the divisions of the solar year (varsha) into two parts or ayanas: Uttara ayana and Dakshin ayana. Pushan rules this auspicious time for death and rebirth of the Sun. At the dawn of the

New Year the Sun dies and then is reborn. Its rulership of Revati is the connection to dawn, between night and day, death and rebirth. Revati represents that time of utter stillness that carries within it a promise of light and beginning of new dawn.

Pushan guides both the living and the dead. He is the guardian of the transition stages of man. He helps people reach their right destination without fear or worry. This can be just a direction in life or the higher direction where the soul transits from one realm to another. Pushan represents the semen, an indication of the seed of creation. He connects to the marriage ceremony. This is where two souls are joined together and the merging of their beings can create another being, another soul. In vedic thought when couples marry, they are no longer two but become one – a divine union.

Planetary Ruler – Mercury

According to the vedic myths, Mercury is the son of the Moon. The Moon is the mind and Mercury is the rational, practical conscious mind but it is still a fragment of total consciousness. What Mercury perceives as reality is only a small part of the ultimate reality. Mercury nakshatras rule the ending of the nakshatra cycles, where the change of individual consciousness takes place by understanding and going beyond the limitations of intellect. Revati ends a major cycle of life where the consciousness meets the intellect to form new realities for the future.

Mina Rashi

Revati is entirely in Mina Pisces which is a highly spiritual sign. In Revati, it is the end of a cycle, but within this ending there is a new beginning. Something is conceived in Pisces, to be born into a new cycle in Aries. Time moves on a different pace for Revati Pisces. The fish is finally emerged in spirituality and higher consciousness. This is where they are the happiest. Intuitive wisdom and deep knowledge are the Pisces inheritance, so practical issues are not their forte.

Symbol – The Fish

Vishnu, one of the holy trinity of the vedic gods, appeared in the form of a fish. He is known as Matsya Avatar or the fish god. Brahma chanted the four Vedas in yoga nidra (sleep with awareness, typical to yogis).

Hayagriva, a demon, heard the vedic chants and memorized them, though he did not understand their meaning. Hayagriva was a horse-faced demon and he took the four Vedas into the ocean. Vishnu took his first incarnation as Matsya avatar in order to save the Vedas from falling into the wrong hands and he rescued them by defeating Hayagriva. Read about Hayagriva's more divine form in Shatabhishak. Revati people are concerned about vedic knowledge and will do anything to protect it.

The fish has another important symbolism. It can only live in water; therefore Revati can only find true happiness when it immerses its soul with the ocean of spirituality.

Puranic Myth – Revati and Balarama

Revati was the only daughter of King Kakudmi, a powerful monarch who ruled Kusasthali, a prosperous and advanced kingdom under the sea, and who owned large tracts of land. Feeling that no human could prove to be good enough to marry his daughter, King Kakudmi took Revati with him to Brahma-loka (the plane of existence where Lord Brahma resides) to ask his advice about finding a suitable husband for Revati.

When they arrived, Lord Brahma was listening to a musical performance by the Gandharvas, so they waited patiently until the performance was finished. Then, Kakudmi made his request and presented his shortlist of candidates. Lord Brahma laughed and explained that time runs differently on different planes of existence and that during the short time they had waited in Brahma-loka to see him, 27 catur-yugas[9] had passed on Earth.

Lord Brahma said that all those you have chosen have already died and so have many generations of their descendants. Now, Kali Yuga is about to come and Kakudmi must find Revati another husband. He told the king not to be alarmed as Lord Vishnu was incarnate on earth as Krishna and his elder brother Balarama, the incarnation of Adi Shesha. Balarama would make the ideal husband for Revati.

They found Balarama and proposed the marriage. Because she was from an earlier age, Revati was far taller and larger than her husband-to-be, but Balarama, tapped his plough on her head and she shrunk to the normal height of people in that Yugas.

---

9. A catur-yuga is a cycle of four yugas, hence 27 catur-yugas total 108 yugas. Yugas are the Ages of Man.

This myth links Revati to time travel and the relativity of time – how it means different things to different people. Godly time is different to human time and as they develop they can move in differing time dimensions and this can sometimes make it difficult to settle in the world they are in.

Revati Aim for Moksha

Moksha or the need for self-realisation becomes intense for Revati people, who want to merge into the infinite and become one with its source. They want to let go of the individual ego and become mukta, or the person who has realised the highest truths while living on earth.

The Revati spiritual path is sacrifice. To give up what you desire for the good of others. Revati does that through service to humanity, working, doing jobs that get no appreciation. Vedic philosophy teaches that all should make their life one of sacrifice. It is a difficult path to follow for others which Revati makes its own.

Sacred Animal – Flying Elephants

Revati's animal is an elephant. Elephants originally had wings and could fly. One elephant was tired of flying around, and rested on a tree. The tree was not strong enough to take his weight so he fell. Unbeknown to him, sage Dhirgatamas was meditating under the tree and the elephant's fall broke the sage's meditation. In anger, he cursed all the elephants that in future they will only walk on earth. Revati's connection is with the flying elephants before they got cursed, Revati has that ability to fly high and for it to live on earth appears like a curse. It further stresses Revati's ability to live in differing dimensions – in the air as well as on earth.

Ayurvedic Dosha is Kapha

Kapha people are philosophical, calm and contented. They will work calmly through the greatest of stresses. Revati's being Kapha shows the further harmony with its greater indication. Revati people will stay calm in crises.

Lagna and Planets

People with planets in Revati are idealistic and want to nourish others and to create something powerful. They can feel their life is full of disappointments, as they are extremely idealistic. They can live in a different reality from the rest of us and this makes them hard to understand. The end of Revati is the final gandanta and all planets placed there can suffer.

People with the lagna here will be idealistic, creative and very spiritual. They can be misunderstood as more materially-based individuals question their motivation and do not understand the true under-pinning of this highly developed soul. These souls do not have many material skills so they can make mistakes regarding money and finances. The position of Mercury and Jupiter has to be taken into account.

The Sun feels the change in its energy. It is nurturing and creative, but the creativity is not expressed outwardly. These people can be idealistic, wanting to create a world of their own. Their talents can go unrecognized unless they make sure to pass their knowledge and wisdom onto others.

The Moon is highly spiritual and idealistic. These people are totally immersed in their spirituality and so can also lose the skills of the material world. They can be full of insecurities and their inner storms make them feel troubled. They can feel disappointed with life as others do not match up to their ideals. They will try to be excellent in whatever they do, but unless their aim is spiritual, they may feel a failure. The first dasha of Mercury can be quite good unless the person is born at the end of Revati on a gandanta point, in which case it indicates major changes right from birth. With the start of Ketu dasha immediately after birth, the insecurities of Revati can be quite pronounced.

Mars is the spiritual warrior. He will be interested in keeping the flame alive but there can be turbulence. These people will not worry if their brand of spiritualism is acceptable to others or not.

Mercury is in its own nakshatra and has passed the degree of its debilitation, so the intellect works very differently in Revati than it does in Uttara Bhadra. Revati allows the mind to expand its horizons. These people are never good at material things, so they have to train themselves to be practical. But if you are looking for a profound thinker, then they are the ones to find. Their thinking knows no restrictions, they know no boundaries, and can therefore be great ideas people, thinkers and writers.

Jupiter can be both strong and weak here. This wisdom has to be used to build something good for the future. These people have strong links to spirituality, creativity and nourishment. The soul needs to be nourished. Future ideas have to be incubated. This usually involves teaching and passing on of knowledge. If the teachers do not do this, the seed does not flourish. There is one pada to be careful about as Revati can debilitate Jupiter.

Venus is exalted. It provides the semen, the ideas, the seed for future development. Pushan, as the deity of the marriage ceremony, encourages people to find the right marriage that will keep their next generation alive. Marriage, children, ideas, future generations are all ensured by Venus placed here.

Saturn can be wise and give the ability to face pain and deal with the transformations. Two padas of Revati are ruled by Saturn, so it still has a role to play. Pay the last debts to society and do what is right, so that it can flow with the river of creation. Saturn deals with death and old age – a part of Revati's remit.

Rahu Ketu begin their journey from Revati as they retrograded out of Aries into Pisces. They face the transformational power of Revati. The turbulence and deep secret wisdom make both Rahu Ketu confused. Rahu works to understand the spiritual aspect of Revati and like the demon Hayagriva it wants all the knowledge without truly understanding. These people need to know that they have many lessons to learn before the true knowledge opens up to them. Ketu people carry all this profound wisdom yet they do not know how to fully express it. They may reject their wisdom but understanding the gift of past lives and using their intuitive knowledge will help them find themselves.

Padas in Revati: Sagittarius, Capricorn, Aquarius, Pisces
The last pada of Revati is vargottama. No pushkara or ashtamamsha. Rahu Ketu retrograde back and begin the journey in Revati – coming into deep spirituality where they have no understanding.

16°40' to 20°00' Pisces – Sagittarius pada
The 1st pada of Revati and 6th navamsha of Pisces is Sagittarius. These are the last steps to be totally one with the spiritual connection. It is great for Jupiter which is in its own sign and own pada. The wisdom is

deep, the teaching great, the knowledge is passed on so that others can benefit. No planet is exalted or debilitated. All have a strong message and are involved in a spiritual journey.

20°00' to 23°20' Pisces – Capricorn pada
The 2nd pada of Revati and 7th navamsha of Pisces is Capricorn. Mars is exalted and Jupiter debilitated. There is a residue of practical karma to be faced before the soul can be immersed completely in spirituality.

Mars goes from its friend's house to being exalted. This is an extremely powerful position of Mars to make spiritual changes. It will fight for the right causes, try to make a good way of life. It will structure its life to achieve its divine goals.

Jupiter goes from strong in rashi to weak in debilitated pada. Jupiter in Pisces people are rooted in its deep spiritual practices; Capricorn is a practical sign. It usually wants to quantify and put a price to everything. This can make a person spiritual from above and calculating within. They should not try to hide their practical nature as hiding it only gives them a bad name.

23°20' to 26°40' Pisces – Aquarius pada
The 3rd pada of Revati and 8th navamsha of Pisces is Aquarius. No planet is exalted or debilitated. All planets will be thinking of others, trying to complete their worldly responsibilities. Aquarius is an air sign and can create storms within the Pisces ocean and make for confusion and turbulent emotions.

26°40' to 30°00' Pisces – Pisces pada
The 4th pada of Revati and 9th navamsha of Pisces is the vargottama Pisces. The last 48' of this pada is gandanta. This is the final ending of the sign, nakshatra and navamsha/pada. All planets here give potential for pushing the soul to the next level of its development. Planets according to their karakas can bring pain to your life usually to enlighten and bring awareness of another facet of your subtle personality.

Venus is exalted and Mercury debilitated. Rahu Ketu come into Revati as their first sign so the move is into the ocean of knowledge where they want everything but may not understand their profound gifts.

Mercury is debilitated by rashi and pada. The old rules do not work, the mind has to expand and reach for new horizons. These people do not know how to think practically. The vargottama says that it is right for the mind to be so unconcerned. They will be happy in their spiritual role but not so good at practical matters or making decisions.

Venus is exalted, its exaltation degree is 27° Pisces and it is vargottama. Venus as the significator of semen and new life force, sows the seed for a new generation, sowing ideas in the fertility of Pisces to flourish another day, another lifetime. The purity of Venus is emphasized. Venus is exalted and beautiful. This position should give very good relationships. These individuals can be undermined by extreme idealism just like Revati in the myth. Gandanta Venus will create difficulties in relationships.

Rahu finds the spiritual turmoil fascinating as it begins a new cycle of development. It will want to embrace everything but does not always want to understand the deeper meaning behind the spirituality of this pada. Ketu knows everything but it is cut off and hidden. It can feel insecure if it does not take refuge in its own intuition and trusts its inner voice.

Planets in Pisces Gandanta – 29°12 to 30°00 Pisces

The end of Pisces is gandanta, the karmic knot where most of the toxins and poisons are collected. Pisces is the last sign and nakshatra, therefore crossing this gandanta is very complex. People with planets placed here are unable to move forward and are stuck in either personal weaknesses or lack of support from family or circumstances that do not allow them to complete this journey.

All planets placed in gandanta will be troubled according to their karaka and house rulerships. It is a complex situation and suffering can come with gandanta. The karmic knowledge is extremely difficult to unravel as this junction ends a complete cycle of soul growth and the planet stuck in a gandanta is not able to move forward. It is important to accept the position and forgive the experiences that have come with this position. Only then can the soul be privy to great secret knowledge.

5
Nama Nakshatra

The Technique of Choosing the Right Name

Nama means name. Nama nakshatra is an ancient tradition of choosing the right name for the incarnating soul. Each pada of the nakshatra resonates with a consonant known as *akshara* which means imperishable, indestructible. These akshara were sacred and the name is chosen with great care. The name is like a mantra and whenever someone says your name it creates an auspicious energy. The consonants are taken from the position of the Moon's nakshatra. Depending on the pada the Moon was at birth, that consonant is chosen.

Naming of a Child

A male child is born on 19 February 2014 at 4:43am in Los Angeles, California. His Moon is in Chitra nakshatra pada 2. Chitra has four akshara Pay, Po, Raa and Re. What would be the right name for him according to nama nakshatra? The pada two akshara would be Po. An Indian name suitable could be Poorna, Poorna Chandra – both connected to the Moon or Poojan (worship). Western names could be Pollux, Polar, Pomeroy – there is a wide choice. This name will resonate with the nama nakshatra at birth and be forever like an auspicious chant.

Checking the Given Name's Alignment to the Nama Nakshatra

Another way to use nama nakshatra is to study what nakshatra your given name resounds with. Quite often we do not have the choice in our names as by the time we are studying Jyotish and come across this technique it may be too late. Then it is good to know which nakshatra your given name resounds with and study what house this name corresponds to. If the birth name links to the nakshatra pada of the Moon at birth, there is no need to check if the Moon is in a positive house or not. People embrace the nama nakshatra qualities. Transits to these nakshatras can have effect according to their nature. Saturn transiting the nama nakshatra can bring obstacles, Jupiter can enhance the status and so on.

Nama Nakshatra Table: Special Sounds for the Nakshatras

	Nakshatra	Pada			
		1	2	3	4
1	Ashwini	Chu	Chey	Cho	La
2	Bharani	Li	Lu	Ley	Lo
3	Krittika	Aa	Ee	U	A
4	Rohini	O	Va	Vee	Vo
5	Mrigasira	Vay	Vo	Ka	Kee
6	Ardra	Koo	Ghaa	Jna	Chcha
7	Punarvasu	Kay	Ko	Ha	Hee
8	Pushya	Hoo	Hay	Ho	Daa
9	Ashlesha	Dee	Doo	Day	Do
10	Magha	Maa	Mee	Moo	May
11	P Phalguni	Mo	Taa	Tee	Too
12	U Phalguni	Tay	To	Paa	Pee
13	Hasta	Pu	Shaa	Na	Thaa
14	Chitra	Pay	Po	Raa	Re
15	Swati	Ru	Ray	Pa	Ta
16	Vishakha	Thee	Thuu	Thay	Thou
17	Anuradha	Naa	Nee	Nou	Nay
18	Jyeshta	No	Ya	Yee	You
19	Mula	Yay	Yo	Baa	Bee
20	P Ashadha	Bu	Dha	Bha	Dha
21	U Ashadha	Bay	Bo	Jaa	Jee
22	Shravana	Ju	Jay	Jo	Gha
23	Dhanishta	Gaa	Gee	Goo	Gay
24	Shatabhishak	Go	Sa	See	Sou
25	P Bhadra	Say	So	Daa	Dee
26	U Bhadra	Du	Tha	Aa	Jna
27	Revati	De	Do	Chaa	Chee

Bob Dylan Singer/Songwriter: 25 May 1941, 21:05, Duluth, MN

Robert Allen Zimmerman is more commonly known as Bob Dylan, so we will be concerned with his popular name. His birth Moon is Krittika and the akshara for Krittika pada 1 is Aa. However his birth name begins with Bo so we need to check how this relates to his natal chart. Bo is the consonant of the 2nd pada of Uttara Ashadha, which is in

Capricorn. Bob Dylan is Scorpio lagna and this pada falls in his third house of communication and motivation. It is connected to writing and creativity too. Uttara Ashadha is a loner nakshatra and the name itself will encourage Bob Dylan to be private, spiritual and self-effacing. Whatever fame or wealth he has, he would never show off, mostly using his wealth to work for society.

Transits to Uttara Ashadha pada 2 will affect his life. The name is to do with recognition and status. In February 1961 he came to New York to follow his musical career. At the time Jupiter and Saturn were conjoined at 1°53' Capricorn in pada 2 Uttara Ashadha (19 February 1961). This was the most significant moment of Bob Dylan's life and two key planets influencing his nama nakshatra in the right pada would have been the key.

Changing the Name to Resonate with Nama Nakshatra

Many people change their names or adopt a spiritual name. It would be a good idea to get the Moon nama nakshatra name. However if the Moon is in a troubled conjunction or placed in any of the dusthana houses, it may be better to choose the nakshatra that trines the Moon or lagna.

In the case of Bob Dylan, his lagna is in Scorpio, and his Moon is in Krittika pada 1 with a close conjunction of Saturn, so his name at present is fine and there is no need to change it. Changing his name to the Moon nakshatra would bring up the Saturn Moon conjunction which would have a more depressing influence. He would be better off choosing the name connected to a nakshatra that is well placed from both the Moon and lagna. My suggestion would be the trinal nakshatra of Krittika which falls in his 10th house from lagna and 5th from the Moon – this is Uttara Phalguni Leo. The akshara are Tay, To, Paa, Pee. He could choose pada 1 of Uttara Phalguni as his name is in pada 1 of Krittika.

The nama akshara could be Tay – Taylor would also have been appropriate.

Using the Nama Nakshatra as Lagna

Another technique to use the nama nakshatra if the birth time is not known, is traditionally to choose the first consonant of the given name and identify its nakshatra to use as the degree of the ascendant.

A person name Cathy has the consonant Ca which is similar to Ka, as in Sanskrit we do not have a different between C and K.

This resounds with Mrigasira pada 3 which is in 00°0' to 03°20' Gemini. These degrees can be taken as an ascendant and a chart constructed if the date of birth is known. Any transits to these degrees – despite natal chart – will be sensitive. Malefic transits would create problems while benefics bring opportunities.

I have seen this technique used with great proficiency in Northern India. Many astrologers will give an accurate prediction just from knowing your nama nakshatra.

6
The Gunas or Qualities of the Mind

The nakshatra is about the mind and the guna reflects the quality of the mind. Studying the guna of the nakshatra is very important as it reveals how the mind is operating. *Guna* also means 'strand', the strands of twine that make up a rope. The rope is seen here as an allegory to personality as the various strands, or gunas, entwine to produce the individuality of a person. The attribute of each guna is usually seen as mental rather than physical, but the mind has a great capacity to affect the physical side of our life.

We all have a balance of the gunas within us. They express themselves as a mental attitude that leads us to see life in a certain way and have particular priorities, and it is vital that we recognise both the gifts and the challenges that they have to offer in our lives. While sattva is considered the best guna to have, too much of it can make us dysfunction in the material world we live in.

- **Rajas** is the cause of activity in mankind. It is the searching quality that as humans, we all have. It can be translated as 'pollen of the flowers', 'a particle in the sunbeams' or 'emotional, moral or mental darkness'. 'Pollen of the flowers' indicates the potential of pollen to create new flowers; humans activating more life; experiencing life and birth. 'A particle in the sunbeam' – a sunbeam is pure and the particle introduces a new element in its purity. 'Moral, emotional or mental darkness' is the inability of humans to see the answers within themselves, with the result that they seek fulfillment in the material, illusionary world. Rajas is a mental attitude that emphasizes strong emotional impulses. Rajasic nakshatras are forever active, always seeking answers in the outer world. They remain dissatisfied because answers do not lie in the outer world. The first to ninth nakshatras from Ashwini to Ashlesha are rajasic by nature.

- **Tamas** is the attribute of darkness. The Sanskrit word can be translated as 'ignorance', making it plain that the darkness is a mental one. Tamasic people have a mental attitude that emphasises sensuality. They can be described as being led by a lack of knowledge or of spiritual insight to a life focusing on human sensual desires. Vedic philosophy encourages tamasic people to dispel their darkness with the light of spiritual insight. The tamasic attitude is to embrace desires. They usually view life in the here and now. These desires keep them tied to the world of happiness and unhappiness; through their own needs they create their own problems. Tamas nakshatras are passive and inert. They can be dispassionate and disinterested in the world around them, which can be taken as selfishness and laziness but at times it is only allowing things to be the way they are. If these people decide to connect, they can be highly spiritual. The tenth to eighteenth nakshatras from Magha to Jyeshta are tamasic by nature.

- **Sattva** is the attribute of purity. *Sat* means being, existing, pure, true and real. *Va* means where purity dwells. A sattvic person believes in purity of being, thought, and action. Water is pure sattva. Vegetarianism is sattvic because it rejects killing animals to fulfill the need to eat. Sattvic people have a mental attitude that emphasises purity. Sattva works very much on the abstract level and sattvic nakshatras are usually happy aspiring to their higher self. They will be calm and collected within relationships. They tend to work on a sense of fairness and love. The nineteenth to twenty-seventh nakshatras from Mula to Revati are sattvic by nature.

The Three Levels of Consciousness

The nakshatras have the gunas entwined in their psychology and all the planets will embrace the guna of their nakshatra. The Moon's position continues to be key, but others should not be ignored. While the guna divides nakshatras into three groups of nakshatras on a primary level, each of them reflects the gunas on three levels. This reveals three levels of consciousness of the planet. The mind organizes itself in multi-layered levels of consciousness and the soul works in many dimensions.

The Primary Level of Gunas
The primary level guna is the one whose quality is most obvious. This generates action and the planets will work according to this guna primary:

> The 1st to 9th (Ashwini to Ashlesha) will reflect rajas
> The 10th to 18th (Magha to Jyeshta) will reflect tamas
> The 19th to 27th (Mula to Revati) will reflect sattva

The Secondary Level of Gunas
The secondary level of gunas reflects hidden mental attitude and helps in generating ideas and thoughts.

> *Rajas on the second level*
> 1st to 3rd (Ashwini, Bharani, Krittika)
> 10th to 12th (Magha, Purva Phalguni and Uttara Phalguni)
> 19th to 21st (Mula, Purva Ashadha and Uttara Ashadha)

> *Tamas on the second level*
> 4th to 6th (Rohini, Mrigasira, Ardra)
> 13th to 15th (Hasta, Chitra, Swati)
> 22nd to 24th (Shravana, Dhanishta, Shatabhishak)

> *Sattva on the second level*
> 7th to 9th (Punarvasu, Pushya, Ashlesha),
> 16th to 18th (Vishakha, Anuradha, Jyeshta)
> 25th to 27th (Purva Bhadrapada, Uttara Bhadrapada, Revati)

Third Level of Gunas
The third level of gunas reflect a deeper, inner level, that remains hidden from others. This inspires spirituality but can remain dormant until developing spiritually can activate this level of consciousness.

> *Rajas on the third level*
> Ashwini, Rohini, Punarvasu, Magha, Hasta, Vishakha, Mula, Shravana, Purva Bhadrapada

> *Tamas on the third level*
> Bharani, Mrigasira, Pushya, Purva Phalguni, Chitra, Anuradha, Purva Ashadha, Dhanishta and Uttara Bhadrapada

Sattva on the third level
Krittika, Ardra, Ashlesha, Uttara Phalguni, Swati, Jyeshta,
Uttara Ashadha, Shatabhishak and Revati

Studying the nakshatras for their guna qualities helps in understanding the journey of the soul and pinpoints certain important stages of the soul's development.

Nakshatras having all the gunas in their nature will express all the qualities of a particular guna. The first level of guna is always the one that is obvious and which the others recognise. If all the three levels of gunas are the same, this shows a concentration of the quality. If two are the same, then the third guna helps to bring out the balancing. If all are different, then the individual will have many facets and the mind moves within the three qualities constantly.

Ashwini, Chitra and Revati have all three levels of the same guna gunas – the first, middle and last nakshatras. Ashwini is rajas on all levels, the drive to find answers motivates Ashwini. After that all nakshatras will reflect various combinations of guna but the purity of rajas impulse is only in Ashwini.

The gunas concentrate again in Chitra, the 14th nakshatra. Here the expression is tamas on all three levels. The soul is completely caught up in the material work immersed in it yet the tamas can break in Chitra and a special light shine for them. Nakshatras from Ashwini to Chitra are searching in the outer world, becoming involved in it and going down to tamas.

From Chitra onwards, tamas starts to unravel. There is disenchantment with the tamas and the soul is not seeking anything else. Sattva dominates from Mula onwards but the pure sattva on all three levels in only reached by the last nakshatra Revati. Here the soul is pure, idealistic and in one with the divine message, using the qualities of the mind to the right direction. Yet the pure sattva of Revati may be tough to deal with in the world we live in, which needs some rajas and tamas too.

Six nakshatras express all three gunas within: Ardra, Pushya, Uttara Phalguni, Vishkha, Purva Ashadha and Shravana. They have the ability to achieve the balance of the gunas as all qualities will be prominent at some time and their mixture gives a more complete personality.

The rest are 18 nakshatras that have guna imbalance with one guna missing from their triplicity. While this guna may be there in their mental makeup it will not be prominent. The table below explains the guna makeup of the nakshatra.

Nakshatras and the Gunas Triplicity

S.No.	Nakshatra	Primary	Secondary	Tertiary
1	**Ashwini**	**Rajas**	**Rajas**	**Rajas**
2	**Bharani**	Rajas	Rajas	Tamas
3	**Krittika**	Rajas	Rajas	Sattva
4	**Rohini**	Rajas	Tamas	Rajas
5	**Mrigasira**	Rajas	Tamas	Tamas
6	**Ardra**	*Rajas*	*Tamas*	*Sattva*
7	**Punarvasu**	Rajas	Sattva	Rajas
8	**Pushya**	*Rajas*	*Sattva*	*Tamas*
9	**Ashlesha**	Rajas	Sattva	Sattva
10	**Magha**	Tamas	Rajas	Rajas
11	**P Phalguni**	Tamas	Rajas	Tamas
12	**U Phalguni**	*Tamas*	*Rajas*	*Sattva*
13	**Hasta**	Tamas	Tamas	Rajas
14	**Chitra**	**Tamas**	**Tamas**	**Tamas**
15	**Swati**	Tamas	Tamas	Sattva
16	**Vishakha**	*Tamas*	*Sattva*	*Rajas*
17	**Anuradha**	Tamas	Sattva	Tamas
18	**Jyeshta**	Tamas	Sattva	Sattva
19	**Mula**	Sattva	Rajas	Rajas
20	**P Ashadha**	*Sattva*	*Rajas*	*Tamas*
21	**U Ashadha**	Sattva	Rajas	Sattva
22	**Shravana**	*Sattva*	*Tamas*	*Rajas*
23	**Dhanishta**	Sattva	Tamas	Tamas
24	**Shatabhishak**	Sattva	Tamas	Sattva
25	**Purva Bhadra**	Sattva	Sattva	Rajas
26	**U Bhadra**	Sattva	Sattva	Tamas
27	**Revati**	**Sattva**	**Sattva**	**Sattva**

Bold = gunas are the same *Italics* = gunas are in balance

Gandanta and Guna

The gandanta points between Ashlesha and Magha (29°12' Cancer to 0°48' Leo); Jyeshta and Mula Magha (29°12' Scorpio to 0°48' Sagittarius); and Revati and Ashwini Magha (29°12' Pisces to 0°48' Aries) are where the guna shifts on a primary level. This is the most physical level of manifestation and the changing guna causes a crisis for planets placed at these degrees.

Ashlesha to Magha gandanta is when the guna changes from rajas to tamas - action to involvement. The soul struggles to accept the ties that tamas brings, but slowly settles into this mode.

Jyeshta to Mula gandanta is the shift from tamas to sattva. This is the most challenging as the soul is caught in the grip of tamas which is hard to let go of and sattva has to break that.

Revati to Ashwini is from sattva to rajas. The soul wants to remain in sattva but rajas has energy and will easily take over the sattva energy. The main aspect in these gandantas is that the two gunas blend together on the primary level causing confusion, karmic stress and issues that are not easy to resolve.

Guna Analysis

Adele 5 May 1988, 3:02 (+1:00 BST) London, England

Rashi (D-1) General   Navamsha (D-9) Dharma/Spouse

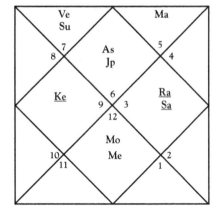

Planet	Nakshatra	No	Rashi	Special
Asc	Dhanishta	23:2	Capricorn	
Sun	Bharani	2:3	Aries	
Moon	Jyeshta	18:4	Scorpio	Gandanta
Mars	Dhanishta	23:1	Capricorn	
Mer	Krittika	3:4	Taurus	
Jup	Bharani	2:2	Aries	
Ven	Mrigasira	5:3	Cancer	
Sat	Mula	19:3	Sagittarius	
Rahu	Purva Bhadra	25;3	Aquarius	

Adele is an English singer, songwriter and musician. She is internationally known and has many awards to her name. Adele has a powerful voice which is packed with emotions. Her father abandoned her at the age of 2 and a bad breakup lead to her writing some of the most emotional music.

		Guna primary	Second level	Third level
Ascendant	Jyeshta	Tamas	Sattva	Sattva
Sun	Bharani	Rajas	Rajas	Tamas
Moon	Jyeshta	Tamas	Sattva	Sattva
Mars	Dhanishta	Sattva	Tamas	Tamas
Mercury	Krittika	Rajas	Rajas	Sattva
Jupiter	Bharani	Rajas	Rajas	Tamas
Venus	Mrigasira	Rajas	Tamas	Tamas
Saturn	Mula	Sattva	Rajas	Rajas
Rahu	P. Bhadra	Sattva	Sattva	Rajas
Ketu	U Phalguni	Tamas	Rajas	Sattva

In order to analyse the guna the following steps should be followed:

Step one – check the balance of primary guna. This gives the visible quality of the individual. Adele's Ascendant, Moon and Ketu are tamasic and therefore will encourage involvement in the material world. The Sun, Mercury, Jupiter, and Venus are in rajas and the search in the outer world and the dissatisfaction with what that reveals is the rajas qualities. Mars, Saturn and Rahu are in sattva nakshatras. The malefics being influenced by sattva can indicate that her motivation is in the higher realms. The planets, though challenging, are using their qualities for higher ends. While the primary level is being expressed by all three gunas, there is a need to dig deeper.

Step two – is there any signature that stands out? Adele's guna on three levels appear to be imbalanced, in all the planets with the exception of Ketu they reflect only two of the three gunas. This may give her emotional highs and lows, moving from detachment to attachment, search to complacency, while she seeks the balance given by the past life planet Ketu.

Step three – each planet needs to be analysed separately. Adele's Moon is in gandanta Scorpio in tamas, sattva, sattva – the inner purity is being sought but the gandanta position confuses this with sattva rajas rajas of Mula and is creating emotional storms and uncertainty.

Step four – study the guna of the dasha ruler to analyse what guna quality is prominent now. Adele is in a Venus dasha now. Venus is in Mrigasira, whose qualities are rajas tamas tamas. Tamas can bring inner darkness, complacency and repetition of patterns of behaviour. While the outer search is ongoing during this dasha, the inner tamas may hold back from making progress, especially in relationships. Venus is karaka of relationship. The inner tamas may make her compromise and choose a partner, as there is an inner urge to settle down.

7
Nakshatra Gandanta, the Spiritual Knot

Gandanta describes the junction where the rashi and nakshatras end together. These points at the junctions of Pisces (Revati) and Aries (Ashwini), Cancer (Ashlesha) and Leo (Magha), Scorpio (Jyeshta) and Sagittarius (Mula), are times of soul growth. The nakshatra gandanta is when the Moon or other planets is situated within 48 minutes either side of these points.

Gand means a knot, *anta* means the end, so gandanta is the knot at the end. A well-tied knot is one that is very difficult to unravel, as the more you try to untie it the tighter it becomes. Gandanta represents a knot within, a complex spiritual issue to which we are trying to become reconciled. The gandanta degrees are:

Degrees	Rashi	Nakshatra
29°12' - 30°00'	Pisces	Revati
0°00' - 0°48'	Aries	Ashwini
29°12' - 30°00'	Cancer	Ashlesha
0°00' - 0°48'	Leo	Magha
29°12' - 30°00'	Scorpio	Jyeshta
0°00' - 0°48'	Sagittarius	Mula

The significations of all planets suffer by being in gandanta, although the Moon experiences it as the most challenging. Being born at nakshatra gandanta is considered very tough and remedial measures are given for this birth. Planets in gandanta are not about success or failure, luck or lack of it, it is an internal feeling that hides the inner truth and makes it difficult to understand the self. At times there are difficulties and challenges to relationships that do not give support, for example the Sun in gandanta can show a complex relationship with the father whereas the Moon will show a tough one with the mother. It is important to remember that for the gandanta to be true, the planets should be hugging the 0° of Aries, Leo and Sagittarius – this is where the storms are at the maximum.

When the planets are placed in these powerfully karmic degrees it shows uncertainty as we try to unravel the secret knot that will take us to the next level. There would be an immediate change of dasha from Mercury to Ketu after birth if the Moon is placed at the end degrees of a sign/nakshatra or the start of life at the beginning of a Ketu dasha if the Moon is placed in the early degrees of the sign.

The gandanta degrees are usually between water and fire signs. Water and fire are inimical elements in the Panchamahabhuta – fire can steam up water while water can put out fire. Together they create steam, mists, and when hot and cold collide in nature hurricanes and tornadoes happen. These take place within us too and are therefore most complicated. All planets placed in this junction are adversely affected.

The Moon in Gandanta

The Moon in the nakshatra gandanta is particularly troubled as it shows that one is born either at the end of a Mercury dasha or the beginning of Ketu dasha. The end of a Mercury dasha usually reveals a soul reconciling with past karma and there can be many debts to pay. Mercury dashas usually have poisonous endings whereas Ketu represents the past life and the soul is burdened with its karma. The problem is that at this time the individual is only a child and does not have the personal resources to deal with this. Although parents can be affected by this gandanta, a child is subtly aware of what is happening and its influence stays with it for life. There can be many difficulties to be faced and adjustments to be made. For those who are spiritually inclined and desiring to develop on to the higher self, planets in gandanta degrees will help them understand the serious blocks karma has created so that they can work to unravel them.

The Gandanta

The Pisces/Revati and **Aries/Ashwini Gandanta** shows the ending of one cycle of soul growth and the beginning of its next stage. If the planets are in the Pisces portion of the gandanta, it relates to ending experiences, where the soul has reached its full maturity at the present level of growth and is ready to move to another cycle and a different set of issues. The soul is closing the door to one cycle and it does not end easily; there can be inner storms as the soul destroys one way to make way for a new life. In the Aries/Ashwini portion of gandanta, the soul is connected to the past life but has begun a new cycle of soul growth. The soul is insecure as it has not yet understood its role in the new incarnation. This creates confusion and brings powerful influences, which are at times difficult to understand. Both these positions are vargottama so there is strength as well as challenges.

The Cancer/Ashlesha and **Leo/Magha Gandanta** is where the soul ends its search in the world of rajas and moves into tamas. The soul has been searching from place to place to seek answers about its incarnations and true identity. This is an outer journey and the result does not bring any answers but it creates an involvement in the world of tamas, the material life. The Cancer/Ashlesha stage is where freedoms must end and it must give up its search to settle down. The poisons have been collected at this point that need to be purified. The transition from rajas to tamas is never easy. The ruling deity of Ashlesha is Naga, the wise serpents. At this stage there is a shedding of the skin to grow another; an experience which changes the mind and psyche and can be extremely painful, but is necessary for the soul to grow into another dimension. The soul is vulnerable and exposed at the gandanta point. At the Magha/Leo stage, the soul is finally getting ready to experience life in tamas. It has not as yet grown a new skin and it is idealistic, exposed and as yet not fully aware of the rules of materialism. The intellectual changes already experienced at the Cancer/Ashlesha level are still very intense.

Scorpio/Jyeshta and **Sagittarius/Mula Gandanta** is the most difficult of the three gandanta as it moves the inner soul in its final direction towards merging with the universal consciousness. This is the stage where the material ties need to be cut and the soul must realise its true spiritual direction. It is where the maximum churning of inner turmoil takes place. Even when the soul knows this path is towards its true self, it fights against it. This is never an easy task and it creates many psychological or physical blocks that need to be tackled with patience and maturity. This is a most challenging position for the Moon to be placed in.

At the Scorpio/Jyeshta stage, there is an immense churning of inner emotion, where material sheaths break up and lead to inner change. If there is resistance to change it makes it even more difficult for the person. On a material level this can be tough whereas on a spiritual level it leads towards activating latent spiritual power.

At the Mula/Sagittarius stage, the soul recognises it has to change and in many ways it already has. But it still remains tied to its past and its earthly needs, which Mula, meaning 'the root', suggests. This root is buried in the ground or in deep material realms. There are two ways for Mula to react: one is to cut away completely from its material roots and begin the spiritual journey and the other is to trim the excess of negativity while remaining still rooted in this world. At the Mula stage one has to be very careful not to be self-destructive and destroy what is still valid. The person should treat their life as a precious plant which needs pruning, so that new shoots of spirituality can grow while the dead wood of materialism is cut out. If they cut the roots, their insecurity can lead to the spirituality dying away.

Jyeshta has to wean itself away from its desires whereas Mula must avoid destroying all that is precious to them when they are ridding themselves of karmic debris.

Jennifer Aniston, 11 Feb 1969, 22:22, PST +8.00
Sherman Oaks, CA, USA

Rashi (D-1) General

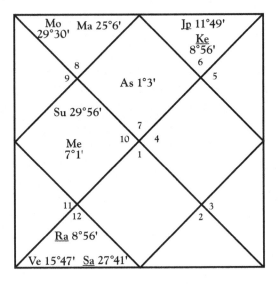

Planet	Nakshatra
Ascendant	Chitra
Sun	Dhanishta
Moon	Jyeshta
Mars	Vishakha
Mercury	Uttara Ashadha
Jupiter	Hasta
Venus	Uttara Bhadra
Saturn	Revati
Rahu	Uttara Bhadra
Ketu	Uttara Phalguni

Vimshottari				
Start Date			**Age**	**Dashas**
28/	4/	2001	32.2	Su	Ve
28/	**4/**	**2002**	**33.2**	**Mo**	**Mo**
26/	2/	2003	34.0	Mo	Ma
27/	9/	2003	34.6	Mo	Ra
28/	3/	2005	36.1	Mo	Jp
28/	7/	2006	37.5	Mo	Sa
26/	2/	2008	39.0	Mo	Me
28/	7/	2009	40.5	Mo	Ke
26/	2/	2010	41.0	Mo	Ve
28/	10/	2011	42.7	Mo	Su
27/	**4/**	**2012**	**43.2**	**Ma**	**Ma**
23/	9/	2012	43.6	Ma	Ra

Actress Jennifer Aniston is famous for being part of the hugely successful *Friends* TV series and her marriage and subsequent divorce from Brad Pitt. Her Moon is 29°50' Scorpio in deep gandanta. Her Jupiter is in Hasta nakshatra which is ruled by the Moon and therefore influenced by the gandanta energy. While the gandanta Moon does not prevent her success in being the 10th richest woman in showbusiness, it does bring great emotional unhappiness. Her relationships and their breakups are well documented in the press. Her divorce from Brad Pitt was finalized on 2 October 2005 in a Moon Jupiter dasha. The combined influence of the gandanta on both the planets would have made this time an extremely painful period and his involvement with Angelina Jolie further added to this pain.

8
The Sexuality of the Nakshatras: Yoni and Animal

Each nakshatra has a yoni of a particular animal which is connected to their sexuality. The yoni and their animals of the nakshatras fascinated me and I wanted to explore further as it had such an important influence on the nature of the individual. I researched animal behaviour and have included them in the information about the nakshatras and their patterns of behaviour and sexuality.

There are 14 types of yoni that reflect 13 pairs of animals of either male or female gender and the fourteenth animal is the mongoose who has no female counterpart.

The Nakshatra Yoni

Animal Sign	Male	Female
Horse	Ashwini	Shatabhishak
Elephant	Bharani	Revati
Goat/Sheep	Pushya	Krittika
Serpent	Rohini	Mrigasira
Dog	Mula	Ardra
Cat	Ashlesha	Punarvasu
Rat	Magha	P Phalguni
Cow	U Phalguni	U Bhadra
Buffalo	Swati	Hasta
Tiger	Vishakha	Chitra
Deer	Jyeshta	Anuradha
Monkey	P Ashadha	Shravana
Lion	P Bhadra	Dhanishta
Mongoose	U Ashadha*	

*The mongoose has no female

The yoni is usually referred to as the female sexual organ, however it has several meanings: womb, vulva, vagina, place of birth, source, origin, an abode, a receptacle. The nakshatra yoni takes on the wider significance of receiving the influence of the planets placed there, either in the natal chart or by transit. Planets in the nakshatra vitalize this energy and therefore create a connection between Shiva (male) and Shakti (female). In the Kama Sutra, the yoni is discussed but it has not been connected to the nakshatras as most translators are unlikely to have studied vedic astrology.

Sexual Compatibility

When comparing two charts for understanding the compatibility, sexual compatibility was given great importance. The yoni of the couples was analysed and from the natural relationship of the various animals a conclusion was reached as to whether there was a good connection or not. The Moon nakshatra at birth decides your primary animal yoni and its counterpart gender will be the best match sexually. Ideally a male should have a male yoni animal which should connect to the female of a female yoni of the same animal, but life is a lot more complex, people with different yoni connect, and gender roles can also get confused within a relationship. Generally sexual compatibility is considered perfect if two people have the same yoni.

Remember that for long-term relationships just matching the yoni is not enough. While a pair of yoni animals are the best match, sexual compatibility varies with other animals and with a few there is actual hostility.

Sexual compatibility of all the nakshatras is given on p. 296.

Animal Adversaries

Each pair of animals has another pair which is inimical to them and therefore a relationship between these two can lead to problems. While the yoni is studied primarily for sexual relationships, I have noticed in life that a relationship between two inimical animals can become negative early on unless there are other strong links.

The sexual relationships of the following pairs do not work, as they are natural enemies in the wild. Relationships between sexual adversaries makes sex a bone of contention and the nakshatras fight to establish supremacy through sexual power play. The sexual adversaries can become involved in a contentious relationship.

- Horse (Ashwini and Shatabhishak) and Buffalo (Swati and Hasta)
- Elephant (Bharani and Revati) and Lion (Purva Ashadha and Dhanishta)
- Goat/Sheep (Krittika and Pushya) and Monkey (Purva Ashadha and Shravana)
- Serpent (Rohini and Mrigasira) and Mongoose (Uttara Ashadha)
- Dog (Mula and Ardra) and Deer (Jyeshta and Anuradha)
- Cat (Ashlesha and Punarvasu) and Rat (Magha and Purva Phalguni)
- Cow (Uttara Phalguni and Uttara Bhadra) and Tiger (Vishakha and Chitra)

Some of these animal adversaries are deadly enemies in the wild, like the serpent and mongoose, while other adversaries do not have anything in common with their animal adversary like the elephant and lion. This quality needs to be taken into account when analysing these relationships.

In the relationship between two sexual adversaries, one can take over the power of the other and become dominant. One person can come under the unhealthy influence of the other.

There is cancellation of antagonism if the lagna lords or Moon lords of the couple are friends or trine to each other.

Yoni and the Kuta System in Relationship Compatibility

Kutas are units that are used for judging traditional compatibility in marriage. There are 12 factors to be considered of which 8 are very important. The eight Kutas have gunas or points given to them which total 32. At least 18 are required for basic compatibility. Yoni kuta is one of the links of compatibility which gets points.

Kuta uses nakshatras and the rashi chart in order to decide compatibility and this was important in India, where many marriages were arranged.

In this book I only deal with yoni compatibility as space precludes me from covering the kuta system in full.

Nakshatra Couples

Two nakshatras are coupled together as male and female energy of the same animal. The male is usually dominant and the female represents the passive quality of the nakshatra, so for example, a female Uttara Phalguni's animal is the bull. She will have bull type characteristics and behaviour as well its sexual needs and desires. A man who has the Moon in cow nakshatra Uttara Bhadra may be more passive and embrace the softness of the female impulse.

In life, an individual can connect with other animals with differing yonis and while their sexual relationship is not considered perfect there can be up to 75% compatibility. Check the sexual compatibility of the various nakshatras on p. 296.

The Horse Couple – Ashwini and Shatabhishak
Yoni – Ashwini: Male Horse   Shatabhishak: Female Horse

Horses are fiercely independent and beautiful. They need to roam free in wild pastures. It is not easy to tame them and they can be commitment phobic; sexual freedom is important to them. They can be nervous and highly-strung. They are usually fussy about who they love and set high standards for their sexual partners. Those who succeed in getting close to them never feel a sense of security as even the most domesticated horses are self-reliant.

The Ashwini male horse is active and dominant. These people have the need to conquer. If they are attracted to someone, they will be the hunters. They are sensuous and can be wonderful lovers. Ashwini will need to be free of all entanglements; they can be selfish in love, not always caring for their partner's desires.

Shatabhishak, the female horse, is more passive. These individuals rarely make the first move. They like finesse in their lovers and enjoy love in special surroundings. They need partners who are sophisticated and cultured. They have a strong sexual drive but will keep it firmly under control lest they express the darker side of their Shatabhishak nature. Being a horse and Shatabhishak with all its mystical energy is often difficult for them as they can think of their sexuality being a darker element that needs to be hidden. They trust very few with their sexual secrets, not always sure that their partners will be comfortable with their sexuality.

Ashwini and Shatabhishak may not be the best companions for each other even though their sexuality matches. The horses may be fussy and fearful of commitment so there is difficulty in making a greater connection. Ashwini are too independent and never give Shatabhishak enough attention. Ashwini are highly strung and need careful wooing, something Shatabhishak are not inclined to do. This relationship will usually struggle to establish an overall connection.

Sexual Adversaries – the Buffalo (Hasta and Swati)

Hasta and Swati are the buffalo nakshatras and they are sexually antagonistic. Buffalo people are practical and earthy so Swati and Hasta may be too unimaginative to satisfy the horse nakshatra's sexual needs. They are never fully sexually confident and therefore do not project the sexual aura necessary to attract horses or keep them interested for long. Horses are fastidious and will continually remind the buffalo of their inadequacies. With Hasta they may experiment sexually, but they will hate themselves for giving into their weakness. They can get on in other aspects of relationship with Swati and despite their sexual antagonism it can be a good relationship.

The Elephant Couple – Bharani and Revati
Yoni – Bharani: Male Elephant   Revati: Female Elephant

Elephants are the kings of the jungle. They are dominant, tend to live in herds and are vegetarian. They are powerful yet gentle. Bharani and Revati seek different things for relationships; Revati wants sacred whereas Bharani is sensuality itself and is more passionate in its demands..

Bharani is the male elephant who is independent and only joins the herds for mating. These people can be selfish and can get into a pattern of only seeking out partners when they are ready for sex and ignore them otherwise. One of the conundrums of Bharani is that it is a female nakshatra but its sexuality is male. The female energy comes from its karma to be the receptacle for the soul. The male sexuality indicates that both male and female Bharani will be active in seeking partners to fulfill their divine mission to help creation. Their nature is earthy and sensuous. They will fight for and relentlessly pursue the person who takes their fancy. They enjoy the victory. Once they have won the partner of their choice, they can become bored easily or take their partners for granted. The male elephant can go into a state of musth or sexual frenzy and this is a very destructive state. If Bharani people go into this state of excessive passion, they can be very damaging and not bother about who they destroy in the process.

At Revati's state of consciousness, they are seeking a relationship that is sacred. They want to create a new generation for tomorrow, therefore their sexuality is precious and not to be misused. According to the Vedas, sexual power should be conserved; it will then become Ojas, an inner radiance that glows from those who are at peace with their desires and learnt to conserve their sexuality. The female elephant will rarely go out seeking a partner and can be puritanical in her sexual habits. These people mature late sexually but they also remain sexually active till a late age.

The male elephant Bharani, connects intimately with the female elephant Revati, who wants to use their sexuality sparingly. They can consequently feel guilty about enjoying sex whereas Bharani takes the enjoyment of sex as a divine right. These two are compatible in other areas with Bharani, so the elephants can have a good overall relationship.

Sexual Adversaries – The Lions (Dhanishta and Purva Bhadra)

Dhanishta and Purva Bhadra are sexually incompatible with Bharani and Revati as elephants and lions are adversaries in the wild. They are both kings of the jungle in their different ways and are possessive of their territory. Bharani can get extremely aggressive with Dhanishta and Purva Bhadra; there can be fighting and arguing over every aspect, just to assert their strength. They will try to show this dominance through sex and sexual power play. While Revati people may appear as soft and spiritual, they can be strong and stubborn. They do not take easily to bullying.

They can learn to live with their enemy. In the wild, the lion and the elephant live together in apparent harmony, each respecting the other. The lion rarely enters the elephant's patch and the elephant does not go into the lion's den. A relationship with clearly marked areas of operation and power sharing can work, but patience and calmness has to be exercised. Take care that the lines of demarcation do not become insurmountable barriers in the relationship.

The Goat Couple – Krittika and Pushya
Yoni – Pushya: Male Goat   Krittika: Female Goat

Goat people are intelligent and inquisitive. They tend to follow the herd so they can be very conscious of what the world is doing and follow fashion and trends. This can create problems within relationships as they get involved in new things and in extreme cases leave a relationship for a new one if they feel the present one is out of sync with new trends. They recognise the need to serve others and are rarely ever aware of them individually. In their sexual relationships they will try to please as well. They can have an unerring sense of what is present and current.

The male goat will be dominant whereas the females are followers. Pushya sexuality is linked to the male sheep/goat which makes them active in seeking sexual fulfillment; they need to be in control of their sexuality. However both sexes of Pushya like to pursue their partners. The ram is passionate and aggressive. They are serious yet they enjoy frivolous sensuality and lighthearted sex.

The female sexuality shows the passive side of Krittika. These individuals are leaders in every other aspect of life but when it comes to expressing their sexuality they become passive spectators. Agni, their deity, has strong sexual desires, and if Krittika's sexual urges are not controlled they can easily get excessive. Unfulfilled, they may resort to having affairs or secret liaisons. They let their sexual partners do all the hard work and initiate a more sensual relationship. Once they get seriously involved they can be fiercely loyal and are liable to hold onto good as well as negative relationships. One of the great qualities that Krittika possess is the ability to get along with most of the nakshatras. Even with their worst partners, they have areas of compatibility.

The ram Pushya connects passionately to the sheep, Krittika. They relate harmoniously in all areas of life so these are good partnerships, sexually satisfying and emotionally complete.

Sexual Adversaries – The Monkeys (Purva Ashadha and Shravana)
The monkeys, Purva Ashadha, and Shravana, are incompatible sexually. Monkeys and goats have no relationship in the wild and this is expressed in this relationship – there is nothing to bind them together. Monkeys are naughty, manipulative, and complicated and they can be at times too devious for the straightforward goat. Monkeys cannot provide

the sexual loyalty that the goat nakshatras need. They will tease and manipulate Pushya and Krittika, never making a commitment. Krittika have average compatibility in other areas with Purva Ashadha so that can make this relationship work but they have poor connections with Shravana, making this a much tougher relationship to manage. Pushya is the opposite, they can overcome the sexual hostility with Shravana as this is a good connection in all other areas, but with Purva Ashadha the connections are complex.

The Snake Couple – Rohini and Mrigasira
Yoni – Rohini: Male Snake   Mrigasira: Female Snake

Snakes are mystical and secretive, they radiate their sensuality and hidden power. The serpent sexuality is intensely private and very passionate and they can hypnotize others with their sensual aura. They will keep their sexuality under wraps, and only a person they really desire would activate their inner passion. But be careful in attracting a snake partner; they can walk away from a relationship in the early stages, but once involved they can be jealous and possessive. They will not let go easily. The snake nakshatras will wrap themselves around their lovers and cling to them. At the same time they like their freedom, as they will not like to feel captive. Snake people should be careful not to let their possessiveness and jealousy get out of control.

Rohini is the male snake and these people will pursue the object of their affections but only express their interest if they know they are receiving that special signal. They often mistake sexual attraction for love, which can lead to disappointments and disillusionment. Other aspects of Rohini suggest a weakness for having inappropriate relationships and this can add to sorrow in relationships.

Mrigasira is the female snake and will not be the aggressive partner. These people may need someone else to take the first steps in a sexual relationship. They need a partner to feel complete within and find it difficult to be casual in relationships. They can also be jealous and possessive; they must try to control their vicious streak which usually comes out when relationships are not going their way and their lovers or partners are being openly defiant and challenging.

Mrigasira and Rohini understand each other's sexual needs perfectly. They are compatible in other areas of life as well, so this can be a mutually satisfying relationship that flourishes on many levels. Mrigasira are more intellectually dominating while Rohini are sensuously so. Snakes have a habit of killing each other. They have to be careful not to go on a warpath, then neither snake will give up and they will fight viciously unable to let go, and it can become a seriously negative situation. In order for extreme negativity to flow between the snake couple there must be other challenging aspects in the chart too.

Sexual Adversaries – The Mongoose (Uttara Ashadha)

Uttara Ashadha is the worst sexual relationship for Rohini and Mrigasira as in nature the mongoose and snake are deadly enemies. Whenever they meet they fight to the death. Snake nakshatras have a subconscious antagonism towards Uttara Ashadha and they are unable to accept the existence of the other. In a relationship the passion can quickly turn sour and in extreme cases sexual competitiveness, irrational jealousies, and vindictiveness can come into this sexual relationship unnoticed. Then they may want to destroy each other without thinking of the consequences. If the relationship does last, one person can dominate the other and completely take over their personality, thoughts and life, to the detriment of the other.

Mrigasira people are better equipped to rationalize than Rohini. They will analyze the hidden undercurrents and not be afraid to cross the barriers that block their relationship, intellectually at least. Their planetary ruler Mars is naturally friendly with Uttara Ashadha's ruler, the Sun.

The Dog Couple – Mula and Ardra
Yoni – Mula: Male Dog   Ardra: Female Dog

Dogs have two sides, wild and domesticated. The dog in the wild is a vicious animal and hard to control, while the domesticated dog can be trained to be loving and caring. Both Mula and Ardra have a fierce side to their nature which needs to be managed; if unleashed it can bring trouble to the relationship. Dogs usually give unconditional love and support. They can be forever seeking approval. If they are sexually attracted to someone they tend to show their love immediately. This can lead them to be treated shabbily by their partners who do not appreciate love so readily given.

Mula, the male dog will actively pursue those that they love. These people can quickly become involved in a sexual relationship but give it up easily; their strong sexuality worries them and this is the part of their nature that they want to transform. They want to be in control of their sexuality rather than be controlled by it. They can be faithful if their partners demand it, otherwise they enjoy exploring their sexuality with no thought to fidelity or commitment.

Ardra people are the female dogs who will wait for their mates to make the first move. They are not necessary faithful either, and just like Mula they too need love, caring and will be forever seeking approval. On the negative side they can be fierce, angry and dissatisfied with their partners. They can give up a good relationship to pursue another one. This can turn out to be a big disappointment. Ardra have to avoid being destructive in relationships

The overall relationship between Mula and Ardra is average; Mula needs more than just sexual compatibility in their true partner. Ardra can thrill them sexually but they remind them too much of their animal instincts, the instincts they are trying to control in their spiritual mission to embrace spirituality. Mula can give Ardra an exciting time sexually but their personal journey is complex and in the opposite direction to Ardra. They can mentally mess with Ardra and hurt them.

Sexual Adversaries – The Deer (Anuradha and Jyeshta)
Mula and Ardra's worst lovers are the deer Anuradha and Jyeshta as in the wild dogs corner and kill deer. Mula and Ardra can become very hostile to Anuradha and Jyeshta once the initial glow of the relationship has faded. They can try to restrict the deer's freedom and independence. Deer people like to be loving, fun and frivolous, but Mula can become perversely practical and unimaginative with them.

With Jyeshta, the relationship is extremely difficult. Jyeshta can make them feel cornered by their constant manipulations and Mula/Ardra can be goaded into attacking them. This may not be physical, but more emotionally and mentally cruel. Jyeshta and Mula/Ardra can be equally guilty of it to each other. Anuradha have the capacity to give unrequited love and they will try to balance the negativity to work through their differences.

The Cat Couple – Ashlesha and Punarvasu
Yoni – Ashlesha: Male Cat   Punarvasu: Female Cat

This is not just the domesticated cat but cats in the wild, like cheetahs and leopards. Ashlesha and Punarvasu people can be instinctively catty, fiercely independent and are not above clawing, if anyone dares to invade their space. They will only want to be loved when they are ready. Once involved, they are extremely possessive and want they lover's attention all the time.

The male cat, Ashlesha, is a promiscuous animal. These individuals can be commitment phobic, moving from one relationship to another or even becoming involved in more than one relationship at a time. Both male and female Ashlesha will be hunters and actively seek relationships when they desire someone. Just like cats, they will only be interested in partners who are not interested in them. Ashlesha people can be selfish and may not bother about their partners too much.

Punarvasu is the female cat and is slightly less dominant than the male. They like their independence and in relationships too they want freedom. They can be jealous of their partner's relationship with others; they mark their territory. The same rules do not apply to them however, they must keep their independence. If their partners accept their nature, then they will show them their true side by being loving, sensuous and committed.

The cats can share a sizzling relationship full of passions, sensuality, possessiveness and true independence. They will fight passionately as both of them are strong personalities, unwilling to give an inch. The overall relationship between them is good; they can find complete fulfillment from their animal counterpart.

Sexual Adversaries – The Rats (Magha and Purva Phalguni)
The worst sexual partners for the cats are their natural enemy the rat, Magha and Purva Phalguni. Though the rats like sex in quantity and they are usually unable to deliver the quality of sex the cats demand, their sexual needs have no common ground and there is a hidden danger of this relationship becoming one between a predator and its prey. They can move from emotional passion to sexual rivalry in an instant. In nature the cat kills the rat and therefore this relationship has the capacity to turn very nasty.

The Rat Couple – Magha and Purva Phalguni
Yoni – Magha: Male Rat   Purva Phalguni: Female Rat

The rat nakshatras develop their sexuality early. They want lots of sex and often. Their voracious sexual appetite can be tiring for those who are not equally sensuous. If their partners are unable to keep up with them sexually, they can look for other lovers. They do not recognise sexual boundaries. Different backgrounds, ethnicity, socially unacceptable – these factors do not concern them. The rat is the smallest in the animal kingdom and therefore has to be careful of predators. They can meet lovers who will try to dominate them.

Magha people are sexually connected to the male rat and express dynamic energy. Magha means mighty, but being the smallest in the animal kingdom, the rat has an image problem. These people can feel inferior sexually and develop unnecessary complexes so they over-express their sexual power, to compensate for the perceived inner inadequacies. Magha is a very virile sign; they should be practising birth control if they do not want unplanned pregnancies.

Purva Phalguni is the female rat, but unlike Magha these people won't always be pursuing sex. Purva Phalguni is family oriented and wants children so they can sacrifice their sexual needs for their family. They may feel frustrated, but the family comes first. Purva Phalguni people suffer a lot emotionally if they are unable to produce children. This can spoil even the best relationships for them. If having children is not an option, they should pursue creative endeavors together.

Rats are good lovers for each other and their compatibility in other areas of life is excellent, so this has the ability to be a match made in heaven. Both of them understand sex, they do not dress up their need in fancy romantic words. This fulfillment leads to them finding love together.

Sexual Adversaries – The Cats (Ashlesha and Punarvasu)
The worst sexual partners are their natural enemy, the cats, Ashlesha and Punarvasu. A relationship with the cat is dangerous for the rat. Cats kill the rat and this relationship can become very negative if other factors in the chart do not compensate. The rat has no power over the cat except to irritate them and in return cats will try to play tricks, involve them

in games and try to undermine their confidence. Rats enjoy sex and the cats will question their need for sex, limiting the sexual part of the relationship. Cat people prefer quality to quantity, which can also be the way of the cats controlling and dominating the rat nakshatras. Magha and Purva Phalguni can feel frustrated at not having their sexual needs met, but their feeling of inadequacy can keep them tied to this deeply unsatisfactory relationship. As natural enemies this relationship takes a very short time to move from ardour to antagonism.

Purva Phalguni may compromise for the sake of the children or family, but this relationship may not bring them happiness.

The Cow Couple – Uttara Phalguni and Uttara Bhadra
Yoni – Uttara Phalguni: Male Bull   Uttara Bhadra: Female Cow

The cow and bull are sacred animals in vedic thought and these animal nakshatras are big-hearted and givers of themselves. Their generosity can be taken for granted. They have a slow-burning temper and usually remain placid but when annoyed they can be destructive. They are possessive and jealous.

Uttara Phalguni sexuality is connected to the bull. Shiva's Nandi bull is the symbol of divine virility. Indian women pray to the bull to give them the ability to bear children, which makes Uttara Phalguni symbolic of fertility and creativity. Both the sexes will have a powerful sex drive; it can become a divine mission to experience sex. They will work hard to make sexual conquests but when they are sexually content, they forget to please. This causes huge problems for them as their lovers do not take kindly to being ignored. They also believe that sexuality should be within commitment and should bear positive results. Bulls can get angry if provoked and partners should be careful not to do so.

Uttara Bhadra is the cow. Like the Kamdhenu, a special holy cow who had the ability to fulfill all desires, they try to fulfil their partner's demands, however difficult and impossible they may be. If someone is in need, they will try to satisfy it. People can also take advantage of them or feel jealous of their generosity. This can leave them open to manipulative partners. They can become victimized by their refusal to see the true picture.

The cow is sacred in India and the sexual act was considered a sacred expression of love for their partner. Uttara Bhadra people do not base their relationships purely on sex and this can make them uncompromising as they struggle to find their ideal relationship. Due to their idealism and good nature they can work well with nakshatras like Uttara Ashadha who have complex sexual issues.

The cow and bull connect together well. They are compatible in other areas of life as well making this a relationship that is happy and long lasting. Both of them view their sexual relationship as sacred and will honour the other with their loyalty and commitment.

Sexual Adversaries – The Tigers (Vishakha and Chitra)

Their worst sexual partners are Chitra and Vishakha. In the wild the tiger kills the bull and the cow, who are afraid of its power. In life, tiger people will exercise this fear factor and try to control and dominate the cow/bull nakshatras. This is usually an unusual position for Uttara Phalguni to be in, as they do not take kindly to being subjugated. The sexual power struggles can mar their relationship. Uttara Bhadra want divinity and their giving nature can be tested with the tigers – the fear can make them over generous and it can become a one-way relationship easily. The tigers seek excitement from sex and Uttara Bhadra seek divinity. The tiger's lack of commitment and their philandering nature makes it a painful partnership for them.

The overall relationship remains challenging for Vishakha and Chitra as the cow and the tiger do not want the same things from life.

The Buffalo Couple – Swati and Hasta
Yoni – Swati: Male Buffalo   Hasta: Female Buffalo

Buffaloes in the vedic system are the water buffalo that have long been domesticated in India. They till the lands and provide milk, yet in mythology they do not have the same respect as the cow. This is a huge issue with the buffalo nakshatras. They are hardworking and industrious yet are not appreciated. Buffalo people can be earthy, powerful and wild. On the negative side, they could be aggressive and crude, and their persona can instill fear in others. They keep a tight control over their baser instincts, afraid of unleashing the animal within them. They can have very fragile egos and hardly ever forget a sexual slight. They hold grudges for a long time and can be vindictive and obsessive. If their partners stir up their inner beast, they can lash out, regardless of the cost to themselves.

Hasta people tend to keep this part of their nature under wraps. They appear refined but have an earthy side to them. Just as buffaloes are domesticated in India so Hasta have the ability to control their nature. They wait until they know they are desired before they reveal themselves and prefer that their mate make all the effort for them.

Swati people have a wild, untamed side but they can harness it to be restrained and civilized. They try to keep a tight control over their baser instincts, afraid of unleashing the animal within them, but they do not always succeed. Libra is the sign of relationships so this hidden earthiness creates inner conflicts. For Swati, sex can take a back seat to their other ambitions.

Swati and Hasta find sexual happiness with each other. Both usually keep their sexuality under wraps and never express their more earthy nature, afraid that others may not understand this as it does not square with the outer personality. With each other there is no need for subterfuge, as they instinctively connect to their natural self.

Sexual Adversaries – The Horses (Ashwini and Shatabhishak)
They are hostile to the horses, Ashwini and Shatabhishak. This is a relationship where there is nothing in common. Between the exotic horse and the unappreciated buffalo, everything is piled in the horse's favour; the horse wastes no time in letting their buffalo counterparts know that they are not attracted to them.

However, Hasta aren't put off by this and are fascinated and attracted to them. They usually feel that they are able to overcome the restrictions posed by destiny. Here is the frustrating part, they cannot do that without losing their self-esteem. They bear the pain of loving Ashwini or Shatabhishak but find it difficult to let go.

Swati is one of the few nakshatras that has good relations with both their sexual antagonists. They know how to give prominence to other human needs such as love, emotion and happiness. Ashwini and Shatabhishak are not always able to appreciate their more earthy nature and Swati find it hard to understand their highly-strung and finicky attitude. Their sexual relationship may not be totally fulfilling, but they try to override the issues that usually split others apart.

The Tiger Couple – Vishakha and Chitra
Yoni – Vishakha: Male Tiger   Chitra: Female Tiger

The tiger is exotic, elemental, and unspoilt; it is the most attractive animal in the jungle yet it hides from view. Tiger sexuality is the strongest amongst the animal kingdom so these people need equally strong sexual partners. They are virile and potent and struggle with their intense sexual needs. They may learn to conquer them and move towards celibacy and temperance, but their sexuality smolders below the surface and given the right conditions can come back to its full force instantly.

Vishakha is the male tiger, the sexual predator of the zodiac. These individuals have strong sexual appetites and will hunt out their partners. They need partners who can match their strong sexuality. This is an area they should never compromise. If their partners do not match their sexual needs, they look elsewhere.

Chitra is the female, very exotic, and people are attracted to them, but Chitra will keep their distance. They have a strong sexuality like their male counterpart but the female quality means they are not so obvious in expressing it.

They have a good partnership with each other that is full of sensuous promise and exciting sex. They are very compatible in other areas of life, so this makes their relationships sexually satisfying and emotionally fulfilling.

Sexual Adversaries – The Bull and Cow (Uttara Phalguni and Uttara Bhadra)

The worst sexual partners are Uttara Phalguni and Uttara Bhadra. In the wild the tiger kills both of them; tiger nakshatras are not in awe of their cow partners, in fact they can create awe and fear in them. They will subconsciously try to exercise their power and the relationship goes downhill fast. Tigers have the strongest sexual desires among the nakshatras and is not an option for them to have a relationship that is not sexually exciting. Uttara Phalguni and Uttara Bhadra are diametrically opposite to them, pragmatic, industrious and staid. The hidden sexual issues will make them frustrated and Vishakha and Chitra can take it out on them emotionally.

The Deer Couple – Jyeshta and Anuradha
Yoni – Jyeshta: Male Deer   Anuradha: Female Deer

Deer are like the Moon and they love passionately and emotionally. The Moon god, Soma, enjoys relationships with all 28 nakshatras (symbolically his wives). Similarly deer nakshatra people can become involved in multiple relationships and sexual intrigues and this can be the weakness of them.

Jyeshta is the male deer who is sexually aggressive. Jyeshta is a stormy nakshatra and their sexuality can create a dilemma. The male deer can get into a state of *musth*, where ecstasy of passion takes over, so these people can get involved so intensely that they lose all sense of what is good or bad for them. In this state Jyeshta allows possessiveness to get out of control. Indra, the deity of Jyeshta, had an affair with his guru's wife and suffered. Jyeshta can get into an inappropriate relationship that causes much sorrow.

Anuradha is the female deer who allows others to take the initiative. Anuradha people need sex that includes love and they avoid purely sexual relationships. However more often than not they mistake lust for love and become involved in a superficial sexual relationship.

Deer will be good for each other as Anuradha people will love Jyeshta with their heart and soul. They fulfil Anuradha's sexual passions while being sensitive to their emotional needs. The male deer, Jyeshta, knows how to woo with love as pure sexual happiness is never enough for Anuradha.

Sexual Adversaries – The Dogs (Mula and Ardra)
The dogs Mula and Ardra are the worst sexual partners. They try to be dominant and controlling but it is never as simple as that. The deer people's relationship with the dogs can be exciting but also destructive. In the wild dogs corner deer and will kill them. Sexually the deer nakshatra are subconsciously afraid of provoking the ferocious side of the dogs, but are unable to help themselves from egging them on. This can lead to a relationship that alternates between dominance and aggression. In extreme cases it can take them over the edge and create extreme unhappiness.

The Monkey Couple – Purva Ashadha and Shravana
Yoni – Purva Ashadha: Male Monkey   Shravana: Female Monkey

Monkeys are fun-loving and enjoy life and love. They can be charming, playful and impish. They rarely show their lighter side to the world; this is reserved for those they love. They can stay uncommitted and if they do not find a true partner, they can be sexually promiscuous and commitment is not very important.

Purva Ashadha is the male monkey. In vedic mythology, the monkey god Hanuman was known for his devotion, but he was a devout bachelor, so this reveals another side of the Purva Ashadha personality. If these people choose the single path, they will be committed to it. Mostly they are serial monogamists. They want their love life to be full of the fun and joys of the world; they are social and like having a family, but they are never ready to commit. They will lead their partner a merry dance before they allow themselves to be caught.

Shravana people have the sexuality of the female monkey, who has a strong mothering instinct. They skirt around the issue of relationships, proverbially jump from one tree to another and avoid being caught. Unlike their male counterpart, they do make the commitment finally and want the security of family around them.

Monkey nakshatras have to watch they do not deify their partners and stop seeing any defects in them.

Monkeys are good for each other. Both of them are commitment phobic and their relationship remains one of loose ties rather than intense closeness. Shravana and Purva Ashadha know instinctively that they will allow themselves to be caught eventually by the other, but only when they are ready. Commitment comes with time.

Sexual Adversaries – The Sheep/Goat (Pushya and Krittika)

Their worst sexual relationships are with Pushya and Krittika. Monkey and sheep have nothing in common and this relationship is not one of danger, but two people who cannot match the other's expectations. Monkey people are lively and fun, and they can have a ready wit that they use against the sheep/goat. The shy sheep does not enjoy being made fun of by the monkeys. Sheep are unadventurous by nature and will not be able to deal with the boldness of the monkey. Both Krittika and Pushya people need loyalty and commitment and they do not enjoy the monkey nakshatra's free-wheeling attitudes. With Pushya, they are able to override the sexual incompatibility to have a loving and fulfilling relationship, but Krittika will be fiery and angry with them and unable to find a common ground to relate.

The Lion Couple – Purva Bhadra and Dhanishta
Yoni – Purva Bhadra: Male Lion   Dhanishta: Female Lion

Lions are the kings of the jungle; exotic with long flowing manes and powerful strong personalities. They live in wild open places and are masters of all they survey. They dominate the animal kingdom and are proud and beautiful beasts.

Purva Bhadra is the male lion who is dynamic, virile and potent. These people can be arrogant and feel they only have to show an interest in a member of the opposite sex in order to get them. This can be very often true. They are not possessive, believing that if they are not willing to commit, they do not expect commitment from their partners. They fight for their partners only if they are interested, but will readily dump that partner if they find that they are being manipulated.

Dhanishta sexuality is connected to the lioness. Lionesses hunt side by side with the lions. They are strong and powerful and exemplify female power. Dhanishta, male or female will defend their cubs. There is no passivity like other female animals. Dhanishta are in charge of their sexuality. If they desire someone, they will make it obvious. They have a strong sexual appetite, liking plenty of sex, but once satiated they may not look for another sexual encounter until they are ready for it. They stay true to their partners as long as their partners are true to them. If their partners stray, so will they. They do not believe in double standards.

The lion and lioness are good for each other; both are powerful and strong, and they can commit sexually. Exciting and sensual, they find happiness together.

Sexual Adversaries – The Elephants (Bharani and Revati)
They are sexually incompatible with the elephants Bharani and Revati. The elephant and the lion are both powerful in the animal kingdom and naturally inimical. Both of them jealously guard their terrain and

will not allow the other to dictate what they do or don't do. In the wild, the lion and the elephant live together in apparent harmony; the lion rarely enters the elephant's patch and the elephant does not go into the lion's den. A relationship with clearly demarcated areas of operation and power can work. Surprisingly Purva Bhadra gets along well with Bharani and Revati people. They have the ability to overcome sexual enmity through diplomacy and careful sharing of power. Dhanishta people find it impossible to have a good relationship with Bharani.

The Lonely Mongoose – Uttara Ashadha

The animal symbol of Uttara Ashadha is the mongoose. There is no female mongoose in the nakshatra animals. For them, there are no ideal partners; they have no instinctive understanding of their sexuality. To fulfill their spiritual path, they have to learn to compromise on their sexuality. Lack of an animal partner can indicate lack of relationship skills too.

To hide their lack of sexual confidence and their low self-esteem, these people appear active and bold. If they fancy someone they make a play for them. They are fast workers and can get involved quickly, but once involved they do not know what to do with their lovers – the lack of an ideal mate in the nakshatra system is certainly a hindrance. They can be passionate yet cold, self-indulgent yet ascetic. The right partner is one who accepts their intrinsic spirituality and makes them comfortable with their sexuality.

They hate secrecy or deception, so they set a high standard for their partners. If they fail, Uttara Ashadha can be most unforgiving. They will not wait till they have rooted it out. Uttara Ashadha people must avoid becoming suspicious for the sake of it. As they are plain speaking and direct, they may not understand wiles and sexual play from others. They need to work at attracting the opposite sex.

The lack of a female partnership in the nakshatra system suggests that a life of perfect sexual and emotional partnership is not available for Uttara Ashadha. Theirs is a highly spiritual sign, it is a loner nakshatra where the mind is being guided to focus on matters beyond sex. This aspect does create difficulties in finding an ideal sexual partner, but there are many nakshatras that have 75% sexual compatibility with them, like Krittika, Pushya, Purva Ashadha, and Shravana.

Sexual Adversaries – The Snakes (Mrigasira and Rohini)

Rohini, and Mrigasira are their worst sexual partners. In nature, the mongoose is the deadly enemy of the snake and they duel to death whenever they meet. The mongoose regards the snake as vermin and this attitude can filter into the relationship between mongoose and serpent people. Uttara Ashadha will want to completely change the personality of their serpent partners – it is their way of killing the serpent, but the incompatibility between them makes happiness within this relationship a challenge. In extreme cases, sexual competitiveness, irrational jealousies, and vindictiveness can come into this sexual relationship unnoticed. Then they may want to destroy each other without thinking of the consequences.

With Rohini the compatibility is low so this is a relationship best avoided. Of the two, Mrigasira is better equipped to rationalize than Rohini. They will analyse the hidden undercurrents and not be afraid to cross the barriers that block the relationship, intellectually at least. Uttara Ashadha must learn to meet them half way. Mrigasira's ruler, Mars, is the friend of Uttara Ashadha's ruler, the Sun. They can use this friendship to settle the differences.

Yoni Analysis

In order to fulfill the sexual desires, it is best to have the person of the same yoni and be the right gender. Alas, life is not like that and this makes for the diversity of experience as we are attracted to different species. I have used a few charts to show how this develops. In order to judge compatibility, the Moon's nakshatra is used.

Brad Pitt's Relationships

Brad Pitt is the mongoose with the Moon in Uttara Ashadha so he has natural issues with relationships. He had several relationships before marrying and divorcing Jennifer Aniston and then partnering Angelina Jolie. The mongoose has to be careful that they do not get involved with the snake. One of his major relationships was with Gwyneth Paltrow who is a serpent Rohini. This relationship ended abruptly which is often the case in snake/mongoose relationships. His later relationships were with a Jyeshta deer (Jennifer Aniston) and a Revati elephant (Angelina Jolie). As Jennifer Aniston has her Moon in gandanta too, her emotions are insecure and needy and this would have put added pressure on Brad Pitt to cope. As the elephant, Angelina is more likely to want her own space and she would be able to deal with the loner Brad Pitt.

Prince Charles' Relationships

Prince Charles is an Ashwini horse, very fussy and particular. His first wife Princess Diana was a Dhanishta Lioness. There is not much in common; the horse's demands would not have gone down well with the lioness, who did not want different rules for each other and both had an independent streak. Diana was passionate about her boys and guarded them fiercely. Camilla, Duchess of Cornwall, is a dog and so much better to get along with the horse. In the English countryside, you often see the dog faithfully following the horse; this relationship is easier for Prince Charles to deal with. Although the Ardra dog would give a fierce side to Camilla, Duchess of Cornwall, this is not apparent to the public.

How to Study the Sexual Compatibility Chart

Look in the vertical column for your Moon nakshatra and the horizontal column for your partner's Moon nakshatra. The number you arrive at is the % sexual compatibility you have with your partner. E.g. if your nakshatra is Magha and your partners is Ashwini, you find Magha in the vertical column and Ashwini from the horizontal one, you will see the number is 50. Therefore your sexual compatibility with your partner is 50%. Remember that there are other factors involved in compatibility; successful relationships are based on many other qualities

Sexual Compatibility

0 = none, 25= below average, 50= average, 75= good, 100= perfect

	Ash	Bha	Kri	Roh	Mri	Ard	Pun	Pus	Ash	Ma	PP	UP	Has	Chi	Swa	Vis	An	Jye	Mul	PA	UA	Shr	Dha	Sha	PB	UB	Rev
Ash	100	50	50	75	75	50	50	50	50	50	50	25	00	25	00	25	75	75	50	75	50	75	25	100	25	25	50
Bha	50	100	75	75	75	50	50	75	50	50	50	25	75	25	75	25	50	50	50	75	50	75	00	50	00	25	100
Kri	50	75	100	50	50	25	50	100	25	25	25	75	75	25	75	25	50	50	25	00	75	00	25	50	25	75	75
Roh	75	75	50	100	100	50	25	50	50	25	25	25	75	50	75	50	50	50	50	50	00	50	50	75	50	25	75
Mri	75	75	50	100	100	50	25	50	25	25	25	25	75	50	25	50	50	50	50	50	00	50	50	75	50	25	75
Ard	50	50	25	100	100	50	25	25	25	25	25	25	25	50	25	50	50	50	50	50	25	50	25	50	25	25	75
Pun	50	50	50	50	50	50	100	50	25	25	00	50	25	25	50	25	75	00	100	75	50	50	25	25	50	50	50
Pus	50	75	100	25	25	50	100	100	50	00	25	75	25	25	75	25	50	75	50	00	75	00	25	25	25	75	50
Ash	50	50	50	25	25	25	50	50	100	100	50	50	50	50	75	25	75	25	50	75	50	75	25	50	25	75	75
Ma	50	50	25	50	25	25	25	00	100	100	100	50	50	50	100	50	50	50	25	50	25	50	50	50	50	50	50
PP	50	50	25	25	25	25	00	25	00	100	100	50	50	50	50	50	50	25	25	50	25	50	50	50	50	50	50
UP	25	25	75	25	25	50	50	75	50	50	50	100	75	00	75	00	75	75	50	50	25	50	25	25	25	100	25
Has	00	75	75	75	75	50	25	75	50	50	50	75	100	25	100	25	50	50	50	75	50	50	25	00	25	75	75
Chi	25	25	25	50	50	25	25	25	25	50	50	00	25	100	25	100	50	50	25	25	50	25	25	25	25	00	25
Swa	00	75	75	75	25	50	50	75	25	50	50	75	100	25	100	25	25	25	50	25	50	50	25	00	25	75	75
Vis	25	25	50	50	50	50	25	25	25	50	50	00	25	100	25	100	25	50	50	50	50	25	25	25	25	00	25
An	75	25	50	50	50	50	75	50	75	50	50	75	50	25	50	25	100	100	00	50	50	50	25	75	25	75	50
Jye	75	50	50	50	50	50	00	75	25	50	25	75	50	50	50	50	100	100	00	50	50	50	25	75	25	75	50
Mul	50	50	25	50	50	25	100	50	50	25	25	50	50	25	50	25	00	00	100	50	25	50	50	25	50	50	50
PA	75	25	00	50	50	25	75	00	75	50	50	50	50	25	25	25	50	00	50	100	75	100	50	50	50	50	75
UA	50	50	50	00	00	50	50	75	50	25	50	50	50	50	50	50	50	50	50	75	100	50	50	50	50	50	50
Shr	75	75	50	50	50	75	75	00	75	50	50	50	50	50	50	25	50	50	50	100	50	100	50	75	100	50	75
Dha	25	25	50	50	75	25	25	25	25	50	50	25	25	50	25	25	25	25	25	50	50	50	100	25	50	25	25
Sha	100	50	75	75	75	50	50	25	50	50	50	25	00	25	00	25	75	75	50	75	50	75	25	100	25	100	50
PB	25	25	50	50	50	25	50	75	50	50	50	100	25	25	25	25	25	25	25	50	50	50	25	25	100	25	00
UB	25	75	50	50	25	50	50	75	50	50	50	75	75	00	75	00	75	75	50	50	50	50	50	25	100	100	25
Rev	50	100	75	75	75	75	50	75	50	50	50	25	75	25	75	25	50	50	50	75	50	75	00	50	00	25	100

9
Nadi Nakshatra – The Secret Pulse

Nadi means a pulse and these nakshatras offer secret clues to chart analysis. Nadi are pulses which flow in our body and connect the various energy points. Similarly how these pulses are flowing within the birth chart is analysed through the nadi nakshatras to show where the blocks are and where the information is flowing smoothly. This technique uses the navatara as its basis and adds further special nakshatras to complete the picture. Navatara takes into account the three groups of nine nakshatras that are ruled by the same planet and highlights how planets relate to each other in the nakshatra mandala and the positive and negative relationships they form. Nadi nakshatras add to the navatara and put the spotlight on certain nakshatras that relate to our career, parents, creativity, relationships with society, past karma and ability to succeed, plus negative aspects that can destroy the significations of the nakshatras and the planets placed within. In order to know these relationships, one point of view is taken and the planets and their nakshatras are studied. Nadi nakshatras can be studied from the Moon, lagna, Sun, and maha dasha nakshatra lord point of view, although more importance is given to the Moon nakshatra.

They are mentioned in many classics including *Jataka Parijata*, *Phaladeepika* and form the basis of Sarvatobhadra Chakra which uses all information including the panchanga, rashi, nakshatra, and sacred sounds to give a fully rounded picture of an individual's life. This is a very complicated technique and needs a full book in itself so it is not covered here. Transits to these nadi nakshatras are significant and can create issues according to their nature. These are often overlooked as they are not so obvious through other analysis.

27 or 28 Nakshatras
The nadi nakshatra technique uses 27 nakshatras. Abhijit, the 28th nakshatra is intercalary with Uttara Ashadha and Shravana and it is not taken as an extra nakshatra.

Nadi Nakshatra Basics

The basis of nadi nakshatra is the navatara which connect the nakshatras that share the same rulerships. *Nava* means nine and *Tara* is stars. The nine planets rule three nakshatras each and therefore these three nakshatras form a connection with each other. This connection becomes activated in the natal chart and then by transits.

The basic navatara chart is then built upon with added nakshatras that activate the pulse of the chart. While navatara are the group of three nakshatras that share the same rulership, the nadi are specific nakshatras that have one role to perform; the other two rulerships do not perform this role. These connections are vital to understanding the subtle workings of the chart – the entwining nadis. For example if the Moon is placed in Ardra, a Rahu–ruled nakshatra, then this is known as janma or birth nakshatra. The other Rahu nakshatras Swati and Shatabhishak will perform a similar role like the birth nakshatra and show creativity as well. Transits to these nakshatras can affect the mind and the physical health due to their Rahu connection.

In order to understand the nadi nakshatras we must study the navatara first. Navatara form the basis of nadi nakshatras and it is used in Muhurta where it helps in planning an event in relation to the moon's transit. The principle is expanded further for chart analysis. While the Moon is prominent, other points of view like lagna, sun and dasha lord, must also be taken into account.

There are three paryay or similar nakshatras which are connected by their rulerships. For example Krittika, Uttara Phalguni and Uttara Ashadha are all ruled by the Sun, therefore they will share similar characteristics and perform similar roles in navatara and in the nadi nakshatra too. The navatara are:

Janma – birth
Sampat – wealth and prosperity
Vipat – danger
Kshema – prosperity
Prayatak – obstacles
Sadhana – accomplishment
Naidhana – destruction
Mitra – friend
Param Mitra – great friend

Navatara Table

Nakshatra type		1st Paryay		2nd Paryay		3rd Paryay
Janma– birth	1	10		19		
Sampat – Wealth	2	11		20		
Vipat – danger	3	12		21		
Kshema –happiness	4	13		22		
Prayatak– obstacles	5	14		23		
Sadhana – attainment	6	15		24		
Naidhana – poverty	7	16		25		
Mitra– friend	8	17		26		
Param Mitra – grt friend	9	18		27		

In order to create a navatara table, the nakshatra of the Moon or ascendant/ other point of view of analysis is placed in the first column, under Janma, and then the nakshatras are added in their order vertically.

Janma means birth and usually refers to the Moon nakshatra and the other two nakshatras that share the same rulership as the janma. Janma nakshatras are the 1, 10, and 19 nakshatras. If janma is Shravana, then the other two janma are Rohini and Hasta. Janma nakshatra is the key nakshatra and planets placed in the janma rulership will have influence on emotional and physical health. Malefics placed in Janma can influence physical health during their dasha or bring challenges to the overall quality of life whereas the benefics will enhance them. Transits to the janma nakshatra can create positive changes or negative issues.

If children are born with the same janma nakshatra (Moon) as their father, brother, mother or sister, it is not considered good and a remedial measure is advised by Parashara. Also marrying a person with the same nakshatra is not considered good. In my experience, sharing a nakshatra with someone can make for either a very strong relationship or a negative one. The main problem occurs when transits hit the similar nakshatras. If a family share the same Moon nakshatra they can experience similar transits which can lead to a major crisis, especially at times of malefic transits.

Although the main janma is the nakshatra of the Moon, other points of view can be taken into account. We can construct a navatara chart from the point of view of the lagna, the Sun or the ruler of the maha dasha. What we are trying to find out are which nakshatras are playing a similar role in our chart from these various points of view. This is extremely helpful in getting a deeper picture of the analysis.

Sampat means wealth. This nakshatra is positive. Sampat nakshatras are the 2, 11 and 20. Planets placed within it bring prosperity and wealth during their dasha. Malefics placed here can make a person feel deprived, even though they have good finances. The influence of the transit can impact their prosperity depending on their nature.

Vipat means grave dangers. Vipat nakshatras are 3, 12, and 21. In practice planets placed in vipat nakshatras tend to lose some of their power and create obstacles in life. People with planets here can make wrong decisions and their karakas and house rulerships get influenced negatively. Planets in vipat nakshatras do not work well and it is during their dashas that they show their true nature.

Kshema means prosperity and welfare. Kshema nakshatras are 4, 13 and 22. Planets placed here are supported and their karaka prosper. Dashas of planets in these nakshatras are good and the transit will have an influence according to the nature of the planet.

Prayatak means obstacles. Prayatak nakshatras are 5, 14 and 23. Planets placed here suffer blocks according to their karaka or house rulership. They can also influence health negatively during their dasha. If Venus is placed in prayatak nakshatra from the ascendant or the Moon, it can bring obstacles in marriage even if it appears well placed in the rashi chart.

Sadhana means practice and it is usually referred to as a spiritual practice with the aim of achieving specific goals. Sadhana nakshatras are 6, 15 and 24. All planets placed in sadhana nakshatras do well. They bring accomplishments, attainment and realisation of ambitions. The dasha of planets in sadhana nakshatra usually do well. Malefic transits to sadhana nakshatra can block our good practices and create struggles whereas benefics bring opportunities.

Naidhana means liable to death or destruction and perishable. These are not easy nakshatras. Naidhana nakshatras are 7, 16 and 25 and planets placed in them will bring suffering and difficulty. Transits to naidhana nakshatra are especially challenging for malefics. Naidhana nakshatras are linked to the 8th house experience so can bring unexpected events that change the course of life.

Mitra means friend. Mitra nakshatras are 8, 17 and 26. All planets placed here are friendly and help in the progress of the chart.

Param Mitra means eternal friend. This is a positive position. Param mitra nakshatras are 9, 18 and 27. This is the nakshatra preceding the janma. All planets will be friendly and supportive.

Nadi Nakshatras

Nadi nakshatras are specific nakshatras that build on the knowledge of the navatara. They bring added roles to some nakshatras:

Jati is the 4th nakshatra from janma or lagna. *Jati* means a form of lineage fixed by birth, race, family, rank, caste, tribe or class.[1] One can look at a wider definition as in what kind of society we were born into. While in ancient societies this role was fixed, now we can move away from it regardless what our starting point may be. It is a very good nakshatra as it relates to the first paryay and kshema nakshatra. It deals with our life style, community, and society that support and give comfort. This nakshatra is studied for lineage, our ability to share food, to give oblations to the fire god, as well as the future of our family.

Matru is the 8th nakshatra from Janma. *Matru* means mother so the relationship with the mother is studied from this. A malefic placed here can create problems. Transits to the matru nakshatra can improve or create problems both in one's relationship with the mother and in her own life as well.

Karma is the 10th nakshatra from janma and indicates the profession or work that the individual will do. This is the next nakshatra ruled by the same ruler as the janma. If the janma is Rohini, then the karma nakshatra will be the next nakshatra ruled by the Moom, which is Hasta. The nakshatra itself has significance regarding the type of profession chosen and planets placed there will add to the information. Transits to this nakshatra can lead to major career success. Also people who have their lagna or the Moon in this nakshatra can be good for you professionally. If an individual has Vishakha Moon and your Moon is Punarvasu, they

---

1. Definition from *Practical Sanskrit English Dictionary*, VS Apte.

will be good for you in supporting your karma – this loosely translates into their ability to help professionally.

Sanghatika is the 16th nakshatra from janma. *Sangha* means unions, groups, associations and close or intimate relationships. *Tika* means to challenge, to hurt, wound or injure. Sanghatika means close associations that are challenging and have the ability to hurt and injure. This is a difficult nakshatra. Planets placed in this nakshatra suffer according to their significations and house rulership. If the ascendant ruler is placed in sanghatika nakshatra, there can be a tendency to keep bad company that hurts the individual. Relationships with anyone representing the 16th nakshatra from your janma Moon nakshatra usually creates challenging situations and can be destructive. If the janma is Krittika then the sanghatika nakshatra will be Jyeshta. There is incompatibility between Krittika and Jyeshta Moons as Jyeshta has the ability to hurt or challenge Krittika. They can form intimate relationships with each other but these may not be productive for Krittika. It would also create problems when malefic planets transit this nakshatra.

Samudaya is the 18th nakshatra from janma and is an auspicious one. It means ascent, rising, war, battle, auspicious moment, and planets in this nakshatra are positive. It deals with good karma from a past life and is one of the most positive nakshatras in our chart. Planets placed here will give rise and success during their dasha and their significations are positive. Transits to this nakshatra will enhance the chart.

Aadhana is the 19th nakshatra from janma, the creative nakshatra of the chart. *Aadhana* means taking, placing in the sacred pot, deposit, a receptacle, a ceremony performed before conception, keeping the sacred fire. Aadhana is connected to conception and therefore the aadhana nakshatra is where new projects are conceived and ideas created for the future. The root of our creation is seen from this. The father is studied from aadhana nakshatra. If malefic planets are placed in this nakshatra or the ruler of this nakshatra is not well placed, it can lead to a difficult relationship with him. Malefic transits to this nakshatra can influence the father negatively as well as the creative abilities of an individual.

Vinasha is the 23rd nakshatra from janma and it means ruin, annihilation and destruction. Planets placed here can be destroyed. This should be specially studied for medical astrology and health. This nakshatra gives a destructive quality to the planets placed within it and the significations can suffer. Be careful of the transits of Saturn, Mars or Rahu; even the benefics in this nakshatra may not be able to give good results. Relationships with individuals having this nakshatra are not always happy or profitable. Starting anything good when the Moon is in vinasha nakshatra is not beneficial.

Manasa is the 25th nakshatra from janma. *Manas* means the mind and this nakshatra gives a deeper understanding and further clues as to how the mind works. This is a key nakshatra to study on all charts. The nakshatra that rules the manasa especially from the Moon shows how the mind works, and planets placed in the manasa nakshatra will express the quality of the mind. Saturn, Rahu or Mars or Ketu placed here will give many mental stresses and can create emotional problems like depression too. Malefic transits to this nakshatra are challenging.

Transits to 25th nakshatra are times of great emotional stress and there is a possibility of wrong thinking and making difficult decisions. The transits that need to be watched are of Saturn, Rahu, Ketu and malefic conjunctions that take place in the manasa nakshatra. A Mars transit can be studied too but as it is a fast–moving planet, it does not stay in one nakshatra for too long. In 2014, Mars and Rahu were both in Chitra nakshatra, and due to its retrogression Mars remained in Chitra with Rahu for a much longer time, so people with Chitra as their manasa nakshatra would have felt its influence acutely. A Rahu Ketu transit suggests that the solar and lunar eclipses during that time may be in manasa nakshatra too, bringing added fears and anxieties.

When Saturn enters the 25th nakshatra, this can be taken as the start of sade sati. Although technically sade sati begins when Saturn moves into the 12th house from the Moon, in practice the transit to the manasa nakshatra is when the mind starts feeling restless. Saturn's transit through manasa nakshatra creates pressures, stress and mental uncertainty which can lead us to make unwise decisions that lead to the crisis situations when Saturn is transiting over the exalt degrees of the natal Moon.

Abhishekha is the 27th nakshatra from janma. Abhishekha is connected to power and achievement. It is param mitra too and all planets placed here are positive and supportive. Transits to this nakshatra, especially benefics, can raise the status of an individual and bring many good opportunities.

Navatara and Nadi Nakshatra

Nakshatra type		1st Paryay		2nd Paryay		3rd Paryay
Janma– birth	1		10	Karma	19	Aadhana
Sampat – Wealth	2		11		20	
Vipat – danger	3		12		21	
Kshema –happiness	4	Jati	13		22	
Prayatak– obstacles	5		14		23	Sanghatika
Sadhana – attainment	6		15		24	
Naidhana – poverty	7		16	Vinasha	25	Manasa
Mitra– friend	8	Matru	17		26	
Param Mitra – grt friend	9		18	Samudaya	27	Abhishekha

Nadi Nakshatra Analysis Rules

There are many ways to use nadi nakshatras. A navatara and nadi nakshatras table is made and analysed for static and dynamic chart analysis. It is also used for compatibility.

- Static
- Dynamic to include Dasha and Transit
- Compatibility

Static analysis is how the planets relate to each other via nadi nakshatra in the natal chart. This will give clues as to how the nadi nakshatras affect the chart, dasha and bhuktis and its karakas. Karakas placed in negative nakshatras can be damaged. Analyse from the Moon, Sun and lagna points of view, and study what energy each nakshatra is reflecting.

Maha Dasha analysis – first the nadi position of the maha dasha ruler is studied from the Moon and then the maha dasha ruler's relationship with the bhukti rulers is studied from its point of view. Two sets of information need to be synthesised. It is complex and needs practice to become comfortable with all the differing information that this brings forth but the result is very good. It gives a deeper understanding to the roles nakshatras play during each period and how planets will change their role as the mahadasha alter. Planets placed in positive nadis from the

Moon and the dasha ruler will give great opportunities, whereas difficult nadis can bring crisis.

Transit analysis – this is extremely useful; as the planets move through the nakshatra mandala, they will connect to the different nadis and create situations that may not be understood through normal analysis.

Compatibility analysis – Nadi nakshatras are important in compatibility. Certain nakshatras from the natal Moon nakshatra are extremely negative. Choosing partners with those nakshatras can bring unhappiness and sorrow.

Key to decide the point of view – When analysing the nadi nakshatra, we need to decide what is the janma nakshatra or the point of view from which the other nakshatras are viewed. More importance should be given to the Moon nakshatra as the nakshatras are connected to the Moon, but others should not be ignored. Vedic astrology is very concerned about taking in many different points of view to give a more complete picture. When we study the nadis from these differing points then a fuller picture emerges.

Chart Analysis – Oprah Winfrey
Oprah Winfrey at 04:30 (+6:00) CST on 29 January 1954, Kosciusko, Mississippi, USA

Rashi (D-1) General

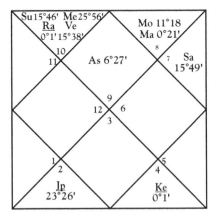

	Nakshatra	Rulership
Lagna	Mula	Ketu
Sun	Shravana	Moon
Moon	Anuradha	Saturn
Mars	Vishakha	Jupiter
Mercury	Dhanishta	Mars
Jupiter	Mrigasira	Mars
Venus	Shravana	Venus
Saturn	Swati	Rahu
Rahu	Uttara Ashadha	Sun
Ketu	Punarvasu	Jupiter

Oprah Winfrey is an American talk show host, actress, philanthropist, and producer. Oprah is one of a kind who brought out a new genre in television which dealt with the emotions and inner feelings of her millions of viewers. She is best known for *The Oprah Winfrey Show* which was on air from 1986 to 2011. She is now running her TV channel called OWN.

We can make a navatara grid for all these points of view, but in this book I am only analysing from the Moon and lagna. Often different points of view bring conflicting information of the activated nadi nakshatras and these have to be integrated into the analysis.

A few key aspects come out from the nakshatras of Oprah Winfrey:

- Moon in Anuradha, Sun in Shravana and Lagna is Mula.
- The lagna lord Jupiter is in Mrigasira which is ruled by 5th lord Mars. Parivartana or mutual reception between Jupiter and Mars ruled nakshatras. Jupiter is in a nakshatra ruled by Mars and Mars is in a nakshatra ruled by Jupiter. This is connecting the 1st house ruler with the 5th house of creativity.

Oprah Winfrey: Navatara and Nadi Nakshatras from the Moon							
Nakshatra type	Pl		1st Paryay		2nd Paryay		3rd Paryay
Janma – birth	Sat	1	Anuradha – Moon janma	10	U Bhadra karma	19	Pushya – aadhana
Sampat – Wealth	Me	2	Jyeshta	11	Revati	20	Ashlesha
Vipat – danger	Ke	3	Mula – Lagna	12	Ashwini	21	Magha
Kshema – happiness	Ve	4	P Ashadha – jati	13	Bharani	22	P Phalguni
Prayatak- obstacles	Su	5	U Ashadha – Rahu	14	Krittika	23	U Phalguni – vinasha
Sadhana – attainment	Mo	6	Shravana – Sun, Ven	15	Rohini	24	Hasta
Naidhana – poverty	Ma	7	Dhanishta – Mer	16	Mrigasira – Jupiter sanghatika	25	Chitra – manasa
Mitra – friend	Ra	8	Shatabhishak – matru	17	Ardra	26	Swati – Saturn
Param Mitra – grt friend	Ju	9	P Bhadra	18	Punarvasu– Ketu– samudaya	27	Vishakha – Mars – abhishekha

Planets and their Nadis		
Planets	Navatara Nakshatra	Added Nadi Nakshatra
Lagna	Vipat	
Sun	Sadhana	
Moon	Janma	
Mars	Param Mitra	Abhishekha
Mercury	Naidhana	
Jupiter	Naidhana	Sanghatika
Venus	Sadhana	
Saturn	Mitra	
Rahu	Prayatak	
Ketu	Param Mitra	Samudaya

The Nadi Nakshatras from the Moon

The relationship between the Moon and lagna needs to be studied. Oprah has lagna placed in the vipat nakshatra from the Moon. This can create lack of understanding between the mind and the body. Her body image (lagna) may be bad. Oprah has suffered from weight issues throughout her life and this may be one of the reasons. Often conflicting or difficult positions are not necessarily negative as it creates the friction that makes an individual keen to succeed.

- The Moon is in Scorpio and its ruler Mars is placed in abhishekha nakshatra, giving her the ability to control it as well as inspiration for the crowning glory that abhishekha promises. This is an excellent position for the Moon ruler to be in. The co– ruler of Scorpio is Ketu and that too is placed in samudaya nakshatra which gives victory and success. Even though Oprah's Moon is in its debilitated sign, the placement of the two rulers in positive nadis further helped in her success.

- Jupiter is in sanghatika or a bad company nakshatra from the Moon. This may be the reason that she had very difficult issues with men in her early years. Even now she remains unmarried although she does have a partner.

- Manasa nakshatra is Chitra. No planet is placed there. Chitra is a creative nakshatra and would give her the many talents she has for acting, writing, presenting etc. She gave up her show in September 2011 at the exact moment Saturn began its transit in Chitra. She would have been emotionally troubled throughout that time following the end of her show. Saturn blocked the mind and delayed all projects and the launch of her TV channel was not successful. The mind would have been troubled with manasa transit of Saturn and she may not have taken the right decisions.

Oprah Winfrey: Navatara and Nadi Nakshatra from Lagna							
Nakshatra type		1st Pariyaya		2nd Pariyaya		3rd Pariyaya	
Janma – birth	1	Mula – Lagna janma	10	Ashwini karma	19	Magha aadhana	
Sampat – Wealth	2	P Ashadha	11	Bharani	20	P Phalguni	
Vipat – danger	3	U Ashadha – Rahu	12	Krittika	21	U Phalguni	
Kshema – happiness	4	Shravana – Sun, Ven jati	13	Rohini	22	Hasta	
Prayatak – obstacles	5	Dhanishta – Mer	14	Mrigasira – Jup	23	Chitra – sanghatika	
Sadhana – attainment	6	Shatabhishak	15	Ardra	24	Swati – Saturn	
Naidhana – poverty	7	P Bhadra	16	Punarvasu–Ketu – vinasha	25	Vishakha – Mars manasa	
Mitra – friend	8	U Bhadra – matru	17	Pushya	26	Anuradha	
Param Mitra – grt friend	9	Revati	18	Ashlesha samudaya	27	Jyeshta – Moon abhishekha	

	Oprah Winfrey: Navatara and Nadi Nakshatra from the Moon and Lagna		
	Nakshatra	Nadis From Moon	Nadis From Lagna
Lagna	Mula	Vipat	Janma
Sun	Shravana	Sadhana	Kshema and Jati
Moon	Anuradha	Janma	Abhishekha
Mars	Vishakha	Abhishekha	Manasa
Mercury	Dhanishta	Naidhana	Prayatak
Jupiter	Mrigasira	Sanghatika	Prayatak
Venus	Venus	Sadhana	Kshema and Jati
Saturn	Swati	Mitra	Sadhana
Rahu	Uttara Ashadha	Prayatak	Vipat
Ketu	Punarvasu	Samudaya	Vinasha

The nadi nakshatra from the lagna:

- The relationship between lagna and the Moon needs to be studied. Oprah has the Moon placed in the abhishekha nakshatra from the lagna. This is very positive and her mind helps the lagna to resolve any issues that were created by the difficult position of lagna from the Moon.
- Jupiter in prayatak nakshatra from the Moon is not well placed from both the lagna and the Moon, which can further add to relationship issues. Jupiter is the ruler of the lagna and being placed in the prayatak or obstacle position may have made her very competitive, always treating every block as an opportunity.
- Manasa nakshatra from the lagna is Vishakha. Mars is placed there. Mars would give a fiery intellect. She may have anger issues that can at times spoil her thinking. Vishakha stands at the threshold of the higher experience and she could have used this quality to create a show where self–improvement was the key. Saturn is in Vishakha nakshatra in 2013 and 2014 and this would continue to block her thinking and bring challenges and uncertainties. Saturn moves out of Vishakha on 30 Nov 2014.

10
Analysis: Revealing the Mind

There are many techniques using the nakshatras but the most important and the first one to analyse is the influence of the nakshatras on the natal chart. The nakshatras exercise a profound influence on the planets, and the planets reflect the way the mind works. By understanding the nakshatra positions of all the planets we gain a deeper insight into both the material and spiritual aspects of our lives. We can work out the gunas and nama nakshatra too.

Then we can move onto analysing the nadi nakshatras. This is an advanced and complex technique which needs time and effort to master, the effort will be more than rewarded with many revelations and clearer understanding.

There are two ways to analyse the chart. One is from the natal chart and what it reveals. The second is from the dynamic influences which show how the chart develops through the experience of the various maha dasha, its sub periods and transits. We can analyse the following:

Static Analysis
- The nakshatras of the ascendant and the planets with extra emphasis on the moon's nakshatra
- The rulers of the nakshatra, its qualities and relationship with the planet that is placed in it
- What is the pattern of rulership? Any unique patterns revealed by the nakshatras
- What houses does the nakshatra ruler rule?
- Navamsha, pushkara, ashtamamsha and vargottama
- Nama nakshatra and gunas
- The animal sign of the moon nakshatra and how this impacts the sexuality
- Nadi nakshatras – how the planets fall and how they relate to each other
- The importance of the manasa (25th) nakshatra from the Moon

Dynamic Analysis
- What is the nakshatra ruler of the dasha ruler and its subtle influence?
- Nadi nakshatra analysis from the dasha lord
- Transits through the nadi nakshatra

The nakshatras need to be analysed along with other rules of vedic astrology which are not discussed in this book. You can refer to these in my earlier book *The Essentials of Vedic Astrology*.

Chart analysis: Steve Jobs
I am using the chart of Steve Jobs, the co-founder of Apple. He is recognised as a visionary, a pioneer of the personal computer and for giving us many products including smart phones, iPods, iPads etc., which revolutionised the way we use the telephone, music and computers. He co-founded Pixar Animation Studios and transformed the genre of animation movies too through his groundbreaking film *Toy Story*. Steve Jobs is an iconic figure; I especially chose to analyse him as studying the nakshatras will reveal the inside workings of this great personality who used his mind in a unique way.

His life was very interesting and had many ups and downs. He was adopted at birth and throughout his life he faced both rejections and opportunities in equal doses.

Steve Jobs, born at 7:15pm (+8:00 PST) on 24 February 1955, San Francisco, CA, USA

Rashi (D-1) General

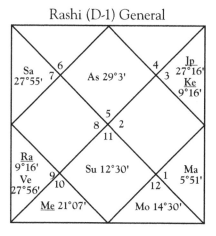

Navamsha

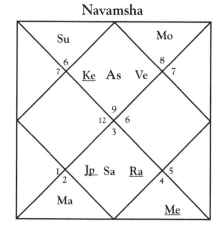

Moon as Lagna Chart

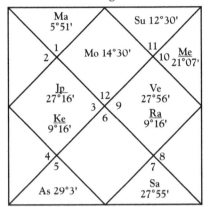

Panchanga & Yogi

Day Lord, Mth	Jupiter	Phalguni
Tithi	3 (66%)	Bright Half
Karana	6 Gara	
Yoga	23 (27%)	Shubha
Nakshatra	26 UttaraBhadra	
Pada	4 (35%)	Hora Sat
Sound	ta/bha/gya(k)	
Devata	AhirBudhnya	Muh: P.b
Overall	Auspicious	
Gandanta: None		
DagdhRashis	Leo Cap	
Yogi Point:	0° 21' Tau	
Yogi: Sun AvaYogi: Sat Duplicate: Ven		

Steve Jobs: Vimshottari Dasha

Sat	24 Feb 1955 to 23 March 1958
Mer	23 March 1958 to 23 March 1975
Ketu	23 March 1975 to 23 March 1982
Venus	23 March 1982 to 23 March 2002
Sun	23 March 2002 to 2008
Moon	23 March 2008 to 5 Oct 2011 - died in Moon dasha

Steve Jobs: The Nakshatras of the Ascendant and the Planets

Planet	Nakshatra	Ruler	Rashi Sign	Pada	Special
Asc	U Phalguni	Sun	Leo	Sag	Pushkara
Sun	S'bhishak	Rahu	Aq	Cap	
Moon	U Bhadra	Sat	Pisces	Scor	
Mars	Ashwini	Ketu	Aries	Taurus	
Mercury	Shravana	Moon	Cap	Cancer	
Jupiter	Punarvasu	Jup	Gem	Gemini	vargottama
Venus	U Ashadha	Sun	Sag	Sag	vargottama, pushkara
Saturn	Vishakha	Jup	Libra	Gemini	
Rahu	Mula	Ketu	Sag	Gemini	
Ketu	Ardra	Rahu	Gem	Sag	

The Nakshatras of the Ascendant and the Planets

Each planet and its nakshatra should be examined. The nakshatras impart their own energy through their many characteristics depending on the planets placed within them. Although we are only influenced by the nakshatras when they are activated due to their position in the ascendant or when planets are placed in them, the characteristics of the 25th nakshatra (the manasa nakshatra) show the workings of the mind even if there are no planets placed there. The house positions of their rulers are significant too. The nakshatra ruler acts as a controller of the mentality of the planet. The ruler of the rashi manages the outer story and the ruler of the nakshatra the inner one, and both of these need to be blended together to make a full analysis. Sometimes it enhances the energy or detracts from it. If Saturn is placed in a nakshatra of Mars (Mrigasira, Chitra, and Dhanishta) it intensifies the stress factor within, as Mars and Saturn are enemies. Saturn's qualities are responsibility, duty, and a good work ethic, so these can suffer while under the influence of action-oriented Mars. The following need to be ascertained about the nakshatra ruler:

- Strength of the nakshatra ruler and house placement
- What other dignity does the nakshatra ruler acquire – is it an atmakaraka, yogi planet, lagna lord?
- Is it in rajayoga or any other planetary yogas?
- Ruler of the lagna nakshatra is always good and in its dasha gives a rise in status

Lagna Nakshatra: Uttara Phalguni

The lagna nakshatra shows the underlying influences of the nakshatra on the rashi lagna. Both the lagna and the lagna nakshatra ruler have to be taken into consideration for a good analysis; the lagna sign decides the temporary benefics and malefics for the natal chart, but the ruler of the lagna nakshatra always works well for the chart by giving its supportive qualities to the person and by creating positive situations during their dashas. If the ruler of the lagna nakshatra is placed in difficult houses or with challenging conjunctions, this can bring inner weaknesses too.

Steve Jobs has Uttara Phalguni as his lagna nakshatra, in the first pada of Sagittarius in Leo rashi. Aryaman, the deity of Uttara Phalguni, is recognised for his leadership qualities and insight, and the ability to see beyond the practical realities of life. Steve Jobs expressed these qualities perfectly; he was not only the founder and leader of Apple, but his insight into the future created a massive market for products that people did not even know they wanted.

The Sagittarius pada of Uttara Phalguni is one of the best places to express the nakshatra's qualities. The lagna being pushkara helps to strengthen any weakness created by the placement of the lagna lord. Both rashi and nakshatra rulers are the same which adds to the intensity of the Sun's expression. Steve Jobs' pinnacle of success came during his Sun dasha too.

The Sun: Shatabhishak

The Sun is the lagna ruler. It is placed in Shatabhishak nakshatra and Capricorn pada. Shatabhishak is a powerful nakshatra where the gods and demons are fighting within themselves in order to find enlightenment. The mystical nature of this nakshatra was shown by Steve Jobs' interest in India, Buddhism and spiritualism in general, and despite his great wealth he always lived a simple life. His inner struggles relating back to his adoption may have shaped his personality. In his biography *Steve Jobs*,[1] Walter Isaacson refers to Steve Jobs being both chosen and abandoned. The lagna shows all the leadership qualities of Uttara Phalguni, whereas the Sun in Shatabhishak is aiming to be much more democratic and egalitarian. A lagna in Leo Uttara Phalguni would have given him the sense of being chosen whereas the Sun in Shatabhishak would have felt the opposite.

It has been widely documented that Steve Jobs was not an easy person to understand or be close to, and the combined influence of Uttara Phalguni and Shatabhishak may have caused his restless nervousness along with a highly demanding personality. His search was for the flowering of the crown chakra, which in material terms could have been the search for perfection.

Capricorn pada would have given a double Saturn influence and made him conscious of his responsibilities which he would have taken very seriously. Capricorn would have encouraged his workaholic tendencies.

---

1. *Steve Jobs*, Walter Issacson, Simon & Schuster, 2011.

Moon: Uttara Bhadra

The Moon has more significance than other planets in the nakshatra analysis as it is the overall ruler of the nakshatras. The quality of the Moon will give added flavour to the other planets and their mental qualities. The Moon is in Uttara Bhadra and Scorpio pada. It rules the 12th house and is placed in the 8th. Uttara Bhadra gives the blessings of Saturn; hard work, responsibility and as it is the second to last nakshatra, the soul is thinking of all the responsibilities it must finish before it can move on to the next dimension. This would have given Steve Jobs a sense of urgency in how he lived his life. He always wanted things done immediately and he demanded that from his workers in Apple too. He was in a hurry to fulfil his material responsibility so that he could move on to a higher more spiritual plane.

He had a fierce nature that could be related to Bhadra, the sister of Saturn, whereas Ahir Budhnya gave him deep knowledge beyond the normal intuition which he used successfully in his business.

Steve Jobs' mind may have remained a mystery to those close to him as Uttara Bhadra can be very private and only comes up to connect with others when it is essential. The 8th house position of the Moon would have added to this mystical and private quality.

The Moon was in Scorpio pada which magnified the intensity of his personality. This is the highest vibration of Scorpio at work, transformational, intuitive and full of deep secret knowledge. The Moon can go from an idealistic Pisces to an intense Scorpio, both signs creating emotional storms. Here the poisons of Uttara Bhadra can be in evidence. The adoption made him feel abandoned and the scars left from that in his early childhood may have caused emotional uncertainty which would have coloured his personality and other decisions in life.

The debilitation by pada of the Moon and its placement in the 8th house would have added to his physical weakness and health crisis. He died in his Moon dasha.

His first dasha was Saturn, which can cause frustration and even misery in childhood, even though he was too young to understand what was happening. Although Saturn is strong in the chart, the detachment of Uttara Bhadra would remain with him throughout his life.

Mars: Ashwini

Mars is the best planet for a Leo ascendant as it rules the 4th and 9th houses. It is placed in Ashwini nakshatra in its own sign of Aries in the 9th house. At first glance that looks like an excellent position, but there is an underlying problem as the 9th house is considered badhaka, or a blocking house for Leo. There is weakness in the strength.

Ashwini is the first nakshatra and is extremely idealistic, trying to complete its mission with zeal and focus. It does not recognise any boundaries. Ashwins are the harbingers of dawn and Steve Jobs brought the dawn of many new ideas and gadgets that changed the way we live. Ketu, the ruler of Ashwini, is seeking moksha or perfection from life and when life does not match up there is a sense of rejection. Steve Jobs was seeking flawlessness and in his absolute need to find it he created many new ideas and inventions and went way beyond expectation.

The pada is Taurus which brings a practical and maybe indulgent side to this dynamic Mars.

The badhaka quality may have made him feel blocked in some of his ideas and this could have made him struggle harder. The main area in which the badhaka expressed itself was connected to his birth father, with whom he never reconciled, and Ashwini would have moved on to a new tomorrow, leaving the emotions or darkness of his adoption/parentage behind. Even the relationship with his birth mother was distant.

Mercury: Shravana

Mercury is in Shravana nakshatra which is ruled by the Moon. Mercury was stationary retrograde when Steve Jobs was born and it turned direct at 2.15 am, just hours after his birth. This adds to the intensity of the Shravana experience. Shravana deals with listening and hearing the sounds of silence. It gives the ability to hear what is left unsaid. For Steve Jobs, this meant he could understand the potential of products that others had rejected and he was able to transform them into something useable and extremely sellable. He was not an engineer or a techie, his success was in recognising the quality of the product and its true usage; this powerful Mercury with its listening abilities helped.

The deity associated with Shravana is Vishnu, the preserver. Steve Jobs tried to preserve his ideas and the honours that were bestowed on him by the adoring public have elevated him to a godly status. The Leo

Uttara Phalguni and added Sharva influence would have helped.

The Moon, the ruler of Shravana, is placed in the 8th house of secret knowledge and transformation. Its rulership of Mercury made him a deep thinker.

Mercury is placed in a Cancer pada, which enhances the intuitive quality of the Moon's rulership of the nakshatra. Steve Jobs could go beyond the inquiring mind to trust his instinct.

Jupiter: Punarvasu

Jupiter is vargottama in Punarvasu and Gemini, which brings the multiplicity of Gemini to the wisdom of Jupiter. Steve Jobs had success in many areas: computers, smart phones, music and as co-founder of Pixar films too. This is definitely a signature of vargottama Jupiter in Punarvasu, a special ability to live on multiple dimensions of consciousness and to move seamlessly from one to the other.

Aditi, its deity, is the divine mother giving birth to the creative Aditya. Steve Jobs gave birth to many ideas and concepts way beyond what an average person could create. He nurtured talent like a mother though he was a hard task master.

Jupiter is retrograde, and retrograde planets are full of ideas, often reflecting them in unconventional ways. Sometimes these ideas are not expressed and at others they can get over-expressed. In Steve Jobs' case, the vargottama position of Jupiter helped in securing the Jupiter quality – powerful, quirky, outside the box. I am sure he felt he had many more ideas than he brought out and this may have made him feel as if he was not fully expressing his talent.

Jupiter rules the nakshatra, therefore enhancing the Jupiterian qualities as well as the Gemini ones.

The pada is Gemini creating a vargottama position and adding strength to Jupiter. The wisdom and creativity as the 5th house ruler and the research and intensity as the 8th house ruler are strengthened. There was immense depth in his creativity and research – he knew what he was doing.

Venus: Uttara Ashadha

Venus is in Sagittarius, in Uttara Ashadha. It is vargottama and pushkara. Venus is the atma karaka as it is the planet with the highest degree, giving it added influence. Uttara Ashadha is a 'loner' nakshatra, all its symbolism is connected with being alone. As atmakaraka Venus is strongly placed, but it will add to his loner temperament. His life's journey was lonely even though he had partners, a wife and children, and this focus was what created his personality. Uttara Ashadha is the start of personal sacrifice in the quest for spirituality, but for Steve Jobs no sacrifice was enough in the pursuit of his vision. While the search is meant to be spiritual, people tend to express it in material terms. Uttara Ashadha wants to complete its material responsibilities first so that it can move on. Uttara Ashadha reveals new talents and there were many revelations for Steve Jobs through the Venus atmakaraka.

The austere symbols of this nakshatra were ever present in his life. His house was sparsely furnished, he walked barefoot – Venus was indoctrinated into the Uttara Ashadha philosophy, no luxury or comforts despite the wealth.

The deity Vishwedevas are the gods of the world, they reflect all the deities of Hinduism. Steve Jobs was multi-talented but also achieved a mythical godly status amongst his many followers, which continues after his death. The pada is vargottama Sagittarius and pushkara, which is a great position for Venus, even when placed in the rival guru Jupiter's sign and pada. The competition between Steve Jobs and Bill Gates for the hearts and minds of the computer-consuming public could be indicated here. Steve Jobs was in harmony with his soul's ambitions – the outer and inner vision was the same. Uttara Ashadha brings philosophy, new ways of thinking, development of talent and a great outer world. Pushkara allows the planets to heal themselves. Usually the vargottama position suggests that all planets are comfortable with what they need to achieve.

Saturn: Vishakha

Saturn is in Libra and Vishakha. It is exalted and almost stationary. Vishakha stands at the threshold of life. The threshold still needs to be crossed as this is the soul looking from without to within; Vishakha brings the aspiration to enter the heavens to connect with the eternal. Saturn brings positive energy in making the aspiration into a reality. This is an exalted Saturn which is made even stronger by being almost stationary. The ideas and aspirations of Vishakha are translated into reality by the efforts of Saturn.

Agni and Indra are the two power deities that rule Vishakha. Steve Jobs could have embodied either. Indra, the king of Gods, adds to the influence of Aryaman and Uttara Phalguni on the lagna, and Agni brings the fire of inspiration and ideas. Saturn may have felt guilty about all these desires for power and success, yet was given the drive and structure to succeed.

The pada is Gemini which adds to the intellectual prowess of the exalted Saturn; it also enabled him to excel at many different tasks simultaneously.

Rahu: Mula

Rahu is in Mula, a Ketu-ruled nakshatra in Sagittarius. The first thing to check when a planet is in Mula is whether or not it is gandanta. In this case Rahu is not in gandanta as it is in pada 3 of Mula.

Mula means a root and Rahu will want to go right to the bottom of the root to find the right answers. Mula is an intense experience and people with planets here find that at least once in their lifetime they will be cut away from their roots and try to create new ones. In Steve Jobs' life this happened a few times; at birth he was cut away from his parents, he left his education at Reed College incomplete, and the control of Apple was taken away from him (while this was not a personal choice, his actions may have contributed to it).

Rahu in Mula seeks spirituality but maybe at the wrong places to begin with. Steve Jobs was always searching for his spiritual roots and even went to India in the search for divine wisdom, but his guru Neem Karoli Baba had died before he reached there. So he wandered through India to find the answers. His quest for spirituality continued throughout his life.

Niritti, the deity of Mula, is fierce and destructive, and there was a side of Steve Jobs that has been much talked about – his fierce and angry nature. Mula demands that we sacrifice our human desires to move on the path of divine. This experience can be fearsome for those who are not ready for this sacrifice, but enlightening for those who are. He was willing to sacrifice a lot in his search for success and although this path appeared to be in the material world I think his motivation was always towards a higher aim.

Rahu was in Gemini pada which gave it the ability to think and analyse the wisdom of Mula and Sagittarius.

Ketu: Ardra

Ardra means moist and green, and this is also a fierce and destructive nakshatra which indicates the sharpness of the mind. The green element of Ardra brings the creativity and Ketu usually shows past life knowledge. This knowledge or talent that he had inherited from a past life gave him the uncanny ability to recognise the talents in others.

Rudra is the deity and Ardra represents the anger of Rudra Shiva; those that knew him were aware that Steve Jobs could lose his temper easily when presented with obstacles or blocks to his path.

The pada was Sagittarius and again it confirms that the spiritual search for answers within the intellectual Gemini was a past life inheritance.

Both Rahu Ketu are in destructive nakshatras – this may reflect the destruction of his birth family due to adoption and then being given a new family.

Nama Nakshatra

The birth is in Uttara Bhadra nakshatra and the consonant for this is Jna. This consonant can give Indian names like Jnaneshwara, Jnanda or Jnana but is difficult to translate to a western name. The consonant Sa which relates to Steve falls in Shatabhishak pada 2; interestingly this is where his Sun is placed and therefore it was the perfect name for him.

Guna Analysis – Predominance of Sattva

Five planets (the Sun, Moon, Mercury, Venus and Rahu) are in sattvic gunas which aim for purity. It is interesting that most Apple products were predominantly white, the colour of Sattva. Sattvic people know how to use their talents in the right way. This is a person aiming for purity who may not have been too grounded. The lagna and Saturn in tamas nakshatra gave the necessary grounding or practical approach to life. Mars and Ketu are rajas, giving activity and the quest for the search. Steve Jobs knew what he wanted to do from a young age – the search of rajas would have been in the past life as reflected by Ketu.

		Guna primary	Second level	Third level
Ascendant	U Phalguni	*Tamas*	*Rajas*	*Sattva*
Sun	Shatabhishak	Sattva	Rajas	Sattva
Moon	Uttara Bhadra	Sattva	Sattva	Tamas
Mars	Ashwini	Rajas	Rajas	Rajas
Mercury	Shravana	*Sattva*	*Tamas*	*Rajas*
Jupiter	Punarvasu	Rajas	Sattva	Rajas
Venus	U Ashadha	Sattva	Rajas	Sattva
Saturn	Vishakha	*Tamas*	*Sattva*	*Rajas*
Rahu	Mula	Sattva	Rajas	Rajas
Ketu	Ardra	*Rajas*	*Tamas*	*Sattva*

The Moon is in the 8th house, hidden away. It has two levels of sattva, with tamas holding it back. The high sattvic quality in his chart would have made Steve Jobs aspire to perfection and purity, whereas the deep down tamas of Uttara Bhadra would have made him feel that there are practical ambitions to fulfill, and still some work to do on earth before he could truly move into the higher realm. He would have always aspired to achieve divinity on earth and the lack of sattva in others would have been disappointing to him.

The ascendant, Mercury, Saturn and Ketu reflect all three gunas. This could have given him the motivation to develop all the qualities. The first three dashas were Saturn, Mercury and Ketu and all of them had the gunas in balance. The leading guna needs to be examined more. Saturn had tamas as the leading guna, this was the first dasha till the age of three, and it would have caused a feeling of darkness or being locked in circumstances beyond his control. Even at a young age, these subtle impressions would have guided his life. Mercury has rajas as the primary guna and the Mercury dasha was when his search would have been most intense; these were his school years, then towards the end of this dasha he went to India to search for his spiritual roots. Ketu has sattva as its primary motivation. He founded Apple in this dasha, which has the highest sattvik ambitions of creating something sublime and previously unattainable for the public so far.

The other planets' internal picture is shared mostly between sattva and rajas. Sattva gives the desire for purity and reflects the outer picture too, whereas the restless search of rajas which included both reaching the heights of success and feeling the depths of darkness, is evident. There is minimal tamas and this could have made Steve Jobs lack a stable core within.

Nakshatra Sexuality: Cow of Uttara Bhadra
The best way to judge the sexuality of the nakshatra is through the Moon's position. The Moon is in Uttara Bhadra whose animal is the cow. Interestingly his ascendant is in Uttara Phalguni whose animal is the Bull. These two animals would have strongly influenced his personality; he was bullish and hardworking. Like the cow of his nakshatra, he always felt that he had to give to his people (Apple employees and consumers). People are always demanding of cows, who in turn want to fulfill the public's every wish. In personal relationships he would have been giving too, and when he was unable to give he would have felt guilty about it. Although not known as a giver, his inner motivation was always generous.

Steve Jobs' wife, Laurene Powell, would have had her Moon in either Punarvasu or Pushya. She was born on 6 November 1963, Milford, New Jersey, time unknown. Punarvasu is the cat and Pushya is the female goat. Both these animals would relate with Uttara Bhadra and this shows good sexual compatibility.

Nadi Nakshatra
Nadi nakshatras are a complex technique which need time and effort spent to master. The technique reveals how the planets connect with each other and adds to the information provided by the other chart analysis rules. The chart is analysed first and then the nadi nakshatra information is added to it. Basic chart analysis is covered in my previous book, *The Essentials of Vedic Astrology*.

Nadi nakshatras need to be analysed from the Moon's position. They can be analysed from other points of view too, like the ascendant and the Sun as ascendant; they are not covered here but they would be a good area of further research for readers. When studying time or life events, analyse the maha dasha ruler with the nadi nakshatra system – this is done below in the dasha analysis.

Steve Jobs: Navatara and Nadi Nakshatra from Moon

Nakshatra type	Pl		1st Paryay		2nd Paryay		3rd Paryay
Janma – birth	Sat	1	U Bhadra – Moon **Janma**	10	Pushya **Karma**	19	Anuradha – **Aadhana**
Sampat – Wealth	Me	2	Revati	11	Ashlesha	20	Jyeshta
Vipat – danger	Ke	3	Ashwini – Mars	12	Magha	21	Mula – Rahu
Kshema – happiness	Ve	4	Bharani – **Jati**	13	P Phalguni	22	P Ashadha
Prayatak – obstacles	Su	5	Krittika	14	U Phalguni – Lagna	23	U Ashadha – Venus **Vinasha**
Sadhana – attainment	Mo	6	Rohini	15	Hasta	24	Shravana – Mercury
Naidhana – poverty	Ma	7	Mrigasira	16	Chitra **Sanghatika**	25	Dhanishta – **Manasa**
Mitra – friend	Ra	8	Ardra – Ketu **Matru**	17	Swati	26	Shatabhishak – Sun
Param Mitra – grt friend	Ju	9	Punarvasu – Jupiter	18	Vishakha – Saturn **Samudaya**	27	P Bhadra – **Abhishekha**

Planets and their Nadis			
Planets	**Nakshatra**	**Navatara Nakshatra**	**Added Nadi Nakshatra**
Lagna	U Phalguni	Prayatak	
Sun	Shatabhishak	Mitra	
Moon	Uttara Bhadra	Janma	
Mars	Ashwini	Vipat	
Mercury	Shravana	Sadhana	
Jupiter	Punarvasu	Param Mitra	
Venus	U Ashadha	Naidhana	Vinasha
Saturn	Vishakha	Param Mitra	Samudaya
Rahu	Mula	Vipat	
Ketu	Ardra	Mitra	Matru

The lagna is in prayatak (obstacles). This suggests that Steve Jobs felt a conflict between his emotional (Moon) and physical needs and ambitions (lagna). Often a conflicted personality can achieve a lot as they try to resolve their inner agitation through their work in the world. The lagna placed in a difficult position from the Moon may have led him to neglect his body or physical health. As it happens, his dietary habits were erratic and he worked almost 24 hours a day managing Pixar and Apple simultaneously, and neglecting his physical body. This attitude was emphasised when he did not take urgent action after being diagnosed with cancer.

The Sun is in mitra nakshatra, which would have given him a healthy respect for his ego and inner soul. He was lucky that his adoptive father, Paul Jobs, always made him feel like 'the chosen one'. This was due to the karaka Sun being in a good position from the Moon. He would have felt emotionally fulfilled by this relationship.

The Moon is in the janma or the starting nakshatra. Challenging transits to Janma nakshatra bring emotional stress to the person too and are usually negative for health.

Mars is in Vipat or danger. Vipat means reverse or bringer of calamities. As Mars rules the 9th house from both the Moon and the ascendant, its position in Vipat shows the reverse fortune he suffered through his adoption as he lacked the presence of a birth father and could never re-ignite the relationship with him. The strength of Mars in its own house gave a great adoptive father.

Mercury is in sadhana or attainment. His powerful Mercury had the added positive influence of being in sadhana nakshatra and gave him intellectual achievements plus business acumen. He was not afraid of putting in hard work and his life was dedicated towards his goals.

Jupiter is in param mitra. Jupiter is the ruler of the Moon and being in param mitra gave him status and the ability to think wisely and expand his horizons. Jupiter is also vargottama which added to its power.

Venus is in prayatak and vinasha nakshatra. Prayatak brings obstacles and vinasha destruction. Steve Jobs had difficult personal relationships with women at a younger age. The main influence of Venus being in Vinasha was on his health. Venus rules the pancreas and he was diagnosed with pancreatic cancer which finally took his life in 2011. Venus' other strength of being vargottama and pushkara gave many positive experiences despite the vinasha status.

Saturn is in param mitra and samudaya (good karma from past lives) nakshatra. Saturn would have given him great strength and hard-working qualities with it being in best friend and samudaya nakshatra which brings forth positive karma from past lives. His work ethic was amazing and is much written about. Despite all the apparent obstacles he made a great and inspirational life.

Rahu is in vipat nakshatra. This would have brought problems to him, again affecting his health too. Vipat may have made him overly competitive and feeling the struggles internally.

Ketu is in Mitra and matru nakshatra. *Mitra* means friend and *matru* is mother. Ketu the past life nakshatra being in matru may have given him a deep connection to his mother and he would have suffered from feelings of rejection from his biological mother. His adoptive mother was a great influence on him and the position of Ketu shows that his adoptive mother had old karma to be his real mother in this life and the positive aspect of Ketu would have helped him to reconcile these issues. He founded Apple in Ketu dasha and this shows positive past karma helping him in this life.

Manasa, the 25th nakshatra: Dhanishta

The 25th nakshatra is manasa nakshatra and it reflects the quality of the mind and thinking. Planets placed here can influence the mind. Steve Jobs has no planets in the 25th nakshatra but we can still analyse the quality of the nakshatra itself to see how it affects him.

Dhanishta people are wealthy in mind and spirit. Their nature is more spiritually inclined. Spiritual wealth does not come easily to Dhanishta, but through self-less work and letting go of their personal egos to work with compassion and high ideals for the universal good. These people have to fight for their rights, but also give a lot of service for others.

Ashta Vasu, the eight deities of Dhanishta, can give thinking on many levels. They transform the ideas from life experiences and use that knowledge to move towards the higher planes of existence. The thinking connected to this multi-layered deity showed his ability to think on many levels and succeed in transforming ideas into major developments.

Dhanishta can have a connection to music and Steve Jobs transformed the way we listen to music. It shows at first his deep love for it so that he could understand the need to consume it in a different way from the previous century.

Timing: Mahadasha, Bhukti and Transits

Timing is studied from maha dasha and transits, and vimshottari dasha is the best way to analyse timing. This is calculated from the ruler of the Moon nakshatra – the nakshatra rulers of the maha dasha and sub dashas are vital to get the true analysis. The nakshatra ruler of the maha dasha lord is important as it exerts a subtle yet powerful influence. Its rulership of positive houses enhances the dasha. If it is placed in a yoga, it further adds to the power.

In analysing the dashas we first study the maha dasha and its nakshatra and its position from the nadi nakshatra from the Moon. Then we go a step further and study the nadi nakshatra from the dasha ruler point of view too.

Steve Jobs: Vimshottari Dasha
Saturn – 24 Feb 1955 to 23 March 1958
Saturn is in Libra and in Vishakha nakshatra. Saturn is not the best planet for Leo Lagna as it rules the 6th and 7th houses. Steve Jobs was adopted at birth as he was given up by his birth parents. The nakshatra lord Jupiter is both the 5th and the 8th house ruler. It is vargottama and brings strength to the nakshatra. The adversity of being given up by his parents was transformed into a positive situation as he got very good adoptive parents.

Saturn is in param mitra and samudaya nakshatra from the Moon and this adds to its strength; it brought victory in the face of adversity.

Mercury – 23 March 1958 to 23 March 1975
Mercury is in Shravana nakshatra. This is the nakshatra for study and learning. Shravana specially deals with what is left unsaid or listens to the sounds of silence, and from an early age Steve Jobs would have had the ability to understand the nuances of the knowledge he studied. He was frustrated by formal education but he took in what was necessary. The ruler of Shravana is the Moon and this is placed in the 8th house.

While this would have helped him in research, it would have created inner turmoil and the insecurities experienced during this dasha led to him going to India in search of a guru. Mercury is in sadhana (practice or working towards a goal) nakshatra and this would have instilled stability, the appetite for hard work and the ability to focus on a goal.

In 1960 during Mercury mahadasha Mercury bhukti the Jobs family moved from San Francisco to Mountain View, California which came to be known as the Silicon Valley. It was here that Steve Jobs began his life-long love of electronics. In 1968 – Mercury Rahu – he met Steve Wosniak with whom he later founded Apple. In 1974 towards the end of Mercury dasha he visited India for 7 months.

Ketu – 23 March 1975 to 23 March 1982
Ketu is in Ardra nakshatra and is placed in mitra and matru nakshatra. This is a positive nadi nakshatra and Ketu dasha was very productive. Ardra deals with excellence of mind. The ruler Rahu is placed with atmakaraka Venus – Rahu is very ambitious. Ketu dasha would have given the past life ability of intuition and talent whereas Rahu would have given ambition and striving for success. It was on 1 April 1976 at the start of Ketu dasha that Apple was founded.

Venus – 23 March 1982 to 23 March 2002
I am analysing the Venus dasha in more detail and studying all the bhukti within it so that the analysis of nadi nakshatras from the dasha-ruler point of view can be explained. His Venus dasha had many ups and downs. Steve Jobs was thrown out of Apple. He founded and created Pixar, then triumphantly returned to Apple.

Venus is in vinasha nakshatra. It is atmakaraka as the planet with the highest degree. Vargottama, pushkara, yet the vinasha (destructive) aspect should never be ignored. In May 24, 1985 he was fired from Apple. This was the start of a Venus dasha and Venus exercised the Vinasha potential. Venus was in Punarvasu ruled by a retrograde Jupiter. Jupiter is placed in the 11th house. As the sixth house from the sixth, the 11th house is the significator of disease. Jupiter also ruled the 8th house which shows long term health matters. Although his cancer was not diagnosed in the Venus dasha, Venus' negative potential shows that the cancer was developing during this time and was only revealed in the Sun dasha.

The Venus dasha brought marriage, children, the launch of many products and the coming back of Apple to its prime position. This was the impact of its vargottama, atmakaraka and pushkara qualities.

Venus Maha Dasha and Nadi Nakshatra Relationship with the Bhuktis

It is important to study each maha dasha and its nadi nakshatra. A new chart is created and the point of view of the chart of the mahadasha ruler is taken and how the bhuktis relate to it. Are the nadi flowing smoothly or are they blocked? This gives us a bigger picture and allow us to see things that are not visible from the normal chart points of view. In order to make this chart for Venus maha dasha, Venus becomes the janma nakshatra and all nakshatra grids are drawn accordingly. Venus is in Uttara Ashadha nakshatra which is ruled by the Sun. The other nakshatras ruled by Sun (Krittika and Uttara Ashadha) will perform the janma role. The next or sampat nakshatra from Venus would be Hasta which is ruled by the Moon and will express the sampat qualities during the Venus dasha. All Moon nakshatras will reflect sampat qualities, and planets placed within them will bring wealth during their bhuktis.

Steve Jobs: Navatara and Nadi Nakshatra from Moon – Venus Mahadasha point of view

Nakshatra type	Pl		1st Pariyaya		2nd Pariyaya		3rd Pariyaya
Janma – birth	Su	1	U Ashadha – Venus **Dasha Lord**	10	Krittika **Karma**	19	U Phalguni – Lagna **Aadhana**
Sampat – Wealth	Mo	2	Shravana – Mercury	11	Rohini	20	Hasta
Vipat – danger	Ma	3	Dhanishta	12	Mrigasira	21	Chitra
Kshema – happiness	Ra	4	Shatabhishak – *Sun* **Jati**	13	Ardra – Ketu	22	Swati
Prayatak – obstacles	Ju	5	P Bhadra	14	Punarvasu – Jupiter	23	Vishakha – Saturn **Vinasha**
Sadhana – attainment	Sa	6	U Bhadra – Moon	15	Pushya	24	Anuradha
Naidhana – poverty	Me	7	Revati	16	Ashlesha **Sanghatika**	25	Jyeshta **Manasa**
Mitra – friend	Ke	8	Ashwini – Mars **Matru**	17	Magha	26	Mula – Rahu
Param Mitra – grt friend	Ve	9	Bharani	18	P Phalguni **Samudaya**	27	Ashadha – **Abhishekha**

Mahadasha Ruler Venus Point of View – Nadi Nakshatra		
	Bhukti	**Nadi Relationship**
23 Mar 1981	Venus	Venus is vinasha from Moon
23 July 1985	Sun	Kshema
23 July 1986	Moon	Sadhana
22 June 1988	Mars	Mitra and Matru
23 May 1989	Rahu	Mitra
22 May 1992	Jup	Prayatak
21 Jan 1995	Sat	Vinasha
23 March 1998	Mercury	Sampat
21 Jan 2001	Ketu	Kshema
23 March 2002	Venus Dasha ends	

As a new mahadasha starts, we first need to study the relationship of the mahadasha ruler from the Moon janma. This decides the beginning of the experience. Usually mahadasha are experienced through their bhuktis – the intense flavor of Venus' vinasha nature would be felt in Venus dasha bhukti. Venus would continue working silently on his health throughout the dasha period too.

Venus Dasha was an extremely creative period for Steve Jobs as all planets are working for the dasha lord except for Jupiter and Saturn who are in difficult nadis which made him struggle, but in the end it made him even more creative and strong. Jupiter and Saturn bhukti followed each other; Jupiter bhukti was from 22 May 1992 to 21 January 1995 and Saturn was from 21 January 1995 to 23 March 1998.

Venus Venus – 23 March 1982 to 23 July 1985
As Venus is the dasha lord itself, we study its relationship from the Moon nakshatra which is vinasha. There has to be some destructive element to it. The start of the Venus dasha coincided with conflicts within Apple and by 1985 they had come to a head. On May 24, 1985 Steve Jobs was fired as the head of Macintosh. Later in 2005 while lecturing at Stanford University, Steve Jobs said that being fired from Apple was the best thing that could have happened to him; "The heaviness of being successful was replaced by the lightness of being a beginner again, less sure about

everything. It freed me to enter one of the most creative periods of my life."

During this time he met Tina Redse with whom he had a long relationship and, according to his biography, she was the first person he was truly in love with. Venus is the karaka for relationship and therefore the start of the dasha brought a significant relationship in his life.

Venus Sun – 23 July 1985 to 23 July 1986

The Sun is the ruler of the natal lagna and is in Shatabhishak nakshatra which is ruled by Rahu. There were some interesting connections in this dasha bhukti which made it very creative and powerful for him. The Sun is the ruler of Venus' nakshatra Uttara Ashadha, and the Sun's nakshatra-ruler Rahu is placed with Venus in the 5th from the ascendant and the 10th from the Moon. The Sun is placed in prayatak from the Moon and Kshema (happiness) from Venus. Both factors would come into account. This period was creative and sad. He founded NeXT computers and bought into Pixar, the animation company that went on later to produce *Toy Story*. His adoptive mother was diagnosed with lung cancer and he was sued by Apple for starting NeXT and poaching some of its employees. This lawsuit was settled out of court in January 1986 at the same time as he invested $10 million in Pixar for a 70% ownership. Although NeXT computer was started in a Venus Sun dasha its official launch was in 1988.

Venus Moon – 23 July 1986 to 22 June 1988

The Moon is placed in the 4th house from Venus, and the 8th house from the lagna. Moon is sadhana from the dasha lord Venus. Sadhana means a regular practice in order to accomplish a goal – his goal may have been to meet his birth mother.. It is in Uttara Bhadra nakshatra which is ruled by Saturn, placed in the 3rd house in exaltation. This was a sad time for him as his adoptive mother, Clara Jobs, died on November 7, 1986. After her death, he began the search for his birth mother Joanne Schieble. The Moon bhukti would have created emotional uncertainties that brought about transformation within. From his meeting with his birth mother Joanne Schieble, he discovered that he had a sister, Mona Simpson, whom he subsequently met. Saturn's nakshatra ruler in the 3rd house of siblings from the ascendant indicated this.

Venus Mars – 22 June 1988 to 23 May 1989
Mars rules and is placed in the 9th house from the ascendant. It is in Ashwini nakshatra, the nakshatra of new dawn. Ketu the ruler of Ashwini is placed in the 11th house with Jupiter. Mars is placed in vipat from Moon and matru and mitra from the dasha lord Venus. The differing relationships of the planet would be reflected during the dasha. His relationship with his biological mother developed during this time. The vipat role of Mars was reflected in Steve Jobs' refusal to meet up with his birth father Abdul Fattah Jandali, when his sister Mona Simpson had contacted him. NeXT computer was launched in October 1988 with much fanfare, although the vipat nature came to the fore when the computer did not do well commercially. The positive outcome of the Mars bhukti was the Oscar that Pixar received for its short film *Tin Toy* on March 29, 1989.

Venus Rahu – 23 May 1989 to 22 May 1992
Rahu is in Mula, ruled by Ketu, it is vipat from the Moon and kshema from Venus. This was when he broke up with his long term love Tina Redse and met Laurene Powell, who was to become his wife. He met Laurene Powell in October 1989, and they married on 18 March 1991. The continuing Venus dasha was all about relationships but why did the marriage take place in Venus Rahu? Rahu is in Ketu nakshatra which is placed in the 7th house from Rahu. Venus was in the Sun nakshatra and the Sun was in the 7th house from the ascendant and in a Rahu nakshatra. These secret links made the dasha of Venus Rahu the prime time for marriage. Transiting Jupiter was in Gemini activating Venus and the Rahu Ketu axis of the natal chart.

Venus Jupiter – 22 May 1992 to 21 Jan 1995
Venus Jupiter dasha is usually not a good time as they are rival gurus and do not work for each other. Jupiter is placed in Punarvasu and ruled by it. Jupiter was placed in param mitra from the Moon but from the dasha ruler Venus it is in prayatak. Jupiter rules the 8th house of transformation from the ascendant. This was by all accounts an unsettled time with NeXT computers not doing well and he lost his father Paul Jobs on March 5, 1993 from lung cancer.

Venus Saturn – 21 Jan 1995 to 23 March 1998
Saturn is placed in Vishakha nakshatra which is ruled by Jupiter, and Jupiter is in the 11th house of profit. Saturn is in param mitra and samudaya (ascent) from the Moon but it was in Vinasha (destruction) from the dasha ruler.

There is a peculiar rule for Venus Saturn dasha bhukti. Usually these are transformational. Often if they are well placed from each other they bring negative transformations, whereas if they are negatively placed from each other they bring a positive result. I don't know the source of this rule but it always works in practice. In this case, Saturn being in vinasha from the Venus dasha ruler actually became a positive transformational experience for Steve Jobs, and Saturn bhukti was extremely good for him. This is when he returned to Apple, first as a temporary advisor and then as the CEO; *Toy Story* was also premiered and there was a public offering of Pixar shares, which brought him immense wealth. *Toy Story* was released on November 22, 1995 and the Pixar public offering was on 30 November 1995. The Pixar IPO was so successful that Steve Jobs not only recouped his original investment, he grossed many times over.

The difficulties from the dasha ruler could have been reflected in the problems both Pixar and Steve Jobs had with Disney who was distributing the film, plus on-going issues with NeXT computers but his Saturn dasha at birth had created a positive situation despite these drawbacks and Saturn bhukti brought success despite all the other tensions.

Steve Jobs' triumphant return to Apple was also a big pressure on him as he was now holding down two jobs – one with Apple and the other with Pixar. This must have had a negative impact on his health which could have been brought on by the Saturn dasha being vinasha from the dasha ruler.

Venus Mercury – 23 March 1998 to 21 Jan 2001
Mercury is in Shravana nakshatra, the listening nakshatra. It gives the ability to hear what is left unsaid, an extraordinary talent which enabled Steve Jobs to understand the hidden needs of his consumers. Many innovative products were launched during this period. Mercury is well placed from both the Moon and the dasha lord. It is in sadhana from the Moon and sampat (wealth) from Venus. When both nadis are in

harmony, much progress can be made. Mercury is friends with Venus and is strong by being stationary. Steve Jobs was back at the helm of Apple. He re-launched the iMac computer in 6 May 1998 and it was an unqualified success. He also conceived the idea of the digital hub which was to became the center-piece of his strategy to move from being a computer company to one of the biggest and most valuable companies in the world.

Venus Ketu – 21 Jan 2001 to 23 March 2002
As the old dasha ends, it is an important time for change. We need to study the role of the next dasha to understand whether the change will be positive or not. Ketu is in Ardra, Rahu's nakshatra. Rahu is placed with atmakaraka Venus in the 5th house of creativity. Ketu is well placed nadi nakshatra from the Moon and the dasha lord. It is mitra and matru (friends and mother) from the Moon and kshema (prosperity) from Venus. This was when Steve Jobs consolidated his Apple family. Although he was known as a fierce personality, he was fiercely protective of Apple and he nurtured talent within it like a mother.

Ketu bhukti would have further emphasised this quality. Often we do not know how Ketu will manifest as it is a past life planet, but his Ketu dasha was extremely positive and while it suggested all change for him, Ketu bhukti brought some excellent opportunities. The iPod was launched on 23 October 2001. This was an innovative product that could store up to a 1000 songs on a small unit, and with it began the rebranding of Apple computers to Apple.

Sun – 23 March 2002 to 23 March 2008
The Sun dasha was the most successful time when the dream was realised with all the different product launches, and it took Steve Jobs finally to the top. But the Sun is in prayatak and the huge obstacle facing him at this time was his health. Often in the dasha of the ascendant ruler, health issues can come to the fore. The Sun was placed in the 7th house from the lagna and 12th house from the Moon. It is in Shatabhishak which is ruled by Rahu.

So despite his success, the struggle with mortality was a constant companion, and his cancer was diagnosed in October 2003 during Sun Rahu dasha. Rahu is in vipat nakshatra from the Moon – both dasha and bhukti rulers are in challenging nadis which created a crisis. Rahu is in Mula, ruled by Nritti, the goddesses of destruction and by being the ruler of the Sun, Rahu brought the destructiveness of Nritti to it. This could have added to the health pressures. Rahu was also placed with Venus, significator of pancreas and aspected by Jupiter, the 8th house ruler and Saturn the 7th house ruler. Rahu being the nakshatra ruler of the Sun and therefore ruler of the three Janma nakshatras from Sun dasha point of view, would have added to the health issues. When Rahu bhukti happened in Venus mahadasha, he was not the ruler of Venus nakshatra and Venus was not the lord of the lagna, so the health issues did not manifest.

Moon – 23 March 2008 to 5 Oct 2011 (He died in a Moon dasha)
The Moon is the janma nakshatra during which health issues often become apparent. The Moon is placed in the 8th house and its nakshatra is Uttara Bhadra. The deity was Saturn which is the ruler of the 6th and the death giving 7th house, plus placed in the 3rd house which is another house connected to death. The start of the Moon dasha brought his health issues to the fore and finally he gave up the control of Apple and left his body on 5 October 2011 during a Moon Jupiter dasha.

Transits and Nadi Nakshatras
We can refine the study of timing by using the transits from the nadi nakshatras. Transits of the malefics to the difficult nadis (vipat, prayatak and naidhana) are challenging. If all the malefics combine to influence the difficult nadis then the experience can be extremely intense. Benefics bring opportunities when transiting the good nadis.

Transits to janma and the other nakshatras ruled by the same nakshatra affects the mind and can have health issues too.

Saturn's transit to manasa, the 25th nakshatra from the Moon is especially intense and it signals the start of sade sati. Other malefics transiting manasa nakshatra, especially Rahu or Ketu, will also bring emotional stress.

The Founding of Apple
Apple was founded as a partnership on April 1, 1976, by Steve Jobs, Steve Wozniak and Ronald Wayne. Ronald Wayne opted out of it soon after

the founding. The time of birth of Apple is unknown. I usually erect a sunrise chart for the event when time is unknown. The Moon could have been in Ashwini or Bharani on 1 April 1976. According to the Steve Jobs' authorised biography by Walter Issacson, 'Jobs and Wozniak went to Wayne's apartment in Mountain View to draw up the partnership agreement for Apple'. Therefore this had to be sometime during the day. The Moon changed from Ashwini to Bharani at 15:31 hrs. and we can say with some certainty that the nakshatra for the founding is Ashwini as it is unlikely they would have waited for the evening with such an urgency to form the company. The Moon would be in Aries at the time of the transit which is Steve Jobs's 9th house of good luck and higher knowledge. Ashwini shows a new dawn and the promise of new ideas and the light that Apple products were going to bring into the life of their consumers. If the Moon was in Bharani then it would indicate the incubation of ideas that Bharani promises. The Moon would move during the day from vipat to kshema nakshatra – one is negative and the other positive from the birth nakshatra. The vipat nakshatra may have shown the stress Steve Jobs was facing and the many challenges Apple had to face before it finally gained global dominance, including losing one partner within a few days of founding.

The dasha at the time of founding was Ketu Venus. Ketu is in Ardra which is mitra and matru nakshatra and Venus is in Uttara Ashadha which is in prayatak and vinasha nakshatra in the nadi. Venus as the bhukti ruler being vinasha may have contributed to the immediate resignation of the third partner, Ronald Wayne. At that fledgling stage of the company, Steve Jobs would have felt that loss acutely. Venus has many strengths, being atmakaraka, vargotamma and pushkara, so the setback was only temporary and the rest of course is history. Transiting Ketu was in Aries Bharani which is kshema nakshatra, bringing a wealth of ideas and prosperity, although that was not the motivation for creating Apple. The bhukti lord Venus was in Purva Bhadra which is param mitra and abhishekha. Venus in abhishekha shows achievement of life's dearly held ambitions and the crowning of a new king of technology. Venus is the atmakaraka for Steve Jobs and for him this would have been the first important step on his soul's path.

Founding of Apple: Sunrise chart for 1 April 1976 (+8:00 PST), Mountain View, CA, USA

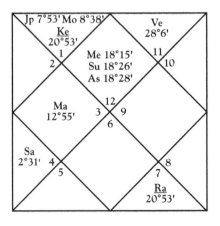

Nakshatra type	Pl		1st Pariyaya		2nd Pariyaya		3rd Pariyaya
Steve Jobs: Navatara and Nadi Nakshatra from Moon – Founding of apple 1 April 1976 *Transit planets in italics*							
Janma – birth	Sa	1	U Bhadra – Moon **Janma**	10	Pushya **Karma**	19	Anuradha – Aadhana
Sampat – Wealth	Me	2	Revati, *Sun, Mercury*	11	Ashlesha	20	Jyeshta
Vipat – danger	Ke	3	Ashwini – Mars, *Moon, Jupiter*	12	Magha	21	Mula – Rahu
Kshema – happiness	Ve	4	Bharani – *Ketu* **Jati**	13	P Phalguni	22	P Ashadha
Prayatak – obstacles	Su	5	Krittika	14	U Phalguni – Lagna	23	U Ashadha – Venus **Vinasha**
Sadhana – attainment	Mo	6	Rohini	15	Hasta	24	Shravana – Mercury
Naidhana – poverty	Ma	7	Mrigasira	16	Chitra **Sanghatika**	25	Dhanishta – **Manasa**
Mitra– friend	Ra	8	Ardra – Ketu **Matru** *Mars*	17	Swati	26	Shatabhishak – Sun
Param Mitra – grt friend	Ju	9	Punarvasu – Jupiter *Saturn*	18	Vishakha– Saturn, *Rahu* **Samudaya**	27	P Bhadra– *Venus* **Abhishekha**

Planets & their Nadis – Founding of Apple 1 April 1976			
Planets	**Transit Nakshatra**	**Navatara Nakshatra**	**Added Nadi Nakshatra**
Sun	Revati	Sampat	
Moon	Ashwini/Bharani	Vipat/ Kshema	Jati if Bharani
Mars	Ardra	Mitra	Matru
Mercury	Revati	Sampat	
Jupiter	Ashwini	Vipat	
Venus	Purva Bhadra	Param Mitra	Abhishekha
Saturn	Punarvasu	Param Mitra	
Rahu	Vishakha	Param mitra	Samudaya
Ketu	Bharani	Kshema	Jati

Transit to 25th Nakshatra

The manasa nakshatra for Steve Jobs is Dhanishta. The main malefic transits over that nakshatra were:

Saturn   16 April to 10 September 1992
                7 January 1993 to 1 Feb 1994

Rahu   20 May 1989 to 27 Jan 1990
                25 December 2007 to 2 September 2008

Ketu   31 January to 19 October 1980
                6 September 1998 to 16 May 1999

Ketu's transit to Dhanishta from 31 January to 19 October 1980 signalled turbulent times for Steve Jobs as Apple was going through growing pains and this would have created mental stress. There may have been some wrong judgements. His behaviour was disruptive, and the Apple management allowed him to remain the public face of Mac but took away some of his roles, especially as the head of Lisa division. He felt rejected by this lack of faith in his talents. He was in a Ketu dasha and Ketu transiting over this nakshatra may have also given him special insight into many of the products which were later introduced.

There were four transits to manasa nakshatra during his Venus dasha. This would have been stormy, giving him times of real emotional darkness and despair. Rahu transited Dhanishta from 20 May 1989 to 27 Jan 1990 and Saturn had two transits to Dhanishta from 16 April to 10 September 1992 and 7 January 1993 to 1 Feb 1994. The period from 1990 to 1994 was an uncertain time for him; he was no longer with Apple and had founded NeXT computers which had many ups and downs and never reached the pinnacle he desired. The revised, second generation NeXT cube was released in 1990, but this was a commercial failure despite its many advanced features. We can see from the transits that this was a mentally stressful time for him.

Ketu transited Dhanishta from 6 September 1998 to 16 May 1999. During this time there don't appear to be any problems to cause him mental stress but his infamous temperamental outbursts could have been caused by the impact of the manasa transits.

Rahu transited Dhanishta from 25 December 2007 to 2 September 2008 when there was much speculation about his health. Professionally he was at his peak, but facing his mortality. Rahu moving through his manasa shows that this was a worried and maybe fearful man coming to terms with his mortality.

Titles from The Wessex Astrologer
www.wessexastrologer.com

Martin Davis	Astrolocality Astrology From Here to There	Joseph Crane	Astrological Roots: The Hellenistic Legacy Between Fortune and Providence
Wanda Sellar	The Consultation Chart An Introduction to Medical Astrology Decumbiture	Komilla Sutton	The Essentials of Vedic Astrology The Lunar Nodes Personal Panchanga The Nakshatras
Geoffrey Cornelius	The Moment of Astrology		
Darrelyn Gunzburg	Life After Grief AstroGraphology: The Hidden Link between your Horoscope and your Handwriting	Anthony Louis	The Art of Forecasting using Solar Returns
		Lorna Green	Your Horoscope in Your Hands
Paul F. Newman	You're not a Person - Just a Birthchart Declination: The Steps of the Sun Luna: The Book of the Moon	Martin Gansten	Primary Directions
		Reina James	All the Sun Goes Round
		Oscar Hofman	Classical Medical Astrology
Jamie Macphail	Astrology and the Causes of War	Bernadette Brady	Astrology, A Place in Chaos Star and Planet Combinations
Deborah Houlding	The Houses: Temples of the Sky		
Dorian Geiseler Greenbaum	Temperament: Astrology's Forgotten Key	Richard Idemon	The Magic Thread Through the Looking Glass
Howard Sasportas	The Gods of Change		
Patricia L. Walsh	Understanding Karmic Complexes	Nick Campion	The Book of World Horoscopes
M. Kelly Hunter	Living Lilith	Judy Hall	Patterns of the Past Karmic Connections Good Vibrations The Soulmate Myth The Book of Why Book of Psychic Development
Barbara Dunn	Horary Astrology Re-Examined		
Deva Green	Evolutionary Astrology		
Jeff Green	Pluto 1 Pluto 2 Essays on Evolutionary Astrology (edited by Deva Green)	John Gadbury	The Nativity of the Late King Charles
		Neil D. Paris	Surfing your Solar Cycles
Dolores Ashcroft-Nowicki and Stephanie V. Norris	The Door Unlocked: An Astrological Insight into Initiation	Michele Finey	The Sacred Dance of Venus and Mars
		David Hamblin	The Spirit of Numbers
Martha Betz	The Betz Placidus Table of Houses	Dennis Elwell	Cosmic Loom
Greg Bogart	Astrology and Meditation	Gillian Helfgott	The Insightful Turtle
Kim Farnell	Flirting with the Zodiac	Christina Rose	The Tapestry of Planetary Phases

9 781902 405926